Consumerism and the Co-operative movement
in modern British history

Manchester University Press

Consumerism and the Co-operative movement in modern British history

Taking stock

edited by
Lawrence Black and Nicole Robertson

Manchester University Press

Manchester and New York

distributed in the United States exclusively by Palgrave Macmillan

Published by Manchester University Press
Oxford Road, Manchester M13 9NR, UK
and Room 400, 175 Fifth Avenue, New York, NY 10010, USA
www.manchesteruniversitypress.co.uk

Distributed in the United States exclusively by
Palgrave Macmillan, 175 Fifth Avenue, New York,
NY 10010, USA

Distributed in Canada exclusively by
UBC Press, University of British Columbia, 2029 West Mall,
Vancouver, BC, Canada V6T 1Z2

British Library Cataloguing-in-Publication Data
A catalogue record for this book is available from the British Library

Library of Congress Cataloging-in-Publication Data applied for

ISBN 978 07190 7684 8   *hardback*

First published 2009

18 17 16 15 14 13 12 11 10 09   10 9 8 7 6 5 4 3 2 1

Typeset in Minion
by Servis Filmsetting Ltd, Stockport, Cheshire
Printed in Great Britain
by CPI Antony Rowe, Chippenham, Wiltshire

Contents

List of contributors

Matthew Anderson is a doctoral candidate in Modern History at the University of Birmingham, writing a thesis on 'The British Fair Trade Movement, 1960 to 2000: A New Form of Global Citizenship?' His research explores the dynamics of Fair Trade as a social movement and looks to explain how socio-economic networks have evolved between co-operatives, development agencies, religious groups, trade unions and consumers.

Lawrence Black is Senior Lecturer in Modern British History at Durham University. He has published on the political left and consumerism and his next book *Defining Politics* (2009) explores modern British political culture.

Espen Ekberg is a Research Fellow at the Forum for Contemporary History, University of Oslo. His doctoral thesis was on the comparative development of consumer co-operation in Norway and the UK. Recent publications include *Organisert Kjøpekraft: Forbrukersamvirkets historie i Norge* (2006), a centenary history of the Norwegian Co-operative Association, co-authored with Even Lange, Eivind Merok, Iselin Theien and Jon Vatnaland.

Andrew Flinn is Lecturer in Archival Studies at University College, London and he is interested in grass-roots activism in a range of campaigns and organisations, and the public histories of those activities. He has published on twentieth-century British labour politics, most recently with K. Morgan and G. Cohen, *Communists and British Society 1920–1991* (2006). At present he is working on an AHRC-funded research project examining community archives and histories within minority ethnic communities.

Mary Hilson is Senior Lecturer in Scandinavian history at University College London. She has published on British and Swedish labour history, including most recently *Political Change and the Rise of Labour in Comparative Perspective: Britain and Sweden 1890–1920* (2006). She is currently finishing a new book on the Nordic model since 1945 and her next research project will examine internationalism in the Nordic co-operative movements during the inter-war period.

Conor McCabe completed his PhD in 2006 at the University of Ulster on 'The Amalgamated Society of Railway Servants and the National Union of Railwaymen in Ireland, 1911–1923'. He has published in *History Studies* and *Saothar* and is currently working on a history of Edenmore housing estate in Dublin.

Nicole Robertson is Lecturer in History at the University of Northumbria. She was the Economic History Society's R.H. Tawney fellow (2006–7) at the University of Nottingham. Her doctoral research was on the co-operative movement in the Midlands. She has published on the Co-operative Party and its relationship with the Labour Party and member activity within co-operative societies. She is currently completing *The Co-operative Movement and Communities in Britain, 1914–60: Minding their Own Business* (forthcoming, Ashgate) on the impact of the co-operative movement on communities in Britain.

Stefan Schwarzkopf is Lecturer in Marketing and Communications at Queen Mary College London. His doctoral thesis was on the history of the British advertising industry between 1900 and 1939. He has published widely on Cold War advertising communication, on the transatlantic relationships between British and American advertising, on the rise of market research, and on the reception of Ernest Dichter's 'Motivation Research' in post-war Britain.

Rachael Vorberg-Rugh is a doctoral candidate in Modern History at The Queen's College, Oxford, where she is writing a thesis on the co-operative movement, 1880–1920. She earned a master's degree from Portland State University, investigating the Women's Co-operative Guild in the same period. She has also been Project Officer for the National Co-operative Archive and Rochdale Pioneers Museum.

John K. Walton is Professor of Social History in the Institute of Northern Studies at Leeds Metropolitan University. He has published extensively on histories of resorts, tourism and consumer societies in Britain, Spain, Belgium, France and the Americas, and on regions and identities, and is editor designate of the new *Journal of Tourism History* (Taylor and Francis). He has sustained an interest in popular politics and the co-operative movement in the nineteenth and twentieth centuries, including a Lancaster Pamphlet on *Chartism* (1999) which has been translated into Chinese.

Lesley Whitworth is Senior Research Fellow (Assistant Curator) at the University of Brighton's Design Archives and a Visiting Research Fellow at the Business History Unit, London School of Economics. She has recently co-edited *Women and the Making of Built Space in England, 1870–1950* (2007) and was a contributor to the ESRC-AHRC Cultures of Consumption Research Programme.

Chris Wrigley is Professor of Modern British History at Nottingham University. His books include *David Lloyd George and the British Labour Movement* (1976), *Arthur Henderson* (1990), *Lloyd George and the Challenge Of Labour* (1990), *Lloyd George* (1992), *British Trade Unions since 1933* (2002), *A.J.P. Taylor: Radical Historian of Europe* (2006), *Churchill* (2006) and an edited *A History Of British Industrial Relations*, 3 vols (1982–96). He was President of the Historical Association, 1996–99.

Stephen Yeo taught and wrote history at the University of Sussex from 1966 to 1989 when he became Principal of Ruskin College Oxford. Since 1997 he has been a Visiting Professor at the Centre for Civil Society at the London School of Economics and at the University of Warwick, chaired the Board of Management of the Co-operative College, and currently leads a College bid to the Heritage Lottery Archives Fund to develop the National Co-operative Archive in Toad Lane, Rochdale and Holyoake House, Manchester. He is writing a history of the CWS from *c*.1970 to *c*.2000.

Acknowledgements

First thanks must go to Joy Cushman, who was involved from the inception of this book and conference. For funding support we would like to thank the Economic History Society, Royal Historical Society, Society for the Study of Labour History, Durham University and the People's History Museum in Manchester. Also to other participants at the original conference – Peter Ackers, Jim Garretts, Valerie Wright, Eileen Yeo and a lively audience of academics and co-operators. For research support Nicole Robertson would like to thank the economic history society and the institute of historical research and Lawrence Black would like to thank the AHRC and British Academy. For the reproduction of images thanks are due Associated Newspapers and the British Cartoon Archive at the University of Kent; the Design Archives, University of Brighton; the various Co-op institutions and especially for the cover image (of Newgate Street department store, Newcastle-upon-Tyne) the North Eastern and Cumbrian Co-op.

Editors' comment

As a rule of thumb, we have capitalised 'Co-op' when referring to a specific organisation (the British Co-op, the local Co-op, the Co-op in Norway) but used lower-case for general discussion (co-operation in Britain, the co-operative movement in Sweden, French co-operators).

List of figures and tables

List of abbreviations

AAM	Anti-Apartheid Movement
AMSAB	Amsab, Institute of Social History (formerly Archives and Museum of the Socialist Labour movement)
AUCE	Amalgamated Union of Co-operative Employees
BCS	Birmingham Co-operative Society
BIM	British Institute of Management
BMRB	British Market Research Bureau
BSI	British Standards Institution
BWP	Belgische Werkliedenpartij
CA	Consumers' Association
CAFOD	Catholic Agency for Overseas Development
CHORD	Centre for the History of Retailing and Distribution
CIC	Co-operative Independent Commission
CmIC	Consortium of Independent Co-operatives
CMEs	Co-operative and Mutual Enterprises
CNWRS	Centre for North West Regional Studies
CoID	Council of Industrial Design
COPRODUCT	Bangkok Co-operative Farm Product Marketing Society
CRDS	Co-operative Retail Development Society
CRS	Co-operative Retail Services
CRTG	Co-operative Retail Trading Group
CTS	Co-operative Tea Society
CU	Co-operative Union
CWS	Co-operative Wholesale Society
D&SER	Dublin and South Eastern Railway
FDB	Fællesforeningen for Danmarks Brugsforeninger (Danish Co-operative Wholesale Society)
FINE:	
FLO	Fairtrade Labelling Organisations International
IFAT	International Fair Trade Association
NEWS!	Network of European World shops

EFTA	European Fair Trade Association
GSWR	[Irish] Great Southern and Western Railway
IAOS	Irish Agricultural Organisation Society
IAWS	Irish Agricultural Wholesale Society
ICA	International Co-operative Alliance
ICAS	Irish Co-operative Agency Society
ICTA	International Co-operative Trading Agency
ICWG	International Women's Co-operative Guild
ICWS	International Co-operative Wholesale Society
ILO	International Labour Office
ILP	Independent Labour Party
ITGWU	Irish Transport and General Workers' Union
ITUC	International Trade Union Confederation
KF	Kooperativa Förbundet (Swedish Co-operative Union)
KICS	Kettering Industrial Co-operative Society
LCS	Leicester Co-operative Society
MNCs	multinational corporations
NA	National Archives, Kew
NAI	National Archive of Ireland
NCO	No Conscription Fellowship
NGOs	non-governmental organisations
NIACE	National Institute of Adult Continuing Education
NKL	Norwegian Co-operative Association
NLI	National Library of Ireland
NMWM	No More War Movement
NUR	National Union of Railwaymen
PEP	Political and Economic Planning
PPU	Peace Pledge Union
RACS	Royal Arsenal Co-operative Society
RCA	Railway Clerks Association
RIBA	Royal Institute of British Architects
RICA	Research Institute for Consumer Affairs
RPM	Resale Price Maintenance
SCWS	Scottish Co-operative Wholesale Society
SEI	Social Enterprise Institute, Heriot-Watt University
SET	Selective Employment Tax
SMEs	Small or Medium-sized Enterprises
SPD	Sozialdemokratische Partei Deutschlands
SWCG	Scottish Women's Co-operative Guild
UDC	Union of Democratic Control
USDAW	Union of Shop, Distributive and Allied Workers
USP	unique selling point

WCG	Women's Co-operative Guild
WDM	World Development Movement
WDWC	Waterford and District Workers' Council
WNC	War Emergency: Workers' National Committee
WTUA	Women's Trade Union Association
WTUL	Women's Trade Union League

1

Taking stock: an introduction

Lawrence Black, Nicole Robertson

Historians and the Co-op

Despite the abundance and quality of recent historical writing on consumerism, it cannot be said that the modern co-operative movement has been well served.[1] The reasons for this can be found in the widely perceived decline of the Co-op since the 1950s, but also in various historiographical agendas that have resulted in its relative invisibility in modern British history. This book, by demonstrating the variety of broader issues that can be addressed through the Co-op and the vibrancy of new historical research into it, seeks to address this.

In the Co-op, historians can peruse an impressive range of debates about production and consumption; retailing and manufacturing; workplace, class and gender relations; ethical consumerism; self-service and consuming practices; democracy, participation and civil society; working-class nostalgia and tradition; debates about institutional decline, management and capitalism; consumer protection, advocacy and politics; the design of buildings, commodities and marketing strategies; regional differences and international comparisons. Discriminating historians should not confine themselves to the Co-op in seeking to address such debates, but no other institution housed so many under one roof. In short, attention to the Co-op can pay dividends for historians of a host of issues. This doubtless explains and has contributed to the renewed interest amongst historians in the co-operative movement in recent years. But while *taking stock* of new approaches and issues raised elsewhere in the history of consumption and modern British history and applying these to and testing them out in the Co-op, this volume also builds on seminal works by G.D.H. Cole, Jack Bailey and Arnold Bonner.[2]

While celebrating past achievements of co-operation and updating earlier texts in light of developments within the movement, such as Fred Hall and W.P. Watkins's 1934 study,[3] these three works sought to reevaluate its role in post-war society. They addressed how co-operation could adapt itself to the demands of the public 'in a rapidly changing world which is on the eve of vast further technical and social advances',[4] in a period where in seemingly 'every field of its activity it has to meet intense competition' with trading rivals that had become 'consumer conscious'.[5] In a similar fashion, this book, subtitled *Taking Stock*, seeks to place the co-operative movement firmly within the context of debates relevant to contemporary historiography and society.

Even though the Co-op has lost market share through the last century, notable recent trading successes remain in banking, in insurance or as Britain's third-largest pharmacy chain, and its turnover today still outranks Marks & Spencer, ICI and British Airways, that of United Co-operatives alone was £2.1bn in 2006.[6] In 2007, the amalgamation of the Co-operative Group and United Co-operatives created the world's largest consumer co-operative with 4.5 million members, 4,500 trading outlets in the UK and a turnover of £9 billion.[7] And the patterns of its mixed fortunes nonetheless inform historians *taking stock* of shifts in consumer politics, identities, behaviour, patterns of taste and broader issues. What this collection does *not* seek to do is to overlook the Co-op's manifest difficulties and critics, which a number of chapters detail. However much it asserts its relevance – and Yeo's chapter is really a manifesto for co-operative and mutual enterprises – this remains historical relevance rather than a Co-op celebration.

Hilton's audit of consumerism in twentieth-century Britain foregrounds the Co-op until rival voices – notably the Consumers' Association (CA) – eclipsed its claim to represent the consumer from the 1950s. For Hilton, the Co-op was marginalised because in the new context of material well-being, it 'lacked the imagination to step beyond an old politics of necessity'.[8] Peter Gurney has questioned the extent to which this constituted a new consumer movement, and instead emphasised how this period 'witnessed the effective marginalisation of the one significant consumer movement Britain ever had'. Both identify the same process that from the 1950s the 'atomized figure of the individual consumer began to shape a hegemonic influence across both polity and civil society, shaping the epistemologies and languages through which the political and economic domains were thought and represented'. While Hilton regards this as the basis for new forms of citizenship and a new consumer movement, Gurney argues it 'undoubtedly helped undermine the co-operative alternative to mass consumption'.[9] Either way – and there is a case to be made that both neglect the extent to which the CA conceived of itself as an 'information co-op' – the co-operative movement was no longer setting the agenda of consumer politics.[10]

There were internal causes for this that made the Co-op the agent of its own situation – a resistance to change that hampered the Co-op while defending sacred and worthy principles. But there were also external and structural factors – demographic and cultural shifts in the industrial working class and, besides competition in the consumer information market, increasing competition from multiple traders. Moreover, as Mercer has shown, the Co-op was often, it seemed, the unspoken target for legislation on trusts, monopolies, pricing and competition policy that favoured capitalist enterprise. Evidence either of a concerted effort to marginalise it or that it was already marginal enough to be excluded was to be found in its exclusion from membership of the Molony Commission to review consumer legislation in 1960 and its submission of evidence treated sparingly.[11] And many of the chapters in this *Taking Stock* collection deal with the relationships between wider structural forces and the Co-op as an agent of its own destiny, the interplay between external and internal and institutional and cultural factors in explaining its history.

In the 2002 special edition of *Mitteilungsblatt des Instituts für soziale Bewegungen*, Chris Wrigley provided a detailed thematic survey of co-operative literature published during the previous ten years.[12] This article highlighted the renewed interest historians have shown in the movement. In particular, attention has focused on the role women and gender politics played in the Co-op.[13] There has also been innovative work on the cultural aspects of co-operation. Most notably, Gurney's influential work on co-operative culture and the politics of consumption considered the co-operative alternative to emerging capitalist forms of mass consumption through the movement's educational work, social life, internationalism and the responses to co-operation from the middle class.[14] Jayne Southern and Jean Turnbull have also explored this culture of co-operation and the ways in which the movement's role within the community went beyond the provision of groceries.[15] An important element of this culture was the visual representations of co-operation. Stephen G. Jones discussed the co-operative movement in his study *The British Labour Movement and Film* and the establishment of the National Co-operative Film Archives in 1992 enabled further research to be carried out in this area, notably by Alan Burton.[16]

By examining organisations at the grass-roots level, studies of the co-operative movement in specific areas have sought to provide comparisons with the image created in national surveys. These case studies help to create a more varied and complex picture of how the co-operative movement developed and functioned. In an important essay, Martin Purvis provided a geographical study of the development of co-operative retail in England and Wales from 1851 to 1901 and highlighted the variations in co-operative expansion.[17] The collection of essays published by the North West Labour History Group, to celebrate the 150th anniversary of the founding of the modern British co-operative movement, included a number of local and regional case studies.[18] *Towards the Co-operative Commonwealth* also incorporated case studies focusing on the origins and developments of the movement in the north of England, notably Lancashire, Liverpool and Cumbria.[19] In addition to these cases studies of co-operation in the north of England, Mary Hilson has studied the co-operative movement in Plymouth, and Rita Rhodes has published a volume on The Royal Arsenal Co-operative Society in London.[20] Nicole Robertson has explored the movement in the Midlands, and has also published a study of the movement incorporating a variety of individual societies throughout Britain.[21] Similarly, comparative perspectives, most notably with that of Scandinavia, have contextualised national Co-operative experience.[22] Work in co-operatives in North America, Asia and Africa has highlighted the broad and diverse nature of the movement.[23]

But there are historiographical silences or omissions too. Most notably, the Co-op scarcely figures in Zweiniger-Bargielowska's anatomy of wartime and post-war austerity and consumption in Britain.[24] This is remarkable given both the Co-op's associations with an austere style, the book's attention to gender and the scale of the Women's Co-operative Guild in this period. The Co-op was *the* shopping experience for Britons at mid-century, but at a moment when post-war affluence was reshaping consumers' political and social identities in ways that the Co-op would struggle to influence. In 1962 one quarter of Britons were Co-op members and half a million worked for it. One-third of milk came from Co-op dairies and one in every seven packets of cigarettes were bought from Co-op shops. The Board of Trade's 1961 Census of Distribution found just over 5 per cent of *all* retail outlets in Britain were Co-operatives. One could live within the Co-op – besides factories and shops, there were the Women's Guilds, it had an Insurance Society, bank and building society (that became the Nationwide), college, flagging youth movement, newspaper and political party – and even end life with it, since around one-third of the UK funeral trade was undertaken by the Co-op. Indeed its ubiquity might have been the Co-op's downfall, insulating it from external developments and fostering an inward-looking, complacent, conservative culture. Such was its size, omnipresence and durability that 'the Co-operative movement', as Elizabeth Gundrey, editor and founder of the British Standards Institute's *Shopper's Guide*, wrote in a Penguin handbook for shoppers in 1962, 'scarcely needs to be described'. So while there were more 'divi' numbers than phone numbers in 1962 and they were just as readily remembered, forty years later the launchers of a new Co-op profit-share scheme admitted they faced a generation who were unlikely to even know even where the nearest Co-op outlet was.[25] In other ways its virtual absence from modern British history is more surprising, since the post-Cold War burgeoning of popular interest in ethical and environmental consumerism and in anti-capitalism since the 1990s, lends piquancy to the Co-op's history. In this respect, Co-op traditions, however flawed as Anderson shows, have returned to favour, rather than hampering the movement.

This oversight of the Co-op is less remarkable if read as symptomatic of certain trends in historiography. In business history the Co-op has rarely been seen as offering examples of best practice – innovation in areas from advertising to self-service, supermarkets and ethical trading has been less apparent than a conservative and amateurish management culture and dowdy style. Cultural history has tended to have had its eye more readily turned by luxury items, sumptuous department stores and the symbolism of consuming practices rather than the more everyday utilitarian and institutional focus necessitated by the Co-op. Here the Co-op's austere, pedestrian, old-fashioned reputation has worked against it. The heckler who responded to Labour MP Herbert Morrison's post-war boast of shopping at the Co-op with a derisive, 'and my god, you look like it', might have been a cultural historian for all attention they have paid the Co-op! Roy Hattersley wrote two decades later of how the Co-op remained 'the home of drab uniformity . . . and shapeless clothes'.[26] Hattersley was most significantly the protégé of Tony Crosland, the chief author of the 1958 Report lacerating the Co-op's conservatism. Hardly a style guru, his opinion was uncontroversial – these were long-standing and recurring opinions. Beatrice Webb, well before co-producing the Webbs's epic 1921 survey, expressed her reluctance to write an official history since she could generate little interest in a 'movement that now appeared as ponderous and unimaginative as it was public-spirited'.[27]

Like cultural history, labour history has preferred to focus on production-based identities and the fireworks of industrial conflict in trade unionism and the political dramas of the Labour Party. It also echoes the Co-op's own historical bent, well developed as Wrigley illustrates, its nostalgia for some 'Golden Age' whose precise moment after 1844 was elusive other than that it was by way of contrast with a sense of decline since the 1950s. Tangible or perceived, that decline has turned attention away from the recent period – anniversary editions such as *North West Labour History* in 1994 passed over the last 50 years.[28]

Stock take

But that decline, like supposedly more halcyon or pioneering days, merits examining rather than taking for granted – not least, to free the Co-op's history from the same introspective, antiquarian tendencies that can be seen in Co-op culture and reconnect it with wider debates. Moreover, as we have argued, decline is a useful register of trends and changes. But the language of decline seems in many ways rather presumptuous, whiggish even – one that our *taking stock* itself interrogates and eschews in favour of a language of change. As many chapters here demonstrate, debates such as how to expand trade without operating to market values or the propagation of Co-op values were recurrent. Declin*ism* is increasingly established as a salient facet of post-war British culture and of debates beyond the Co-op. Indeed, in Walton's hands, decline becomes something to revel in and explore the material culture and make-up of Co-op identities, memories and representations.

Our collection highlights a medley of themes in Co-op history. Robertson, Whitworth, Black, Schwarzkopf and Anderson specifically relate it to a recent historical literature and debates about consumerism – from consumer protection to design and advertising. McCabe, Flinn and Vorberg-Rugh focus upon the interplay between the co-operative and other parts of the labour movement and tensions within the Co-op in its dual roles as employer, producer and consumer. Ekberg and Hilson take international and comparative European perspectives. Walton and Wrigley, in quite different ways – Walton in the imagery and memory of the Co-op, Wrigley through its material culture and commemorations – explore the sense of the past within the Co-op. Yeo protests how the Co-op's history has become 'hidden', but outlines and urges a philosophical recovery package and the enduring potential of co-operative principles (read, variously, as social capital and mutual enterprise) to inform seemingly more modern counter-balances and alternatives to capitalism.

The book's chronological reach extends from the nineteenth century to the present day. It endeavours to transcend and yet detail the multi-layered histories of the wholesale and retail societies plus the Co-op Union in themselves and as a whole, a *movement* – a multiple and fluid identity that helps account for its relative invisibility in modern British history. Likewise, for the historians in this book, consumerism is taken to include a range of practices, ideologies and cultures; they explore facets and groups under the umbrella of the co-operative movement and, in doing so, the ways in which its diverse activities provided various opportunities for consumer-members to engage with *their* organisation. Wrigley, Flinn and Hilson's chapters notably consider the ideals propogated by the movement in educating its members in the ideology behind the shop front.

Individual chapters intersect in other ways too. Due focus is given by Flinn and Vorberg-Rugh to the Women's Co-operative Guild. Both Black and Ekberg emphasise the cumbersome culture that impeded innovation in the 1950s and 1960s and with Walton engage with debates about the idea, causes and legacies of the Co-op's post-war 'decline'. Anderson stresses the compromises that were experienced with ethical practices of fair trade up to the 1980s. But other contributors – Robertson's defence of the Co-op's consumer-protection credentials, Schwarzkopf's outing of the modernity of Co-op advertising in the first half of the century and Whitworth's account of its engagement with the Council of Industrial Design – stress the resources that the Co-op could deploy more positively.

Others use the Co-op to interrogate broader historical terrains. McCabe uses the case of retail co-operatives to demonstrate the importance of social and economic factors in Ireland after the Great War that have been marginalised in a historiography that showcases nationalist and Unionist politics; Black locates the 1958 Co-operative Independent Commission in a broader context of post-war consumerism; Hilson questions the veracity of notions of the exceptionalism of British working-class movements given how the Co-op's aspiration to be a social movement paralleled European models. Likewise, Whitworth's chapter on design queries the evidence and precise processes of how (and indeed, whether) the Co-op lost touch with consumers; and Schwarzkopf situates the Co-op in the trajectory of the history of advertising, at once reconfiguring familiar narratives of both Co-op and advertising history. Most chapters deal with the Co-op's distinctive interface between practical, everyday issues and grander idealist concerns – all take into account and demonstrate the cornucopia of choice the Co-op offers historians and its utility for a broader historical stocktake.

Notes

1 For an overview, see Frank Trentmann, 'Beyond consumerism: new historical perspectives on Consumption', *Journal of Contemporary History* 39:3 (2004).

2 G.D.H. Cole, *A Century of Co-operation* (Manchester: George Allen & Unwin, 1944); Jack Bailey, *The British Co-operative Movement* (revised edn, London: Hutchinson, 1960); Arnold Bonner, *British Co-operation* (revised edn, Manchester: Co-operative Union, 1970).

3 F. Hall and W.P. Watkins, *Co-operation: A Survey of the History, Principles, and Organisation of the Co-operative Movement in Great Britain and Ireland* (Manchester: Co-operative Union, 1934).

4 Cole, *A Century of Co-operation*, p. 401.

5 Bailey, *The British Co-operative Movement*, p. 165.

6 *Guardian* (9 February 2001, 13 April 2007). *Manchester Evening News* (21 September 2006).

7 www.co-operative.co.uk/en/corporate. Accessed 3 September 2007.

8 Matthew Hilton, *Consumerism in 20th-century Britain* (Cambridge: Cambridge University Press, 2003), p. 170.

9 Peter Gurney, 'The battle of the consumer in postwar Britain', *Journal of Modern History* 77:4 (December 2005), p. 959.

10 Michael Young and Marieanne Rigge, *Mutual Aid in a Selfish Society* (London: Mutual Aid Centre, 1979), p. 22.

11 Helen Mercer, *Constructing a Competitive Order: The Hidden History of British Antitrust Policies* (Cambridge: Cambridge University Press, 1995); M. Hilton, 'Consumer politics in post-war Britain', in M. Daunton and M. Hilton (eds), *The Politics of Consumption: Material Culture and Citizenship in Europe and America* (Oxford: Berg, 2000), pp. 250, 254.

12 Chris Wrigley, 'The Co-operative movement', *Mitteilungsblatt des Instituts für soziale Bewegungen* 27 (2002).

13 Jean Gaffin and David Thoms, *Caring and Sharing: the Centenary History of the*

Co-operative Women's Guild (Manchester: Co-operative Union, 1983); Gillian Scott, *Feminism, Femininity and the Politics of Working Women, The Women's Co-Operative Guild, 1880s to the Second World War* (London: Taylor & Francis, 1998); Barbara Blaszak, *The Matriarchs of England's Cooperative Movement: A Study in Gender Politics and Female Leadership, 1883–1921* (London: Greenwood Press, 1999).

14 Peter Gurney, *Co-operative Culture and the Politics of Consumption in England, 1870–1930* (Manchester: Manchester University Press, 1996).

15 Jayne Southern, 'The Co-operative Movement in the North West of England 1919–1939: images and realities' (PhD, Lancaster University, 1996); Jean Turnbull and Jayne Southern, *More than just a Shop: The History of the Co-op in Lancashire* (Preston: Lancashire County Books, 1995).

16 Stephen, G. Jones, *The British Labour Movement and Film* (London: Routledge, 1987). Alan Burton, *The People's Cinema: Film and the Co-operative Movement* (London: BFI Publishing, 1994); *The British Co-operative Movement Film Catalogue* (Trowbridge: Flick Books, 1997) and *The British Consumer Co-operative Movement and Film, 1890s–1960s* (Manchester: Manchester University Press, 2005).

17 Martin Purvis, 'The development of Co-operative retailing in England and Wales, 1851–1901: a geographical study', *Journal of Historical Geography* 16 (1990).

18 *North West Labour History* no.19 (1994/95).

19 Bill Lancaster and Paddy Maguire (eds), *Towards the Co-operative Commonwealth* (Manchester: Co-operative College, 1996).

20 Mary Hilson, 'Consumers and Politics: the co-operative movement in Plymouth, 1890–1920', *Labour History Review* 67 (2002), pp. 7–27; Rita Rhodes, *An Arsenal for Labour: The Royal Arsenal Co-operative Society and Politics 1886–1996* (Manchester: Holyoake Books, 1998).

21 Nicole Robertson, '"A Good Deal . . . and a Good Deal More": The Impact of the Co-operative Movement on Communities in the Midlands, 1914–60' (PhD, University of Nottingham, 2006); 'The political dividend: Co-operative Parties in the Midlands, 1917–39' in M. Worley (ed.), *Labour's Grass Roots* (Aldershot: Ashgate, 2005); *The Co-operative Movement and Communities in Britain, 1914–60: Minding Their Own Business* (forthcoming, Ashgate).

22 Katarina Friberg, *The Workings of Co-operation: A Comparative Study of Consumer Co-operative Organisation in Britain and Sweden 1860 to 1970* (Växjö: Växjö University Press, 2005); Mary Hilson, *Political Change and the rise of Labour in comparative perspective: Britain and Sweden 1890–1920* (Lund: Nordic Academic Press, 2006) which includes the Co-op. For more recent coverage, I. Theien and E. Lange (eds), *Affluence and Activism: Organised Consumers in the Post-war Era* (Oslo: Oslo Academic Press, 2004). On France see Ellen Furlough, *Consumer Co-operation in France: The Politics of Consumption, 1834–1930* (London: Cornell University Press, 1991).

23 Ellen Furlough and Carl Strikwerda (eds), *Consumers against Capitalism? Consumer Co-operation in Europe, North America and Japan, 1840–1990*

(Lanham MD: Rowman & Littlefield, 1999); Johnston Birchall, *The International Co-operative Movement* (Manchester: Manchester University Press, 1997).

24 Ina Zwieniger-Bargielowska, *Austerity in Britain: Rationing, Controls and Consumption, 1939–55* (Oxford: Oxford University Press, 2000).

25 Research Institute for Consumer Affairs, *British Co-operatives: A Consumer's Movement?* (London: RICA, 1964), pp. 7, 20–21. Elizabeth Gundrey, *Your Money's Worth: A Handbook for Consumers* (Harmondsworth: Penguin, 1962), p. 20. *Guardian* (30 August 2006).

26 B. Donoughue and G.W. Jones, *Herbert Morrison* (London: Weidenfeld & Nicolson, 1973), p. 20; R. Hattersley, 'New blood', in G. Kaufman (ed.), *The Left* (London: Blond, 1966), p. 152.

27 S. Webb and B. Webb, *The Consumers' Co-operative Movement* (London: Longmans, 1921). K. Morgan, *The Webbs and Soviet Communism* (London: Lawrence & Wishart, 2006), p. 92.

28 *North West Labour History* no. 19 (1994/95).

Part I

Debating and constructing post-war decline

2

The post-war decline of the British retail co-operative movement: nature, causes and consequences

John K. Walton

Writing in the aftermath of the Dunfermline by-election of February 2006, which produced a startling Liberal Democrat victory in a normally safe Labour seat on Gordon Brown's doorstep, Ian Jack (the editor of *Granta*) used the outcome as a peg for an extended rumination on the transformation of British town centres, urban economies and urban living over the past half century.[1] He mused on the significance of the ruins of the old central Co-operative store in Dunfermline's Randolph Street, and of the role the Co-op had played in the life of this and many similar towns in the 1950s:

> Through the 1990s they stood tall, shuttered and abandoned on both sides of the street . . . Nobody knew what to do with them. And yet the buildings had once been so busy, so central to this town . . . that the Co-op was known simply as 'the store' . . . In the tea-room on the top floor my grandparents celebrated their golden wedding with 'store' steak pie. For years I remembered my mother's 'store' dividend number. The Scottish Co-operative Wholesale Society supplied own-brand goods to local co-operative societies across the country. Store tinned puddings, store mops, store custard creams, store slicing sausage . . . all of them often delivered in store vans to the outlying villages.

The Co-operative Directory for 1957 endorses this vision of past glories. The Dunfermline society then had over 23,000 members on the books, and thirty-five branch stores, sixteen of them in the surrounding villages and small towns (out of over 31,000 in Britain as a whole). It did its own baking, painting and decorating, footwear repairs, upholstery and slaughtering; it had its own farms, and its retail specialities went beyond the basics to include sports goods, dog and bird food, flowers, jewellery, millinery, optical goods, radio and television, and wines and spirits. It also provided a range of services, including hairdressing, laundry, funeral furnishing and a travel bureau, as well as the café referred to above. It was capable of meeting new desires as well as supplying old essentials, and it looked after its members' needs from the cradle to the grave. And on Thursday afternoons its Education Committee met to supply the educational aspirations of the members, while the general management committee considered the practical needs and policies of the society and its enterprises.[2]

After commemorating the lost glories of the Co-op, Ian Jack moved on to develop a nostalgic but sharply analytical argument about, in effect, the impact of globalisation on the provincial towns of Britain in the late twentieth century, the uprooting and displacing of family firms and 'decent Georgian and Victorian architecture', and their replacement by international supermarkets on the urban fringe, 'developers' shanty-town', a plague of charity shops, downtown dereliction, the loss of the informal weekly sociability of town-centre routine, and the demise of an array of clubs, voluntary associations and shared activities and enthusiasms. These changes accelerated at the end of the twentieth century, as between 1995 and 2000 the United Kingdom lost 20 per cent of what the New Economics Foundation defined as 'local' economic outlets, such as corner shops, grocers, post offices and pubs. A process of High Street 'cloning' that leached local character out of townscapes, with the loss of distinctive facades and building materials accompanying the replacement of local shops by national and international chains, continued to accelerate.[3] The Co-operative Societies of the 1950s were emphatically 'local', not least in the architecture of their established stores and in the recruitment of staff and customers alike, and the decline of the old *modus operandi*, coupled with the movement's embrace of amalgamation and modernism in the late twentieth century, made the Co-op a harbinger of these wider developments. Indeed, the decline of the Dunfermline incarnation of the Co-op (which was, as we shall see, to be replayed endlessly across Britain in the last third of the twentieth century) was one early symptom among many of the wider changes he goes on to sketch. The private traders who were to share in its decline were among the Co-op's fiercest enemies while they lived, while the changes within the Co-op that brought about its own retreat from town centres and neighbourhood streets were part of a general process of transformation in townscape, retail provision, consumption and ways of life. But Jack is right to begin his account of the process here, for the Co-operative Societies, whose local demise was an early warning of what was soon to gather momentum on a broader front, were not just about the distribution of a particular range of branded products or the sharing out of an agreed rate of dividend on goods purchased among customers who were also members of the Co-op itself. They were also about a range of shared values, social activities, democratic participation and aspirations to a better, fairer society on the wider national and international stage. For the committed, the greater purpose entailed building the Co-operative Commonwealth, a fair society of ethical socialist communities founded on mutuality and collectivity rather than individualism, profit and greed.[4] The village or town society was a local manifestation of a global movement; and the decline in the retail co-operative movement's vitality, ubiquity and distinctiveness that, in hindsight, was already setting in by the late 1950s was a symptom of wider generational changes in values, assumptions and popular culture.

This chapter addresses this broader agenda by focusing on the problems faced by the British retail co-operative movement over the generation after the Second World War, with particular reference to the relationship between retailing provision and practices and the Co-op's identities as an ethical provider of necessary goods of high quality at fair prices and as the potential basis for an alternative society, and to explaining the declining vitality of this mass movement of the first half of the twentieth century. The decline of the Co-op has not just been a matter of the loss of imposing central retail premises, but of the networks of neighbourhood and street-corner branches that formed the veins and capillaries through which the life-blood of the movement circulated into the minutiae of everyday shopping. Beyond this, it has entailed the loss of active members and real shareholder democracies rooted in the civic pride of communities, an alternative system of provision not only of goods but also of sociability expressed through dance halls, billiard halls, libraries, theatres, meeting rooms, women's and men's guilds, concerts, carnivals, sporting activities, children's summer camps, cinemas (including mobile ones, and showing the movement's own films), and even (mainly in the South Midlands) fish and chip shops.[5] Membership of what were still, in the late 1950s, locally rooted Co-operative societies, often expressing rivalries between neighbouring communities as well as civic pride, was not only the core of a way of life but also, for a significant and articulate minority, a political statement about the desirability and attainability of an alternative, peaceful, uncompetitive, equitable system of social and economic organisation. The movement had been linked to the Labour Party, through the Co-operative Party, since 1918, but was never assimilated to it nor looked after by it, as Labour's masculine and trade-union base inclined it toward an emphasis on regulating the social relations of production rather than consumption, while underestimating the importance of the Co-op itself as producer and employer, which in turn inhibited the necessary recognition and enhancement of the organic and systemic links between the two imagined spheres.[6]

As a national movement, paradoxically, the Co-op probably reached its peak around 1944, the centenary of the founding of the Rochdale Pioneers, just before the post-war Labour government's disappointing neglect of its ideals, resources and legislative needs, failure to recognise its importance, and adoption of a public corporation model of nationalisation that ignored its principles, all combined to play their part in the initial stages of the movement's decline. This was when G.D.H. Cole's centenary history was published, with its impressive maps of local co-operative society distribution in the endpapers, coinciding with the release of the movement's epic (if endearingly

creaky) commemorative film about the Rochdale Pioneers and their enduring purpose, and coexisting with the continuing mass circulation of the
Co-operative press (especially *Reynolds Newspaper* and the *Co-operative
News*), and the extensive take-up of co-operative societies as the vehicle for
individuals' access to rationed goods, with two and a half million people reg-
istering with their local Co-op over and above the 'official' aggregate Society
membership. This evidence of strength, vitality and ambition fed into a more
general growing confidence in an equitable and idealistic post-war settle-
ment, and put the evidence of stagnation and complacency that was already
apparent to some in the northern industrial towns of the 1930s into temporary eclipse.[7] The number of individual co-operative society members 'on the
books' in Britain continued to grow through the early post-war period, from
just over 9,000,000 at the centenary, and 9,730,000 in 1946, to 12,594,000 in
1958, at about the point on which Ian Jack's memories of Dunfermline were
focused; and this expansion, as was remarked at the time, took place in the
absence of any sustained or targeted post-war membership drive, and from
a level at which saturation point was already assumed to have been reached,
at least in the established strongholds. It may well have reflected a failure
to remove lapsed or deceased members from the books, giving rise to false
optimism about the movement's continuing attractiveness to new recruits,
for the Guilds and youth movements were already haemorrhaging members
at an alarming rate, as the disruptions of the Second World War proved to be
'a decisive turning point' from which these organisations never recovered,
and despite a limited revival during the immediate post-war years of Labour
government, membership numbers had declined to little more than half the
immediate post-war level within a decade.[8]

By the late 1950s consolidation and amalgamation had begun to reduce
the number of individual societies, but as yet only very slowly; and there
was already unease about the present and future competitiveness of the
movement in a rapidly changing world, not least because the expansion of
trade per member had not kept pace with the growth of the multiples, while
diversification beyond the grocery core of the movement's business was still
limited in scale and range. But there was also continuing innovation, not
least in building on the Co-op's early lead in the introduction of self-service
stores (the Royal Arsenal Society had pioneered this concept in Britain in the
late 1940s, and was operating thirty such stores by 1954 and eighty by 1960,
although this seems to have been an unusually dynamic record), and dis-
playing a proud commitment to modernist new buildings and fitments. The
Co-operative News publication *This is Progress*, which presented a pictorial
record of Co-op retailing innovation during 1958, demonstrated an enthusiastic embrace of modernity in architecture and design, featuring new stores
and supermarkets in unglamorous strongholds of the movement from Grays

(Essex), by way of Plymouth, Luton, Eccles, Scunthorpe and Hartlepool, to Ian Jack's own Dunfermline, where the Co-op itself had opened a new crescent-shaped supermarket for food, drapery and furnishings, with a café and chemist's shop and new features that included conveyor belts and individual bag lockers at check-out points, a public address system and under-floor heating. This relocation of important parts of the business from Randolph Street to Abbey View must have played its own part in the early stages of the lamented decline of Dunfermline's town centre and the Co-op's remembered place in it. Captions capture the spirit of the time and the enterprise: Colchester's footwear department featured 'cut-out silhouettes in peg-board', rightly described as 'a unique feature'; at Luton 'a mosaic column and striped furniture give sparkle to the corset salon'; while Worcester's central store boasted a 'charcoal-black ceiling'. Some of this was to date with alarming speed.[9]

Whatever the durability of such innovations, the fact that they could occupy 153 pages of text and illustrations for a single year is compatible with their representing only a small minority of all co-operative societies; and unease about a wider *malaise* in the movement at large had already led to the commissioning, in 1955, of an Independent Commission to report on the current state of the movement and its trade. The Commission was appointed at the behest of the Edinburgh congress of the Co-operative Union in that year, and chaired by Hugh Gaitskell, leader of the Labour Opposition. Its members included Dr J.B. Jefferys, the leading academic expert on retailing, and its highly active and influential Secretary was the modernising Labour intellectual Anthony Crosland, whose *The Future of Socialism* was published in 1956 and who was to hold high ministerial office under Harold Wilson and James Callaghan. In the introduction to the Commission's Report, which was issued in 1958, Crosland was said to have 'made by far the most important contribution' to its preparation, and his 'capacity for presenting our views concisely and clearly' was lauded: 'If any one name is to be associated with this Report, it should be his.' The Report drew attention to the retail co-operative movement's overall stagnation over the previous twenty years, and its failure to move beyond its strong position in food and drink retailing to develop its volume and market share in other sectors, especially clothing and footwear, where there was already evidence of decline since the end of the war. There were also weaknesses at the core of the traditional food-retailing business, especially in meat, fruit and vegetables. The Co-op's share of total retail trade was stagnating at around 11 per cent during the early 1950s, while that of the private multiples, which were emerging as its main challengers, had grown from 17.1 per cent in the late 1930s to 21.7 per cent in 1956. These were hardly revolutionary changes, but the share of a greatly expanded total retail trade had fallen away from around 20 per cent at the end of the war, and such trends sat uneasily with aspirations toward continuing growth and expansion into new sectors.[10]

The Commission was critical of aspects of management and financial structure, and of aspects of the location of existing stores; and it noted a widespread failure to engage with an emergent consumer society, which was (as applied to the Labour Party) a key theme in Crosland's *The Future of Socialism*. In particular:

> In men's wear, women's wear and children's clothes, few Co-operative stores are able to offer the quality of goods, at the price, which is offered by some private chains of specialist shops and variety bazaars. There is a tendency, perhaps, to a certain dowdiness. The goods are no doubt solid and durable, but they are not always stylish or 'smart' enough to appeal to the younger generation . . . many societies, not yet awake to the higher and more varied expectations . . . of to-day's shoppers, are still stocking too narrow and old-fashioned a range of goods. The Movement must beware of aiming too low in this respect. It is no longer appealing to a working class which is barely above the subsistence line, but to consumers whose tastes are changing and rising rapidly. Increasingly, they demand such 'non-traditional' merchandise as a larger variety of cheeses, continental viands, wines and spirits, gramophone records, high-fashion textiles, and the like; and the Movement must, as some societies are already doing, adjust its range of merchandise to meet these new demands.[11]

It is easy to imagine the influence of the *bon viveur* Crosland on the production of this text, and the availability of alcohol from retail Co-operative stores is quite a good indicator of the movement's level of engagement with the new popular consumer preferences the Report identified. 'Wines', 'wines and spirits', 'wines and beers' or (in the eccentric case of Penrith, which also manufactured clogs) 'wines and cider' were on offer at 123 co-operative societies in England and Wales in 1957. This was a substantial minority, but the level of sophistication of the providers may not always have matched Crosland's preferences, especially in the case of Shiremoor (Northumberland) where the only wines and spirits available were 'medicated'. One-third of the alcohol-vending societies had a strong coal-mining presence in the local economy, and there were concentrations in north-eastern England, the Lancashire and Yorkshire Pennines, and the north Midlands, including many village and small-town societies. Some of the big-city and regional societies supplied wines and spirits, including Birmingham, Bristol, Exeter, Leicester, Newcastle, Oxford and Reading, as well as the enormous London, Royal Arsenal and South Suburban co-operatives in the metropolis. But societies that were still 'dry' included giants like Barnsley, Leeds, Liverpool, Manchester and Salford, Derby, Plymouth, and Birmingham's Ten Acres and Stirchley, as well as Grays and Enfield Highway in the London suburbs. The absence of alcohol was not a necessary indicator of general failure to identify new needs: Enfield

Highway had a theatre agency, a nursery, coach hire, sports goods and toys, while Coventry had its own holiday camp, Derby offered car hire, Oswestry cosmetics, Ipswich petrol, and Plymouth a camp and caravan site. But these were isolated and random initiatives. Meanwhile 'wet' societies might also offer older kinds of service such as chimney sweeping (Bristol), blacksmiths and cartwrights (Middlesbrough), and saddlery (Royal Arsenal). But having a licence to sell alcoholic beverages in the late 1950s was a convincing indicator of 'keeping up with the times', and such an aspiration was still capable of generating conflict within societies where an older ethic of temperance and Nonconformity was still strong, as in the case of Barnsley. Changes were beginning, but the Co-op lagged behind its competitors in this field as, no doubt, in other areas identified by the Report.[12]

The Commission probed into the roots of the problems it identified, noting the existence of a high proportion of under-performing societies, and identifying a positive relationship between size of society and economic performance. It also noted the growing democratic deficit in many local societies, with tiny percentages of the membership actually participating in elections, especially in the larger societies. It recommended the introduction of management training, to expose managers to ideas from outside the movement, though only on the 'technical' as opposed to the 'cultural' side, to overcome a perceived 'certain isolation and consequent conservatism in the field of ideas, techniques and innovation'. In the main body of the text it stopped short of recommending an optimum size of society, recommending amalgamations between adjacent societies where current arrangements were wasteful of resources, especially in big cities, but insisting on the importance of retaining the ties between society and locality, and recommending a very limited optimum minimum size of fifteen grocery branches. But the concluding recommendations were much sharper, pushing strongly for consolidation through (effectively) imposed amalgamation, to avoid wasteful local competition and because 'there should only be one society to each main shopping-centre and its catchment area'. The key recommendation that the 'ideal' number of societies should be 'in the region of 200–300', to be achieved through a national amalgamation plan, envisaged revolutionary change; and it may well have been at the point of defining the recommendations that Crosland's influence really came into play in what is, overall, an internally contradictory document. The proposed report on amalgamations was commissioned by the new Central Executive, and published two years later, proposing a reduction in the number of societies to 307. This was followed in December 1967 by the issuing of a Regional Plan, which envisaged the rationalisation of the movement into fifty geographical regions each with its own single society. This went a great deal further than the Commission's recommendations. Significantly, however, the Commission endorsed the principle of the dividend on purchases, which was the distinguishing feature of Co-op shopping for most of the retail movement's customers, although it recommended caution in setting dividend levels and a preference for allocating surpluses to bolstering reserves rather than increasing dividend.[13]

Those who were young in the late 1950s, with Ian Jack, share a very widespread characteristic: the ability to remember the family's dividend number, and to conjure up Proustian memories of the distinctive aroma of the local Co-op grocery store, a compound of beeswax polish, sawdust, ripe cheeses (cut with a wire), loose tea and freshly sliced bacon.[14] In university classes with a leavening of mature students, those who were born before mid-century can usually recall the magic number, and are able to explain its significance to younger colleagues to whom this is an arcane mystery. In the late 1950s and early 1960s the present writer was sent on errands to the New Bolsover Model Village branch of the Pleasley and Pleasley Hill Co-operative Society, a store that epitomised this remembered environment perfectly, with the injunction not to forget to answer the counter assistant's invariable, almost liturgical question with '6169'.[15] This was a society with more than 11,000 members on the books in 1957, with nineteen branches spread across the small towns and industrial villages of the then coal-mining district between Chesterfield and Mansfield on the Nottinghamshire/Derbyshire border, and its own bakery, dairy, slaughterhouse and shoe-repair facilities; and the dividend was central to its operations.[16] The dividend was a way of saving while you spent, accumulating money for 'lumpy' purchases like the annual holiday, festive clothing or the payment of local taxes, and shoppers took care to level up their expenditure to make sure of the maximum return. It was built into the regular rhythms of family life.[17] The generational watershed described above may reflect a decline, setting in during the 1960s, in children's errands to local Co-op branches; but it also shows the deep significance of the subsequent abandonment of the dividend on members' purchases, which had been such a strong distinguishing feature of Co-op practice, and the parallel shedding of branches like this one in the face of competition first from multiples, then from a new breed of 'open-all-hours' grocers using family labour, and from the transformations of shopping culture associated especially with generalised automobility in the late twentieth century. Associated with this, in places like New Bolsover (which was 'new' when the Bolsover Colliery Company's pit was sunk in the 1890s), has been the decline of the jobs, communities and cultures into which such Co-ops were embedded, as part of a 'traditional' working-class way of life that had its roots in the late nineteenth century, generated its own version of the common sense of everyday life, and appeared indestructible until the eve of its demise.[18] Linda McCullough Thew saw the Co-op in the big pit village or small town of Ashington, Northumberland, in the 1930s as '[w]oven into the fabric of my life from the beginning. Allegiance to the church might waver, schools change, our stay in various houses be short-lived, work at the pit be unpredictable, but our attitude to the store was steadfast. It claimed our whole-hearted fealty and esteem'.[19] Like the coal mines that generated its income, its disappearance from the scene was simply unthinkable.

It is fitting, therefore, that one of the most popular features of the '1913 street' at the North of England Open-Air Museum at Beamish, County Durham, commemorating the recently lost industrial culture of a distinctive region, should be the reconstructed Co-op store from nearby Annfield Plain. As recently as 1957, and for some years afterward, this had been the central store for a wide area of the Durham coalfield. In that year the society had 15,000 members on the books, 23 branches (with the recurrent 'Front Street' address showing their prominent positions in village after village), a funeral parlour and coffin workshop, and its own market gardens to supply fresh local produce.[20] The recent nature of memories of prosperity and decline, and the negative connotations of association with the collapse of old certainties, may have helped to make the store's incorporation into Beamish controversial when proposed in 1976, with public objections to the 'absurdity' of putting such a commonplace building on display; and the significance of the Co-op had to be defended forcefully as an essential part of the fabric and social life of every town in north-east England in the recent past.[21] The store itself seeks to recreate the lost smells, atmosphere and retailing technologies associated with this version of the past, and necessarily abandoned (of course, as part of the innovatory purpose) by the re-sited and re-imagined Co-op supermarkets of the late twentieth century. But it is, inevitably, stronger on the nostalgic conjuring of archaic retail technologies, goods and trading practices than on imparting information about the Co-op's ideals, aspirations and inner workings.

Where a more 'authentic' version of this past is still accessible, if only in the sense that it still lives on in its own right, it can be found in the surviving village or small-town Co-operative stores, as in the case of Coniston or Penrith (and branches) in Cumbria, that have resisted (or evaded) the modernising and rationalising drive of the national movement, and sustained an independent existence of their own.[22] A distinctive example is the village store at Grosmont in North Yorkshire, founded by miners, ironworkers, railwaymen and farmers in 1867, which in 1957 still had 770 members and offered crockery, drapery, furnishing, footwear, hardware, ladies' and men's outfitting, paints, wallpaper, radio and even television, over and above the standard basics of groceries, bread, greengroceries, confectionery and tobacco, as befitted a time when for that majority of inhabitants without a car even the six-mile trip to Whitby was a significant journey.[23] This venerable society, run on the basis of genuinely local democracy, continues to offer a seven-day retailing service and a regular dividend to its 400 shareholder members, although it has lost all but the basic 'corner shop' functions as its premises have shrunk over the intervening years. It survived by resisting amalgamations into larger societies, which would have rationalised it out of existence, and by seeing off an attempt in the early 1990s to close it down and sell it up, apparently for the benefit of a small clique who had taken over the management committee. Rescue came through the management committee elections, at which a caucus of concerned villagers took over control, installed a manager and kept the shop in business.[24] What has enabled Grosmont Co-op to keep going economically, however, after the loss of the village's industries and the Co-op's ties to the surrounding settlements of the lower Esk Valley, has been the transformation of the local economy wrought by railway-heritage tourism in the form of the North York Moors Railway, whose locomotive sheds and ancillary workers provided much of the support for the counter-coup that kept the society in business, and whose tourist passengers buy the ice cream, sweets and souvenirs that form an essential part of the village store's highly seasonal trade.[25]

Grosmont's Co-op, however businesslike it might be in catering efficiently for villagers and tourists, is kept alive by what might be called a nostalgia economy, in contrast with the fate of village stores in other nearby settlements; and its survival is, in its own way, as poignant an irony as those enshrined in the reinstatement and refurbishment of the Annfield Plain buildings at Beamish.[26] It could, indeed, be reinterpreted, in the exceptional and paradoxical nature of its survival, as further reinforcement of the strong messages in the existing literature about the Co-op's widespread failure to respond adequately or appropriately to the post-war retailing and wider social trends which brought about decline in its old industrial strongholds. To add a further dimension, at the beginning of the twenty-first century a search for archival remains in the roof space of the old Co-op building in Grosmont turned up two telling caches of unsold goods from the early 1950s: a large container of rusting clog irons, and an equally substantial consignment of wicks for oil lamps. These had clearly been purchased in bulk, following long-established routines, even as the demand for them was collapsing with the advent of new forms of footwear and the adoption of electricity in the village and surrounding area; and it would be tempting to use them as a metaphor for the Co-op's failure to adapt to the post-war world on a broader front. But there is, of course, much more to the story than this.

The changes in the fortunes and nature of the co-operative movement that were beginning at the very point in the late 1950s when the Independent Commission produced its report, were far-reaching and cumulatively revolutionary. 'On-the-books' membership continued to increase until 1968, when it reached nearly 13 million; but a downward trend in membership had long been evident in the old industrial areas, and in the late 1960s a general and continuing decline set in.[27] In south-eastern England the membership numbers of the immense Royal Arsenal Society were regularly refreshed by mergers, but in between these events the trend was already downward by the late 1950s. A brief recovery between 1966 and 1968 proved illusory, and between 1971 and 1979 the number of members on the books fell steadily year on year from 510,000 to 416,000. How many of these memberships were or became purely nominal is another question; and there is no reason to believe this trajectory to be at all exceptional.[28] A Lancashire example is, indeed, much starker: in 1957 the four societies that were to make up the Lancastria Co-op in the north-west of the county had a combined recorded membership of 153,852, which had apparently fallen to 30,000 by 1975 after seven years of successful trading in its amalgamated guise.[29] This suggests that a precipitous fall in membership could be combined with survival and even recovery in a business sense; but nationally, against this backcloth, the Co-op's share of total retail trade fell from 12 per cent in the early 1960s to 4 per cent (admittedly of a greatly expanded figure) in 1994, and over forty years from the mid-1950s that of the grocery trade declined from 20 per cent to 7.2. The number of separate retail societies had peaked as early as 1903, at 1,455, but there were still 1,065 in 1940 and 1,000 ten years later.[30] Contraction in society numbers, through amalgamation and rationalisation, then began apace: there were 562 in 1955, 467 in 1967, 312 in 1976 and 55 in 1994. This could be, and was, regarded as evidence of efficiency and adaptability. Indeed, it almost matched the target of 50 envisaged by the Co-operative Union's Regional Plan of 1967; but it also diluted local identity and accountability.[31]

To take a regional example of a complex set of processes, the amalgamations which began in earnest in the late 1960s, following the Regional Plan, pulled thirty Lancashire societies under the capacious umbrella of United Norwest between 1968 and 1991, including proud local organisations in such towns as Bolton, Blackpool, Preston, Rochdale, Oldham and Stockport. Three societies in north-west Lancashire merged in 1968 to form Lancastria, and three more in the centre of the county in 1970 to form Bolton and Wigan, before these societies were pushed together in their turn in 1976 to form Greater Lancastria. This failed to match the business success of Lancastria, and in 1983 it drew in another group of merged societies, North Midland, to consolidate again as United, pulling in several additional independent societies over the next four years. Meanwhile, a further set of amalgamations in the Manchester region between 1970 and 1982 produced Norwest Pioneers, which also drew in further local societies in the mid-1980s, before the two new retail giants fused into a single body in 1991.[32] By this time members, and customers, of the older societies might be forgiven for having lost touch completely with what had been happening, especially as these changes coincided with extensive closures of local stores and the concentration of business into large new premises on the urban fringe, often rebranded with names that lacked obvious Co-op connotations, which were difficult to differentiate from the supermarkets of commercial chains. The Co-op thus became uprooted and divorced from local communities which had given birth to it and nurtured it over, in many cases, more than a century. There was no great outpouring of celebratory centenary histories to match the substantial expressions of pride in lasting achievement, strongly bound and often printed on high-quality paper, which had been issued by society after society to mark their golden jubilees in the Edwardian years;[33] indeed, there were hardly any surviving local societies to organise such commemorations, nor were there many active members to commission them.

The decline of the retail co-operative movement as an expression of local pride, identity and (in many cases) idealism ran parallel to the collapse of its educational and political activities. The decline of the Women's Guild and similar ancillary organisations continued apace: the Guild at its peak had 87,000 members nationally in 1938, but 50,000 in 1959, 35,000 in 1965 and only 5,000 in 1991. In the former stronghold of Lancashire, Women's Guild membership fell from 12,000 in 283 branches in 1945, to 340 in 20 branches by 1992. The Men's Guild began its decline earlier, falling nationally from 11,000 members in 1938 to 1,500 in 1959. The Co-operative Youth Movement, founded in 1944 to bring all of the movement's youth organisations together, fell into decline nationally from the mid-1950s. It was disbanded in 1979, although the Woodcraft Folk, whose relationship with the movement had ebbed and flowed, continued to recruit and flourish locally. A survey of the closing dates of Co-operative publications, as listed in the catalogue of the national archive in Manchester, shows that at least nine periodicals targeted at educationalists, young people, consumers and activists gave up the ghost between 1959 and 1968, several after repeated renamings that betokened a loss of confidence in the Co-op label: the *Co-operative Home Magazine*, for example, dropped the Co-operative prefix in 1959 and became *Good Shopping* for its last two years between 1964 and 1966. The widespread abandonment of the old Co-op Halls, which had been focal points of urban social life in small towns like Carnforth and Chorley in the inter-war years, both reflected and exacerbated these trends, as societies vacated their central premises and failed to include meeting facilities in the new supermarkets.[34]

It will be clear that during the half-century after the Second World War the British retail co-operative movement declined not only in economic terms, but also, and more deeply, as an ethos and a way of life. Efforts within the movement to modernise it as a business or set of businesses helped to bring this about. Peter Gurney has advanced a persuasive set of explanations for these developments, focusing on the Labour Party's failure to recognise the value of the movement or to protect it against its competitors, the Conservatives' support of big private business interests through their policies on television advertising, credit sales and retail-price maintenance, the rise to dominance of a post-war ideology based on the sovereignty of the individual consumer who merely needed perfect information (as provided, it was hoped, by the Consumers' Association),[35] and the failure of the movement to come to terms with the new post-rationing culture of media-driven consumerism, abundance and the rhetoric of innovation and choice in a way that might have preserved its integrity.[36] There are, however, additional dimensions to co-operation's decline as a ubiquitous, popular and democratic institution with its own distinctive values, and these need to be teased out a little further. The implications of the loss of local identity and the semblance of working democracy through successive mergers were discussed above; but there are several other key themes to consider.

The great symbolic and practical issue was the abandonment of the dividend. This was a response to symptoms of decline that were already apparent: it was part of a package of economic reforms within the movement that sought to assimilate it to 'best-practice' business methods in mainstream retailing, as with the amalgamation programme, but damaged its distinctive ethos and identity in the process. The dividend came under increasing pressure in many societies during the 1960s, and as it declined – from 1s 5.5d (7.4p) in the pound in 1946 to 6d (2.5p) through the 1960s, maintained with great difficulty, in the Royal Arsenal Society – the administrative costs began to look disproportionate in relation to the return.[37] As the Independent Commission had emphasised, 'In a Co-operative society the members are both consumers, who want lower prices, and members, who want a higher dividend; and we do not clearly know how they weigh their claims in these respective roles.' It also pointed out that members' capital was no longer accumulating automatically as it had done before the war, and that even the conservative savers who continued to leave their unspent dividends in the societies might eventually start to notice that they could get better returns elsewhere.[38] As retail competition intensified and the societies failed to recruit a new generation of members, the push to put lower prices ahead of dividend maintenance gathered momentum; and during the 1960s the movement's leaders shifted from intransigent opposition to the trading stamps that the multiples were introducing, to adopting them in place of the dividend. In 1967 the Co-operative Wholesale Society introduced its own stamp scheme without consulting the retail side of the movement, and, as Attfield remembered, 'For some years the question of stamps became a battleground within the movement nationally between those who saw them as an essential trading weapon, and those for whom stamps represented part of a general retreat from co-operative principles, abolishing one of the most distinctive features of co-operative trade and diminishing the advantages of membership.' The advocates of stamps gained an almost universal victory.[39]

The process by which trading stamps were introduced at Royal Arsenal was representative of a series of battles across the movement during the late 1960s and early 1970s. In 1970 the Royal Arsenal General Committee's proposal to introduce stamps in place of the dividend provoked fierce opposition from the Education Committee and the auxiliary organisations (such as the Women's Guild), and when at the March quarterly meeting it failed to gain the requisite two-thirds majority the executive insisted on returning two months later to secure it and press ahead. The defeated advocates of the dividend could only muster 660 votes on the latter occasion, out of a nominal membership of over half a million; and the view of the Society's historian that '[m]any saw (the vote) as representing, in effect, the wishes of the officials and senior staff against the views of the active grass-roots membership', suggests how small that active, principled membership had become. It could be overridden by a combination of General Committee members, who put business efficiency as they saw it before the traditions and distinctive ethos of the movement, with managers and 'senior staff'; and the defeated campaigners for the dividend had to fall back on trying to redress what they saw as the failure of active democracy in the Society that had permitted such an outcome. They quoted a senior official's remark that, 'We cannot allow a decision of this magnitude to be left in the hands of the members', as a classic expression of what had gone wrong. The abandonment of the dividend, a complex and contested process which deserves a research project of its own, was widely seen as a symbol and expression of the triumph, orchestrated from within, of 'mainstream' business culture over the values the movement was supposed to represent.[40]

The struggle over the dividend exacerbated existing fault-lines within the movement. The tensions are clear in Attfield's account of the Royal Arsenal Society: the internationalist interest in socialism and pacifism of those who still pursued the ideal of the Co-operative Commonwealth in post-war South London was in permanent conflict with the efforts of 'mainstream' supporters of the Gaitskellite Labour Party, or indeed people of any political allegiance or none, to keep business separate from politics, to sustain membership by denying ideology rather than achieving conversions, and to adapt to a changing consumer environment rather than resisting or rejecting it. The employees, at least implicitly, endorsed this non-ideological approach as a matter of common sense: the Co-op's relations with its workforce had long been problematic and conflict-ridden in many societies, and educating them in its higher ideals was always difficult. The decline of member democracy gave them disproportionate power in many societies, and educational provision for members and the general public was among the sufferers. Attfield's main focus is on Royal Arsenal's education division and on the youth movements, but differences of this kind clearly prevented many societies from achieving their full potential, whether as businesses or as idealistic communitarian democracies.[41]

To make matters worse, the divided co-operative movement was also an ageing one: it was failing to recruit a new generation of members. An important aspect of the decline of the guilds and the educational activities, and of the lack of democratic participation, was an ageing membership, which in turn became set in its ways and unwelcoming to younger people; and the unresponsiveness of management committees to new fashions and the new consumerism probably had a similar demographic dimension as established post-holders grew old together without benefit of democratic refreshment. The movement's reluctance to embrace the new consumerism through advertising and public relations, as analysed by Gurney, may have arisen from a combination of the conservatism of the elderly and the principled opposition of radical groups within the membership, some of whom were themselves ageing.[42] Investigations by the Co-operative Independent Commission suggested that by the mid-1950s 'few people under 25 are Co-operative members and capital-holders', which raised a 'disturbing' question about 'the appeal of Co-operation to the younger generation' which was deemed to lie beyond the Commission's remit.[43] In 1960 Brian Groombridge's report on the guilds and other auxiliaries found that (for example) nearly 40 per cent of Women's Guild branches had no members under 40 and nearly half had an average age of over 60. There were some bright spots, but the report criticised lack of energy and innovation and a commitment to maintaining empty routines and rituals that was calculated to exclude and discourage new recruits. In this respect the Co-op suffered from the same malaise as (for example) many churches, chapels and youth and labour-movement organisations during the post-war decades, though, as Groombridge pointed out, the success of Townswomen's Guilds, Women's Institutes and other voluntary bodies showed that this was not inevitable.[44]

As the co-operative movement came under increasing pressure, it also suffered from denigration in much of the media, in common with the nationalised industries. William Crofts has shown how private enterprise used propaganda through the advertising media against the Attlee government's nationalisation programme, deploying characters such as 'Mr Cube'.[45] Media attacks persisted after nationalisation, and it seems clear that the co-operative movement was tarred with the same brush as British Railways or the National Coal Board, although it seems not to have been found guilty by association with post-war rationing.[46] This theme would repay further investigation: images of the Co-op as 'antiquated, shabby and lower-class', or as a 'retail dinosaur', do not come from nowhere, although this is not to suggest that they had no basis in fact: the Independent Commission commented that 'in many areas, the word "Co-operative" is, we fear, associated with a drab, colourless, old-fashioned mediocrity'.[47] Cartoon evidence is relevant here. As early as 1950 even David Low in the sympathetic *Daily Herald*, identifying 'Empire Free Trade' with the idea of 'Labour's World Co-op Stores', combined a modernist image of the stores themselves, complete with Attlee as the bell-boy presiding over a capacious lift, with a depiction of plump, dowdy, elderly customers that was more than just a caricature of the politicians concerned.[48] Ten years later, Low's response (see cartoon 1 after this chapter) to the Co-operative Commission Report showed a gas-lit two-storey Victorian Co-operative store front, flanked by a 'Gigantic Chain' and 'Colossal Multiple' and assiduously ignored by fashionable young female shoppers. The manager of this anachronism eyed a quizzical Gaitskell loitering at the door with grave suspicion, and warned his assistant to '[b]eware of suspicious characters trying to bring the business up to date' and 'conspiring to make it a success'. By 1974 the Co-op was a sitting duck for Mac in the *Daily Mail*, whose fantasy about the consequences of a Co-op takeover of the great white-elephant tower block Centre Point, in central London, had elderly customers collapsing with exhaustion as they trailed trolleys up the stairs to the fifteenth floor, only to be told by a cheerful white-coated manager that 'Good heavens no, madam – beans and butter are on the 27th floor . . .'[49] Image problems involving old-fashioned stock, inefficiency and bureaucracy were at the core of the Co-op's problems in recruiting new generations, whether of customers, members or activists, and the press coverage both responded to and reinforced them.

These image problems reflected widespread realities in the post-war retail co-operative movement. They were echoed in the decline and disappearance of the Co-op as manufacturer, but they were not replicated in the broader movement's recovery or continued success in banking, insurance and (for example) milk and funeral services in the late twentieth century.[50] There is a great deal here to explain, and it is hoped that this chapter, coupled with the highly stimulating work of Peter Gurney, will help to encourage the necessary local, regional and thematic studies that will pursue these questions in greater depth. Meanwhile, the sustained neglect of the British retail co-operative movement by historians of post-war consumption and consumerism is remarkable, and needs to be redressed: this is still an immensely significant set of organisations with a distinctive identity and the scope for making a difference, but at the moment, outside its own internal historiography, it seems to be almost invisible on the wider historical stage. The reasons for this neglect would themselves repay investigation; but the more important task is to remedy the distorted view of post-war British society that pushes the co-operative movement to the margins. Even within the specialist field of historiographies of decline, the cotton industry, already insignificant on the national stage by the post-war years, has attracted more attention from historians than the Co-op, which was still a mass movement across the whole nation in the 1950s, when it was still growing on the basis of many key indicators. It is time to redress the balance.

Notes

1 Ian Jack, 'Things that have interested me', *Guardian Saturday Review* (18 February 2006), p. 15.
2 Co-operative Union Ltd, *The Co-operative Directory* (Manchester: Co-operative Union, 1957), pp. 450–1; Co-operative Union Ltd, *Co-operative Independent Commission Report* (Manchester: Co-operative Union, 1958), p. 88. Co-operators recognised the power of the phrase 'from the cradle to the grave', and made use of it: for example John Attfield, *With Light of Knowledge: A Hundred Years of Education in the Royal Arsenal Co-operative Society, 1877–1977* (Crouch End: RACS, 1981), p. ix.
3 M. Conisbee, P. Kjell, J. Oram, J. Bridges Palmer, A. Simms and J. Taylor, *Clone Town Britain* (London: National Economic Forum, 2004).
4 This is well articulated in Attfield, *With Light of Knowledge*, Chapters 6–8.
5 For the range of activities see, for example, L. and A. Chew, *The Co-op in Birmingham* (Stroud: Sutton, 2003), pp. 91–102; S. Mullins and D. Stockdale, *Taking Shop: An Oral History of Retailing in the Harborough Area during the Twentieth Century* (Stroud: Sutton, 1994), pp. 95–110. For cinemas and film-making, Alan Burton, *The People's Cinema: Film and the Co-operative Movement* (London: National Film Theatre, 1994), and *The British Consumer Co-operative Movement and Film, 1890s–1960s* (Manchester: Manchester University Press, 2005); for fish and chips, *Co-operative Directory*, 1957, pp. 75, 115, 125, 271, 333.
6 A. Bonner, *British Co-operation* (Manchester: Co-operative Union, 1961), Chapter 11; G.D.H. Cole, *A Century of Co-operation* (London: George Allen & Unwin, 1944), Ch. 19.
7 Peter Gurney, *Co-operative Culture and the Politics of Co-operation in England, 1870–1930* (Manchester: Manchester University Press, 1996), pp. 234–6.
8 Cole, *Century of Co-operation*, p. 377; Bonner, *British Co-operation*, p. 251, 289; P. Gurney, 'The battle of the consumer in postwar Britain', *Journal of Modern History* 77:4 (2005), p. 963; Attfield, *With Light of Knowledge*, p. 94.
9 Bonner, *British Co-operation*, Chapter 10; Attfield, *With Light of Knowledge*, p. 66; Co-operative News Publications, *This is Progress: A Pictorial Record of Co-operative Store and Shop Development in 1958* (Manchester: Co-operative Union, 1959), pp. 23, 26, 52–4, 99.
10 Attfield, *With Light of Knowledge*, p. 67.
11 *Co-operative Independent Commission Report*, p. 49–50.
12 *Co-operative Directory* (1957); Gwen Cropper, 'The Retailing of Alcohol within the Co-operative Movement in England, *c.*1930–1980', Centre for the History of Retailing and Distribution, conference on 'The Commercial World', University of Wolverhampton, September 2001.
13 *Co-operative Independent Commission Report*, Chapters 1–6 and 14, especially

pp. xi, 49–50, 79, 237–8, 241–2; J. Turnbull and J. Southern, *More Than Just a Shop: A History of the Co-op in Lancashire* (Preston: Lancashire County Books, 1995), p. 21; D. Flanagan, *A Centenary Story of the Co-operative Union of Great Britain and Ireland, 1869–1969* (Manchester: Co-operative Union, 1969), p. 128; Gurney, 'Battle of the consumer'.

14 Linda McCullough Thew, *The Pit Village and the Store: a Portrait of a Mining Past* (London: Pluto, 1985), pp. 147–56, provides a full first-hand description of such a shop.

15 Bernard Haigh (ed.), *Around Bolsover* (Bath: Chalford, 1994), p. 101, provides a photograph of the New Bolsover store and some interesting commentary.

16 *Co-operative Directory* (1957), pp. 296–7.

17 Mullins and Stockdale, *Talking Shop*, pp. 98–9; McCullough Thew, *Pit Village*, pp. 109–12.

18 E.J. Hobsbawm, *Worlds of Labour* (London: Weidenfeld & Nicolson, 1984), Chapters 10–11, for the 'making' and longevity of this working class.

19 McCullough Thew, *Pit Village*, p. 71.

20 *Co-operative Directory*, 1957, pp. 8–9.

21 G.S. Cross and J.K. Walton, *The Playful Crowd: Pleasure Places in the Twentieth Century* (New York: Columbia University Press, 2005), pp. 235–6.

22 Jean Turnbull, 'The Co-op: a brief survey of development in North-West England *c.*1820–1994', *CNWRS Regional Bulletin*, Lancaster University, new series, 9 (1995), p. 26.

23 *Co-operative Directory* (1957), pp. 158–9.

24 Ian MacKinnon, 'Village at war as factions vie for control of co-op', *Independent* (21 August 1993), p. 7.

25 Grosmont Co-operative Society, Front Street, Grosmont, North Yorkshire: card indexes of members and their purchases at various points since the 1890s. Thanks to Dave Templeman for information on Grosmont.

26 For the general problems of village shops in the late twentieth century, Jonathan Brown and Sadie Ward, *The Village Shop* (Newton Abbot: Rural Development Commission, 1990).

27 Turnbull and Southern, *More Than Just a Shop*, p. 18.

28 Attfield, *With Light of Knowledge*, pp. 62–3.

29 Turnbull and Southern, *More Than Just a Shop*, p. 23; *Co-operative Directory* 1957, pp. 40–1, 140–1, 196–7, 306–7.

30 Gurney, *Co-operative Culture*, Appendix 1, pp. 241–2; *Co-operative Independent Commission Report*, p. 85, Table 13; Turnbull and Southern, *More Than Just a Shop*, pp. 19–21.

31 *Co-operative Independent Commission Report*, p. 87, Table 14; Turnbull and Southern, *More Than Just a Shop*, p. 21; Attfield, *With Light of Knowledge*, p. 72.

32 Turnbull and Southern, *More Than Just a Shop*, pp. 54–5.

33 For example, F.W. Peaples, *History of the Great and Little Bolton Co-operative Society Limited, Showing Fifty Years' Progress, 1859–1909* (Bolton: Bolton Co-op Society, 1909); or, on a smaller scale, David Lawton, *Village Co-operation: A Jubilee Sketch of Greenfield Co-operative Society Ltd, 1856–1906* (Manchester,

1906): a 128-page hard-back history of a Lancashire society which had 608 members in 1905 (p. 122). Liverpool was among the Societies that did produce centenary histories, but it had begun early enough to lay claim to the milestone in the inter-war years: W.H. Brown, *A Century of Liverpool Co-operation* (Liverpool: Liverpool Co-operative Society, 1929).

34 Attfield, *With Light of Knowledge*, pp. 95–7, 116–20; Turnbull and Southern, *More Than Just a Shop*, pp. 43–4, 48.

35 Matthew Hilton, *Consumerism in Twentieth-Century Britain* (Cambridge: Cambridge University Press, 2003), in which the co-operative movement receives little attention.

36 Gurney, 'Battle of the consumer'.

37 Attfield, *With Light of Knowledge*, p. 72.

38 *Co-operative Independent Commission Report*, pp. 28, 138–43.

39 Flanagan, *Centenary Story*, pp. 126–7; Attfield, *With Light of Knowledge*, p. 73.

40 Attfield, *With Light of Knowledge*, pp. 63, 73.

41 Ibid., Chapters 4–6; J. Southern, 'The co-operative movement in the North West of England, 1919–1939: images and realities' (PhD, Lancaster University, 1996).

42 Gurney, 'Battle of the consumer'.

43 *Co-operative Independent Commission Report*, pp. 139–40.

44 Attfield, *With Light of Knowledge*, pp. 95–6; Callum Brown, *The Death of Christian Britain* (London: Routledge, 2001).

45 William Crofts, *Coercion or Persuasion? Propaganda in Britain after 1945* (London: Routledge, 1989), Ch. 14.

46 See Ina Zweiniger-Bargielowska, *Austerity in Britain: Rationing, Controls and Consumption 1939–1955* (Oxford: Oxford University Press, 2000).

47 Turnbull and Southern, *More Than Just a Shop*, p. 27; *Co-operative Independent Commission Report*, p. 24.

48 *Daily Herald* (23 August 1950): National Cartoon Archive, University of Kent (NCA), David Low, LSE7796.

49 *Daily Mail* (17 December 1974): NCA, Mac (Stan McMurtry), 27110. There is a suggestion in the top right-hand corner of the cartoon that the Co-op had not yet caught up with the introduction of decimal currency three years earlier.

50 J. Birchall, *Co-op: The People's Business* (Manchester: Manchester University Press, 1994).

Figure 3.1 'Business pitfall', David Low's cartoon in The Guardian (10 June 1960), shows the verdict of the Co-operative Independent Commission (1958) and the Co-op's uneasy reception of its report. A suited Gaitskell, affluent shoppers and modern retail competitors are warily eyed by the Co-op. Copyright: British Cartoon Archive, University of Kent (LSE8652). See Walton, Chapter 2 and Black, Chapter 3.

3

'Trying to sell a parcel of politics with a parcel of groceries': the Co-operative Independent Commission (CIC) and consumerism in post-war Britain

Lawrence Black

The Co-op's quantitative claim to represent consumers in the 1950s and 1960s was formidable. Its submission to the Molony Committee on Consumer Protection reckoned two in three Britons had regular contact with the Co-op.[1] Yet its trading position was more parlous than this and qualitatively too, the Co-op seemed a fading rather than dynamic presence. It was this that the CIC (1955–58) was charged with interrogating.

Between 1957 and 1961 Co-op retail trade increased by 6 per cent, that of multiples (like Marks & Spencer) by 37 per cent; its market share fell by a third 1957–70 to under 8 per cent. Its strengths were in necessities like food and coal where spending was static rather than in dry goods or consumer durables, such as cars and radio-electrical (up 371 and 131 per cent respectively, 1952–62) and where margins were in any case greater. The motoring revolution overtook it, with less than a tenth of societies selling petrol and many fewer cars. As Sidney Pollard put it in 1964, it was 'tied to the geography of the tram rather than the bus or motor car'. It was poorly represented in the suburbs, newer housing estates and the South, where population growth was stronger. More than half of its clothing shops were located in areas that accounted for 18 per cent of national trade. Glasgow, Liverpool and London's West End had no Co-op outlets on the main shopping streets. Pollard admitted the Co-op's image was 'coloured by the drab and semi-derelict nature of their strongholds in the North', whereas 'there clings to the South . . . an aura of success and glamour which the chain stores . . . bring.'[2] If there was a Northern chic to post-industrialising 1960s Britain, then it was not acquired from the Co-op. The Co-op's problems were those of relative rather than absolute decline and the difficulties of being an early innovator.

In less tangible ways too the Co-op seemed at odds with the main trends of change. The defining Co-op value, its unique selling point (USP), was the dividend. Accrued on Co-op purchases, dividends were based on earned and deferred pleasure and rewarded loyalty. But post-rationing consumerism was edging rather more toward immediate gratification than toward self-restraint in the realm of goods. Hire-purchase and credit detached spending from earning power and were used to attain luxuries rather than immediate needs. Co-op traditions of (if not preference for) cash-only trading were long gone – it offered generous credit terms in mutuality clubs, but remained attached to the dividend rather than to price cuts or trading stamps, at least until the symbolically seismic advent of a national stamp scheme in March 1968. Its puritan moorings were apparent in that the majority of societies did not sell alcohol, and in its unease toward newer fashions. Such frugal instincts were not absent from shoppers, but commentators like journalist Robert Millar believed the Co-op was past its sell-by date and bypassed it in their tours of the emergent high street.[3]

There were structural reasons for the Co-op's post-war malaise. As Mercer, Gurney and Hilton have shown, it was systematically excluded or marginalised from markets by trade associations and competition legislation, politically by both parties, from government committees like Molony and even by price regimes, despite having long campaigned against Resale Price Maintenance (RPM) that ended in 1964. As Hilton argues, struggling to meet the demands of relative affluence, the Co-op's status as a consumer advocate was also challenged by comparative testing organisations aiming to inform consumer choice, most notably the Consumers' Association (CA).[4] Where the CA flourished, the Co-op seemed afflicted by the new consumption. Yet the CIC reported that many of the Co-op's difficulties were self-inflicted rather than the result of social change. Without discounting structural factors, the emphasis here is on the internal culture, inherited traditions and instincts of the Co-op's ethos, suggesting these were at least as weighty.

The report

Prescient warnings abounded before the Commission. In 1955 Jack Bailey, National Secretary of the Co-operative Party, anticipated 'intense competition' from the multiples, that the rate of amalgamation was 'too slow' and of how 'modern methods of advertising and publicity' and their power to 'influence . . . public taste and consumer demand . . . threaten the accustomed levels of the dividend'. He welcomed the CIC as breaking down the Co-op's fear of outsiders. A 1951 survey of the Co-op's 607 self-service shops found that it could reduce wage costs, satisfy customers and boost sales. It 'predicted that self-service will extend', but recommended 'greater study' to refine the practice and since the Co-op 'cannot afford . . . to allow this new method of retailing to settle into a routine business operation' and there were 'signs that this may be happening'. Its authors, the Co-op Union's Research Officer (Hough)

and manager of the Co-op Wholesale Society (CWS) market research department (Lambert), felt 'it would be a pity if, having played the role of pioneers,
the movement were to allow others to take advantage of its work'.[5]

The CIC was chaired by Hugh Gaitskell, and was composed of the author
of the seminal 1954 study *Retail Trading in Great Britain, 1850–1950* and
secretary of the International Association of Department Stores, J.B. Jeffreys;
J.T. Murray, industrial consultant and member of the Scientific Advisory
Council; economics Professor D.T. Jack; Alderman Pette, Middlesbrough
Society general manager; Margaret Digby, the secretary of the Agricultural
Co-operative Producers Federation and the Horace Plunkett Foundation
(which furnished the CIC with London offices); and Colonel Hardie, whose
minority report argued for national co-operative societies for Scotland and
England-Wales.

This composition was controversial. 'Is Gaitskell the right man?' wondered
Co-operative Consumer. Gaitskell's election as Labour leader late in 1955
placed the onus on Tony Crosland, who replaced the Co-Op Union's assistant
general secretary as CIC secretary early in 1956, the same year as he published
the revisionist text, *The Future of Socialism.* Later that year economist Lady
Margaret Hall joined and the pro-revisionist Alan Sainsbury was also touted.
The Co-op Union's general secretary expressed anxiety at the appointment
of 'one of our competitors', borne out by Sainsbury apologising for missing
a scheduled meeting because of opening the first New Town self-service
Sainsbury's.[6]

Those of revisionist tendency were regarded uneasily by many who feared
the CIC was a lever to modernise the Co-op and its conclusions pre-meditated.
Crosland was up-front that 'our proposals to be of any use must be . . . so
radical that the movement will not accept them *in toto* the year after we report'.
He anticipated 'the minority of progressive leaders – the Jacques', Forsyths . . .
should accept the rightness of our proposals straight away', but 'that the movement as a whole should adopt them in 10 years time'. The CIC tackled cher-
ished Co-op principles, deemed some outdated (cash trading), and updated
(democratic control) and reconfigured others. Crosland, for instance, figured
the Co-op wasn't a non-profit organisation so much as one that distributed its
surplus to customers in a way that offset private capital gains.[7]

Democracy was the linchpin of the Co-op's claim to represent and be
controlled by its consumers. For all its benefits, Crosland believed market
forces might be 'more efficacious' at making producers and managers sensitive to consumers, given the low level of participation in Co-op affairs. A
1954 Co-op College survey found 0.24 per cent attended meetings and 2.78
per cent voted in local board elections. This could lead to 'faction-packing' at
meetings, either political (Jefferys reported 'mutterings' about Catholics in
Beswick battling Communists in Manchester and Salford) or by employees,

trumping the interests of consumers. But given the movement's growth (the average society was thirty times larger in the 1950s than in the 1880s), lower participation was, Crosland deduced, neither surprising nor necessarily problematic. Where democracy might be 'an obstacle' was if lay boards interfered in management or local societies derailed national initiatives (like amalgamations or the proposed retail development society).[8]

Such thinking trod on hallowed traditions of local autonomy and egalitarianism. This was also true of management, where the CIC wanted better-educated recruits from outside besides within the movement. Post-war educational changes meant recruitment from school leavers no longer guaranteed the Co-op the best working-class students and left it with what a later critic described as 'largely inbred' management, prone to reproduce its culture. In 1958 not 1 per cent of societies had a full-time personnel officer. Moreover, the Commission supposed – echoing Crosland's belief in the 'managerial revolution' – management to 'have become more complex, more specialized'. To this end and to negotiate low participation levels, the role of lay elected boards (inexpert, amateur, but democratically accountable) should be clearly differentiated from that of professional, specialist management. The Commission saw no principled reason why efficiency, skilled management and democratic control could not operate in tandem.[9]

Streamlining CWS and Scottish CWS production to better coordinate it with retail societies was laboriously discussed. There was no doubting the advantages of vertical integration (the retail societies owned the wholesale societies), but since Co-op factories didn't make everything the retail societies bought, it was felt the two wholesale societies might best wield their market power to buy for retail societies. The latter lacked modern layout and design (in 1957 the CWS market-research department found only 20 per cent of window displays were dedicated to Co-op goods) or a national marketing strategy for almost 200 CWS brands. The existing CWS retail society was 'a defensive mechanism', a last resort. What was needed, the CIC decided, was a professional, dynamic Co-operative retail development society (CRDS), able to surmount local resistance, propagate best practice and develop national specialist chains, especially in dry goods.[10]

Another concern was mobilising the movement's capital, tied up by conservatively accounted liquidity ratios and a prudent preference for saving. The Co-op was 'supposed to be a dynamic trading organization, not a giant investment trust', the CIC complained, but exhibited a 'preoccupation with the balance sheet at the expense of the premises.'[11] Jeffreys and Crosland visited Sweden and were impressed by its central advisory services and Domus stores. Crosland found it more 'venturesome' than the British movement.[12]

The Commission's UK visits made for a doleful audit of mid-century Co-operation. At the Royal Arsenal, Britain's largest Society, there was plenty of capital, but little imagination. Self-satisfaction emanated from the 'unimpressive' general manager and committee. At its Powis Street store, Jeffreys found that 'lighting was dull, the fixtures were 30 years old . . . signing was ugly and careless'. The CWS directors were only the most senior managers to impress the Commission with their amateurishness and complacency. If these were recurrent themes, field findings ranged from the ridiculous to the sublime. Huddersfield really agitated Crosland. Its 'fantastic number of huge shops of a positively Edwardian size and majesty' if 'often tarnished', caused 'vast waste', since they belonged to no fewer than 37 different societies in the city. The economist in Crosland saw it as 'a textbook example of the advantages of rationalization'. He compared Huddersfield with 'a late Roman Emperor whose proud bearing and splendid robes conceal a fatal weakness'. Accounting for its management, Crosland turned to the Renaissance: '15th century Italy can offer nothing to compare with the ancient feuds . . . passed on from generation to generation' that blighted meetings. Crawley provided modernist relief. Its expansive plans were funded via a low liquidity ratio and its Epstein sculpture and 'remarkable' lunch with wine and Irish coffee, left Crosland contemplating 'what a dreamworld it would be if all Co-operative societies were like this'.[13]

The '"image" of a Co-operative shop in the public mind', the CIC report declared, was an 'unimaginative grocery-cum-butchery-cum-drapery, built in the early 1900s, still operating counter-service, the window display old-fashioned, the exterior clumsy and badly in need of paint, the interior frowsy'. There were 'too many such Co-operative premises, especially in parts of Scotland and the North' that lent the 'whole movement a name for . . . drabness'. This ill suited the modern consumer. The commission was bluntly told: 'women in Southampton don't buy their clothes [at the Co-op] because they are made of cheap, shoddy material and not modern in style and at a dear price' and that the grocery department had a reputation 'for very bad service'.[14]

If this common impression of the Co-op was partly a hangover from rationing, it also stemmed from the Co-op's instinctive focus on subsistence needs and propensity to regard consumers as equals. But it ill fitted the relative affluence of the later 1950s. J.T. Murray welcomed the 'creative minority of experts' – designers, advertisers – aiming to 'create new satisfactions for the consumer of which he would unaided probably never have dreamed'. Murray warned those in the Co-op who thought this 'amoral' were failing to 'recognize their creative responsibilities'. Crosland concurred, rejecting distinctions between innate needs and invented wants and insisting the Co-op 'must give the consumer what he thinks he wants as well as what it thinks he wants'.[15]

The CIC aspired to highlight how consumer control made it responsive to customer demands, but also to the high standards it saw at Macy's or Printemps. The report declared the Co-op's slogan 'should be that "nothing is too good for the co-operator"'. Its ambition was 'that the word "co-operative" comes to be a synonym for both leadership and dependability in respect of price, quality and service' instead of, as at present, 'associated with a drab, colourless, old-fashioned mediocrity'. 'It must be said dogmatically that this is not good enough for the consumer in 1958' and 'betrays a somewhat patronising and insulting attitude to the wants and expectations of the ordinary co-operative member'. To rectify this it insisted 'the greater proportion of co-operative capital expenditure in the next few years should take place, not in the production, but in the retail field' and that the wholesale societies should become 'more retail-minded'.[16]

Reception

Among historians Birchall considered the CIC report was received, if not implemented, with enthusiasm; Pollard felt it went 'largely unheeded'. Battle was joined well before it was published. The Newcastle Society's General Manager, J.T. Fair, confessed he was 'not interested in the Independent Commission . . . we have the brains . . . let us get down to the job'. Others, like Jacques, defended ideas of smaller, potent management structures.[17] What most clearly impressed through the weight of evidence in the Report were the Co-op's Byzantine structures and traditions – qualities that were to outweigh and assimilate the report's proposals.

Within Co-op circles the sense was that the CIC proposals modified 'the traditional conception of Co-operative democratic control in the pursuit of business efficiency'. Critics of the Co-op agreed it amounted to 'bouquets for capitalism'. Both the revisionist *Socialist Commentary* and David Ainley, a communist London Society member, doubted the loss of lay democratic control was worth the gains in efficiency.[18] *Tribune* and *The Economist* agreed that if 'apathy is often a greater enemy than capitalist competition', then this was 'a radical report aimed at a stuffy, conservative organization'.[19] There was a suspicion of the agenda of the modernisers (as Low's 1960 *Guardian* cartoon shows: Figure 3.1 preceding this chapter).

The report was delivered in May 1958 and Gaitskell urged 'don't defer and defer and defer!' Alive to the resistance, a group (including Co-op MP Bert Oram and future Co-op MP George Darling) held a conference in Nottingham in July. Its pamphlet, *Four Things First*, urged establishing the CRDS, a national chain of specialist stores, amalgamations and Wholesale reorganisation.[20] Leonard Cohen, Managing Director of a Manchester store, depicted a depressingly complacent organisation that saw fit to leave the report for six months before formally debating it. The ensuing debate at November's

Special National Congress in Blackpool served to vindicate Robert Millar (the socialist, not journalist) wondering whether 'history and tradition can be overthrown so ruthlessly?'[21]

In November the Co-op Union's Central Executive rejected parts of the Report. Gaitskell expressed his 'disappointment' (not surprise) and with Crosland saw the attempt to absorb the CRDS within the CWS as evidence that producers dominated consumers in the Co-op.[22] The case for amalgamation – 44 North East societies with under 1,000 members were described by the Barnsley British delegate as a 'colossal waste' – a minority thought best handled independently rather than by the Executive. When a delegate suggested that 'parochial instincts . . . in the average board' might work against the wider movement, the Executive and several smaller societies invoked the spectre of compulsory mergers to defend their independence.

The proposed CRDS exposed further divisions. St Albans, Pontycymmer and Stockton's resolution K to have the central executive initiate the CIC's proposal for an independent CRDS narrowly passed. The Executive assured congress it was 'not running away from the problem' but had alternative proposals, reminding local societies that an independent CRDS might overrule them. The Executive promised to action the resolution nonetheless, prompting one delegate to complain that the 'approach of the central executive to this matter is completely inadequate'. To complicate matters, Resolution M to have the Co-op Union develop its own retail services, rather than a separate CRDS, was passed by a majority of 6,790 votes, compared to 91 for K.

As fractious was the debate on recruiting more skilled personnel. A delegate from Redding welcomed the executive's efforts not to *implement* but *encourage* societies to examine recruitment, insisting 'do not let us allow too many of these educated men into this movement', otherwise rather than '"These Things shall be" we shall be singing "Land of Hope and Glory"'. University types would 'bankrupt us' and 'think it below their dignity to enter a co-operative shop'. Though roundly denounced, the effect of the intervention was to deflect the question of implementing reform.

The Executive wanted to *refer* the report to the wholesale societies, but modernisers wanted *acceptance* recommended. Edinburgh's G. Gay argued the executive were as 'mild as lambs when making proposals – or failing to make proposals! – with regard to the future of the wholesales'. The Executive argued they could not prejudge the CWS (whose directors had been too quiet on the Report, a Royal Arsenal delegate held) response and were abetted by a delegate arguing that discussion was best deferred since the wholesale societies difficulties ought not be aired in the presence of 'our enemies' in the press. Others argued too many decisions were being deferred. Pontcymmer's H.C. Greening argued the 'report cannot be treated in bits and pieces', only as 'an integrated whole', but central indifference and local autonomy triumphed.[23]

In 1959 the Executive admitted it did 'not see eye to eye with the Commission on . . . the amalgamation problem'; would not rein in local societies nor specify whether it would prioritize Resolution K or M in developing retail services. But reports in *Co-operative News* through 1959 corroborated CIC findings. Forty societies were accused of having 'fallen hook, line and sinker' for a deal from a combine of Westons, Ranks and Spillers that was 'crippling the co-operative baking trade' and showed the lack of co-ordination between retail and wholesale. Mark Abrams, another revisionist who supplied data for the CRDS negotiating Committee, showed multiples' market lead in areas like clothing and electricals and tied this to the CIC's argument that they were more adroitly winning clientele from the newly prosperous working class.[24]

By 1960 the CRDS was the site on which pro-Commission modernisers took on conservative critics. At Blackpool for the spring congress, the modernisers on the CRDS committee – Gay, Greening, Oram and Cyril Forsyth from Nottingham – issued a minority report. They accused the Central Executive of stalling negotiations, trying to 'frighten the movement about its capital position in relation to CRDS' and of exploiting the majority Resolution M had over K to downgrade the CRDS to a CWS chain. The executive countered that neither the minority (who argued for an autonomous retail division of the Co-op Union) nor majority reports argued for an independent CRDS, as the Commission had (and as Watford and Stockton societies still wanted). It argued that the CWS had already commenced a national chain (Shoefayre) and accused the modernisers of 'guerrilla tactics'. As think-tank Political and Economic Planning (PEP) concluded, 'the rebels, even if successful, will go only part of the way to implement the independent commission's report'.[25]

Shopfloor modernisation flawed

Evidence of resistance to change was abundant. The Co-op's submission to the Molony Committee harked back to the 1940s Utility scheme as 'a guarantee of good quality and a fair deal'. Its preference for state regulation rather than the voluntary efforts that replaced Utility after 1952 was not tempered by any consideration of consumer pleasure or empowerment at the ending of such regulation.[26]

Leslie Adrian, consumer correspondent of *The Spectator*, thought the Co-op had been overlooked in the attention lavished on the newer CA. Its goods were by no 'means as bad as the Co-op's opponents like to claim', but its public image was such that its 'virtues tend to be overlooked and vices exaggerated'. Adrian dwelt on why despite efforts at retail modernisation, it maintained an old-fashioned image, surmising that in Co-op culture 'the past has too much influence on the present and may undermine the future'.[27]

The editor of *Stores and Shops* thought 'parochialism' was the Co-op's 'besetting sin'. It had 'an inbred, subconscious reluctance to make too much money or to join too vigorously in the . . . battles which rage up and down our High Streets'. Management consultant Nancy Hewitt highlighted this 'inward looking attitude' that meant it tended 'to concentrate on existing members' rather than on new trade. Difficulties 'more properly . . . ascribed to bad public relations', were put down 'to political prejudice and lack of loyalty and idealism' among shoppers. Hewitt felt the Co-op underestimated shoppers. Most people did 'not care less what party ticket the directors of a business wear', but the Co-op's ethical brand as 'a living symbol of its belief that people do not exist to make a profit out of each other' could yield idealistic dividends, particularly in youth markets.[28]

The Co-op 'boasted, perhaps too quietly' of its forty goods approved by the Council of Industrial Design (CoID)'s Design Index. A Croydon co-operator complained in 1960 that her local store and staff ('lax about assisting') didn't push CWS brands in tandem with TV ads. PEP felt the Co-op did 'not sell its worthwhile consumer educational publications as energetically as a private enterprise publisher would'.[29] But modern publicity seemed to adulterate Co-op values, emphasising image (for Bonner, the 'biggest and most persistent lie' prevailed) over ideals. This was despite its long history and ranking in the UK top 20 for expenditure. This unease was apparent toward commercial television, which despite busting the BBC's monopoly, was feared by the Co-op as evidence of private commercial power and beyond the finances of individual societies. Burton shows the Co-op's attitude toward ITV combined its fears with a pragmatic outlook (which can be read into its brand of TV sets, the 'Defiant'). The CWS applied for a commercial licence to force the government to address the danger of control of programmes by manufacturers. CWS took out advertisements from ITV's outset and, overriding the anxieties of local societies, developed national strategies for its brands and for the Co-op itself in 1968's 'Operation Facelift', with a uniform blue on white logo.[30]

Modernisation met resistance. Woodham has related the difficulties the CoID experienced in bringing modern furniture design and marketing to the Co-op from the late 1940s. The CA painted a mixed picture. Positive reports in *Which?* suggested 'Co-operative products may be among the best available', whatever 'shoppers' casual gossip' insinuated. CIC supporters, like Forsyth, saw potential in progress in his own society on credit trading and management, but could not demur from more generic criticisms.[31]

The Co-op's relationship to self-service was paradigmatic of this flawed modernisation. It was a pioneer – 90 per cent of self-service stores in Britain in 1950 were Co-ops, but just one quarter by 1968. A similar pattern occurred with supermarkets – the Co-op ran two-thirds of these in 1953, but scarcely a third by 1960. In 1957 three-quarters of Northern Co-ops were self-service, but in the South less than one-third, well behind the multiples. Shaw, Curth and Alexander have stressed how self-service and supermarket development was constrained until 1954 by rationing, building restrictions and RPM. Once these passed, so did the Co-op's advantage, which was in conversions rather than costlier building of new, larger outlets.[32] Mobile shops were an alternative. Serving housing estates and rural areas, they commanded 3 per cent of national trade. The Co-op ran around half these by 1959, mostly in Scotland and Northern England. And bar fifty self-service mobiles, their success drew upon the expertise of their salespeople.[33]

The Self-Service Development Association reckoned Co-ops lagged behind competitors in having a higher ratio of storage to sales area. A Board of Trade survey of self-service had the Co-op behind the pace in sales per checkout or shopfloor area.[34] In 1960 the Nottingham society compared the performance of forty-five product groups in an experimental self-service store (Farnborough Road) against a yardstick store (Dungannon Road). Techniques such as grouping related products and the marketing of Co-op brands (Shieldhall coffee outstripped the brand leader without price incentives) saw the experimental store increase sales significantly. The authors concluded that 'the counters of stores have been removed, but the attitude of many managers is still a counter service attitude . . . apparent in the lack of . . . adventurous merchandising and unprofitable control and utilization of floor and shelf space'. Hough's fears in 1951 had been realised.[35]

Self-service was a useful but not definitive register of modernising trends. Contemporary research found that for all the time it gave shoppers, they complained of checkout queues (complicated in the Co-op by the issue of dividends), lack of a personal sales touch and knowledge and the anonymity of supermarkets. The CA's rapid growth, after all, had much to do with the dilemmas of choice posed by self-service.[36]

Uncertainties in modernisation stemmed from a sense that that economic, political and democratic attachments to the Co-op were slipping. The fate of the *Sunday Citizen*, as *Reynolds News* had been rebadged in tabloid form in 1962, was symptomatic. It struggled on until June 1967, but its almost exclusively working-class readership made for a poor advertising profile, which impeded efforts to win advertising – including from the Labour government.[37]

Halsey and Ostergaard found that the Rochdale Pioneers meant nothing to 89 per cent of members, who saw the Co-op as a shop not a social movement, and concluded the 'drift towards apathy' was pronounced in the Co-op. Participation beyond shopping, they described in 1965, was 'a *diminuendo* on small numbers'. This made for a trading and democratic deficit. A 1960 survey found that besides being more male, middle-class and likely to be a Co-op employee than the average Co-op member, those who actively participated in the local Co-op also shopped there more.[38] The issue of dividends could be, the Central Executive explained in 1958 – arguing for less publicity for a dividend day and for societies to encourage members to retain them in share accounts – as beneficial to other traders as an advertisement for Co-op shopping. 'What are we to do', a Coventry Co-operator asked MP Richard Crossman in 1955, 'when our members draw the "divi" to spend at M&S'? Even such loyalty as could be detected in the Co-op's insularity had the effect, PEP reckoned, of robbing Co-op consumers 'almost completely of their sense of discrimination'. They were poorer because 'the devoted co-operator will prefer to buy at his own shop even though a manifestly better buy is on offer in a free enterprise shop'.[39]

Average capital holding per member fell by two-thirds in the period 1938–59, leaving many with merely nominal shareholdings. This problem grew through the 1960s as a younger generation withdrew parents' holdings, leaving societies with runs on capital. Rotherham suspended repayment in 1967 and even large societies like Barnsley British were impacted. Meeting with the Friendly Societies Registrar in 1971, Senior CWS officials 'fully accepted' that this 'arose from poor management' and the 'failure to adopt up-to-date ideas'. The CIC suggested that withdrawable schemes in local societies might be supplemented by longer-term investment opportunities. This was realised in a CWS ten-year escalator bond scheme, but only by 1971. Critics feared it would supplant traditional local schemes with central control.[40]

The Co-op's political and social aspect generated limited interest. The Co-op opined that its distinctive problem was 'trying to sell a parcel of politics with a parcel of groceries'. No irreconcilable task, but one that evidence here suggests was tough given what was being sold, how and to whom. At Royal Arsenal, the only society to affiliate direct to Labour, the CIC found this put off as few members as it attracted. Only one of 204 respondents to a 1958 survey of new Manchester members joined for political reasons – a third joined for the 'divi', 41 per cent were introduced by family, 14 per cent by Co-op Roundsmen.[41]

Most commentators assigned sluggish modernisation – typified by amalgamations which reached the upper level of 300 societies proposed in the 1958 Report only by 1972 and were made more out of financial necessity than conviction or choice – to a failure of will, not of knowledge. This sustained the Co-op in a hamstrung state of anxious self-examination alongside complacent conservatism. Through the 1960s, surveys and commentators reprised the CIC's case. The managing secretary of Nottingham Co-op and Director of the Hyde Equitable, restated the case for accelerating amalgamations to 30–40 regional societies. Bernard Rhodes, head of the London College of Distributive Trades' management department, highlighted weakness in 'trades where fashion . . . style and design are of great importance' such as clothing, hairdressing and record sales. No Co-op restaurants featured in the

Good Food Guide, it ran no wimpy bars and few espresso bars. A 1960 Alfred Bird & Sons survey found 40 per cent of Co-op shoppers were aged 55 or over and only 17 per cent under 35. Local boards elected by and from 'a restricted circle', Rhodes believed, encouraged 'an unwillingness to experiment and a narrow conception of a specifically "co-operative type" of consumer'. This made for familiar reading to those versed in the CIC Report.[42]

A 1963 Co-op College survey underscored the CIC case on management. Woeful contact with careers offices at Grammar schools or Universities meant few managers had a degree (1 per cent at assistant department-head level or above). Of 885 senior vacancies 1956–61, only 10 per cent were filled from outside the movement. College diploma recipients – only three of whom since the 1930s had been women – felt that lay boards favoured length of service over talent in promotion and that the multiples offered better salaries. (The Co-op feared alienating managers from the shop floor.)[43]

Pollard reconciled his initial criticisms with the CIC report. The CWS, SCWS and Co-op Union should merge, a move that retail societies and the SCWS scotched at the 1964 congress. Only such a body would have the power to effect reform and sustain the 'divi' in the anticipated onslaught from multiple retailers after the abolition of RPM. Pollard drew on Hewitt's assessment of Co-op management, but his advocacy was not simply business-minded. Consumer societies should 'remain proselytizing agencies for their own form of trading as a superior form'. To reject the new affluence was aimless, because while he shared the Co-op's 'healthy suspicion' of advertising, 'the saving and . . . dull and unglamorous routine of the Victorian working class home were not ideal for the development of the human spirit'. Instead Pollard referenced the Co-op Union Education Department's collaboration (further detailed in Whitworth's chapter 11 in this volume) with the CoID and their pamphlet, *Eating, Sleeping and Living*. The slogan 'only the best was good enough for their members' was apt, marrying the Co-op's hope of making capital servant not master of people's lives with modern post-materialist agendas of the quality of life.

Pollard noted the rise of a new consumer movement, the CoID and notably the CA. Such developments had 'bypassed the co-operative movement' and garnered media attention, although Pollard was uncertain whether this was because of their vocal criticisms of goods or by virtue of being more compatible with a liberal market economy. Pollard believed the new movement was too middle-class and had structural limits to its influence. Their initiatives were 'static and passive . . . they cannot by themselves initiate production or use the purchasing power of a large membership or of a large chain of shops'. In this lay the potential for the Co-op to 'recapture the initiative in this field' and realise the consumer movement's 'countervailing power'.[44]

For its part, the CA saw the Co-op as 'the neglected opportunity of the contemporary consumer revolution' and its Director, Casper Brook, suggested 'what the Co-ops need is a Dr Beeching' to enforce the CIC's Report. Its failure to involve shopper-members in decisions on goods, prices and quality negated its democratic potential and claims to represent consumers. It was a 'producer-oriented organization' where the CA maintained independence from producers. It represented Co-op, not *all* consumers.[45]

The International Co-Operative Alliance's head of economics research retorted that 'to inform a consumer about the relative merits of different products enables him to become a *discriminating* consumer rather than an *active* consumer'. 'Only when consumers are organized and their consumption becomes creative' did they 'become active consumers'. 'By feeding back to producers and distributors, whose activities they control by ownership' it was possible for consumers 'in Co-operative societies to do something that the new consumer movement cannot'. Its submission to Molony bemoaned collaboration with the CA being limited (by CA's strict independence from producers) to work on consumers' legal rights, but suggested CA's testing was of more interest to traders than consumers.[46] That *Which?* aided manufacturers was a common charge, one CA claimed as testimony to its facilitation of consumer-producer dialogue (except where it was perceived as in the pay of business). Other Co-op critiques of the CA's approach disclosed its resistance to change. Bonner thought 'scepticism of advertising by the more intelligent consumer' was 'not enough' to compensate the consumer 'deprived of the assistance of knowledgeable retailers' in the self-service era.[47]

At stake here was the form of modern consumer politics – CA's consumers asserting their individual power and right to choose in the marketplace, vying with the Co-op's collective attempt to provide an alternative system to the market. But there were resemblances. Crosland's Co-op associations were used to question the impartiality of the CA (on whose executive he sat from 1958 to 1964) toward Co-op goods.[48] And like the Co-op, the CA's claim to speak for consumers was limited. One in four Britons might see *Which?*, but CA's membership, like the Co-op's, saw it as a value-for-money guide and was more apathetic toward its broader social movement aspirations. For this reason, Crosland's proposed CA constitution separated policy-making from membership control. Like other CA leaders, he was anxious to develop an audience beyond the middle class.[49]

Epilogue

Historians and biographers have overlooked Crosland's relationship with the consumer movement. Not least, the £2,000 he was paid as CIC secretary was welcome since he had lost his parliamentary seat in 1955, and Co-op associations helped him become MP for Grimsby in 1959. His frustration at the report's rejection and closeness to CA founder Michael Young is noted, but not his formal CA links. Hilton has detailed Young and Crosland's rethinking of social democracy along less productionist lines.[50] But the Co-op also informed his thinking on modernisation, Labour, professionalism, Scandinavia and management, besides consumer politics.

The CIC helped forge leitmotivs of Crosland's thinking, not least that democratic society need not have notably high levels of political participation. Discussing 'Co-operative First principles' in February 1956, Crosland noted that 'we do not want the entire population to "participate" or . . . fuss around in an interfering manner constantly attending meetings. An evening, for the ordinary citizen . . . should be spent at home or with friends . . . an active minority of 3 per cent is quite sufficient. Let the rest of us cultivate our gardens'. Such thinking was evident in the final report, *The Future of Socialism*, and was revived in 1970 to caution uncritical celebration of pressure-group advocacy of popular participation.[51]

Crosland returned to the fate of the Co-op in 1971, addressing the Co-op Party's conference. He welcomed the integration of the retail side and CWS, which had seen the latter buying *for* societies and the national advertising strategy and insignia. He endorsed the Co-op Union regional plan, the performance of the Nottingham Society, Insurance society and Bank and (now Lord) Jacques's idea of a national society. But this was tempered by the continuing downward trends in market share and capital position. Above all, consumer representation agitated him. The CA was too middle-class, but nor had the Co-op 'found the right formula to mobilize and express working-class needs and opinions'. With the 'murder' of the state Consumer Council in 1970, Crosland sensed an opportunity, since 'the Tories have deserted the field'. Crosland remained 'a firm believer in competition', but shared Ralph Nader's anxieties that the economy was presently semi-monopolistic and 'immune from the full rigours of competition'. So opposition to monopoly but also educating of consumers were grounds for the Co-op to tend.

Crosland wound up by arguing that the Co-op should expect help from Labour, but had to demonstrate its viability 'and this it has not shown unambiguously in the last ten years'.[52] Co-operators might have felt this was rich, given how fraught relations were with the Wilson government. Most fractious was the Selective Employment Tax (SET), introduced in the 1966 budget and doubled in 1968. An attempt to shift the tax from manufacturing (to aid exports) to distribution and retailing, its burden fell particularly heavily on the Co-op. By 1969 SET payments absorbed half the net profit of consumer co-operatives.[53]

Many societies thought SET 'a vicious stab in the back'. The Co-op Party warned that such 'political spite' questioned 'the whole basis of . . . our relationship with Labour'. But evidence of the Co-op's faltering modernisation weighed against it in meetings with the government. The Prime Minister was briefed in 1969 on its 'old-fashioned image' and 'reluctance . . . to adapt itself to modern conditions'. This came a year after 'Operation Facelift' had sought to renovate the Co-op. In 1966 the CWS management was replaced by professional executives and a part-time board elected by retail societies – bifurcating management and democratic control. By 1971 several senior figures resigned, including Keith Willoughby who introduced the new logo (and joined Woolworth's), and the trading position continued to decline.[54]

The Co-op's resilient culture would seem to disclose much to historians about its fortunes. Its enduring ethical appeal has revived its fortunes since the 1990s. Equally, in 2000, shortly before Andrew Regan's bid to buy CWS, another report critiqued the trading performance, directors and 'old-fashioned image of grocery stores' of the Co-op. Chaired by TUC general secretary Alan Monks and with Alan Donnelly, former Labour leader in the European Parliament, as secretary, the Commission's evidence and conclusions were distinctly reminiscent.[55]

Notes

1 Co-operative Union, *Consumer Protection: A Memorandum Submitted by the Co-operative Union Ltd to the Molony Committee* (Manchester: Co-operative Union, 1960), p. 3.

2 Research Institute for Consumer Affairs (RICA), *British Co-operatives: A Consumer's Movement?* (London: RICA, 1964), pp. 5, 14, 26; C.A.R. Crosland, *A Critical Commentary on Co-operative Progress* (Manchester: Co-op Party, 1971), p. 1; S. Pollard, *The Co-operatives at the Crossroads* (Fabian Research Series 245, 1965), pp. 12–15, 25.

3 P. Gurney, 'The Battle of the consumer in postwar Britain', *Journal of Modern History* 77:4 (2005), pp. 976, 962, 982; R. Millar, *The Affluent Sheep* (London: Longman, 1963), p. 107.

4 M. Hilton, *Consumerism in 20th-century Britain* (Cambridge: Cambridge University Press, 2003); H. Mercer, *Constructing a Competitive Order* (Cambridge: Cambridge University Press, 1995); Gurney, 'Battle of the consumer', p. 984.

5 J. Bailey, *The British Co-Operative Movement* (London: Hutchinson, 1955); J.A. Hough and F. Lambert, *Self-Service Shops* (Manchester: Co-operative Union, n.d., *c*.1951), pp. 10, 13, 15.

6 *Co-Operative Consumer* (January 1956), p. 12; CIC minutes (22 December 1955, 26 October 1956), Hugh Gaitskell papers (University College London, hereafter HG), C309/1: Crosland (9 February 1956); R. Southern (29 October 1956); Sainsbury (11 October 1956) to Gaitskell, HG C309/3.

7 'Co-operative First principles' (28 February 1956), pp. 33–7, Crosland papers (LSE, hereafter, Crosland), 14/1.

8 'Structure of the movement' (n.d.), Crosland 14/1; J.A. Banks and G. Ostergaard,

Co-operative Democracy (Co-op College paper 2, 1955); RICA, *British Co-operatives*, p. 18; Jeffreys report (27 April 1956), HG C309/2.

9 *Co-operative Independent Commission Report* (Manchester: Co-operative Union, 1958), pp. 17, 61, 67–68, 249; RICA, *British Co-operatives*, p. 27.

10 RICA, *British Co-operatives*, p. 35. A. Bonner, *British Co-operation* (Manchester: Co-operative Union, 1970), p. 260. Letter to Crosland (2 November 1956) and 'CWS retail society', 'Production' in Crosland 14/1.

11 *CIC Report*, pp. 45–6, 238.

12 CIC minutes (15 March 1957), HG C309/1; C.A.R. Crosland, *The Future of Socialism* (London: Jonathan Cape, 1956), p. 494.

13 Vis/Carc/2–4, 9, 12, 14, 19, 21, 24, Crosland 14/1.

14 *CIC Report*, pp. 44–9; Elizabeth Wilson (31 January 1956) to Gaitskell, HG C309/3.

15 Mass Observation, Topic Collection 21/F, G, E (1947); J.T. Murray to C.A.R. Crosland (7 March 1957), HG C309/3; 'Co-operative First principles', p. 10.

16 'Co-operative First/Four principles', Crosland papers 14/1; *CIC Report*, pp. 24, 49–50, 235–53.

17 J. Birchall, *Co-op: The People's Business* (Manchester: Manchester University Press, 1994), p. 153; Pollard, *Co-operatives at the Crossroads*, p. 8; *Co-operative News* (3 November 1956, 7 April 1956).

18 A. Perkins, 'First impressions of the Commission's report', *The Bulletin* (Co-Op Educational Secretaries Association, July 1958), p. 11; 'Bouquets for capitalism', *Sunday Times*, 13 July 1958; 'Co-Operator's choice', *Socialist Commentary* (June 1958), pp. 22–3; *Daily Worker* (21 May 1958).

19 *Tribune* (May 9 1958); *Economist* (10 May 1958).

20 *Co-Operative News* (31 May 1958); Oram to Gaitskell (29 July, 13 September 1958), HG C309/3.

21 L. Cohen, 'The future of the Co-ops', *Trading Interest* (n.d., c.June 1958) pp. 17–23, Crosland 14/2; R. Millar, 'A blueprint for co-ops of the future?', *Tribune* (2 May 1958).

22 Gaitskell to R. Southern, 7 November 1958, HG C309/3; Crosland, 'I disagree with the Central Executive', *Scottish Co-Operator* (8 November 1958).

23 *Report of Proceedings Special National Congress, Blackpool* (Manchester: Co-operative Union, 1958), pp. 19–33, 43–65, 69–74, 84–96.

24 *Report of Action by the Central Executive on Resolutions of the Special National Congress* (Manchester: Co-operative Union, 1959), pp. 13–17. *Co-operative News* (28 February, 6 June 1959).

25 *Report of the CRDS Negotiating Committee* (Co-operative Union: Manchester, 1960); Central Executive statement (9 May 1960), leaflet *The Co-ops Must Fight Back*, Mark Abrams Papers, Churchill College Cambridge, Box 82, File 'CRDS, 1959–60'; PEP, 'Consumer protection and enlightenment', *Planning* XXVI:441 (1960), p. 122.

26 Co-operative Union, *Consumer Protection*, p. 14.

27 'Choice improved', *Spectator* (17 April 1964).

28 RICA, *British Co-operatives*, pp. 29–30; N. Hewitt, 'Some causes of Co-op failure', *Agenda* XI:3 (1962).

29 Bonner, *British Co-operation*, p. 249; 'Woo your customers', *Labour Woman* (July 1960), pp. 83–4; PEP, 'Consumer protection', p. 122.

30 Bonner, *British Co-operation*, p. 260; Gurney, 'Battle of the consumer', pp. 969–71. A. Burton, *The British Consumer Co-operative Movement and Film 1890s–1960s* (Manchester: Manchester University Press, 2005), pp. 224–8.

31 J. Woodham 'An episode in post-utility design management: the Council of Industrial Design and the Co-operative Wholesale Society', in J. Attfield (ed.), *Utility Reassessed* (Manchester: Manchester University Press, 1999); RICA, *British Co-operatives*, pp. 30–6.

32 London Press Exchange, 'Self-Service in the UK' (10 September 1957), Abrams Box 81, 'Retail Trade I'; G. Shaw, L. Curth and A. Alexander, 'Selling self-service and the supermarket: the Americanisation of food retailing in Britain, 1945–60', *Business History* 46:4 (2004).

33 Bonner, *British Co-operation*, pp. 248, 250; Leonard M. Harris, Mass Observation Ltd, *Buyer's Market* (London: Business Publications Ltd, 1963), p. 31.

34 *Self-Service and Supermarket* 8:4 (April 1959), p. 46; Ralph Towsey, *Self-Service Retailing* (London: Iliffe Books, 1964), p. 186.

35 L.A. Cherriman and R. Wilson, *The Operation of a Self-Service Store* (Co-op College Papers no. 9, 1962).

36 Towsey, *Self-Service Retailing*, pp. 19–22, 167. Hough and Lambert, *Self-Service Shops*, p. 13.

37 Correspondence from W.R. Richardson, Harold Wilson papers, Bodleian, c.889.

38 A.H. Halsey and G.N. Ostergaard, *Power in Co-operatives* (Oxford: Blackwell, 1965), pp. 70–8, 94–5; *Co-operative News* (7 May 1960).

39 *Special National Congress*, p. 36; Crossman in G. Hodgkinson, *Sent to Coventry* (Oxford: Pergamon, 1970), p. xxvii; PEP, 'Consumer protection', p. 123.

40 S. Musson (Chief Registrar of Friendly Societies) to B.E. Fensome (Treasury) (2 February 1971), National Archives (NA), T326/1303; *CIC Report*, 168–173, 248–9. *Guardian* (28 May 1971).

41 *Co-Operative Consumer* (January 1956), p. 12; Royal Arsenal (Vis/Carc/2), Crosland 14/1; CWS Market Research Department: *Survey among New Members of the Manchester and Salford Society* (February 1958), pp. 33–7, HG C309/6.

42 Birchall, *People's Business*, pp. 147, 159; L. Harrison and J. Roper, *Towards Regional Co-Operatives* (Fabian Research Series 260, 1967); RICA, *British Co-operatives*, pp. 19–28.

43 F.A. Wells, M.D. Skillicorn and J.R. Straker, *Recruitment, Selection and Training for Management in Retail Co-operative Societies* (Co-Op College Papers no. 10, 1963).

44 S. Pollard, 'Tradition versus efficiency', *Socialist Commentary* (July 1958); *Co-Operatives at the Crossroads*, pp. 5, 12–15, 21, 28, 34, 39; Henry and Lillian Stephenson, *Eating, Sleeping and Living: a Guide to Design in the Home* (Manchester: Co-operative Union, 1964).

45 RICA, *British Co-operatives*, pp. 31–6. L. Tivey, 'The politics of the consumer', in R. Kimber and J.J. Richardson (eds), *Pressure Groups in Britain* (London: JM Dent, 1974), p. 197.

46 F.D. Boggis, 'Which? way', *Co-op Party Monthly Newsletter* (September 1963), p. 53; Co-operative Union, *Consumer Protection*, pp. 12–13.
47 Harris, *Buyer's Market*, p. 53; Bonner, *British Co-operation*, p. 249; Millar, *Affluent Sheep*, pp. 194–6.
48 J. Douglas to Casper Brook (16 February 1959), Conservative Party Archive, Bodleian, CRD2/8/19.
49 L. Black, 'Which?craft in post-war Britain: The Consumers' Association and the politics of affluence', *Albion* 36:1 (2004), pp. 70–1; Harris, *Buyer's Market*, p. 53; Tivey, 'Politics of the consumer', p. 199.
50 Co-operative Union accountancy department to Gaitskell (1 December 1956), HG C309/3; Susan Crosland, *Tony Crosland* (London: Coronet Books, 1983), pp. 88, 90; Kevin Jeffreys, *Anthony Crosland* (London: Richard Cohn Books, 1999), pp. 64–5; Hilton, *Consumerism*, pp. 270–6.
51 Crosland, 'Co-operative First principles', p. 7. *CIC Report*, p. 17; Crosland, *Future of Socialism*, pp. 341–2; *A Social Democratic Britain* (Fabian Tract 404, 1971).
52 Crosland, *Critical Commentary*, pp. 1–9.
53 'Summary of objections' (21 July 1969), NA PREM13/2857.
54 Sittingbourne Co-op to Wilson (16 May 1966), Wilson papers, c.1298; T.E. Graham memo to Co-op Parliamentary Group (17 April 1969), 'The Co-operative Union' (17 July 1969), NA PREM 13/2857; *Financial Times* (12 February 1971).
55 'The future of the co-operative movement', *New Statesman* (30 October 2000), p. 3.

4

Consumer co-operation and the transformation of modern food retailing: the British and Norwegian consumer co-operative movement in comparison, 1950–2002

Espen Ekberg

A prominent question in the recent resurgence of interest in studying the historical development of consumer co-operation has been why so many Co-operatives failed to sustain their market position in the post-war period. While important insights have been gained from these studies, they have largely failed to recognise that the post-war history of the consumer co-operative movement is not merely one of decline. True, in the UK, the decline in terms of market shares and membership has been dramatic.[1] While in countries such as the Netherlands, Belgium, France, Germany and Austria once large and vibrant consumer co-operative organisations have simply collapsed.[2] Still, there are important exceptions to this trend. The Norwegian co-operative movement experienced a steady strengthening of its position from the 1950s onward, securing a stable market share of approximately 24 per cent.[3] Similarly, consumer Co-ops in the other Nordic countries, most notably Finland, as well as in Italy and Switzerland have also managed to retain a substantial share of their respective home markets.[4]

To fully account for the post-war developments in consumer co-operative organisations this divergent development pattern should be investigated in more detail. This calls for comparative investigations, systematically analysing co-operative organisations showing a divergent development path. The present chapter seeks to show the possible merits of such an approach. It does so by analysing the post-war decline of the British consumer co-operative movement in light of the overall successful development of the Norwegian Co-ops.

This chapter specifically deals with the question of how the Norwegian and British co-operative organisations confronted major transformations in the competitive climate in which they operated. Throughout the post-war period, the food industry – the core business of most consumer co-operative organisations – was transformed from a structure dominated by small counter-serviced shops, owned individually by independent shopkeepers, to a structure where self-serviced supermarkets and hypermarkets owned by a few large, integrated businesses controlled the majority of the market.[5] These changes fundamentally challenged the market position of the Co-ops and called for drastic reorganisations of their operational and organisational structures. The chapter identifies the main differences between how the UK and Norwegian consumer co-operatives confronted these challenges and discusses how they can be explained.

Co-ops and the development of new retail formats

The post-war period witnessed several radical transformations in the way food was sold to the consumer. The introduction of self-service, the rise of large retail formats such as supermarkets and hypermarkets, and the development of a diversified structure of retail stores aimed at serving different segments of consumers were among the most important.[6] In both Norway and the UK these developments started in the early 1950s. The ultimate result was a dramatic reduction in the number of food stores and a corresponding rise in their average size. The ability of the co-operative societies to confront these changes was fundamental in shaping their subsequent development. As it turned out, the challenges were met with varying success by the British and Norwegian consumer Co-ops.

In 1942 the London Co-operative Society opened what has come to be regarded as the first self-service store in the UK.[7] Five years later, in October 1947, Oslo Co-operative Society opened Norway's first outlet based on self-service. In the following years, consumer co-operative societies were to take a leading role in the implementation of self-service trading in the two countries. By 1954, Norwegian Co-ops controlled close to 40 per cent of all self-service stores, even if they controlled less than 20 per cent of the market.[8] Figures for the UK were even more impressive. As late as 1957, Co-ops in the UK controlled at least 60 per cent of all self-service stores in operation. When *The Co-operative Review* reported on these figures the editor proudly announced that 'a big majority of all the Self-services in this country are co-operative stores'. Even if private traders were trying to catch up they were, in the confident words of the editor, 'still behind the co-operatives in the technique of retailing and . . . likely to stay so for years ahead'.[9]

As it turned out, however, only three years later the majority of self-service stores in the UK were no longer run by Co-ops. Even more problematic was the fact that the Co-op's share of the growing supermarket segment was even lower. Having controlled 66 per cent of all supermarkets in 1953, Co-ops controlled only 37 per cent of supermarkets by 1960.[10] Gradually, several more fundamental problems in how the transformations to self-service and super-market trading had been approached by the UK Co-ops were also revealed.

First of all, while the Co-ops had been quick to transfer their stores to self-service, the outlets had generally been small and were, in many instances, unsuitable for hosting an efficient and modern self-service business. It soon turned out that these early conversions failed to live up to the standards offered by private competitors. As early as 1953, the manager of the CWS market-research department, Fred Lambert, warned members of co-operative management committees that the 'many co-operative conversions carried out some years ago were quite inadequate to present day trade requirements'. The stores opened by multiple retailers 'outshone' the co-operative self-service stores, many of which, in the blunt words of Lambert, were already in danger of becoming 'the slums of self-service'.[11]

A second problem was that the actual running of the co-operative self-service supermarkets was hampered by numerous weaknesses. Space was excessive in relation to sales, average rate of stock turn was too low, and the stores failed to operate on the aggressive price and merchandise policies characteristic of private supermarkets. Rather, as a 1961 report from the Co-operative Union's Food Trades Department pointed out: 'co-operative supermarkets . . . normally trade on the basis of the general price policy of the society operating them and thus co-operative societies in the main have not used the price weapon to attract trade into the larger units'.[12] These problems persisted throughout the 1960s, and according to Co-op researcher Joshua Bamfield, 'even as late as 1968, 73% of Co-op supermarkets had the same price structure as corner shops, would make up orders and provide a delivery service'.[13]

Behind these fundamental trading problems lay a noticeable resentment within the co-op movement itself toward large-scale supermarkets. Conservatism and a reluctance to abandon the small store seems to have prevailed among many of the local societies. Debating at length the report of the newly established Grocery and Provisions Trade Association at the 1961 Co-operative Congress in Scarborough, several of the representatives taking to the podium spoke explicitly against a fast transfer to supermarkets, warning about what they saw as an 'epidemic of supermarket hypnosis'. Some representatives were in fact sceptical of the conclusion that supermarkets would dominate future food trading. Mr Baily of the Midland Sectional Board, for example, argued that the popularity of the supermarkets among the consumer should not be expected to last: 'They go there the first six weeks or so, but sooner or later they feel that dragging the groceries home a mile-and-a-half from the High Street is not so satisfactory as walking 200 yards and getting the goods in our shops as cheaply as they can get them in the supermarkets, and in addition receiving dividend on all purchase.'[14] The ultimate consequence of such resentment was that the co-operative societies fell behind their private competitors in the transfer of trade to larger, more efficient units.

Turning to the Norwegian development, the contrasts are striking. First of all, the Norwegian Co-ops managed to hold on to their initial lead in self-service and supermarket trading. This was the case both in terms of the number of stores operated and in terms of size. One important reason was that private retailers remained chiefly small-scale and hence the race to enlarge and modernise the stores was less fierce in Norway than in the UK. In 1954 it was estimated that the average turnover in co-operative food stores was more than twice that of the private retailers.[15] Twelve years later the situation had changed only marginally, the average turnover of co-operative shops still being close to twice the size of that in the privately owned stores.[16]

The Norwegian Co-operatives also outpaced their British sister organisation in transferring trade toward the supermarket segment. By 1966, 13 per cent of all co-operative shops in Norway were run as supermarkets.[17] The similar figure for the UK movement was 3 per cent.[18] One important reason for this difference may be that while British co-operators continued to express reluctance toward the new retail formats, Norwegian co-operators took pride in leading the modernisation of the retailing business. Norwegian co-operators generally expressed a much more pragmatic stance toward the need for change and for the Co-ops to develop their stores into larger units.

The viability of such pragmatic attitudes was clearly demonstrated when a group of ten co-operative societies around Trondheim, in close co-operation with their national federation – The Norwegian Co-operative Association (NKL) – opened Norway's first hypermarket in 1968. The opening sparked off a process whereby the co-op movement also took on the leading role in developing large-scale hypermarket retailing in the Norwegian market. By the mid-1980s, Co-ops were running seven out of the ten largest food stores in the country.[19]

In Britain on the other hand, Co-op hypermarket development followed much the same pattern as the transfer to self-service and supermarkets. The co-operators took an early lead when considering the number of stores operated. By 1979, 27 Co-op hypermarkets and superstores had been opened, making the Co-op the second largest operator of such stores in the UK.[20] Seven years later the co-op movement was running 65 superstores, still giving them one of the leading positions in the number of stores operated.[21] But the efficiency of the stores, in terms of sales per square foot, remained behind that of their competitors. The stores were also 'spread thinly across a number of societies', causing fragmentation and problems in realising the potential economies of scale.[22] The opening of the large stores also drained the societies of capital, and expansion by way of huge and expensive loans put a heavy cost burden on societies already struggling to produce a profit.

This more general problem of capital formations reflects a further important difference between the Norwegian and UK consumer Co-ops, characteristic of the period as a whole. In Norway a savings campaign started as early as 1954 had a tremendous effect on the total level of share capital. In the period from 1950 to 1980, members' savings grew eightfold in fixed prices. The contrast with capital development in the UK Co-ops is striking. Not only did continuous erosion of sales and generally weak profitability severely hamper their financial situation, negative publicity and increased competition for savings also caused members to withdraw their deposits. Hence, instead of a strengthening of the financial position, in the period from 1945 to 1985 share capital declined by 95 per cent in real terms.[23] In only the short period 1968–70, fifty million or 12 per cent of total capital employed was withdrawn from societies.[24] Government legislation restricting self-investment also forced retail societies to dispose of their employees' pension funds in external equities, without having the possibility of receiving similar investments in return.[25] Finally, capital realised from the selling of assets, which could have eased some of the financial strains, was largely used to cover up trading losses, and not invested in new stores.[26] Even more problematically, large sums were used to retain substantial dividend rates. As Joshua Bamfield has shown, in the period 1981–83 co-operatives paid out dividends totalling £70 million. In the same period the total net profits of the movement added up to £4 million.[27]

Hence, both in terms of capital formation and when it came to the application of the capital actually available, the Norwegian Co-ops had a clear advantage over their British counterparts. The overall consequence was to be seen in the two movements' different ability to expand, and more fundamentally, in the development of their market shares. In the period from 1980 to 2000 alone, the Co-op's share of the UK food retailing market was close to halved. In Norway by contrast, the market share of the co-operative movement remained fairly stable at 23–25 per cent.

The dramatic decline in market shares seen in the UK gradually pushed forward a radical reformulation of the movement's overall strategy. It was believed that in order to survive, the movement had to focus its operations on one distinct market segment. Hence, in 1997 the CWS, by now the largest retail co-operative within the movement, announced that they, after a 'major strategic review' had 'identified [their] particular strengths as being in conveniences stores and . . . medium sized supermarkets'.[28] Similar strategic reorientations were made in other societies, superstores were sold off to competitors and the movement as a whole increasingly came to define itself as a 'community retailer'.[29]

This strategic turn was, however, made in a period when competing multiples were starting to abandon their one-sided reliance on large stores and diversifying their operations into several different market segments. The order of the day within the retail industry of the 1990s was not to focus on particular segments, but rather to be present in different markets through a multi-format strategy.[30] Hence, both Tesco and Sainsbury's started to open convenience stores, while at the same time consolidating their position in the supermarket and hypermarket segments. A similar strategy had already been chosen by the Norwegian co-operative movement from the mid-1980s onward. A separate chain of discount stores had been developed alongside a chain of supermarkets, as well as a chain of local stores. By 2002 the Co-ops were holding leading positions in three out of the four most important segments in the Norwegian food retailing market (the local-store segment, the supermarket segment and the hypermarket segment).[31]

By deciding to leave the large-scale segments and focus specifically on the convenience format, the UK Co-ops went counter to the major trends in the food retail industry. An obvious consequence was further loss of market share. At the same time the Co-ops were faced with strengthened competition in the convenience segment, as major competitors started to diversify their business into a multitude of markets, including the convenience market.[32] An as yet unanswered question is thus whether the Co-ops can manage to run their medium-sized convenience stores as efficient as the large multiples, without having the same possibilities of scale in buying coming from the parallel running of large hypermarkets.

To conclude, the post-war challenge of transforming existing sales premises to larger and more efficient units proved much more difficult in the UK than in the Norwegian co-operative movement. While the British Co-ops lost a large market share and were gradually forced to focus their operations on the limited convenience segment, the Norwegian Co-ops managed to remain in the lead in a broad group of different segments. In part this may be attributed to the different competitive climates of the two countries. Still, different approaches to the transformation to self-service, diverging attitudes toward the value and prospects of co-operative large-scale retailing, and above all, different fortunes in solving the capital problem, also proved vital.

The challenge from the retail multiples

Besides the development of large supermarkets and hypermarkets, perhaps the most notable change within the post-1945 Western European retail market was the growing importance of the large, integrated retail chains.[33] From being dominated by small, independent shopkeepers, the food retail industry was gradually to become completely controlled by large, hierarchically organised enterprises comprising both retail and wholesale functions. The timing and extent of these transformations were different in Norway and the UK, private retail chains not making serious inroads in the Norwegian market before the mid-1970s onward. But the ultimate result of the development was that both the British and the Norwegian food retail markets came to be completely controlled by the large, integrated chains.[34]

The general strategic recipe of these so-called multiple retailers was to standardise operations, stocks and advertising, centralise buying, and create an integrated and dedicated distribution system (either by way of vertical integration or by contracting).[35] The chains showed superior efficiencies in their operations and the consumer Co-ops had to find ways of keeping up with this new competition in order to stay in business. As it turned out, this was again a challenge that was approached differently by Norwegian and British co-operators.

Even though the UK Co-ops in the 1950s were regarded by contemporary commentators as a large-scale retailer, the actual operational structure was based on decentralised, small-scale co-operative societies.[36] The wholesaling function of the CWS was owned by the retail societies, but it was not integrated operationally with the local societies, and even if all societies were part of the wider co-operative movement, the retail operations were controlled locally and the level of standardisation across society boundaries remained limited.

Throughout the post-war period there were numerous attempts to reform this structure. The superior organisational efficiencies of the multiples were clearly recognised among leading co-operators; various commissions, reorganisation plans and committee reports recommended that the movement, at least in parts of its trade, should centralise its decision-making processes and integrate more closely the wholesaling functions of the CWS with the retail operations of the local Co-ops. However, most of these recommendations were either ignored or simply rejected. The fate of the Joint Reorganisation Committee (JRC), presented in 1965, is a telling example.

Even though the CWS accounted for a substantial share of the retail societies' total purchase, the relationship between the wholesale and the retail organisations was based on a traditional buyer-seller association. The basic idea of the JRC report was to transform this structure and create a more integrated organisation where the CWS was 'no longer forced to act as an independent organisation competing for society's trade on a day to day basis'.[37]

The suggestion gained only limited support. Quite to the contrary, the tendency throughout the immediate post-war years was one of reduced loyalty from the retail societies toward the CWS. Even though some progress was made throughout the 1970s and 1980s, most notably through the establishment of regional buying groups and greater use of unified marketing under a common 'Co-op' logo, resentment toward standardisation and vertical integration remained pronounced. The attitude expressed by the chief executive officer of Colchester and East Essex Co-operative Society, Mr F.L. Round, speaking at a 1983 meeting of the Metropolitan and Southern Regions of the Society for Co-operative Studies, is illustrative. As Round saw it, 'in the world of retailing flexibility and freedom of access to alternative sources of supply is an imperative ingredient of survival, let alone success'. In the view of Round, the regularly repeated call for vertical integration was thus nothing but a 'noxious disease'.[38]

The gradual consequence of such resentments was that the CWS drifted away from its initial role as a wholesaler, and started to develop its own retail branch. By 1989 close to one-quarter of total CWS turnover came directly from retailing.[39] And although the organisation functioned fairly well as a retailer, its credibility as a potential national coordinator of co-operative trade was lost. The subsequent consequence was, as historian Franz Müller has highlighted, that the movement as a whole was undermined by 'fragmentation, loss of influence as bulk purchasers, and thus also loss of price and other advantages to be gained through the wholesale society consolidating the co-operative orders'.[40]

The contrast to the Norwegian case is again striking. In the immediate post-war period, a process of purposeful modernisation and rationalisation of the existing structure was initiated.[41] The local societies gradually concentrated their operations in retailing while the NKL strengthened its role as a wholesaler. Production facilities were dissolved or sold, and a country-wide system of NKL-owned, modern, single-storey warehouses was established. Buying power was also gradually becoming more coordinated. Efforts to integrate were made by creating standardised ordering routines between the NKL and the local societies on selected products, while a new bonus system developed by the NKL provided clear incentives for the retail societies to increase the volume of goods bought from the NKL.

The distribution system developed bore a clear resemblance to the so-called 'independent chain-stores' seen in the US. The leading architect behind the system, CEO of the NKL Knut Moe, argued that the co-operative movement had found a system that allowed them to reap the benefits from chain-store organisation, without altering its federative characteristics.[42] While the system fell short of completely centralising purchasing decisions, it allowed for a substantial strengthening of the integration between local retailers and the NKL. In the years 1950–80 the retail societies more than doubled their purchases from NKL, in share of their total purchase, from 21 to 48 per cent.

Returning to the British experience, what the UK Co-ops did manage to some extent was to centralise their operations by way of amalgamation of local societies into larger, more robust units. In the period from 1950 to 2002 the number of societies was reduced from approximately one thousand to forty-two. Still, the centralisation of control across the boundaries of these retail units, so fundamental to operations of the multiple retailers, remained limited. In practice, increased centralisation through the creation of larger societies seems to have reduced the loyalty provided to the common wholesaler. Hence, by increasing centralisation through amalgamation, integration and standardisation suffered. That these were possible consequences of amalgamation had been pointed out already by the JRC report, which argued that there is 'an inherent tendency for retail societies, as they increase in size, to grow away from the C.W.S. and to seek to perform for themselves functions at one time undertaken by the Wholesale'.[43] Generally, it seems as if the strategic plans dedicated to reducing the number of societies, most prominently the *Regional Plan* of 1968, were not sufficiently coordinated with more broadly defined reorganisation reports.[44] Commenting on the possible contributions of the plan in *The Society for Co-operative Studies Bulletin*, vice-principal of Ruskin College John Hughes noted that '[the] thinking is so confined to the traditional autonomy that the reference to scale economies "in the purchase" of goods does not even explicitly link with the J.R.C. programme of integration of retail/wholesale functions'.[45] In short, the plans for merging societies into larger units were not sufficiently followed by a plan for how the activities of these large societies could best be coordinated in order to strengthen the total performance of the movement.

In Norway by contrast, the main strategic focus of the NKL management was on coordination, not size. Even when the Norwegian movement saw a dramatic reduction in the number of societies, the process of amalgamation was paralleled with continuous efforts to strengthen the link between the retail and the wholesale level.[46] The main challenge for the Co-ops, as seen in retrospect by Knut Moe, was not to develop the largest possible societies, but to develop a rational system of distribution.[47] The central association was to stay in charge of wholesaling and buying, while leaving the actual running of the retail operations in the hands of the local societies. Parallel to the ongoing processes of centralisation and integration, the strength of the federative structure was thus repeatedly underlined. In this way, the conflict between the demand for local autonomy and the need for central co-ordination, which was causing so much trouble in the UK movement, seems to have been handled more smoothly by Norwegian co-operators.

This is not to say that the failure to integrate, standardise and centralise operations that had hampered the economic development of the UK consumer co-ops did not cause trouble within the Norwegian movement. As in the UK, safeguarding of local autonomy within the co-operative societies did indeed hinder the NKL-led drive toward a stronger integration of the business operations. In 1984, there were still 595 independent societies, running more than 1,600 shops. Of these shops, only about 22 per cent were organised into some form of centrally developed store concept. Although the local societies had more than doubled their purchase in the NKL since 1950, as a percentage of total purchase, by the mid-1980s the share was still below 50 per cent. Despite these obvious shortcomings, the Co-ops continued to hold on to a leading position in the food retail market. As the private retailers from the mid-1970s onward seriously started to adopt the chain-store model, the dominance of the Co-ops was, however, put under pressure. After one hundred years of continuous expansion, the movement started to lose market share. In 1987 the NKL ran a deficit for the first time in the history of the organisation. A year later, the average surplus recorded by the retail co-operatives reached a historic low, at 0.3 per cent of total turnover.[48]

In many ways, the developments within the Norwegian retailing market throughout the 1980s showed clear parallels with those seen in the UK throughout the 1950s and 1960s. Multiple chains were increasing their share of the market and the dominant position of the co-operative retailers was becoming less obvious. As it turned out, and in contrast to the UK experience, Norwegian co-operators managed to find ways of countering the challenges coming from the chain stores.

By the early 1990s, and as a direct result of the increased competitive pressures, an extensive turnaround process was initiated by the NKL. Within the course of a few years, all 1,300 shops within the co-op movement were converted into four different store concepts. These stores were organised as fully integrated chains, with centralised control over all decisions concerning assortment, branding and overall strategy. In addition, the distribution system was reorganised to make sure that the different food-chains were selling parallel products and purchasing was fully controlled by the NKL. At the same time, the local societies were to keep their independence regarding both ownership and economic responsibility for the shops. Hence, despite the drastic measures, the NKL continued to stay dedicated to a federative model with a clear division of labour between the local and the federative levels. And instead of putting forward a policy of radical amalgamation of all societies, a stronger emphasis was put on how the federative model could be adapted to the integrated chain-store system.

The basic problem of a federative organisational structure is how to secure the necessary loyalty and discipline among the member societies, and especially how to counteract the propensity among the large Co-ops to act on their own. As we saw, this had been an increasing problem in the UK as the regional societies grew larger. To address such challenges, the NKL introduced an innovative system comprising a set of internal economic incentives. So-called 'chain discounts' were offered to enhance the attraction of joining a chain, 'investment discounts' were given to stimulate growth and renewal in the structure of the shops and 'shop discounts' to stimulate a transfer to larger shops. This system gave the NKL an effective means to steer the strategic decisions of the local societies in what they thought to be the most adequate direction. The result was that basically all the local societies converted their shops into the established chains and directed all major buying through the NKL.

The fact that the NKL was the only federative organisation in the movement, comprising both commercial and ideological functions, proved vital in the process of creating this intricate, yet highly efficient system of federative governance. It provided the NKL with the economic means by which to push forward the necessary organisational alterations. Neither the Co-operative Union nor the CWS had the means and legitimacy necessary to develop a similar system in the UK. A further advantage was held in that the NKL, apart from a few failed attempts in the non-food trades, remained primarily a wholesaler.[49] By keeping with the established division of labour between the NKL and the retail societies, it became easier for the local societies to accept the adoption of a chain model.

The drastic reorganisation of the early 1990s substantially enhanced the movement's total competitive strength. Profitability rose dramatically and by 1995 the movement had also regained a 25 per cent market share. The winning formula had comprised a successful blending of the well-known potential for economies of scale immanent in the integrated chain model, with an adapted version of the federative organisational form.

In the UK, the co-op movement's strenuous attempts to create a more coherent and tightly integrated organisation continued throughout the 1980s and 1990s. What seemed to be an important breakthrough occurred in 1993, when the CWS together with three other retail societies formed the Co-operative Retail Trading Group (CRTG).[50] The CRTG was to function as a joint buying group for the member societies, with the goal of improving buying conditions, reducing the duplication of lines carried in Co-op stores, increasing the share of own-label commodities and generally rationalising the system of co-operative grocery distribution.[51] Again, however, the inability to develop a comprehensive strategy including the entire co-operative movement was soon proven, as a group of regional societies only a year later formed a separate buying group, the Consortium of Independent Co-operatives (CmIC).[52] In 1995 the CmIC was joined by the Co-operative Retail Services (CRS), Britain's then largest retail society, to take control of approximately 30 per cent of total Co-op turnover.[53] Further disintegration was the result, as the CRS decided to develop an independent own label and launched its own separate logo.[54]

It was not before 2004, and mainly as a result of a long-awaited merger between the CWS and the CRS, that all co-operative food buying in the UK was finally centralised to a single buying point, the CRTG. The overall structure of the movement remained, however, quite fragmented. The distribution system was not integrated on a common, electronic platform; there were still no national co-operative chains, no co-operative logo used by all the major societies in the movement and no national membership scheme. These are all strategic features firmly established in the Norwegian co-operative movement, and they have proved essential in securing the organisation's competitiveness. The failure of the UK Co-ops to implement a similar degree of centralisation, standardisation and integration needs therefore to be regarded an important reason behind the divergent developments of the two movements.

Conclusions

The present chapter has analysed the divergent development of the consumer co-operative movement in Norway and Great Britain in the post-war period. It has tried to show the viability of systematic comparisons in studying co-operative development and has argued for the advantages of relating co-operative history more closely to the general history of retailing.

The basic premise of the chapter has been that the post-war development of the co-op needs to be analysed in close relation to how the movement confronted major transformations in the food retailing business. The transformations toward larger retail formats, the coming of 'multi-format' retailing and the development of centralised, standardised and integrated chains controlling large proportions of the food retail market challenged the economic viability of the co-operative model. This chapter has shown how the British and Norwegian consumer co-ops confronted these challenges and how differences in approach fundamentally shaped the two movements' development. It has also suggested some possible explanations for these differences.

It is evident that while the UK Co-ops already from the 1950s onward were confronted with keen competition from multiple retailers, the Norwegian food retail sector remained more fragmented. Multiple chains with competitive strength to actually challenge the position of the Co-ops did not seriously start to develop in Norway before the mid-1970s. These differences in the competitive climate of the two countries obviously shaped the development pattern of the co-operative societies. The divergent development observed was, however, also strongly affected by internal operational, organisational and cultural differences.

Dramatic share withdrawals in combination with minimal profits left the UK co-operatives financially weak. The use of existing capital in the form of pension funds was also severely restricted by government legislation. The Norwegian movement on the other hand managed to secure a steady influx of capital through increased member savings as well as by the use of retained earnings. They thus better managed to obtain the capital necessary for investments and expansions.

The federative organisational structure of the Norwegian movement, based on one national association comprising both commercial and ideological functions, also seems to have been an advantage for the Norwegians. Most importantly, it provided the NKL with efficient economic means by which to make local societies follow existing recommendations. Upholding a federative structure with a clear division of labour between the federative and the local level further secured a positive growth. Specifically, it helped the Norwegian retail societies to focus on their core business and allowed for greater integration without denying the importance of local autonomy and authority.

Finally, while the development of the Norwegian Co-ops was supported by an overall pragmatist stance to the changes taking place within the food retailing industry, the UK movement was hampered by a more conservative organisational culture. The two movements also seem to have advocated very different views on the basic meaning of co-operation. While the British view tended to focus on the value of local independence, self-governance and the obligation to serve local communities, the Norwegian co-operators primarily focused on the task of rationalising the system of distribution. It is indicative that Knut Moe, one of the leading executive officer of the NKL throughout the post-war years, when in retrospect was asked what he saw as the essence of co-operation, he answered the following: 'I mean that co-operation represented a simplification of buying, distribution and the setting of prices.'[55]

Notes

1 The most convincing analysis to date of this development is provided by L. Sparks, 'Consumer co-operation in the United Kingdom 1945–1993: Review – and prospects', *Journal of Co-operative Studies* 79 (1994), pp. 1–64. See also L. Sparks, 'Being the best? Co-operative retailing and corporate competitors, *Journal of Co-operative Studies* 35:1 (2002), pp. 7–26.

2 For a broad analysis, see J. Brazda and R. Schediwy (eds), *Consumer Co-operatives in a Changing World*, vols 1 and 2 (Geneva: ICA, 1989). See also I. Williamson, 'Consumer co-operation in the post-war period', in B. Lancaster and P. Maguire (eds), *Towards the Co-operative Commonwealth: 150 Years of Co-operation: Essays in the History of Co-operation* (Manchester: Co-operative College, 1996).

3 A comprehensive account of the historical development of the Norwegian consumer co-operative movement is provided by E. Lange, E. Ekberg, E. Merok, I. Theien and J. Vatnaland (eds), *Organisert kjøpekraft. Forbrukesamvirkets historie i Norge* (Oslo: Pax, 2006).

4 For Italy see P. Battilani, 'How to beat competition without losing co-operative identity: the case of Italian consumer co-operatives', in ACTA of the International

Congress, 'Consumerism versus capitalism? Co-operatives seen from an international comparative perspective' (Gent: AMSAB, 2005); for Switzerland see J. Setzer, 'Switzerland', in Brazda and Schediwy (eds), *Consumer Co-operatives in a Changing World*, vol. 1. Another exception at the positive end is the Co-operative Retailing System in western Canada, for which see B. Fairbarn, *Living the Dream: Membership and Marketing in the Co-operative Retailing System* (Saskatoon: University of Saskatchewan Press, 2003).

5 For an overview of the major changes, see R. Bell, 'Food retailing in the United Kingdom', *European Retail Digest* 28 (2000), pp. 22–8.

6 Bell, 'Food retailing'.

7 The self-service venture in Romford was not strictly speaking a shop; it was a screened-off section in a countered serviced grocery store operating on self-service lines. Still, the opening has been regarded as the first British effort to put into operation the principles of self-service. See F. Lambert 'Self-service review', *Agenda*, September (1954), pp. 81–112. For a more recent account stating the 1942 London opening to be the first self-service venture in the UK, see David Powell, *Counter Revolution: The Tesco Story* (London: Grafton Books, 1991), p. 51.

8 Lange (ed.), *Organisert kjøpekraft*, p. 304.

9 'Pioneering Still', *Co-operative Review* 31:9 (1957), p. 194.

10 G. Shaw, L. Curth and A. Alexander, 'Selling self-Service and the supermarket: The Americanisation of food retailing in Britain, 1945–60', *Business History* 46:4 (2004), p. 574.

11 The address was printed in the co-operative periodical *Agenda*, F. Lambert, 'The nature of competition', *Agenda*, December (1953), p. 61.

12 Co-operative Union Ltd, 'Report of the 91st annual co-operative congress in the Winter Gardens Blackpool June 6th–9th 1960.' (Manchester: Co-operative Union Ltd, 1960), p. 44. Also H.L. Jennings, 'Rapid development of supermarkets', *Co-operative Review* 35:3 (1961), p. 81.

13 J. Bamfield, 'Rationalization and the problems of re-positioning: UK co-operatives caught in the middle', in G. Johnson (ed.), *Business Strategy and Retailing* (Chichester: John Wiley & Sons, 1987), p. 159.

14 Co-operative Union Ltd, 'Report of the 92nd Annual Co-operative Congress in the Spa Grand Hall Scarborough May 22nd–25th, 1961.' (Manchester: Co-operative Union Ltd, 1961), pp. 322, 324.

15 S. Halvorsen, 'De første resultatene fra bedriftstellingen 1953', *Forbrukeren* 10:10 (1954), pp. 237–43.

16 NKLs Utredningskomité, *Forbrukersamvirket under utvikling: Innstilling fra NKLs utredningskomité 1966* (Oslo: NKL, 1968), p. 46.

17 Ibid., p. 59.

18 Co-operative Union Ltd, 'Co-operative supermarkets 1967', *Trade Advisory Bulletin* 38 (1968).

19 As reported by the Norwegian trade journal *Fritt Kjøpmannskap* 3 (1987).

20 Co-operative Union Ltd, 'The 110th Annual Congress of the Co-operative Union Ltd. held in the Congress Theatre Eastbourne May 28th–30th 1979.' (Manchester: Co-operative Union Ltd, 1979), p. 65.

21 A. Hallsworth and J. Bell, 'Retail change and the United Kingdom co-operative movement: new opportunity beckoning?', *International Review of Retail, Distribution and Consumer Research* 13:3 (2003), pp. 301–15, at p. 304.

22 T. Stephenson, 'Confronting competition: Consumer co-operatives in the UK', *Yearbook of Co-operative Enterprise* (1988), p. 111.

23 P. Paxton, 'Consumer co-operative capital', *Yearbook of Co-operative Enterprise* (1989), 67–71.

24 Bamfield, 'Rationalization and the problems of re-positioning', p. 160.

25 Paxton, 'Consumer co-operative capital'.

26 See R.L. Marshall, 'The next bulletin, alarm bells for co-operative retailing? Action stations?' *Society for Co-operative Studies* (1982), p. 18. See also E. Furlough and C. Strikwerda, 'Economics, consumer culture and gender: An introduction to the politics of consumer cooperation', in E. Furlough and C. Strikwerda (eds), *Consumers against Capitalism? Consumer Cooperation in Europe, North America and Japan, 1840–1990* (Lanham MD: Rowman & Littlefield, 1999), p. 32.

27 Figures taken from Bamfield, 'Rationalization and the problems of re-positioning', p. 158.

28 CWS, *Annual Report 1997*, p. 6.

29 On the transfer to convenience retailing, see also Hallsworth and Bell, 'Retail change'.

30 Sparks, 'Being the best?'

31 K4, anteroom of the administration, figures developed by AC Nielsen for the Boston Consulting Group and Coop NKL, 24 January 2006.

32 Sparks, 'Being the best?'

33 For a comprehensive analysis of the rise of the large supermarket chains in the UK, see A. Seth and G. Randall, *The Grocers: The Rise and Rise of the Supermarket Chains* (London: Kogan Page, 1999).

34 For figures see Lange (ed.), *Organisert kjøpekraft*, p. 517, and Competition Commission, *Supermarkets: A Report on the Supply of Groceries from Multiple Stores in the United Kingdom*, vol. 2 (Competition Commission, 2000), p. 47.

35 See J. Vatnaland, 'Stability and change in the organization of industry. The chain store innovation and the transformation of American retailing in a comparative perspective' (PhD, University of Oslo, 2007).

36 J.B. Jefferys, *Retail Trading in Britain 1850–1950* (Cambridge: Cambridge University Press, 1954).

37 Co-operative Wholesale Society Ltd, *Report of the Joint Reorganisation Committee* (Manchester: Co-operative Wholesale Society Ltd, 1965), p. 22.

38 F.L. Round, 'A future for consumer co-operation in Britain? The debate continues: C.W.S/C.R.S restructuring points (and counter-points)', *Society for Co-operative Studies* 47 (1983), p. 84.

39 Co-operative Wholesale Society, *Trading Review 1989*, p. 1.

40 F. Müller, 'The consumer co-operatives in Great Britain', in Brazda and Schediwy, *Consumer Co-operatives in a Changing World*, vol. 1, p. 101.

41 The two following paragraphs are largely based on Lange (ed.), *Organisert kjøpekraft*.

42 Knut Moe was the leading architect behind the strategic reorientations of the NKL in the period 1950–80, first as managing director of the NKL's food trades department and then as a CEO in the period 1968–82.

43 Co-operative Wholesale Society Ltd, *Report of the Joint Reorganisation Committee*, p. 16.

44 Co-operative Union Ltd, *Regional Plan for Co-operative Societies in England, Wales and Ireland* (Manchester: Co-operative Union Ltd, 1968).

45 J. Hughes, 'The co-operative movement: A perspective for the 1970's', *Society for Co-operative Studies* 16 (1972), p. 13.

46 Statistics compiled by Tore Kristoffersen, Coop NKL, *Våre tall 1907–2005*.

47 Interview, Knut Moe, 19 December 2002.

48 Statistics compiled by Tore Kristoffersen, Coop NKL, *Våre tall 1907–2005*.

49 For a comprehensive analysis of these failures see Lange (ed.), *Organisert kjøpekraft*, pp. 545–71.

50 These were Anglia, Central Midlands and the Oxford, Swindon and Gloucester society, see D. Hopwood, 'Conditions for progress', *Journal of Co-operative Studies* 78 (1993), pp. 4–10.

51 T. Stephenson, 'The future of retail co-operatives: A look ahead', *The World of Co-operative Enterprise* (1994), 153–8; Hopwood 'Conditions for progress'.

52 Insight Research, *Co-op 96: Combined Purchasing or Further Fragmentation?* (London: Insight Research, 1996), p. 5. The original member societies were United Northwest, Portsea Island, Tamworth, Leicestershire and Brighton societies – 'Co-ops form £2bn buying group', *Co-operative News* (7 November 1995).

53 *Co-operative News* (7 November 1995). In 1995, CWS controlled the largest share of co-operative retailing, but the CRS was the largest society operating exclusively in retailing.

54 'Signs of the times – CRS unveils new logo', *Co-operative News* (28 May 1996).

55 Interview, Knut Moe, 19 December 2002.

Part II

Ideologies and identities

5

The consumer co-operative movement in cross-national perspective: Britain and Sweden, c.1860–1939

Mary Hilson

Earlier generations of labour historians, whether writing from a socialist perspective or not, tended to regard the co-operative movement with some suspicion. The popularity of consumer co-operation after about 1860 was seen as symptomatic of the defeat and deradicalisation of the British working class following the decline of Chartism, analogous to New Model Unionism in its appeal to self-interest and material gain. The co-operative stores became another example of the enclosed and defensive working-class culture of urban Britain in the late nineteenth century.[1] Other scholars have questioned this interpretation, suggesting that there were important elements of continuity between early nineteenth-century co-operation and the movement founded by the Rochdale Pioneers.[2] In an important study of co-operation published in 1996, the historian Peter Gurney insisted on the need to understand co-operation on its own terms, as an organisation of consumers seeking to challenge the dominant capitalist mode of consumption. Even the humble 'divi' was 'part of the "practical knowledge" used by working people to cope with and simultaneously reconstruct capitalist social relations'. The commitment of the post-Rochdale co-operative movement to political neutrality should not obscure the movement's aspirations for social change, based on an 'association of workers within the sphere of consumption.'[3]

It is thus no surprise that the recent renaissance in co-operative history, of which this book is part, has coincided with the growing interest in the history of consumption and consumerism more generally. American labour historians have noted the role of conflicts over consumption in early twentieth-century working-class politics, while European historians have examined the significance of bread-and-butter politics during the First World War in particular.[4] Debates about food, consumer interests and citizenship were undoubtedly central to the co-operative movement throughout its history, and our knowledge of the movement has been greatly enriched by this new perspective.

There is a potential problem here, however, for the emphasis on consumerism means that less attention has been paid to co-operation as a social movement, and to its relations with other social movements, especially the labour movement. This is a significant omission in my view, given the importance of the co-operative movement in Britain, especially during the period 1918–39. It was one of the largest working-class movements, with over 8.7 million members in 1940.[5] The range of activities with which co-operative societies were engaged was very significant, and went far beyond shopkeeping. Moreover, co-operators regarded their movement above all as an international movement, in which British co-operators shared fraternal contacts with their counterparts across Europe and beyond, and which could offer some hope of future peace amid the tense international relations of the first half of the twentieth century. It makes sense therefore to consider co-operation in an international perspective to a greater extent than has been done before. The study of the international links in the co-operative movement can also help us to understand the transfer of ideas about working-class organisation and protests against capitalism across national boundaries, and the development of the European social movements in a wider comparative context. As this chapter attempts to show, drawing mostly on the example of Sweden, an examination of English co-operation can also provide interesting insights into how Britain was perceived more generally in the rest of Europe.

The spread of the Rochdale model

Knowledge of English consumer co-operation spread quickly following the foundation of the Rochdale Equitable Society of Pioneers in 1844. A major influence on this process was the movement's first historian, G.J. Holyoake, whose *Self-Help by the People: History of Co-operation in Rochdale* (1858) was serialised in the French journal *Progrès de Lyon* in 1862, and provided the inspiration for the foundation of many French consumer Co-ops.[6] For middle-class liberal reformers, Great Britain, as Europe's most advanced industrial country, was the obvious source of ideas about social reform during the mid-nineteenth century. '[T]hat country should be our model and tutor when we wish to follow the same path', wrote the Danish priest Hans Christian Sonne, who also drew on Holyoake in establishing a successful consumer co-operative in northern Jutland in 1866.[7] The attractiveness of Rochdale co-operation lay partly in its potential to soothe class tensions and to promote desirable habits of thrift, self-help and self-education among the working classes. But most importantly, Rochdale co-operation was more than an abstract idea: it offered a practical blueprint which could be successfully transplanted and emulated elsewhere. The co-operative stores themselves provided tangible concrete evidence of the movement's success. Through the divi system, the Rochdale rules provided co-operative businesses with the means to secure the loyalty of their members and to raise the necessary capital for expansion. Holyoake's *Self-Help by the People* not only served in this respect to demonstrate co-operation's potential for promoting peaceful class relations to a middle-class audience, though it was probably interpreted in this way, but was also intended as a practical handbook to guide and inspire working-class activists.[8]

In Sweden, too, early interest in Rochdale co-operation came mainly from middle-class liberals with an interest in social reform. In 1851, the Swedish writer Frederika Bremer described with obvious approval the 'co-operative shops' she had seen in many English towns during a visit to England guided by her contacts in the Christian Socialist movement.[9] Holyoake's *Self-Help by the People* was also a main source for the lecture series given in Stockholm in the early 1860s by the university professor G.K. Hamilton. The rapid growth of the co-operative stores (*samverkande magasinerna*) in England, according to Hamilton, 'bordered on the incredible'.[10] Detailed descriptions of the English Co-ops also appeared in Abraham Rundbäck's *Afhandling om konsumtionsföreningar* (1869), which presented the Rochdale system as a model for Swedish consumer co-operation against the background of the economic difficulties of the 1860s.[11] This flurry of interest had some influence on the liberal workers' societies (*arbetarföreningar*) established in the 1860s and 1870s to promote self-help and education, but there were no lasting successes in consumer co-operation.

One of the principal influences on the establishment of consumer co-operation on a permanent footing was G. Halfred von Koch, who was directly inspired by the English co-operative movement. From a well-to-do middle-class family, von Koch was trained as an agriculturalist, but developed an interest in social reform following his exposure to the wretched conditions under which his peasant neighbours lived.[12] In November 1897 he took leave of absence from his employment as a farm steward in Skåne, and travelled to London with the intention of spending some months investigating social-reform work there. The choice of destination was purely practical – the family had relatives there – but von Koch seems to have set out motivated by a keen desire to discover a practical solution to some of the social problems he had encountered at home. He discovered co-operation apparently by accident when he came across the Co-operative Wholesale Society's large tea warehouse in the East End, and was directed from there to the premises of the largest consumer co-operative society in London, the Royal Arsenal Co-operative Society (RACS) in Woolwich. Here von Koch met T.G. Arnold, then the secretary of RACS, who was to become one of his main contacts in Britain. Later in life, von Koch presented his discovery of consumer co-operation as the big idea he had been searching for. His first main source was Beatrice Potter's recently published book on consumer co-operation. Reflecting on his experience of this in his memoirs, von Koch wrote:

> The more I read the more interested I became. Here, at last, I had found a social movement that was entirely sound, founded on self-help, cash trade, thorough democracy [and] educational work. It was entirely free from any kind of party ties, it received everyone with open arms and fought against that well-known weakness of the workers, the credit system. Above all, I believed then and still believe today that the co-operative movement would give the population in general an insight into the machinery of the world and an education about realities in life, which ought to change the workers' attitudes to life in general for the better.[13]

Returning to Sweden in June 1898, von Koch chose the town of Gävle, several hundred kilometres north of Stockholm, as the ideal site for his ambition to establish a model consumer co-operative. This turned out to be a success, and served as von Koch's base while he undertook speaking tours proselytising for co-operation across the country.[14] Meanwhile, independently of these endeavours, consumer co-operative societies were also established in Malmö, Stockholm and Göteborg during the 1890s. These societies owed much to the changing climate of opinion toward co-operation in the labour movement from this time. Inevitably, middle-class enthusiasm for consumer co-operation as a means of promoting class harmony and social improvement meant that co-operation had been regarded with suspicion by socialists. Until the 1890s, the official line of the Socialist International was that consumer co-operation should be regarded in the light of Lassalle's iron law of wages, and the movement was portrayed as a means of undermining the class struggle. In Sweden, a leader in the social democratic organ *Arbetet* criticised consumer co-operation as 'liberal capitalist', and the party leader Hjalmar Branting suggested that it would 'weaken the class struggle'.[15]

The softening of this hardline attitude from the 1890s was partly due to the great success of the 'Vooruit' consumer co-operative in Gent. Founded in 1880, Vooruit had grown very rapidly to become a self-proclaimed 'socialist Rochdale' which used the profits of its commercial activities to create 'un petit univers socialiste'. The centre of this universe was the People's House and its wide variety of leisure and cultural activities, proudly shown off to delegates attending the 1891 Congress of the Second International in Brussels, but the co-operative was also providing pensions, libraries, banks, pharmacies and a socialist press. By the 1890s Vooruit and its sister organisations had become the main local bases for the Belgische Werkliedenpartij (BWP), providing financial support for its campaigns and election activities.[16] It was thus influential in persuading socialists to discard some of their former hostility to co-operation. The German Social Democratic Party shifted its stance from outright condemnation in 1892, to a grudging neutrality in 1899, to a resolution passed at its Magdeburg congress in 1910 where the party declared its acceptance of consumer co-operatives and actively encouraged its members to join them.[17] In the same year the congress of the Second International formally acknowledged consumer co-operation as a legitimate weapon of the working class.[18]

In Sweden the foremost convert to this new way of regarding consumer co-operation was the Malmö social democrat Axel Danielsson. Before the 1890s he had been a staunch defender of Lassalle's iron law, but following a short spell in prison in 1888/89 he became influenced by the German revisionist debate inspired by Bernstein, and this changed his view of co-operation. A series of articles in *Arbetet* in 1897 outlined his ideas about co-operation as a 'new field for labour organisation'.[19] His views were shared by the Stockholm social democrat Axel Rylander, who wrote to Branting in 1894 advocating the development of Belgian-style socialist co-operatives.[20] In 1899, Rylander and Danielsson joined forces with A.C. Lindblad of the Vooruit-inspired co-operative society Fram in Göteborg to issue invitations to a founding congress intended to establish a national co-operative federation. The congress was attended by representatives of forty-two organisations, and led directly to the establishment of the Swedish Co-operative Union, Kooperativa Förbundet or KF. A year later, the Social Democratic Party's congress adopted a resolution expressing sympathy for consumer co-operation, and the co-operative movement was recognised formally in the party's 1911 programme.[21]

The Belgian socialist co-operatives were undoubtedly influential on this reassessment of consumer co-operation within the Swedish labour movement, but this should not be taken to imply that the Belgian model was seen as representing a competing model to the English liberal one. In Sweden, at least, co-operators drew from both systems in their attempts to form new types of organisation. Axel Danielsson was also influenced by Beatrice Potter's concept of consumer co-operation as the complement to producers' organisations, i.e. trade unions.[22] Rylander's Workers' Consumption Society (*Arbetarnas konsumtionsförening*) founded in Stockholm in July 1897 drew much of its inspiration from Acland and Jones' textbook on the British co-operative movement, which appeared in a Swedish translation in 1894, and which Rylander had reviewed favourably in *Social-demokraten*.[23] The costs of publication and translation were borne by the director of the Atlas publishing house, O. Lamm, who wrote in the foreword that the English model of consumer co-operation offered 'the best and only way to prepare and educate the workers to a more independent situation'.[24]

Once again, therefore, we must ask why the Rochdale model lent itself so well to emulation and attracted the interest not only of middle-class liberals like von Koch but also working-class socialists like Danielsson and Rylander. Its appeal, I would like to suggest, was twofold. The first and most important reason for its attractiveness was simply its success. The achievements of Rochdale co-operation could speak for themselves: few foreign observers could doubt the success of the English co-operative movement on the eve of the First World War. An early edition of the KF journal *Kooperatören* ran a feature on the Royal Arsenal Co-operative Society in south-east London, describing its main building as 'a magnificent palace of commerce, after the arsenal the finest building in Woolwich and without doubt the most beautiful'. The correspondent was also deeply impressed with the new bakery, 'one of the most modern in England, where neither dough nor bread is touched by human hand but all the work is done by machine'.[25] Like its Belgian counterpart, the Co-operative Union was well aware of the means at its disposal to publicise its successes, and by the early twentieth century the annual Co-operative Congresses had become not only a forum for conducting co-operative business, but also a means of extolling the glories of co-operation to the world. In 1907 *Kooperatören* carried a report on the annual co-operative exhibition at the Crystal Palace in London, which included theatre, sports and choral competitions, and a concert involving several thousand children as well as a vast display of co-operative goods from the CWS and its affiliates.[26] The Swedish co-operator Anders Örne was among a party of foreign delegates from various European countries who attended the 1914 congress in Dublin, and participated in an extensive programme of events clearly designed to impress the foreign guests. Reporting on his experience in *Kooperatören*, he wrote that '[one] cannot avoid being struck by the power and influence of British co-operation, of its unshakeably solid economic standing and its unparalleled opportunities for development'.[27]

The guarantee of success was especially attractive to those who had been disillusioned by the frequent failures of co-operative businesses. Writing in *Social-Demokraten*, Axel Rylander acknowledged that many Swedish workers had been put off consumer co-operation following the collapse of so-called 'workers' rings' or purchasing societies in the 1880s. But

> a distribution of goods based on a <u>given</u> and <u>certain</u> circle of customers . . . <u>for the most part</u> trading for <u>cash</u>, under good <u>financial control</u>, strict <u>honesty</u> in both prices and quality, and as far as possible in <u>direct</u> contact with the producers, a distribution of goods like this would undoubtedly be to the great economic advantage of the working class.[28]

The attraction of Rochdale – with the 'divi' system and the prohibition on credit – was that it provided a straightforward set of rules for achieving just this.

Rochdale was thus influential on two different levels. On the one hand, it was the main reference point and source of inspiration for those looking to propagandise for co-operation. Von Koch's short pamphlet on English co-operation was frequently loaned to trade-union branches and temperance societies as the text of a lecture, accompanied by a set of lantern slides.[29] On the other hand, the Rochdale system also provided a straightforward and easily adaptable programme for action. Detailed guidance on the day-to-day running of a co-operative business was forthcoming through various textbooks. The KF's model rules, introduced in 1908 to help improve the success rate of new co-operative societies, were directly inspired by the English system, for example in the provision for setting aside certain proportions of the profits to different funds.[30] On some occasions, representatives of the English co-operative movement also attended KF's conference in order to offer practical advice, though direct assistance was in fact more readily available closer to home. An example of this was the KF's decision in 1900 to establish a co-operative wholesale society. Although the English CWS provided the main source of inspiration, for practical reasons it was decided that the new wholesale should be based not in Stockholm but in Malmö, which would give easy access to the advice and experience forthcoming from the Danish co-operative wholesale society, Fællesforeningen for Danmarks Brugsforeninger (FDB), based across the water in Copenhagen. The 1901 congress was duly held in Malmö, and included a day trip to Copenhagen where the delegates admired the FDB's premises.[31] Danish co-operators were regular guests of the KF congress, where during the early years at least they seemed to assume a role as mediators between the much larger and more advanced English movement and the newer organisations in Sweden. Indeed, as the Danish co-operator P. Eskesen told the congress in 1900, 'the figures from England were almost incomprehensibly large for us; perhaps the Danish conditions would be more interesting, and by telling the history of the movement in Denmark the speaker hoped to answer many of the questions which had emerged during the course of the day'.[32] The FDB also provided a direct link with the CWS, which was its main customer for butter, pork and eggs, and by the turn of the century had its own branches and agents in four major Danish towns.

Although it offered a detail blueprint for running a successful co-operative business, a further advantage of the Rochdale model was that it could be condensed into simple principles. Von Koch laid down five founding principles that amounted almost to a 'catechism for co-operation', including the importance of democratic organisation and education as well as practical considerations such as cash trading.[33]

In 1919 two prominent Swedish co-operators, Axel Gjöres and Anders Örne, distilled the essential characteristics of the Rochdale model into seven guiding principles in their attempt to create a programme for Swedish co-operation and the KF. The principles were written following the international co-operative congress in Paris that year, where Örne had discussed the matter with the French co-operator Albert Thomas, but in many respects the principles show the continuing influence of Rochdale co-operation on the Swedish movement. This is especially apparent in the inclusion of the divi (no. 6) and the exhortation to set aside a fixed proportion of the surplus for educational purposes (no. 7). The seven principles are as follows:[34]

1.   capital loaned by members at a fixed rate
2.   only pure and unadulterated goods to be sold
3.   all goods to be sold at full weight and measure
4.   prices to reflect those in the locality; no credit trading allowed
5.   one member one vote; women considered equal to men
6.   surplus redistributed to members in proportion to purchases
7.   a fixed percentage of surplus to be set aside for educational purposes.

The advantage of Rochdale co-operation, expressed in terms such as these, was that it allowed space for local interpretations of more difficult matters such as the relation between co-operation and the wider labour movement. The initial proposal for the KF rules, reflecting the social-democratic allegiance of the congress organisers, contained the aspiration that the co-operative movement should become 'an important element in the struggle of the working class for its existence and a worthwhile place in society'. However, the delegates attending the congress represented a broad mix of political backgrounds. Von Koch was among them, and his view, that the co-operative movement should be 'an important element in spreading general citizen education and raising the position of the population both economically and morally', eventually replaced the original social-democratic proposal.[35] For von Koch, the significance of consumer co-operatives not only rested on the immediate benefits they provided for their members but also paved the way toward producer co-operation and the unity of labour and capital.[36] As KF's first secretary, von Koch continued to work for co-operation as a broad movement for all classes, but following his departure in 1905 the movement became much more openly aligned with the wider labour movement, especially under the leadership of the working-class socialist Martin Sundell during 1905–1910. KF actively supported the trade-union movement in times of conflict, for example by donating goods and foodstuffs to affected workers, and this support was reciprocated when the trade-union movement supported KF's boycott of the margarine cartels Zenith and Pellerin.[37] Within a few years of its foundation KF had quickly become closely associated with the social-democratic labour movement in practice, even if it remained committed to the principle of political neutrality.

Indeed, the question of political allegiance was to become one of the main sources of friction within the early twentieth-century co-operative movement. In England, the question of co-operative political representation had been debated inconclusively since the turn of the twentieth century. The experiences of the First World War put matters into a different light, and resulted in a famous – or infamous – U-turn on political neutrality made at the extraordinary Co-operative Congress in Swansea in 1917, when the movement decided that it would seek political representation in parliament. The official interpretation of events presented in the co-operative textbooks was that this was a pragmatic response to the movement's grievances against the government in the peculiar circumstances of war. Some historians challenged this view, arguing that the Swansea decision in fact reflected the growing class consciousness within the movement in the years before 1917.[38] In fact, both positions were strongly represented within the movement, at both a national and a local level, and the matter was never really settled satisfactorily.[39] Nonetheless, the resolution for political action was passed by Congress, and from 1918 the co-operative movement – uniquely perhaps in Europe – had its own political party, the Co-operative Party. The handful of Co-operative MPs elected in subsequent elections took the Labour whip, and in 1927 the two parties concluded a formal agreement. Some local societies continued vehemently to oppose this close relationship with Labour. But in other cases there can be no doubt that the co-operative society was very significant in the development of a movement for working-class political representation.[40] Perhaps nowhere was this more the case than in Woolwich, where the RACS had campaigned politically in alliance with the labour movement since 1897, and affiliated to the divisional Labour parties in the area from 1922. The RACS was an extremely important source of funds to Labour in the area, even to the extent that it acted as the party's 'milch-cow', closer perhaps to the Belgian Vooruit model than to the Rochdale Pioneers.[41]

In Sweden, despite the growing dominance of social democrats on KF's national executive committee, the movement remained politically neutral. Indeed, Swedish co-operators were generally critical of the close relationship that developed between the British Labour Party and the Co-operative Party during the 1920s.[42] This was motivated, however, not so much by an adherence to the movement's liberal roots, but more likely by the realistic fear that the movement would be damaged by exposure to the internal divisions within the Swedish labour movement. In England, where support for revolutionary socialism was much weaker, this was less a problem for co-operators. Here, the main faultline remained instead that between Liberals and Labour, and with the decline of the Liberal Party after the end of the war this too was less of a problem. KF's adherence to the principle of political neutrality was also endorsed by the statement from the general secretary of the International Co-operative Alliance (ICA) at its 1930 congress, which advocated political neutrality as essential if the co-operative movement were to achieve the necessary unity to create a 'truly democratic alternative to capitalism'.[43]

The British co-operative movement as an alternative workers' culture?

As the foundation of the Co-operative Party suggests, the English co-operative movement had moved some distance from its roots in mid-Victorian popular liberalism. One of the most striking aspects was the range of activities it encompassed. In the first place, most local retail societies made provision for the social life of their members. Activities available to members of the Banbury Co-operative Society during the 1880s included tea meetings, musical entertainments, singing classes, an orchestra, a debating society, scientific lectures, a flower show, children's parties and annual seaside excursions.[44] In the larger societies these sorts of activity were sometimes very extensive. A report for KF on co-operative education in Britain cited the example of Bolton, with its sixteen reading rooms and clubs for literature, discussion, walking, music and song, concerts and exhibitions.[45] The Plymouth Co-operative Society, with more than 60,000 members by 1918, could boast, in addition to its network of stores, extensive productive operations, including a 2,500-acre farm, a milk depot and dairy, bakeries, sausage and jam factories, also a life-assurance scheme for members, a Junior Comrades group (foreshadowing the Woodcraft Folk), co-operative kitchens and a co-operative crèche, holiday homes and residential courses. It also organised the usual programme of outings, choirs, classes, lecture series and lantern-slide shows, and it was experimenting with the use of film as early as 1916.[46]

Even the decisions to provide these activities could sometimes give rise to debate on key matters of co-operative principle. The Plymouth Co-operative Society faced both internal and external criticism over its house-building scheme in the early 1900s because its decision to sell the houses rather than to rent them out had, it was suggested, put them beyond the means of most ordinary working-class members. As was frequently the case, the debate provoked a reference to the Rochdale Pioneers and claims and counter-claims about how they might have been expected to act in the matter.[47] '[The Education Committee's] ideas of educational work is in striking contrast to the ideas that governed the men of Rochdale,' wrote one disgruntled Plymouth co-operator, 'These latter stood for efficiency and improvement. Whether or not they organised Cinderella dances I leave to the person who cares to study the original programme.'[48] Local education committees often arranged extensive programmes of adult-education classes, covering matters such as co-operative principles and citizenship as well as more mundane subjects such as co-operative bookkeeping. Many also published regular journals and news-sheets – the Plymouth society had both a monthly and a weekly publication circulating at the end of the First World War – which went out in addition to the publications of the Co-operative Union: *Co-operative News*, *Millgate Monthly* and the *Wheatsheaf*.

In some respects the British co-operative press was a direct model for the establishment of similar organs in Sweden. During the first years of KF it was decided to use the journal *Social Tidskrift* as an unofficial organ for the dissemination of co-operative ideas, but from 1903 KF published its own monthly paper, *Kooperatören*. Like the English *Co-operative News* this was intended above all as a newsletter for the movement, and carried reports of local societies, annual congresses and other KF business, and profiles of co-operators and co-operative activity abroad. From 1913 KF also began to publish *Konsumentbladet,* which as its name (literally, *The Consumer Paper*) suggested, was aimed more at ordinary co-operative consumers than at activists. Under the editorship of Axel Gjöres during the 1920s, *Konsumentbladet* was developed into a family journal with a broader appeal, in a direct attempt to emulate the success of popular English co-operative journals mentioned above.[49] The English co-operative movement was also a source of practical inspiration for efforts to develop provisions for co-operative education in Sweden. A report on co-operative education commissioned by KF in 1918 investigated activities in other countries such as Finland and Germany, but found much to learn from the English example. The report described the range of courses available to all co-operators, ranging from classes in social history for children to practical training for co-operative employees.[50]

Another source of inspiration for Swedish co-operators was the Women's Co-operative Guild, founded in 1883 and by the 1920s one of the most important organisations for working-class women. Early editions of *Kooperatören* carried articles on the activities of the Guild as a further example of how England was 'not only co-operation's motherland, but also its model'.[51] Once again, however, the direct influence on the establishment of a women's co-operative guild in Sweden came via Denmark, through the influence of the Danish co-operator Julius Eskildsen. The first women's co-operative congress was organised in September 1907 by Axel Rylander. Though they were probably influential in the later establishment of housewives' organisations in inter-war Sweden, the co-operative women's guilds never achieved quite the prominence of their English counterparts. Here, following a reorganisation in the 1890s, the Guild developed a reputation as the radical left wing of the co-operative movement, and campaigned prominently on controversial issues such as women's suffrage and divorce, thus doing much to extend the role of female co-operators beyond that of the 'woman with the basket'. It has been described as 'the most progressive and intellectually fertile element within the Movement as a whole'.[52] The Guild was also 'the most uncompromisingly pacifist' of all women's groups during the inter-war period, and campaigned prominently for pacifism against the mounting international tensions of the 1930s, most famously through its promotion of white poppies to commemorate Armistice Day.[53]

It has been suggested that one of the features that set British working-class life apart from that of its continental counterparts, in Germany for example, was the failure of the British labour movement to develop an all-embracing workers' culture, similar to the clubs, societies, choirs and sports teams fostered by the Social Democratic Party. According to British historians such as Ross McKibbin, working-class life in Britain was characterised by a rich associational culture which tended, however, to work against class-conscious political activity.[54] British workers were enthusiastic participants in clubs and leisure activities, but these generally were commercially organised. Rather than fostering a shared sense of political purpose, these activities instead competed with political activism for the attention of British workers, and therefore made a limited contribution to the building of an alternative, radical proletarian culture.

But what about the co-operative movement? Could it have fulfilled this role, and in doing so acting like its Gent counterpart in attempting to create 'a little socialist universe'? If we are to believe Peter Gurney, the movement retained at its heart a powerful critique of capitalism and a utopian vision for the future, embodied in the idea of the Co-operative Commonwealth. The problem is that as Gurney himself admits, we know relatively little about what co-operation actually meant for the many thousands of ordinary members who actually shopped at the co-operative store. Were they motivated merely by the thought of the 'divi' and the concern to make ends meet, or did they genuinely support the vision of an alternative to modern, capitalist, economic organisation? What was the role of co-operation in local communities? How significant was co-operation in the construction of working-class culture in inter-war Britain?

It was certainly very prominent. Even a small rural co-operative society with modest ideological aspirations had a 'pervasive' impact on 'community culture and self-esteem'.[55] Larger local societies such as the Plymouth Co-operative Society were inevitably very prominent within the communities which they served. 'We are not only the Co-operative Society; we are the Town!' declared the President of the Plymouth Society in 1917. Even his opponents might have been forced to concede that he had a point, for later that year it was reported that 183,000 people, out of a population of a quarter of a million, had registered with the Society for the distribution of potatoes at a time of severe food shortages.[56] More than twenty years earlier, the Society had celebrated the opening of its imposing Central Premises, right in the heart of Plymouth, with a very public musical parade through the streets.[57] Another large and prominent society – the Royal Arsenal Co-operative Society in Woolwich – was typical in promoting its activities with a Great Co-operative Exhibition held over two weeks in 1927, attended by more than 100,000 visitors including the Prince of Wales.[58] Jubilees, the opening of a new grocery store or, perhaps above all, the hosting of the annual Co-operative Congress were also important occasions on which to demonstrate the strength and vibrancy of the co-operative movement to the wider public.

It was, moreover, a broad and heterogeneous movement, which encompassed many different ideas about what co-operation was and what it should be. As Peter Gurney has shown, even the work of George Jacob Holyoake, who was perhaps the central figure in promoting the myth of the Rochdale pioneers as the founding fathers of the movement, was open to different interpretations. In some ways Holyoake was the authentic representative of the Liberal tradition within co-operation, but throughout his writings he also insisted on the anti-capitalist roots of co-operative practices.[59] While many of his self-professed heirs may have condemned the movement's 1917 decision to abandon neutrality and seek political representation on public bodies in terms of the Rochdale legacy, supporters of the action were just as likely to defend it in similar terms.

This is clearly an area that requires further research. But, even if this interpretation is only partially correct, it cannot be denied that the co-operative movement had an extremely important role in working-class culture in late nineteenth- and early twentieth-century Britain, perhaps especially during the two decades between the wars. Moreover, its influence extended beyond Britain: as we have seen, the English co-operative movement provided a direct source of inspiration for co-operators in Sweden and beyond during the first decades of the twentieth century. It should be pointed out that this influence was returned: Anders Örne's book on Swedish co-operation, for example, was later translated into English for the benefit of those co-operators whose movement had originally helped to inspire him.[60] In some ways, as we have seen, Swedish co-operation could be said – and perhaps understand itself – to represent a 'purer' embodiment of the Rochdale model. Here, cultural and educational activities were generally organised through the wider labour movement, and the role of the co-operative movement was perhaps more narrowly confined to consumer issues.[61] It also remained strictly politically neutral, while the English co-operative movement abandoned its roots with its decision to seek political representation in 1917, and evolved close links with the Labour Party during the 1920s. The wide ambition of British co-operation as a social movement seems to suggest that in some ways it was in fact closer to the Belgian 'Vooruit' model. Nonetheless, the continuing influence of British co-operation, and the international iconic status of the Rochdale pioneers, cannot be denied. There were many other influences on co-operators in Sweden and Britain, but there was a strong perception of Britain as the natural and original home of the co-operative movement during the first decades of the twentieth century. Given the significance of co-operation in inter-war Britain and the range and extent of its activities, this must raise questions about the supposed isolationism and exceptionalism of the British working-class movements in the inter-war period.

Notes

1 Sidney Pollard, 'Nineteenth-century co-operation: from community building to shopkeeping', in Asa Briggs and John Saville (eds), *Essays in Labour History* (London: Macmillan, 1960), pp. 102, 109; John Foster, *Class Struggle and the Industrial Revolution: Early Industrial Capitalism in Three English Towns* (London: Weidenfeld and Nicolson, 1974), pp. 203–24; E.J. Hobsbawm, *Labouring Men: Studies in the History of Labour* (London: Weidenfeld & Nicolson, 1964), p. 342, n. 4.

2 Barbara Taylor, *Eve and the New Jerusalem: Socialism and Feminism in the Nineteenth Century* (London: Virago, 1983), p. xv; Robin Thornes, 'Change and continuity in the development of co-operation, 1827–1844', in Stephen Yeo (ed.), *New Views on Co-operation* (London: Routledge, 1988).

3 Peter Gurney, *Co-operative Culture and the Politics of Consumption in England, 1870–1930* (Manchester: Manchester University Press, 1996), pp. 11, 22.

4 Frank Trentmann, 'Bread, milk and democracy: consumption and citizenship in twentieth-century Britain', in Martin Daunton and Matthew Hilton (eds), *The Politics of Consumption: Material Culture and Citizenship in Europe and America* (Oxford: Berg, 2001); Belinda Davis, 'Food scarcity and the empowerment of the female consumer in World War I Berlin', in Victoria de Grazia with Ellen Furlough (eds), *The Sex of Things: Gender and Consumption in Historical Perspective* (Berkeley: University of California Press, 1996); Mary Hilson, 'Co-operation and consumer politics in comparative perspective: Britain and Sweden during the First World War', in P. Verbruggen and L. Soubry (eds), *Consumerism Versus Capitalism? Co-operatives Seen from an International Comparative Perspective* (Amsab-Institute of Social History, Gent, 2003).

5 Arnold Bonner, *British Co-operation: The History, Principles and Organisation of the British Co-operative Movement* (Manchester: Co-operative Union, 1961), p. 160.

6 Ellen Furlough, *Consumer Cooperation in France: The Politics of Consumption 1834–1930* (Ithaca NY: Cornell University Press, 1991), pp. 48–9.

7 H.Chr. Sonne, *Om Arbeiderforeninger: Til Oplysning og Veiledning* (Copenhagen: H Hagerups Boghandel, 1867); A. Jepsen and L. Harboe Jepsen, *Rochdales redelige Banebrydere* (Copenhagen: Det Danske Forlag, 1944), pp. 119–37.

8 Gurney, *Co-operative Culture*, p. 118.

9 F. Bremer, *England in 1851 or Sketches of a Tour in England* (Boulogne: Merridew, 1853), pp. 104–5; A. Påhlman, *Pionjärerna* (Stockholm: Kooperativa Förbundets Bokförlag, 1944), pp. 223–4.

10 G.K. Hamilton, *Om arbetarklassen och arbetareföreningar* (Lund, 1865), cited in Påhlman, *Pionjärerna*, p. 224.

11 A. Rundbäck, *Afhandling om konsumtionsföreningar tillegnad rikets hushållningssällskaper* (Stockholm: Bonnier, 1869); Påhlman, *Pionjärerna*, p. 229.

12 A. Wirén, *G.H. von Koch: Banbrytare i svensk socialvård* (Stockholm: Rabén och Sjögren, 1981), on which much of the following is based.

13 Wirén, *G.H. von Koch*, p. 60.

14 G.H. von Koch, *Om arbetarnas konsumtionsföreningar i England* (Stockholm: Studentföreningen Verdandis småskrifter nr 78, 1899), p. 13.

15 H. Tingsten, *Den socialdemokratins idéutveckling*, vol. 2 (Stockholm: Tidens förlag, 1941), pp. 374–5.

16 For Vooruit see Carl Strikwerda, '"Alternative visions" and working-class culture: the political economy of consumer co-operation in Belgium 1860–1980', in Ellen Furlough and Carl Strikwerda (eds), *Consumers Against Capitalism? Consumer Co-operation in Europe, North America and Japan, 1840–1990* (Lanham MD: Rowman & Littlefield, 1999); Hendrik Defoort, '"The strongest socialist party in the world?" The influence of Belgian social democracy in international socialism prior to 1914 as a means to study the relations between co-operation and socialism', in Verbruggen and Soubry, *Consumerism Versus Capitalism?*

17 Brett Fairbairn, 'The rise and fall of consumer co-ooperation in Germany', in Furlough and Strikwerda (eds), *Consumers Against Capitalism?*, pp. 383–4.

18 Ellen Furlough and Carl Strikwerda, 'Economics, consumer culture and gender: an introduction to the politics of consumer co-operation', in idem (eds), *Consumers Against Capitalism?*, p. 16.

19 A. Danielsson, *Social själfhjälp* (Svenska folkets öresskrifter 22: 1898), pp. 6, 13, 18; cited in P. Aléx, *Den rationella konsumenten: KF som folkuppfostrare 1899–1939* (Stockholm/Stehag: Brutus Östlings Bokförlag Symposion, 1994), p. 65.

20 Aléx, *Den rationella konsumenten*, p. 66.

21 O. Ruin, *Kooperativa Förbundet 1899–1920: En organisationsstudie* (Stockholm, Lund: Rabén och Sjögren, 1960), p. 139.

22 Aléx, *Den rationella konsumenten*, p. 63.

23 *Social-Demokraten* 8 October, 16 October, 22 October 1894; 24 April 1895. Rylander thereafter maintained his contacts with the British co-operative movement. See K. Nilsson, *Stockholms kooperation 1900–1915* (Stockholm: Kooperativa Förbundets Bokförlag, 1952), p. 10.

24 A.H. Dyke Acland and B. Jones, *Arbetarnes Cooperations-Föreningar i Storbritannien: Hvad de uträttat och hvad de åsyfta* (Stockholm: Nordin och Josephson, 1894; first published in English 1884 as *Working-Men Co-operators*).

25 KF archive: *Kooperatören*, 23 April 1904.

26 *Kooperatören*, 15 September 1907.

27 *Kooperatören*, 1914, pp. 146–54.

28 *Social-Demokraten*, 8 October 1894. Emphasis in original.

29 Von Koch, *Om arbetarnas konsumtionsföreningar i England*; KF archive: KF congress report, 1901.

30 Aléx, *Den rationella konsumenten*, pp. 72–6; Ruin, *Kooperativa Förbundet*, pp. 36–9.

31 KF congress reports, 1900, 1901.

32 KF congress report, 1900.

33 Von Koch, *Om arbetarnas konsumtionsföreningar i England*, p. 45; Wirén, *G.H. von Koch*, pp. 67–8.

34 A. Gjöres, *Konsumentkooperationen i Sverige* (Stockholm: Tidens Förlag, 1925),

p. 1; A. Örne, *De sju grundsatserna: Kooperationens program i kort sammanfattning* (Stockholm: Kooperativa Förbundets Förlag, 1920); see also Aléx, *Den rationella konsumenten*, pp. 104–8.

35 Ruin, *Kooperativa Förbundet*, p. 145.

36 Von Koch, *Om arbetarnas konsumtionsföreningar i England*, pp. 6, 23, 44.

37 Ruin, *Kooperativa Förbundet*, pp. 151–9; for the margarine conflict see Ingrid Millbourn, 'Kooperatismen – ett alternative till capitalism och socialdemokrati 1900–1920', *Scandia* 57:1 (1991), 105–6.

38 The debate is summarised in Mary Hilson, 'Consumers and politics: the co-operative movement in Plymouth, 1890–1920', *Labour History Review* 67:1 (2002), 8–9.

39 Hilson, 'Co-operation and consumer politics', pp. 227–9.

40 See Hilson, 'Consumers and politics'.

41 Rita Rhodes, *An Arsenal for Labour: The Royal Arsenal Co-operative Society and Politics 1896–1996* (Manchester: Holyoake Books, 1998), pp. 50–2 and *passim*.

42 Ruin, *Kooperativa Förbundet*, p. 167.

43 Iselin Theien, 'Two phases of consumer co-operation in Scandinavia: Pre-war pluralism and post-war unification under social democracy', in Verbruggen and Soubry, *Consumerism Versus Capitalism?*, p. 83.

44 Malcolm Bee, 'Co-operation in Oxfordshire 1860–1913', *Southern History* 20/21 (1998/99), p. 203.

45 KF archive: Helge Bäckström et al., 'Kooperationens utbildningsfråga. Utlåtande avgivet av den av KF:s och KFF:s styrelser tillsatta utbildningskommittén', 1918, p. 9.

46 Plymouth and South Devon Co-operative Society archives: *Plymouth Co-operative Record*, October 1916, p. 336; November 1918, pp. 239–44.

47 *Plymouth Co-operative Record*, April 1897, p. 122; July 1902, pp. 78–9.

48 *Plymouth Co-operative Record*, December 1904, pp. 141–2.

49 Aléx, *Den rationella konsumenten*, p. 87; G. Elveson, *Kooperatören – Konsumentbladet – Vi: Konsumentkooperativ press och kultursyn 1899–1974* (Uppsala: Meddelanden utgivna av Avdelningen för litteratursociologi vid Litteraturvetenskapliga institutionen i Uppsala, nr 8, 1974), p. 26.

50 'Kooperationens utbildningsfråga'.

51 *Kooperatören*, 21 January 1905.

52 Jean Gaffin and David Thoms, *Caring and Sharing: The Centenary History of the Women's Co-operative Guild* (Manchester: Co-operative Union, 1983), p. 43.

53 Naomi Black, 'The mothers' international: the Women's Co-operative Guild and feminist pacifism', *Women's Studies International Forum* 7 (1984), 467.

54 Ross McKibbin, 'Why was there no Marxism in Great Britain?', in McKibbin, *Ideologies of Class: Social Relations in Britain 1880–1950* (Oxford: Clarendon, 1990 [1984]), pp. 13–16.

55 Malcolm Bee, 'Pro bono publico: the Chipping Norton Co-operative Society 1866–1968', *Family and Community History* 4 (2001), p. 121.

56 *Plymouth Co-operative Record*, March 1917, p. 76.

57 *Plymouth Co-operative Record*, March 1894, p. 26.

58 Rhodes, *An Arsenal for Labour*, p. 92.
59 Gurney, *Co-operative Culture*, pp. 113–21.
60 Örne's *De sju grundsatserna* was published as *Co-operative Ideals and Problems*, trans. John Downie (Manchester: Co-operative Union, 1926).
61 Aléx, *Den rationella konsumenten*.

6

The identity of co-operative and mutual enterprises and the political sociology of Emile Durkheim: an introduction

Stephen Yeo

'To work out something . . .'

Our political malaise . . . has the same origin as the social malaise we are suffering from. It too is due to the lack of secondary organs intercalated between the State and the rest of the society . . . the primary duty is to work out something that can relieve us by degrees of a role for which the individual is not cast. To do this, our political action must be to establish these secondary organs which, as they take shape, will release the individual from the State and vice versa, and release the individual, too, from a task for which he is not fitted.[1]

. . . but what?

What did Durkheim (1858–1917) mean by this statement? As a founding father of sociology, he was interested in *society* and the *social* not only as facts but as norms, and in regulation as active socialisation. As pioneer *social scientists*, so were early co-operators in Britain. Not only did they invent the term 'social science', they used *rules* or *laws* to refer to what are now known as the values and principles of their Societies. Could co-operative and mutual enterprises (CMEs[2]) substitute for the 'secondary organs' which Durkheim wanted to bring into being, in order that everyone might belong, by means of Societies, to a society which, at last, might be worthy of the name? Might asking such a question cast light on Durkheim as well as on co-operation and mutuality?[3]

An imagined introduction

To address this question, my conceit is to introduce the spirit of Durkheim's political sociology to the 'identity' of CMEs, as if I were host at a party at which they are guests. Durkheim's work should help CMEs to move out of their safe, quasi-heritage sector – true at least of 'The Co-op' in Britain – into the wide-open spaces of a would-be social world. I would also hope that the recently rediscovered identity of CMEs (as in the 1995 International Co-operative Alliance 'Statement of Identity'[4]) will help some of Durkheim's prescriptions for society to look less forlorn, for example his prescriptions for the professional associations or new guilds which were the particular secondary organs he advocated.

In his novel *Elective Affinities* (1809), Goethe explored natures and substances which 'most decidedly seek and embrace one another, modify one another, and together form a new substance'. 'Those natures which, when they meet, quickly lay hold on and mutually affect one another, we call affined'.[5] For Max Weber, the protestant ethic and the spirit of capitalism were elective affinities in exactly this sense. Durkheim also used the concept.[6] My intention here is to explore the identity of co-operative and mutual Enterprises and the political sociology of Durkheim in this alchemical laboratory. I will use CMEs to follow Durkheim's imagination wherever it leads: in the lectures posthumously published as *Leçons de sociologie: physique des moeurs et du droit* (1950), translated as *Professional Ethics and Civic Morals* (1957) (PECM), he talked to his students of 'radical changes beyond our powers of imagining'. I will also use Durkheim to get to a fuller understanding of 'the co-operative difference' (a phrase increasingly used by Co-operators from the late 1990s onward).

My guests are at least present now in forms that could be affined. I will tell the story of how this happened elsewhere. In summary, co-operatives and mutuals began to redefine their identity, manifestly in Britain but also globally, during the last two decades of the twentieth century, at a time when other discourses of 'identity' were also becoming explicit. During the same decades, the radical *politics* in Durkheim's sociology also surfaced, particularly in the work of his English-language interpreters. 'Organic solidarity' as concept took on a more active life. Once seen as a static, conservative description of modern society's escape from the traditional (in Durkeim's term, the 'mechanical'), organic solidarity became a name for a desirable state of affairs unachieved in Durkheim's France or, as yet, anywhere else.

Professional ethics and civic morals

PECM is a key text for Durkheim's sociology as socio-political agendum. For this chapter, I will root my argument in it to the virtual exclusion of the rest of his work and its legions of interpreters. Durkheims's preoccupation in PECM will be read here as practicable, realised mutuality or actual, complex, ethically effective, widespread and in the end, universal co-operation. Durkheim's St Simonian dimensions should not be forgotten, any more than the Owenite roots of CMEs.[7] If the *method* of the lectures in PECM is that of historical sociology, their *project* is society as universal, conscious, socialised, 'organic' belonging, conjugated by individuals differentiated to the limits of their capacities, i.e. within modernising divisions of labour and thereby dependent, all on one, one on all.

In Durkheim's *The Elementary Forms of Religious Life*, it is religion which 'provides the system of symbols by means of which society *becomes* (my emphasis) conscious of itself'. It does this in the only way that it can, by every individual being fully realised as such, by means of association. Society becoming conscious of itself is one possible description of the purpose of co-operative and mutual associations. In modern times and as a constituent of organic solidarity, religion is being progressively earthed (individualised *and* socialised: God and gods alike) instead of being projected, as in most of human history, *ex machina*. When society is fully and consciously present, Durkheim anticipates a socialisation of religion and a sacralisation of society.[8] The lectures in PECM were about the socio-logic of a universally internalised morality – an effective, binding, human ethic. Such an ethic, Durkheim argued, would have purchase (or could have, for he was expert enough in society as constraint always to touch wood when being most prophetic) on the scattered, divided elements of individuals in all our dimensions. These include our psyches, our membership of domestic units, us as economic actors, as citizens of states and, ultimately, as individuals of the species: that is to say as human beings who are separable from lesser-order types of belonging, e.g. to nations, because in the end we have obligations and possibilities which inhere in our humanity.[9]

But the burden of Durkheim's historical sociology is that none of this will happen without 'secondary groups' able to articulate state and individual, the most potentially powerful of which, he argues, could be professional – in the sense of occupation-based – associations. We need 'to work out something that can relieve us by degrees of a role for which the individual is not cast': secondary groups 'which, as they take shape, will release the individual from the State and vice versa'. Are CMEs relevant to 'the task'? How much of what it would take to deliver Durkheim's project do they possess, in principle if not always in practice? To answer this question, a further gloss on Durkheim will help, before addressing the identity of CMEs directly and returning to Durkheim. What exactly would 'organic solidarity', one of Durkheim's signature concepts, consist of?

In most times and most places in human history, when solidarity was more mechanical, we have belonged to what we have belonged to for necessary, local, culture-bound, tribal/domestic, inherited, traditional, in a word 'mechanical' reasons. Individuals have been minimally individuated, with the result that a single individual or group could be replaced in human society without making much difference to a whole which existed as such mainly when seen from the outside. One driving direction of human history, however, has been toward a whole human society which exists also when experienced from the inside, a society belonging to all its members among whom aspiration and desire find social and personal attachment. They are no longer lawless or unregulated (the Greek a-nomos means without law, hence *anomie*). There could be a time, Durkheim wrote in PECM, touching wood again, when *we* becomes an actually-existing first-person plural, when we are what we are for inclusive, cross-cultural/national, synchronic, conscious, relatively autonomous – 'organic' – reasons.[10] Quite a project! Society as *it* becomes society as *us*, which is not a bad summary of the elusive goal CMEs set themselves: 'the co-operative commonwealth' either.

The identity of co-operative and mutual enterprises

To turn to my other guest: the identity of CMEs can be summarised in a brief list of their defining properties. These are not the same, of course, as how they always behave.

CMEs reach for *member ownership*, with an equal emphasis on both words. Without it, they would cease to qualify as either co-operative or mutual. They are associations to which members belong and which belong to members. Ownership is central to CMEs, paradoxically, in its developed, most capitalist, 'private' or modern sense. CMEs do not try to transcend or 'abolish' ownership as many socialisms do, by collectivising it, nationalising it or even by making it 'common'. This could account for their systematic neglect or marginalisation by 'the Left': CMEs want more – even 'private' – ownership not less, in a common-wealth in which more for some will not mean less for others. Impossible? Probably so, without Societies (such as the Co-operative Group [CWS Ltd] or the Midcounties Co-operative) in complex, federal relations with each other. It is as though co-operatives are minute particulars in search of a general system, a practice in search of a theory: their theory within the present system unable to constitute more than their limited practice, able to progress only 'by degrees' and 'as they take shape', not all at once, by 'revolution'.[11]

Membership is central to CMEs also in its most developed sense of voluntary, willed and entire belonging. CMEs are awkwardly pre- and post-capitalist, always *en route* to forms of sociality, which are, in Raymond Williams's useful triad, both residual and emergent but never yet dominant.[12] One of their social inventions as associations of people rather than of capital illustrates this: in the interests of accessibility, members can own before they are fully 'paid up' and while their economic rights fluctuate with their *use*, their governance rights do not vary with their *investment*.[13] These rights derive simply from membership: and they do not have to be 'granted' their rights bit by bit, like political suffrage in nineteenth- and twentieth-century Britain.

Democracy is the intention if, once they have grown large enough in scale and scope to incur the penalties of size, not always the fully realised practice of CMEs. The aim is democracy in its 'classical' sense, rather than in the dominant, dilute, modern, capitalist sense of the word.[14] CMEs came from pre-representative, simple democracy and aspire to post-representative, complex democracy. Their members aspire to grow government/governance by, for and of themselves, in association, often in federation, rendering unto states only that which belongs to them. In the same way in which they sit awkwardly with the idea of a 'managerial class' doing the management of their Societies *for* them, they also challenge the idea of electing and paying a 'political class' to do government for them.[15]

Education is central to CMEs to foster their values and principles. Knowledges and other ways of appropriating the world which belong to the world of competition differ from the knowledges which members posit as coming from co-operative and mutual, less anti-social, relations. Education has often been a driving force behind the growth of the largest and most successful CMEs and it was always seen as more than a preface to the projects they later became better known for.[16] And, turning to my other guest, I almost forgot that education was Durkheim's trade and preoccupation before and while it became sociology.[17]

CMEs are regulated in the same way that private and public corporations are regulated in capitalisms only more so, in case they get too big for their boots. But their offer, indeed their whole *raison d'être*, is to regulate themselves in the widest, least statist sense of regulation. They make their own rules, agreed by members and amendable through highly developed democratic procedures. Self-regulation informs a morality or ethic which aspires to be effective in all the spheres listed above, from psyches to species. The self-regulation – the ethics and morals – of CMEs aspires to deal with: the 'professional' (pertaining to work and the economic sphere); the civic, and 'duties in general independent of any social grouping'. Co-operatives and mutuals deal quintessentially with matters of ordinary, private, everyday, mostly individual or familial choice and detail; 'having in view the most ordinary day-to-day occurrences' (a phrase from Durkheim which could be echoed a thousand times in the history of co-operatives and mutuals). CMEs regulate members as individuals, regardless of family, ethnicity, work, trade, state, nation and place, territory. But they also deal with 'civic', public matters, informing mutual duties between individuals as citizens and 'forms of state' (especially democratic ones) and between both of them and secondary associations. The simultaneity of ordinary, small-scale, private moral choices ('by degrees' and 'as they take shape') and large-scale, public, national and 'world amendment' (addressing Durkheim's 'the social malaise we are suffering from') is the specific alchemy of co-operatives and mutuals.[18] It is the most characteristic of their many social inventions. Their genius is precisely to *connect* Durkheim's levels or spheres, itemised above.

The CME project is exceptionally ambitious. Their connecting work can make it seem as if their members keep out of the political kitchen. In fact the stakes have always been high. To do for themselves that which others in capitalism *systematically* need to do *for* them, constitutes no less than revolution. It is: to own or to belong, members to associations, associations to members; to rule democratically; to educate for themselves; and to regulate for themselves, in a moral sense of regulation, personal and social. And to set about this task as early in the history of capital's socialisation in Europe as CMEs did – with the onset of industrial revolution – was an additional scandal from a capitalist point of view. A different way of carrying on, another mode of production, is disclosed. *Quelle horreur!*[19] The panic which ensues has so far gone largely unrecognised by historians. It takes two public or state forms: first prohibition, then containment by means of regulation. The panic also takes the pervasive private or market form known as 'competition', which licenses the use of either or both of the public/state forms on behalf of 'free enterprise' and its favoured modern form, the private or the public limited company.

In Britain, CMEs quickly grew into large-scale, complex, forward-looking organisations. This was, of course, the age of such organisations. A CWS *Annual* called them 'as large and multi-functional as many states'. By the third quarter of the nineteenth century such was their reach, across consumption, production, finance, insurance, housing, mutual improvement and sociality that it had already become anachronistic to characterise CMEs as 'primitive' or 'archaic' organisations.[20] In the words of Martin Beaumont when Chief Executive of the Co-operative Group CWS Ltd in 2003, they already had what he wanted to restore to them, 'a modern personality'. Attempts continued to be made throughout the twentieth century, however, to patronise them as alternative, 'niche' organisations, good where the state or market cannot reach but bad replacements for both – good, even, for groceries, not so good for airlines or hospitals.

CMEs have been a constitutive part of the history of 'the social' as normative. The 'social' would lack its original vocabulary without them. This is a historical fact, insufficiently celebrated by members.[21] But it is also a theoretical knot which needs to be untied if members are to develop their own socialism in opposition to other forms of socialism.[22] The project of CMEs was to constitute the social as moral destination – a 'new moral world' – from the new, early nineteenth-century 'economic' world, a would-be autonomous zone with its emergent science of economics/political economy.[23] In this respect the affinity with Durkheim is manifest. CMEs, like professional associations, did not set out as ad hoc state, policy or political creations. They set out with their members' sense of their own agency, rather than seeking what others could do for them, thereby making practical contributions to the structure versus agency debate within sociological theory. Member-commitment to making the social bit by bit and all the time held fast. As a member of the Royal Arsenal Co-operative Society once declared, 'we shall eat our way into the future'.

CMEs consist of more than individuals. In associating individuals, the whole becomes more than the sum of its parts. But they do not form individuals into a collectivised mass. CMEs also consist of more than (singular) states. They construct states within *the* state precisely in order to disperse the definite article. CMEs act as additions to ' the individual' and subtractions from 'individual*ism*' and additions to 'the state' and subtractions from 'statism'. They constitute a vital part of the essentially contested zone between such -isms, within which socialism was generated.

The contest in this zone has been central to making the modern world – in its own estimation – modern. So are contests about the division of labour, which is another theoretical knot to be consciously unpicked by every co-operative member. Members lived with its rendings and tearings, its competitive divisions of humans into classes as opposed to the co-operative sharing of tasks, in communities.[24] To an extent necessary for survival as considerable organisations, co-operators replicated modern divisions of labour, but always with some internal agony and chiding from antagonists, and always reaching out beyond the most offensive of the divisions until an entire alternative becomes possible. As a condition of survival, but also as a condition of survival as co-operatives or mutuals, CMEs work with modern divisions of labour, just as they work with the penalties of size and centralisation. But they also work to put things back together again – to articulate them – in emergent rather than recessive ways. A prime example of modern, capitalist divisions of labour is that between producers, consumers and citizens.[25] In capitalist organisations/'societies', such divisions can be resolved profitably. In CMEs the task is more difficult. Associational/cultural – and business – forms have to be invented which allow space for contradictions to be lived by the membership as ways of engaging, as productive contradictions, in and against competition.[26]

Realising Durkheim's project (1)

Hosts worry throughout any party. Is an affinity between Durkheim's political sociology and the identity of CMEs beginning to look plausible without me speaking too much *for* my guests? Is there enough in Durkheim's political sociology to interest members and historians of CMEs who want to engage them in wider practical and theoretical worlds? To be confident of a positive answer, I will turn to Durkheim and focus on four conditions for the realisation of his socio-political project, in the light of the identity of CMEs.

The first of these conditions I will call a Rendered State. In PECM the state is rendered in the culinary sense of rendering fat. Durkheim separates the state in an unusually precise way from the sinew, bone and blood which accumulates round it, in sociologies as much as in societies. He then clarifies it so that it can be rendered in the Gospel sense: unto Caesar the things that are his and unto God those which are his. There are things the state does or has done which must be done by it: there are also things which it does or has done which could be better done by means of other (associational) forms, or even by individuals.

In many cultures, the state has been mystified to the point of deification. Durkheim identified this as a growing danger in his own time. The dividend for holders of political power is obvious. But the state can be abstracted in another and equally immaterial direction. It gets confused with government as well as with the government. This is hard to avoid and Durkheim does not always manage it. When would-be holders of political power such as the *demos* confuse the state in this way, even more so when 'the individual' (a modern object of worship[27]) appropriates the state, it loses its relative autonomy as a relation of government ('the means of government' as the Rochdale Pioneers called it). Such relative or relational autonomy is necessary for general justice and equity, dissolving privilege (private law). Durkheim also warns that actual and would-be holders of economic power attempt a similar appropriation, which is now known as privatisation or, in the case of CMEs, demutualisation. Extremists collapse the state into a seeming-nothing at the level of ideology while in reality they depend on its growth into something of unseemly strength. Theirs is an attempt to fold the state into what they produce and profit from, hiding its essential functions (currency, communications, contract law) behind labels like 'laissez-faire', 'liberalisation', 'neo-liberalism'.

To render the state was not to leave it as an inconsequential stand-alone. The state, for Durkheim, is not 'moi'. Nor is it a secondary group – although secondary groups, Durkheim observed, can become oppressively state-like while, in federal forms, they can also be creatively state-like. [28] To render the state was to give it its own agenda and thereby to render unto secondary groups their related agendas. For Durkheim, some of these would best be taken up by 'professional associations'. It was also to render unto individuals the things they could do within increasingly complex (and therefore mutually dependent) divisions of labour.

The Rochdale Pioneers Equitable Co-operative Society had a characteristic way of expressing their objects: 'to arrange the powers of production, distribution, education and government'.[29] Transposing this to Durkheim makes his *relational* rendition of the state clearer: the state does not, or need not, *do* production, distribution, education or government in a modern, complex society, large in scale and scope. But 'the state' does describe a formation of functionaries/functions at a centre, without which the powers of production, etc. cannot develop and without which these powers cannot be 'arranged', or arrange themselves, to their fullest, most socially effective, extent. It is, at best, a nodal point, or *social* brain – the principal organ, or articulation of *social* thought. Social interactions of all kinds multiply as societies develop, most of them at some distance from the state. As they do so, a central node becomes more and more essential, knowing even as it is known, so that the sociality of relations can be seen through glass less dark than it is in mechanical times. To achieve transparency – impossible without consciously constructed equitability – is the complicated agenda of an adequate modern, democractic state and its (civil) servants, in what could be described as a constructional, associational, or co-operative and mutual social-ism. In such a democracy we would discover 'the political form by which society arrives at the purest consciousness of itself'.[30]

'But when are *we*?':[31] realising Durkheim's project (2)

My three further conditions for the realisation of Durkheim's project are: a relational epistemology, social property and associated individuals.

A relational epistemology

An epistemology which I call relational is clearly not the same as one based on revelation, but should not be dismissed as relativist either. A relational theory of how things are known does not propose that knowledge comes from nowhere-round-here or from it-doesn't-matter-where. It proposes that knowledge is made somewhere: somewhere imbricated in social relations. This means that knowledge is liable to develop as relations change, as they become more, or less, social. How much of what there is to be known how many people know depends, among other things, on how they associate. In plain words, there is a *sociology* of knowledge. One topic for knowledge, therefore, must be its social-ness or, in Durkheim's thinking, a sociology which understands how (or through what varying relations and agents/associations) we belong to society and it to us. In Durkheim's use of 'religion', this becomes a sociology of religion. It is easy to see how useful it might also be to CMEs to know how best to 'surround ourselves with circumstances' in such a way as to make for social knowledge.

CMEs have rarely debated theories of knowledge even though, as we have seen, co-operative learning is their characteristic preoccupation (and one of their Principles) and even though there is something unusually mutual about knowledge.[32] However, it is clear that if Durkheim's epistemology had been of a revealed kind, there could be little affinity with the project of CMEs which, after all, aspire to produce things (including social relations and knowledge of them) and to be co-operative and mutual about how they do so. For Durkheim, religions, as we have seen, are (like CMEs) about the making of social belonging. They are creative, productive forms. They vary with what we belong to and that varies with what exists for us to belong to in any single culture (how much 'society' there is at any time or place is a Durkheimian 'social fact', as well as an agendum). If we are to socialise belonging, we will require adequate associational forms to do so. To a degree which is determined by and which determines how real society is, we know and alter it for ourselves.

As host, I am daring to hope that CMEs may be helpfully understood as religious, in Durkheim's sense of would-be-socialised religion. There could come a time when society will be humanised and we, as its members, socialised: it becoming us and us becoming it. What kinds of association could do this best? Any association is not as good as any other, although recent 'pluralism', 'civil society' and 'social capital' theory, curtseying in the general direction of de Tocqueville, can be as loosely relativist as that. And any individual's knowledge is not as good as any other's. Every association and every person is capable of generating real, social knowledge, to the extent that such knowledge is available in that time and place. Knowledges differ. Those which differ from ours are no more inevitably wrong than ours, though they may be wrong, just as ours may be untrue. Durkheim made that clear in his treatment of aboriginal religions in Australia. Relativism of an intelligent kind acknowledges the mutability of fixed concepts (such as the truth), their historicity, individual plus social specificity and thus their availability for change.

Social property

Property which has become social is, for Durkheim, property which has come to be consciously recognised as such (and thus as legitimate and not anti-social) by non-holders as well as by holders. It has ceased to appear as arbitrary (coming from nowhere-round- here) or as theft (coming from any-old-where, with might characteristically dressing up as right). Legal, juridical forms of ownership are socio-historical products, imbricated in relations of power. Property, once individualised, is commonly passed down by its very powerful holders to their friends and relatives as inheritance. It is at least conceivable, however, that the relations surrounding ownership and contract could become positively and completely 'just'.[33] They could/might grow from historical and social relationships consciously made by and believed in by all individuals working mutually and co-operatively toward this end, in moral and juridical forms which inform their private and public conduct. Durkheim saw signs in his own times that this direction was available for people to take, moving from mechanical forms (such as the inheritance of property) to organic solidarities. Entirely organic solidarity had become conceivable ('to imagine humanity in its entirety organised as a society'). But while less than organic forms of ownership remain as they are, as the context for ethical and moral conduct, things are likely to remain unstable or worse.

Until relations become more deliberately lucid, self-consciously shared, co-operative and mutual, there will be sullen conflict and open struggle in class and/or national conflicts and wars.[34] Somehow a shared, equitable, restitutive sense of justice is to be achieved, allowing the ownership of things, and knowledge, by more than an inherited, property-owning group. And this will change the nature of ownership itself. This is perhaps where 'the co-operative difference', learning directly from Durkheim, most needs to be consciously identified and articulated by members of CMEs: 'making membership meaningful'.[35]

Associated individuals

Real people associate with other real people variously across time and place. Returning again and again in PECM to the sociality of individuals, Durkheim's question was: what forms of association would be most serviceable to his students and followers for the making of *society* as fully organic solidarity?[36] In his social science, Durkheim understands us as deifying individuality in the modern world, abstracting it from association as an object for worship. We do so, however, as with earlier totems and gods, as attempted representations of how we belong to each other: at first mechanically, in the end organically. But again, by means of what associational forms?

Durkheim's answer in PECM, as well as in the more formal 1902, new 'Introduction' to *The Division of Labour in Society*, lay in 'professional associations'. In societies large in scale and scope these fall within a larger category of 'secondary associations' which enable the writ of the state to run where otherwise it would not. They also enable individuals to cluster in ways which enable them to access and be accessed by state and society.

But secondary associations in general are not all that is necessary either for society, or for democracy. If they were, Durkheim would have merely been a pioneer of pluralism or an early advocate of 'civil society' or 'social capital' deploring 'the lack of secondary organs intercalated between the State and the rest of the society'.[37] He pointed to associations which were specifically suited to making economic activity more social/moral because they operated in relation to work or occupation. Roman guilds provided one model.[38] Another model was that of self-regulating modern professions, enabling the details of their specific *mystères* to bind members, while contributing to more general or civic morals. The growth of economic or 'industrial' life was beginning to define the modern world: organic solidarity would increasingly have to be manufactured from it.[39] However, economic life was busy escaping regulation altogether, resulting in anomie. In this economic or industrial climate, it was not likely that ethics and morals which fostered bridging rather than bonding, cooperative rather than competitive, communal rather than class-divided practices would flourish, unless individuals at work (such as his students and followers) did something about it.[40]

Professional associations, were they to be revived as new guilds, had the potential to get close to individuals at work, where it mattered most, and to be accessible to states and to individuals as citizens as well as individual members of human families. They could even be heirs to the family, recipients of inheritances. At work, the rules of life (regulation) could win detailed, day-to-day assent and become components of willed, associated self-government. Civic, state activity – politics and administration – could also re-form around work, to prevent politics separating from society and industry defaulting into permanent class divisions. Sense could be made of 'duties of an entirely different nature for the state', difficult to express except in terms of 'dualities' and 'diverging currents flowing through our moral life'.[41] State, association and individual are in necessary tension. 'It would be failing to recognise the existing state of affairs, if we wished to reduce this duality to unity here and now'. But:

> There *is* (my emphasis) an inward activity that is neither economic nor commercial and this is moral activity . . . It is not merely a matter of increasing the exchanges of good and services, but of seeing that they are done by rules that are more just; it is not merely that everyone should have access to rich supplies of food and drink. Rather is it that each one should be treated as he deserves, each be freed from an unjust and humiliating tutelage, and that, in holding to his fellows and his group, a man should not sacrifice his individuality. And the agency on which this special responsibility lies is the State. So the State does not inevitably become either simply a spectator of social life (as the economists would have it) in which it intervenes only in a negative way, or (as the socialists would have it) simply a cog in the economic machine. It is, above all, supremely the organ of moral discipline.[42]

Such a vision was entirely cognate with that of nineteenth-century working-class 'congresses' in Britain, trades union as well as co-operative, which saw themselves, at their most confident best, not only as collectivities for labour more inclusive than 'the family' but also as parliaments of labour making for a new kind of fair, inclusive, equitable state, rearranging the powers of production, distribution, education and government.

CMEs and Durkheim's professional association: then and now

CMEs are not, of course, *the same* as Durkheim's professional associations. They do, however, belong to the same lineage. Guilds, trades unions, lodges, companies, clubs, building societies, friendly societies, credit unions, educational associations and, overlapping with many of these, co-operatives and mutuals, may all be identified on the same family tree, even where their pre-eighteenth-century origins are controversial and, in a Durkheimian context, interestingly 'religious' or mythological.[43] 'Going into union' – to use an English phrase from the 1830s, before *trades* unions had been specialised as such – seems significantly similar in working-people's lives across time and place, as well as creatively different in detail. Many CMEs which sought variously to include more members began life as associations of workers in a single trade. They started as 'producer/worker co-ops', particularly in France, or as consumer co-ops most of whose members worked in the same trade or in the same plant: the Royal Arsenal is a good example.[44] Some began as co-operatives or mutuals for tradesmen made unemployed by trade cycles or technical change – such as the Rochdale Pioneers. Yet others did not fit into a neatly organised trade: they were oddfellows in the Manchester Unity of Oddfellows sense.[45]

This last point provides the beginning of a positive answer to the question: could the respects in which CMEs differ from Durkheim's professional associations make them a less forlorn hope for our time than his new guilds? Put another way: do the differences between CMEs and Durkheim's professional associations map onto the differences between his time and ours, so that CMEs might even be seen as *the* condition of production of Durkheimian organic solidarity for *now*? The beginning of an answer is all that I offer here, leaving my guests, if they choose, 'to work out something' at greater length, to elect the affinity they may jointly find.

In the circumstances of the early twenty-first century, belonging will be better achieved by CMEs than by Durkheim's professional associations because purely professional associations, whether CMEs or not, are ill-suited to generating change or realising human potential in times when the place and nature of work itself has fundamentally changed. Work in 'post-industrial' times (abstracted as industry, production, etc.) is not the same as it was, for reasons which relate to the continuing 'division of labour in society' which Durkheim traced in the first three lectures in PECM. People no longer belong to single, life-long trades or occupations. Association based upon them would be inelastic, rather as syndicalism would be in a global division of labour. To be confined to such silos would be to reflect where things were, among old, militantly particular interests, rather than to be in a position to anticipate where they could be, in the general interest. It would be like trying to build a new superstructure upon an old base, a metaphor which fits, if it ever fitted, earlier times. Identities are less easily inhabited than they were. Today, adults cannot expect a definitive answer if they ask a child 'what do you want to be when you grow up?' Most trades or occupations are less fully self-contained in a single place even than weaving was in Rochdale in the nineteenth century, and that had cross-continental connections. They are more global, less autonomous from other trades and occupations, more net-worked, less separate from the rest of life, more 'textualised' and continuous with or organic to other life-contexts (not-work, leisure, culture, etc). They are also less bonded, more bridged and less fundamental to other human bonding than was once the case. Life-long, identity-defining occupations are now less central to production, more 'mechanical' in Durkheim's sense, so that asso-ciational forms which simply reflected them would be insufficiently capable of producing the *connections*, bridges and relations upon which production now depends. Information and communications technology has been central to these changes, making the relations of production in general (in a new mode thereof) more central than the relations among any singular group of producers.[46]

Reflecting on the great debate between the proponents of producer and consumer co-operation which informed the history of co-operation during the second half of the nineteenth century in Britain, it is the producer side, the idealists, who now look archaic and the consumer side, the materialists, who may be more and more appropriate for our times.[47] Why? Because what is modern is the web of connection between the production and consumption of a vast and interrelated range of goods, services, and values: food, funerals, meanings of life and death, insurance, travel, health, fair and just exchange, finance, decisions and responsibilities, really useful knowledge and mutual improvement. During the early phase of my current work on the history of the CWS, the Society's Secretary, Bill Shannon, remarked to me in a brilliant aside, 'of course, the product of co-operatives is co-operation'. Less incisively, I now want to ask whether it might help to give the Co-operative Group (CWS Ltd) a 'modern personality' if Durkheimians and co-operators pursued the question: is *society/the social*, understood as organic solidarity, a creative way of understanding the product and furthering the objects of CMEs? Through our Societies, could we be making society better than anyone else can? Is the product of CMEs the creation of new moral, equitable relations of production rather than (but of course by means of) particular goods or commodities?

CMEs and Durkheim: ordinary associations meet an extraordinary thinker. What prejudices, practices and power relations need to be overcome to recognise their joint potential for changing society? What a pity it is, as Goethe wrote in *Elective Affinities* (part 2, chapter 3) that 'when ordinary people get passionately worked up over the common difficulties of everyday we can only give them a pitying smile, but we regard with reverence a soul in which the seed of a great destiny has been sown, which must await the unfold-ing of this conception'. For me, would-be *social* historian and (imagined) host and broker, I will return to my work in progress on the history of the CWS/ the Co-operative Group during the late twentieth and early twenty-first centuries, going back to move forward. For my imagined guests, on with the conversation . . .

Appendix: publications on co-operative and mutual enterprises, co-operation and mutuality by Stephen Yeo

Religion and Voluntary Organisations in Crisis (London: Croom-Helm, 1976).

'Working–class association, private capital, welfare and the state', in M. Rustin and N. Parry (eds), *Social Work, Welfare and the State* (London: Edward Arnold, 1979).

'State and anti-State: reflections on social forms and struggles from 1850', in Philip Corrigan (ed.), *Capitalism State Formation and Marxist Theory: Historical Investigations* (London: Quartet, 1980).

'Co-operative Association' and 'Working-class movements', in Tom Bottomore (ed.), *A Dictionary of Marxist Thought* (Oxford: Blackwell 1983).

'Socialism, the State, and some oppositional Englishness', in R. Colls and P. Dodd (eds), *Englishness, Politics and Culture 1880–1920* (London: Croom Helm, 1986).

'Notes on Three Socialisms: collectivism, statism and associationism, mainly in late nineteenth and early twentieth-century Britain', in Carl Levy (ed.), *Socialism and the Intelligentsia 1880–1914* (London: Routledge, 1987).

'Three Socialisms: statism, collectivism, associationism', in W. Outhwaite and M. Mulkay (eds), *Social Criticism and Social Theory* (Oxford: Blackwells, 1987).

'Rival clusters of potential: ways of seeing co-operation' and, with Eileen Yeo, 'On the uses of "Community" from Owenism to the present', in S. Yeo (ed.), *New Views of Co-operation* (London: Routledge, 1988).

Who was J.T.W. Mitchell? (C.W.S. Membership Services, 1995).

Organic Learning: Mutual Enterprise and the Learning and Skills Agenda (NIACE, Policy Discussion Paper, 2000).

Mutuality: Owning the Solution: The Report of the Oxfordshire Mutuality Task Force (Co-operative Futures, 2000). The report of a Task Force which Yeo chaired from September 1999.

Social Enterprise in the Scottish Borders: An Audit Report (Social Enterprise Institute, Heriot-Watt University and the Co-operative College, July 2001). This report was researched and drafted to Yeo's design, working with Dr Ray Donnelly of the SEI and Mervyn Wilson of the Co-operative College.

'The new mutualism and Labour's third way', in Johnston Birchall (ed.), *The New Mutualism in Public Policy* (London: Routledge, 2001).

The Making of a Successful Co-operative Business: The Co-operative Wholesale Society 1973–2001 (Zeebra Publishing, Co-operative Group (CWS) Ltd, Manchester, 2002). An overview of what will be a history of the CWS, 1973 to the present.

Co-operative and Mutual Enterprises in Britain: Ideas from a Usable Past for a Modern Future (London School of Economics, Centre for Civil Society, Report Series, no. 4, 2002).

'Making membership meaningful: the case of older Co-operative and Mutual Enterprises in Britain', in Nicholas Deakin (ed.), *Membership and Mutuality:*

Proceedings of a Seminar Series Organised at LSE Centre for Civil Society (London School of Economics, Centre for Civil Society, Report Series, no. 3, 2002).

'What value do co-operative and mutual enterprises in general and the co-operative movement in particular add to the citizenship agenda?' *Journal of Co-operative Studies* 35:2 (2002), reprinted as 'Co-operative learning and responsible citizenship in the 21st century', Co-operative College Papers (new series) no. 1, 2003.

'A celebration of the modern personality of 'Co-op Original': revisiting the Pioneers with the help of G.J. Holyoake, their first historian', in *Pioneers of Co-operation: 160th Anniversary Reflections on the Opening of Toad Lane Store* (Co-operative College, Manchester, 2005, with the British Columbia Institute for Co-operative Studies, University of Victoria BC, Canada).

'Living the vision: co-operative principles in contemporary practice: an address to the Society for Co-operative Studies, Sept. 2006', *Journal of Co-operative Studies* 40:1 (no. 119), April 2007.

'Theorising Co-operative Studies: obstacles and opportunities for 21st-century Co-operative and Mutual Enterprises' and 'Co-operation, mutuality and the democratic deficit: remembering democracy', in Ian MacPherson and Erin McLaughlin-Jenkins (eds), *Structuring Diversities and a Complex Heritage: Essays in the Field of Co-operative Studies* (British Columbia Institute for Co-operative Studies, New Rochdale Press, 2007).

Notes

1 E. Durkheim, *Professional Ethics and Civic Morals* (London: Routledge, 1957), pp. 106–9. This is the English translation of *Leçons de sociologie: physique des moeurs et du droit* (Istanbul: Publications de l'Université, Faculté de Droit, 1950). I refer to it as PECM.

2 I have promoted 'CMEs' as an acronym since chairing the Oxfordshire Mutuality Task Force (1999–2000) during which Peter Couchman and Edgar Parnell coined it. See *Mutuality: Owning the Solution: The Report of the Oxfordshire Mutuality Task Force* (Oxford: Cooperative Futures and Oxfordshire Economic Partnership, 2000). The point of the acronym is to offer policy-makers a handle to complement the fashionable acronym 'SMEs' (small or medium-sized enterprises) and to place the co-operative movement or Co-op in Britain back among the wider co-operative and mutual family to which it belongs. The Co-op needs the wider family and the wider family needs the Co-op (now rebranding itself as 'the co-operative . . .'), in ways which were neglected for much of the second half of the twentieth century.

3 Durkheim's place among the pioneers of 'modern social theory' is best described in A. Giddens, *Capitalism and Modern Social Theory: An Analysis of the Writings of Marx, Durkheim and Max Weber* (Cambridge: Cambridge University Press, 1971). A meticulous bibliography of his publications, including English translations is in Steven Lukes, *Emile Durkheim: His Life and Work* (London: Allen Lane, 1973), pp. 561–90. The best-known outside academia are *The Division of Labour in Society* (French publication 1893, 1st English trans. 1933); *Suicide* (French

1897, English 1951); and *The Elementary Forms of the Religious Life* (French 1912, English 1915). The concepts by which he is best known are the *conscience collective*; 'organic' as opposed to 'mechanical' solidarity; 'social facts'; the sacred/ profane binary as the matrix of the many binaries which structure human thought and action; the social/individual difference *but also* mutual dependency; the *social* division of labour; and a definition of religion in *The Elementary Forms* as 'a unified system of beliefs and practices relative to sacred things, that is to say, things set apart and forbidden – beliefs and practices which unite into one single moral community . . . all those who adhere to them'. Ken Thompson, *Emile Durkheim: Revised Edition* (London: Routledge, 2002) is an invaluable brief introduction to his work.

4 International Co-operative Alliance, 'Co-operative statement of identity and principles as approved at the ICA Congress, Manchester, Sept. 1995', for which see *Co-operative Principles for the 21st Century* (Geneva: ICA, April 1996).

5 Goethe, *Elective Affinities* (1809), Part 1 chap. 4, Penguin Classics edn, trans. R.J. Hollingdale (Harmondsworth: Penguin, 1971) pp. 46–57.

6 *The Elementary Forms of Religious Life* (1912), trans. Carol Cosman, with an Introduction and Notes by Mark S. Cladis (Oxford: Oxford University Press, 2001), Book II, chap. 3, p. 115.

7 E. Durkheim, *Socialism and Saint-Simon,* trans. C. Sattler, intro. Alvin W. Gouldner (London: Routledge & Kegan Paul, 1959), from *Le Socialisme: sa définition, ses débuts, la doctrine Saint-Simonienne,* intro. M. Mauss (Paris: Presses Universitaires de France, 1928). In his excellent, long 1992 'Introduction' to PECM, pp. xxiv–v, Bryan S. Turner suggests that Saint-Simon's problematic was also that of Durkheim.

8 Durkheim 'appeared to believe that a secular religion is possible – in other words that people can gain the benefits of religion while regarding it as a social construction', M. Prowse, 'Emile Durkheim', *Prospect* (February 2005), p. 55, 'but no such faith has yet emerged'.

9 PECM, pp 72–4, 220, and Turner, 'Introduction', p. xxxv. This is where Durkheim imagined 'humanity in its entirety organised as a society'.

10 Lukes, *Durkheim,* pp. 147–67 is an excellent place to start for organic versus mechanical solidarity, with on p. 158 a useful one-page tabulation of the ideal types. There could come a time 'under organic solidarity' (Lukes's phrase) when social organisation increasingly loses 'the transcendent character which placed it as if in a sphere superior to human interests'. For the socialism which Durkheim was prepared to identify with, 'it was necessary that . . . society cease to be regarded as a transcendent being, towering high above men'. The vision is far-reaching, well expressed by Giddens in his discussion of the division of labour in his 'Introduction' to Durkheim, *Durkheim on Politics and the State* (Stanford, CA: Stanford University Press, 1986), p. 12: 'Labour is divided spontaneously only if society is constituted in such a way that *social inequalities exactly express natural inequalities*' (my emphasis).

11 T. Lowit, 'Marx et le mouvement coopératif ', *Cahiers de l'Institut de science économique appliquée,* series 129 (1962) ' Etudes de Marxologie'; see T. Bottomore

(ed.), *A Dictionary of Marxist Thought* (Oxford: Blackwell, 1983) pp. 95–6 for Stephen Yeo, 'Co-operative association'; K. Marx, *Inaugural Address of the Working Men's International Association* (1864) and *Capital*, vol. 3 (1894), chap. 27.

12 R. Williams, *Marxism and Literature* (Oxford: Oxford University Press, 1977), pp. 121–8.

13 For 'social inventions as capital for CMEs to draw upon', see Stephen Yeo, *Co-operative and Mutual Enterprises in Britain: Ideas for a Usable Past for a Modern Future* (London: Centre for Civil Society, LSE, 2002) pp. 38–45. For CMEs as associations of people not of capital, see Charles Gide, *Consumers' Co-operative Societies* (Manchester: Co-operative Union Ltd, 1921); E. Furlough, 'French Consumer Co-operation', in E. Furlough and C. Stikwerda (eds), *Consumers against Capitalism?* (Lanham: Rowman & Littlefield, 1999), p. 187, n. 4 has excellent material on Gide whose relationship to the Durkheim school, if any, remains to be explored.

14 J.A. Schumpeter, *Capitalism, Socialism and Democracy* (London: Allen & Unwin, 1943) makes the distinction between classical theories of democracy and 'another theory' adapted for capitalist competition; S. and B. Webb, *Industrial Democracy* (London: Longmans, 1897) remains the most usable work in this field, provided that their advocacy of professional/managerial or expert democracy is kept separate from the cornucopia of material they provide on class and democracy.

15 I have explored the themes of this paragraph at greater length in 'Co-operation, Mutuality, and the Democratic Deficit or Re-membering Democracy', in Ian MacPherson and Erin McLaughlin-Jenkins (eds), *Structuring Diversities and a Complex Heritage; Essays in the Field of Co-operative Studies* (British Columbia Institute for Co-operative Studies, New Rochdale Press, 2007).

16 This was true, for example, of the Rochdale Pioneers, of the Mondragon group of Basque co-operatives and of Credit Unions in Ireland. The imbrication of successful CMEs in educational projects, from their very beginnings, is a theme which deserves global, comparative treatment.

17 Durkheim's posthumous publications major in education. They include: *Education et sociologie* (1922), translated as *Education and Sociology* (Glencoe: Free Press, 1956); *L'Education Morale* (1925), translated as *Moral Education: A Study in the Theory and Application of the Sociology of Education* (Glencoe: Free Press, 1961); and *L'Evolution pédagogique en France* (1938) translated as *The Evolution of Educational Thought* (London: Routledge, 1977).

18 World amending comes from G.J. Holyoake, *Self-Help by the People* (London: S. Sonnenschein, 1907) p. 93.

19 Marx's exclamation in *Capital: A Critique of Political Economy* (1867) vol. 1, chap. 13 (1867) (Harmondsworth: Penguin, 1976), p. 449. The context is a chapter on co-operation, in which Co-operation in Rochdale is also referred to. In n. 15 Marx quotes 'a philistine English periodical', *The Spectator* (26 May 1866) which had attacked 'the Rochdale co-operative experiment'. 'The same paper', Marx writes, 'finds that the main defect in the Rochdale co-operative experiments is this: "they showed that associations of workmen could manage shops, mills, and

almost all forms of industry with success, and they immediately improved the condition of the men, but then they did not leave a clear place for masters." *Quelle horreur!'*

20 Reading Helmut Anheier and Nuno Themudo, 'Organisational forms of Global Civil Society: implications of going global', in Marlies Glasius, Mary Kaldor and Helmut Anheier (eds), *Global Civil Society 2002* (Oxford: Oxford University Press, 2002) pp. 191–216, I was struck by how modern (early twenty-first century), in the authors' typology, CMEs were.

21 A.E. Bestor, 'The Evolution of the socialist vocabulary', *Journal of the History of Ideas* IX:3 (1948), pp. 259–302. 'For a period of twenty years after 1825, the "science of society" carried Owenite implications', J.F.C. Harrison, *Quest for the New Moral World: Robert Owen and the Owenites in Britain and America* (New York: Scribner, 1969), p. 78.

22 Stephen Yeo, 'Notes on Three Socialisms, Collectivism, Statism and Associationism, mainly in late nineteenth and early twentieth-century Britain', in Carl Levy (ed.), *Socialism and the Intelligentsia 1880–1914* (London: Routledge, 1987), pp. 219–70; and 'Three socialisms: statism, collectivism, association-ism', in W.Outhwaite and M. Mulkay (eds), *Social Criticism and Social Theory* (Oxford: Blackwell, 1987), pp. 83–113.

23 For which see Donald Winch, 'The origins of economics as a science, 1750–1870', in Carlo M. Cipolla (ed.), *The Fontana Economic History of Europe*, vol. 3 (London: Fontana, 1967). For socialist economists versus political economy, see Harrison, *Quest for the New Moral World*, pp. 63–87 and the Reports of the first four Co-operative Congresses during the early 1830s listed in Harrison's 'Bibliographies', pp. 355–6.

24 John Ruskin, *The Political Economy of Art* (London: Unwins, 1857) makes the distinction between the division of labour as division between humans and as division of tasks.

25 The building blocks of S. and B. Webb, *Industrial Democracy*. Finding ways of putting them together in modern forms of democracy was their project, as it was the practice of J.T.W. Mitchell in the CWS during the late nineteenth century, which was much admired by Beatrice Webb. See Stephen Yeo, *Who Was J.T.W. Mitchell* (Manchester: CWS, 1995).

26 For contradictions not being 'abolished' but finding forms 'within which they have room to move', and for how 'this is, in general, the way in which real con-tradictions are resolved', see K. Marx, *Capital* vol. 1, p. 198.

27 PECM, pp. 69–70.

28 PECM pp. 61–2 provides a good sociological frame within which to look at not only the 'bridging' but also the 'bonding' function of CMEs.

29 A convenient place to read the 'objects and plans' of the Rochdale Pioneers in 1844, with added commentary, is Holyoake, *Self-Help*, p. 12. Arranging these powers was to be done, in a nice phrase, 'as soon as practicable'.

30 Lukes, *Durkheim*, p. 273.

31 Don Paterson, *Orpheus: a version of Rilke's Die Sonette an Orpheus* (London: Faber & Faber, 2006) p. 5, from a sonnet called 'God'.

32 See Mick Fletcher's insights on this in Stephen Yeo, *Organic Learning: Mutual Enterprise and the Learning and Skills Agenda* (Leicester: NIACE Policy Discussion Paper, 2000) pp. 12, 17.

33 PECM, pp. 212–13.

34 Durkheim had a harder, more 'Marxist' sense of class than is sometimes suggested. PECM, pp. 213–14; Gouldner, 'Introduction', 1962, p. 30; Turner, 'Introduction', 1992; and see David B. Grusky and Gabriela Galescu, 'Is Durkheim a class analyst?' in Jeffrey C. Alexander and Philip Smith, *The Cambridge Companion to Durkheim* (Cambridge, Cambridge University Press, 2005), pp. 322–83.

35 International Joint Project on Co-operative Democracy, *Making Membership Meaningful: Participatory Democracy in Co-operatives* (Saskatoon, Centre for the Study of Co-operatives, University of Saskatchewan Press, 1995).

36 'The key to Durkheim's whole life work is to be found in his attempt to resolve the apparent paradox that the liberty of the individual is only achieved through his dependence on society', Giddens, 'Introduction', p. 45.

37 Robert Putnam, *Bowling Alone* (New York: Simon & Schuster, 2000), suggests that the term 'social capital' was independently invented at least six times over the twentieth century, commencing in 1913 with an educationalist (L.J. Hanifan) who sounds quite Durkheimian and who also called associations 'an accumulation of social capital'. See L.J. Hanifan, 'The rural school community centre', *Annals of the American Academy of Political and Social Science*, 67 (1916), pp. 130–8.

38 PECM, pp. 17–18, 31–3.

39 PECM, Lectures 1–3 analyse this, as does Part 3 of *The Division of Labour*. See Thompson, *Durkheim*, pp. 73, 80, 146–7 for convenient summaries.

40 The distinction between bridging and bonding social capital comes from Putnam, *Bowling Alone*.

41 PECM, pp. 70–1.

42 PECM, pp 71–2, see also Thompson, *Durkheim* p. 148.

43 Andy Durr, 'Ritual of Association and the Organizations of the Common People', *Ars Quatuor Coronatorum: Transactions of Quatuor Coronati Lodge* 100 (1987), pp. 88–108.

44 The Christian Socialists of 1848–54 tried to press the French model onto the British working-class movement, a bit like the editors of the second phase of the *New Left Review* during the 1970s and 1980s. The debate between the producer and the consumer model was conducted with religious fervour, between people coming from opposed religious (and class) positions between *c.*1850 and *c.*1900 in Britain. I now see it as a debate between different forms of membership and belonging, and between different class positions. Through which forms of Society do we (who? from what class position?) best belong to society? Can the most 'economic' actors of all in capitalism, waged labour or the working class, belong to each other rather than to abstract 'society', and thereby construct a universal society worthy of the word and belonging to everyone?

45 This is only one version of the meaning of the use of the word 'oddfellow' in Friendly Society history.

46 For 'conceptualising global labour', global labour markets/divisions of labour and 'distributive justice' as a response, see Guy Standing, *Global Labour Flexibility: Seeking Distributive Justice* (Basingstoke: Macmillan, 1999). For how technology is changing the nature of economic production for 'information goods' from an industrial model based on capital to a networked one, characterised by 'peer-production', see Yochae Benkler, *The Wealth of Networks: How Social Production Transforms Markets and Freedom* (New Haven: Yale University Press, 2006). Each of these are points of entry to a vast new, global socio-economic context and literature which any adequate CME history and think tank for the twenty-first century will have to enter.

47 Furlough and Strickwerda, *Consumers against Capitalism?* explores this question, and particularly in Peter Gurney, 'Labor's great arch: co-operation and cultural revolution in Britain, 1795–1926', pp. 135–72. For consumerism and the missed opportunity of the link with the London Co-operative Society via Michael Young, see Asa Briggs, *Michael Young, Social Entrepreneur* (Basingstoke: Palgrave, 2001).

7

Irish railwaymen and the retail co-operative movement, 1917–23

Conor McCabe

The Great War saw a surge in co-operative activity. High inflation, war profiteering and a food crisis contributed to the moves toward alternative solutions. In Ireland, the majority of these new co-operatives were agricultural, although a small but significant number were 'Rochdale-type' stores. The Irish members of the National Union of Railwaymen (NUR) played a strong role in the growth of these new stores, which took place within a wider radicalisation of the Irish NUR.[1] In 1917 the union emerged as the 'van of progress' within the Irish labour movement, having won a significant pay rise in December 1916.[2] It saw the union's Irish membership grow from around 5,000 to almost 20,000 in eight months. In March 1918 the Stranorlar Co. Donegal NUR branch wrote to the union's Irish journal, *New Way*, to say that 'our activities as a branch have not been confined to union organisation, and we look back in pride to the year 1917 as the year in which we inaugurated the co-operative movement'.[3] Similar initiatives were undertaken by railwaymen in Limerick, Waterford, Dun Garbhan, Coleraine and Clonmel, and built on the existing railwaymen co-operative stores in Inchicore, Co. Dublin and Rosslare, Co. Wexford.

The move to establish co-operative stores by the railwaymen, however, was not just a practical response to the food crisis, but an ideological one as well. These co-operative stores formed part of a wider discussion within the Irish NUR about the role of trade unions, and trade unionists, in society. It was one that saw the principles of guild socialism spread among the Irish NUR activists, especially those associated with *New Way* and the union's Irish executive. 'So many of our readers have shown themselves keenly interested in the co-operative method of killing capitalist exploitation', wrote *New Way* in April 1918, 'that we give [a] list of books which, besides being interesting reading, are convenient to get and give information as to how to get things done.' From 1917 to 1920 the Irish NUR showed an intoxication with the changing and turbulent times in Ireland, constantly making the argument that with a little more organisation, a little more ambition, the railwaymen could achieve a better Ireland, 'the attainment of a nobler existence, when fraternity and equality shall prevail'.[4] The co-operative stores were seen as part of this process, answering short-term needs around food and prices, while putting in place more equitable structures for a long-term future. They reveal an Ireland influenced as much by economic and social forces as by the political and military issues which dominate the written history of the period.

The retail movement in Ireland

The co-operative movement in Ireland suffered a split in its early stages – between the agricultural movement, which became Irish-based, and the retail movement, which remained affiliated to the English and Scottish organisations. The split had a significant effect on the growth of Irish retail co-operatives. The earliest successful co-operative store in Ireland was established in 1859 by railwaymen in Inchicore, Dublin. The initiative, however, remained a solitary venture, and little in the way of co-operation took place in Ireland until the 1880s, when Sir Horace Plunkett sought to establish both retail and agricultural co-operatives in the country. Sir Horace's actions were bolstered by a conference that took place in London in August 1888 to discuss the possibility of extending the co-operative movement in Ireland. It was organised by the Co-operative Union's southern section, and although there were some delegates from Ireland, the majority were from the southern section.

Mr Ben Jones, the secretary of the southern section, in his speech to the delegates, 'urged that steps should be taken to preach the principles of co-operation to Irish workers'.[5] At the same time, he called on efforts to develop new forms of co-operative production in Ireland, principally agricultural production. The proposals were accepted and the union established a propagandist association for the purpose of bringing co-operation to Ireland. The north-western section of the Co-operative Union took on the responsibility of developing the Irish movement, and a separate Irish section was duly established, with Sir Horace as chairman and Mr R.A. Anderson as secretary.

In 1888 the Co-operative Union sent Mr J.C. Gray to Ireland to advise the new board and he met with Sir Horace Plunkett, among others. In his report to congress, he said that at the time there were 'some thirteen societies as comprising the whole field of co-operation in Ireland'.[6] After a few failed attempts to establish retail outlets, the sectional board agreed to focus its attention on creameries and agricultural societies. By 1894, thirty-three co-operative dairies and thirteen retail stores in Ireland were affiliated to the Co-operative Union. Tensions, however, soon arose between the Irish section and the Co-operative Union, in particular with regard to the Co-operative Union's opinion of the Irish movement.

1894 saw the formation of the Irish Agricultural Organisation Society (IAOS) under the leadership of Sir Horace Plunkett. Catherine Webb, in her history of industrial co-operation, rather diplomatically stated that 'it was found at this time that the democratic machinery of the Co-operative Union, with its central office in Manchester, was not sufficiently elastic to meet the requirements of the organisers in Ireland'.[7] In 1895 issues of trade, policy and jurisdiction between the two organisations came to a head. The Co-operative Wholesale Society (CWS) had treated Ireland primarily as a source of produce, and saw the establishment of creameries, 'co-operative or otherwise', as a practical necessity rather than as a propagandist or idealist venture. At the same time, the Irish Co-operative Agency Society (ICAS) established a depot in Manchester – a move which, according to one observer, 'must have presented itself to the agents of the CWS as a direct challenge to their prospects of unfettered buying in Ireland, and caused them to see the new movement as a competitive menace rather than an addition to the co-operative ranks'.[8] Congress that year decided to back the CWS's policy of Ireland as primarily a source of produce, over the concerns of the IAOS. It led the IAOS to disaffiliate from the Irish section of the Co-operative Union. After the split, the IAOS actively discouraged the establishment of general-store societies, focusing primarily on the agricultural movement. The establishment of co-operative stores was left to the Co-operative Union, which 'confined its activities entirely to the towns'.[9]

The Co-operative Union's Irish section, however, did not survive the split, and it was dissolved at the 1896 congress. Responsibility for the development of retail co-operatives in Ireland was placed under the Scottish section. On 19 December 1896, a meeting of the Londonderry, Lisburn, Portadown and Belfast societies was held in St George's Café, Belfast. Also present was Mr James Deans, secretary of the Scottish section. A new body, the North of Ireland Co-operative Conference Association, was formed, and it was in the north of Ireland where retail co-operatives remained strongest.

In 1903 a resolution was passed at the Co-operative Union's annual conference to give the 'Irish societies a measure of home rule' within the organisation. Mr Deans, from New Cummock, proposed the resolution. He said that with the help of the Scottish section, the Irish societies had organised themselves into a district conference association. 'That association had done splendid propaganda work', he told the conference, 'and they now wished to be relieved from the wing of the Scottish section.' The Irish section was re-established, with twenty societies and a combined membership of 5,340.[10] Over the next ten years, the section organised talks and seminars to try to popularise the retail movement, but with limited success. In 1906 the section reported to congress that 'continued depression in several of the smaller centres, together with managerial difficulties, have prevented the expansion and increased stability for which we are looking with some degree of confidence'.[11] In 1907 a retail store was opened in Bray, Co. Wicklow, 'consisting chiefly of railway workers', while correspondence was entered into 'with the projectors of a store near Rosslare harbour' – one that was chiefly the work of railway workers as well.[12] In 1910 the Co-operative Union supplied a full-time organiser for Ireland. At first the position fell under the jurisdiction of the executive, but later passed to the Irish sectional board.[13]

Overall, though, progress was small. By 1912 the number of stores remained at twenty, with a total of 14,413 members.[14] Of this, two stores, Belfast and Lisburn, accounted for 9,200 and 1,060 members respectively – or 71 per cent of the total figure. 'The most casual consideration of the facts as recorded', wrote Lionel Smith-Gordon and Laurence C. Staples, 'will inevitably suggest that the harmonious growth of the co-operative movement in Ireland has been very much retarded by the separation of agricultural and industrial interests.' The agricultural base of Irish society was often put forward as the reason for the lack of growth in the retail movement, but in the eyes of Smith-Gordon and Staples, 'the clash between the CWS and the IAOS must be held responsible as the first cause.'[15] It was not until the economic effects of the Great War had begun to bite that the Irish retail movement saw sustained and significant growth.

War-time inflation, radicalism, and the Irish food crisis

In 1917, Smith-Gordon and Staples observed that 'war conditions have increased the appeal of the co-operative store very greatly, and the movement is exciting interest in quarters where it has been accustomed to meet with indifference or contempt'.[16] From 1915 to 1918, there were 326 new co-operatives registered as friendly societies in Ireland.[17] Of these, 28 were retail co-operatives, an increase of 140 per cent on the pre-war figures.[18] The effects of low wages, high prices and a devastating war had led some people to consider alternative ways of production and distribution. This included elements within the Irish NUR, who helped to establish at least six of these new stores. It took place during a time of increased radicalism within the union, bolstered by a successful wage campaign in 1916. The ideas of syndicalism and guild socialism began to enter the mainstream of the union's leadership in Ireland – ideas that saw co-operation as a natural extension of trade-union activity.

With the outbreak of hostilities in 1914, government policy toward trade unions was shaped by four main issues: war supplies, labour shortages, the cost of living and industrial peace.[19] These four issues combined to give workers a forceful bargaining strength, and saw a move from mass strikes and direct action to arbitration and collective bargaining. In the early stages of the war, however, the railway unions did not see the conflict as a bargaining tool, but a national issue. This soon changed as the sudden jump in prices for such basic items as bread and eggs put a great strain on wages. In the case of the NUR, the union's attempts to keep wages in line with inflation was 'like someone trying to keep his place by running up a downward moving escalator'.[20] In September 1915 the *Railway Review* printed a letter from a member of the Crewe no. 1 branch, who wrote that 'after over a year of war we are not able to supply our children with that which is so necessary to rear them up strong and healthy, while to see one's wife growing paler and thinner through lack of nourishing food makes one pause and wonder whether it is possible to carry patriotism too far'.[21]

Throughout 1915 the Irish railwaymen organised meetings and protests around the need to address wartime inflation and a wage increase. In November a deputation from the Railway Clerks Association (RCA) met with the leader of the Irish Nationalist Party, John Redmond, in order to 'ask for his influence in the remedying of certain marked grievances under which they suffer'.[22] Redmond later met with J.H. Thomas of the NUR, and also with the president of the Board of Trade, in order to discuss the situation. The problem, however, was with the Irish Great Southern and Western Railway (GSWR), who refused to recognise the trade unions, let alone negotiate with them. Although the GSWR asked the government for funds to accommodate a pay increase, the company wanted it in the form of a grant to the companies and not directly to the men as had been the case with the war bonus. The GSWR appears to have accepted that some form of intervention was needed, but it would not agree to a common front with the trade unions. For its part, the NUR would not sanction strike action to force the issue. As the war progressed, the pressure on wages increased. The situation came to a head in September 1916 after the second round of war bonuses were announced, from which Ireland was excluded. The constant failure of the NUR to undertake the necessary campaign to secure a war bonus for the Irish membership passed the initiative to the grass roots, and to the radicals among them.

On 19 September 1916 the RCA held a meeting in the Banba Hall, Parnell Street, Dublin, to discuss wartime inflation, and to demand government intervention. The meeting was chaired by Mr W.B. McMahon. He argued that the recent increase in the war bonus had 'aggravated the situation in Ireland, because in this country they had no war bonus or recognition'.[23] The meeting ended with a resolution to contact the Irish MPs and to press home the need for government intervention. Meetings were held by NUR branches in Limerick and Dublin demanding that the war bonus should apply to Ireland. The men in Limerick said that they were finding it impossible to provide for their families. On 25 September the D&SER railwaymen passed a resolution to the effect that if their application for an increase was not satisfied they would hand in their notice. British railwaymen had now received not one but two war bonuses, both of five shillings each, while Irish railwaymen struggled under a maximum increase of one shilling and six pence.

The Irish NUR finally called for strike action on 16 December 1916, against the advice of the London-based executive. The call for strike action worked, however, and on the eve of the strike the government announced that it would take over the Irish railways for the duration of the war, and meet in part the railwaymen's pay claims. The Irish railwaymen received a 50 per cent pay increase, a result that led in part to the ascent of radicalism within the union.

The year 1916 saw a further deterioration in food supplies. In November of that year the leader of the Irish Labour Party, Thomas Johnson, wrote in the *Dublin Saturday Post* that 'in '46 and '47 the grain harvest was shipped from Ireland to pay landlords' rents; today our food supplies are being sold at high prices for consumption in Britain, and farmers are buying war loan certificates!'[24] Johnson called for a new protectionism, 'to prevent the export of the necessaries of life until the needs of the whole people are conserved'.[25] The partial failure of the potato crop that winter led to talk of famine, and 'a widespread demand for the prohibition of potatoes from Ireland'.[26] On 1 October 1916 the Dublin Trades Council held a food prices meeting in the Phoenix Park, Dublin, which called on the 'organization of municipal depots for the sale of food and fuel at prices fixed by local consumers and government representatives'.[27]

On 16 December 1916 the ITUC held a special congress at City Hall, Dublin, to 'consider the food crisis and the present cost of food, fuel, and the necessaries of life'.[28] The conference passed a series of resolutions that called on the government

> [to] take steps to secure for the Irish people all the advantages which would accrue to a self-supporting country in times of emergency. Among the many demands were the prohibition of all export of food, live or dead, until a census of foodstuffs was taken; the appointment of a national authority to take over the entire business of food, export and import.[29]

It was a call echoed by Waterford Corporation which adopted a trades council resolution on the restriction of food exports, particularly potatoes.[30] The food crisis soon became a political issue, with Sinn Féin urging the public to 'make war on the rabbit', and to be 'careful of your potatoes. Hide them from carrion crows'.[31] The campaign focused not only on food exports but also on rising prices, which were blamed on profiteers. The government responded with the introduction of tillage orders, which obliged all farmers, including cattle farmers, to 'bring at least ten per cent of their arable land under the plough in 1917, and a further 5 per cent in 1918'.[32]

The food-supply crisis had given the Irish trade union movement a social purpose, and broadened its terms of reference from wages and conditions to overall societal change.[33] The Irish NUR's successful pay increase had seen it emerge as the second largest union on the island. Over the next three years it would tackle again issues of wages and conditions, produce a monthly journal, secure 'home rule' for the Irish branches of the NUR, put members up for election to local councils, and engage in a robust and positive manner with the co-operative movement.

The Irish railway retail co-operatives

Railwaymen were instrumental in the establishment of co-operatives in Waterford, Dun Garbhan, Rosslare, Clonmel, Limerick, Stranorlar and Coleraine. Of these, only Waterford, Limerick and Clonmel have files in the Registry of Friendly Societies in the National Archives, Dublin. In Waterford and Dun Garbhan, the Irish NUR's membership rose from 275 to 614 following the 1916 wage action, the result of which was a 'surging radical confidence'. In 1917 a group of fifty workers, including railwaymen, set up the Waterford Co-operative Society as a practical response to wartime profiteering and the food-control crisis.[34] There had been attempts to establish a retail co-operative in Waterford in the past. In 1912, the Co-operative Union's Irish section organised 'a very successful meeting' in the city, and reported that 'the prospects of starting a society are fair',[35] but it came to nothing. According to an unsigned report in *New Way*, March 1918,

> A few NUR men in Waterford have been keen on this question for a long time, and less than a year ago the first preliminary meeting was held, followed at short intervals with other meetings. About twenty men attended. In June 1917, the first business meeting was held and a provisional committee appointed. There were only fifty men at the meeting, but one hundred £1 shares were taken up and £30 in cash paid in. This was the real start, and meetings were held weekly after that, and sums of £35, £43, £38, £32, etc., were paid at each meeting until at the end of six months no less than £300 was paid in cash, and a share of £1,500 guaranteed.

The railwaymen extended invitations to other workers in the city, a move that soon trebled the size of the society, and organised guest lecturers from Belfast and Dublin to speak on the benefits of co-operation. The result was such that by September 1917 the society was in a position to register as a friendly society, 'one of the finest business establishments in the city was secured, and, in spite of the natural opposition from the traders, the venture safely launched'.[36] The report ended by stating that the establishment of the co-operative had 'caused the men of Waterford to realize their power which they intend to be self-respecting and independent in future'. Luke Larkin, a long-time NUR activist and socialist, was among the original committee.[37] Larkin originally worked on the Dublin and South Eastern Railway, and had built up the union's membership in Dublin and Wexford, where he was known as an effective organiser. He was subsequently moved to Waterford, and became chairman of the local NUR branch in 1918.

The Waterford society began trading on 21 December 1917. Its rules were taken from the Manchester Co-operative Union, with a president, elected for three years, and a rotating committee of nine to run the society. Its membership in December 1917 stood at 398, with share contributions of £642. In November 1918 the society finished its first year of trading with sales totaling £8,957, and a balance of £222. Its membership had risen to 498. The society continued to grow. In 1919, membership dropped slightly to 477, but sales grew to £13,594. The next year, membership had risen once again, this time to 546, with sales of £17,387. By 1921, four years after it had been set up as a limited company, the Waterford Co-op had opened its own bakery and was producing what it claimed was the cheapest bread in the country, with four-pound loaves retailing at nine pence each. The society's membership stood at 550, with sales of £18,612, and a staff of seven. By 1923, its membership had risen to 836, its highest ever figure, with sales amounting to £29,753. The society now owned four premises: the original grocery at Barron Strand Street, a drapery and boots at Gladstone Street, a bakery at Mayor's Walk, and a warehouse and Stores on John's Lane. The society's staff now numbered twenty-three – nineteen in distribution and four in production.[38]

From its outset, the society kept track of its political role, campaigning on the food-control issue and setting aside funds for a programme of education on co-operation. In March 1918 it was active in the establishment of a corporation joint committee on profiteering. The Co-op also 'campaigned for direct municipal purchase of food to relieve distress, exposed hoarding of fuel, and protested against the export of live meat.' At the same time, local farmers threatened to withhold milk supplies until there was an increase in prices. The society responded by bringing in milk directly. In April 1920 the Waterford and district Workers' Council (WDWC), of which Larkin was a major figure, declared a two-day stoppage within the city. It was in response to the government's decontrol of food prices and the issue of political prisoners, who were at that time on hunger strike in Mountjoy prison, Dublin. The Waterford 'soviet', as it became known, was led by 'Commandant' Larkin. It was a moment of 'pure theatre', but nonetheless was indicative of the growing class-consciousness.[39] It was one in which the co-operative movement increasingly played a part.

In March 1918, James Nolan, a NUR member from Limerick, wrote in the *New Way* that the local branch had made 'the co-operative question a real live practical issue; and also, we are determined, even though no outside aid should be forthcoming (which, of course, is not the case), to carry our scheme through'. Nolan went on to say that

[w]hen it is remembered that this matter was on the carpet in Limerick for the last twenty years, being murdered in its infancy at every turn, through the influence of small shop-keepers and merchants, its appearance in practical shape now is both surprising and magical. To my knowledge, it is the only movement started here without resolution mongering. Now, how did it start? In order to continue our useful course of lectures, the writer took it on himself to step into the breach and keep the ball rolling. The subject chosen was co-operation. After a little initial difficulty my efforts were rewarded with a good attendance, amongst whom were many outside enthusiasts in the movement. The scheme was outlined, an appeal made for immediate action, and a start made on the spot. Through the co-operation of the other trade union bodies, we hope ere long to launch the Garryowen on the co-operative sea. Let us hope, that from the tiny seed thus sown, will grow a mighty co-operative tree whose influences for good will being blessings unbounded to many a home. Comrades and fellow co-operators, peg away, throw in your lot, invest your money, no matter how small the amount, and be loyal to your store.[40]

On 8 March 1918 the *Limerick Leader* reported that a co-operative store was on the way in the city. The Limerick Co-operative Society was registered on 31 May 1918, and by December it had 242 members. The next year its membership rose to 502, but it did not begin trading until 1920, when it returned end-of-year sales of £13,273, and a balance of £392.[41] Its membership had risen to 1,104. The society's best year of trading was 1921, when it recorded sales of £23,112. Its membership peaked at 1,600 the following year. The society's appearance was linked not only to the food crisis and profiteering, but also to the rise of the NUR in Limerick, the education classes, and the marked sense of confidence that the railwaymen now had about their abilities and future. Furthermore, it showed that while the idea of a co-operative was not new, the circumstances were, and it was these changed circumstances that had led to its foundation.

The issue of profiteering and the NUR education lectures were also raised by the Stranorlar, Co. Donegal branch as motives behind the establishment of its co-operative. 'Just nine months ago,' wrote Mr B. McMenamin, 'when profiteering was acute, and the gombeen man couldn't be satisfied in his lust for greed, brother T. Bell introduced the subject of co-operation at one of our meetings . . . from that date we have never looked back, and with the farmers and labourers of this locality joined with us, we feel justly proud at the result of our combined efforts.'[42] McMenamin said that, initially, the venture was met with scepticism:

We were met with the cry from the profiteers 'this movement won't last long as they have nothing but a few working men at the helm'. We are proud to say we have shown them that working men have brains also, and are endowed with as good business instincts as our opponents . . . we have a very flourishing general

> store going strong, and we have bigger ambitions for the future . . . We should like to hear of other branches embarking on such like projects.

The railwaymen-backed co-operative store in Clonmel was registered on 31 August 1917. In January 1918 it had 164 members, and it began trading in the summer of that year. By January 1919 it had sold £9,196 of stock, with a balance of £564. The next year saw £14,100 in sales, with a membership of 359. The Co-op's membership continued to rise, reaching a peak of 442 in January 1922, with sales of £38,240. In 1923 it operated three stores on three different premises: a grocery, a bakery and a drapery.[43] As with the Waterford Society, the Clonmel Co-op took its rule book from the Manchester Co-operative Union. In its 1926 report and balance sheet, the society reiterated its founding principles. It stated that 'co-operation is the greatest bulwark the working classes have to rely upon for protection against the chaotic industrial conditions, low wages, and a low standard of living'. It went on to say 'what co-operation will do':

> Abolish poverty by promoting a more equitable distribution of wealth. Ensure that the workers shall enjoy the wealth created by their labour. Keep down prices, and increase the purchasing power of wages. Enable the workers to become their own shopkeepers, manufacturers and landlords. Increase the well-being of the community as a whole, and create a new social order based on the great co-operative principle of 'each for all and all for each'.[44]

As with the other retail societies already discussed, the Clonmel society saw clearly the wider potential of co-operation in Irish life, 'the attainment of a nobler existence, when fraternity and equality shall prevail'.[45] And in common with the other societies, Clonmel looked to the Co-operative Union and Manchester, and not the IAOS, when it came to practical advice on committees, constitutions and organisation. This shows that the split in 1895 between the IAOS and the Co-operative Union continued to hold influence more than twenty years after the event. In April 1918, the *New Way* contributor 'co-operator' wrote that those who were interested in setting up a co-operative store 'cannot do better than write to Mr. [William] Knox, Co-operative Hall, 18 Frederick Street, Belfast, who will give the necessary information and literature, free of charge, and will also speak on the subject, if invited to do so'.[46] William Knox had a long career in the co-operative movement, having been auditor of the Belfast society in 1892, president from 1907 to 1912, and assistant secretary from 1912 to *c.*1914.[47] The Belfast society was affiliated to the Co-operative Union as were the more established railwaymen's co-operatives in Inchicore, Co. Dublin, Rosslare, Co. Wexford and Greenore, Co. Louth. The 1895 split continued to exert influence over the development of retail co-operatives in Ireland.

Conclusion

Patrick Bolger, in his history of the Irish co-operation, lamented the lack of trade-union activity in the movement, saying that he was unable to provide a reason for such inaction.[48] In fact, trade unions played quite an active role in the establishment of co-operatives – although it was in retail shops, rather than the agricultural co-operatives, that trade unionists concentrated their energies. Furthermore, the trade-union movement only became a fully active participant in retail co-operatives during and after the Great War – the period in Irish history dominated by issues of nationalism and Unionism. Indeed, the dominance of high political and military themes in Irish historiography can give the impression that were it not for the home-rule and independence question, Ireland would have been a veritable oasis of calm in the tumultuous seas of post-war Europe. The mainstream view was summarised by Mike Cronin and John Regan thus:

> There is little evidence of a social component within the Irish revolution and less again in its settlement. Such potential as there was for social upheaval had to a great extent been defused by the transfer of land back to native ownership under a series of reforming land acts at the end of the nineteenth, and the beginning of the new century.[49]

The analysis that social issues took a back seat to nationalist and Unionist ambitions ignores the fact that while social issues may be ignored, social forces rarely allow such a luxury. Furthermore, the theory that the land acts pacified Ireland ignores the fact that it was the people left out of the 'transfer of land back to the native ownership' – the landless labourers and the semi-skilled and unskilled urban workers – who were joining unions and agitating for better work, and social, conditions. This is not to downplay in any fashion the effect that nationalism and Unionism had on the island during this period – rather, it is to say that not everything can be explained by nationalism and Unionism alone.

In a wider context, the effects of the Great War had radicalised people. High inflation and low wages, coupled with a food shortage and profiteering, saw a move toward alternatives such as co-operation. The cost of living had increased sharply since 1915, and saw increased calls for wage increases to offset the price rises. In Ireland, police reports for 1917 noted a 'breeding suspicion that farmers were withholding produce to maximize prices',[50] and such profiteering was often cited as a reason for the creation of co-operatives, both agricultural and retail, during this period.

The period from 1914 to 1918 saw the number of 'Rochdale-type' stores in Ireland grow from twenty to forty-eight, having remained at twenty for the entire period from 1903 to 1913. Of these twenty-eight new stores, six were established with initiatives from Irish NUR members, while a further six came from the activities of the Irish Transport and General Workers' Union (ITGWU). Both unions had a strong belief in industrial unionism, with the NUR leaning toward guild socialism and the ITGWU accepting the more radical, syndicalist approach.

The Irish railwaymen, however, cited ideological as well as practical motivations for their participation in these co-operatives. Their involvement was linked not only to issues around food prices, but also to ideas around the role of trade unions in society. The radicals among the railwaymen believed in moving trade unionism from the workplace to the high street. The Irish NUR local leadership referenced the success of the union in the 1916 pay dispute, and the subsequent growth in membership, as providing the catalyst for action. They were joined in their enthusiasm for co-operation by the ITGWU, whose members established stores in Cork, Kilkenny, Listowel, Maynooth, Roscrea and Tullamore.[51] The retail societies do not form part of the history of the IAOS, but that is different from stating that they do not have a history at all.

Co-operative activity formed only part of Irish trade-union activity during this period, which was one of the most tumultuous and complex periods in modern Irish history. The Irish NUR co-operative societies offer a window on the social and economic forces that dominated the period. They show that retail co-operatives not only existed in Ireland, but had a relevance to their members' lives, and a commitment on their part to co-operative ideology, that cannot be explained by high politics or military history. The Irish NUR included some of the most radical and forward-thinking trade unionists in the country. These were men who reflected on a daily basis on the role of trade unions in society, on what a society should be, its core principles and ideals, and how best to bring them to life. The retail societies formed a small, but by no means insignificant, contribution to that debate.

Notes

1 For reasons of brevity, the Irish branches of the NUR will be referred to as the Irish NUR.

2 Emmet O'Connor, *A Labour History of Ireland 1824–1960* (Dublin: Gill and Macmillan, 1992), p. 96.

3 *New Way*, March 1918.

4 Ibid.

5 Lionel Smith-Gordon and Cruise O'Brien, *Co-operation in Ireland* (Manchester: Co-operative Union Limited, 1921), p. 70.

6 Lionel Smith-Gordon and Laurence C. Staples, *Rural Reconstruction in Ireland: A Record of Co-operative Organisation* (London, 1917), p. 39.

7 Catherine Webb, *Industrial Co-operation: The Story of a Peaceful Revolution* (Manchester: Co-operative Union Limited, 12th edn, 1929), p. 149.

8 Smith-Gordon and Staples, *Rural Reconstruction*, p. 205.

9 L.P. Byrne, *Twenty-one Years of the Irish Agricultural Wholesale Society, 1897–1918* (Dublin: IAWS, 1918), p. 19.

10 The Co-operative Union Limited, *The 36th Annual Co-operative Congress, Stratford, 1904* (Manchester: Co-operative Union Limited, 1912), pp. 348, 444.

11 The Co-operative Union Limited, *The 38th Annual Co-operative Congress, Birmingham, 1906* (Manchester: Co-operative Union Limited, 1906), p. 172.

12 The Co-operative Union Limited, *The 40th Annual Co-operative Congress, Newport, 1908* (Manchester: Co-operative Union Limited, 1908), pp. 159–60.

13 Smith-Gordon and O'Brien, *Co-operation in Ireland*, p. 71.

14 The Co-operative Union Limited, *The 44th Annual Co-operative Congress, Portsmouth, 1912* (Manchester: Co-operative Union Limited, 1912), p. 199.

15 Smith-Gordon and Staples, *Rural Reconstruction*, p. 212.

16 Ibid., p. 212.

17 National Archive of Ireland (NAI), Registry of Friendly Societies.

18 Smith-Gordon and O'Brien, *Co-operation in Ireland*, p. 73.

19 Teresa Moriarty, 'Work, warfare and wages: industrial controls and Irish trade unionism in the first world war', in Adrian Gregory and Senia Paseta (eds), *Ireland and The Great War: A War to Unite Us All?* (Manchester: Manchester University Press, 1992), p. 77.

20 Philip S. Bagwell, *The Railwaymen: The History of the National Union of Railwaymen* (London: George Allen & Unwin, 1963), p. 347.

21 Bagwell, *Railwaymen*, p. 349.

22 *Waterford News* (5 November 1915).

23 *Freeman's Journal* (20 September 1916).

24 National Library of Ireland (hereafter NLI), LO P113, item 106, 'food prices and Ireland's needs', William O'Brien (labour leader) collection.

25 NLI, LO P113, item 106, 'food prices and Ireland's needs', William O'Brien (labour leader) collection.

26 *Dublin Saturday Post*, 18 December 1916.

27 NLI, Ms 17,113, notes regarding Dublin Trades Council food prices meeting, Thomas Johnson papers.

28 Irish Trades Union Congress and Labour Party, *Report of the Twenty-Third Annual Meeting, Derry, 1917* (Londonderry: Derry Standard, 1917), p. 15.

29 Irish Trades Union Congress, *1917 Annual Meeting*, p. 16.

30 Emmet O'Connor, *A Labour History of Waterford* (Waterford: Waterford Trades Council, 1989), p. 135.

31 NLI, ILB 300 P5, Sinn Féin leaflet on the conservation of food, 1917.

32 O'Connor, *Ireland*, p. 96.

33 O'Connor, *Waterford*, p. 135.

34 Ibid., p. 140.

35 Co-operative Union, *1912 Congress*, p. 200.

36 *New Way*, March 1918.

37 NAI, R/1345/A+B, Waterford co-operative yearly returns, registry of friendly societies archive.
38 O'Connor, *Waterford*, p. 142.
39 Ibid., *Waterford*, p. 159.
40 *New Way*, March 1918.
41 NAI, R/1395/A+B, Limerick co-operative yearly returns, registry of friendly societies archive.
42 *New Way*, March 1918.
43 NAI, R/1338/A, Clonmel co-operative yearly returns, Registry of Friendly Societies archive.
44 NAI, R/1338/A, *Rules of the Clonmel Co-operative Stores Ltd*, Registry of Friendly Societies archive.
45 *New Way*, March 1917.
46 *New Way*, April 1918.
47 Irish Co-operative Conference Association, *Dublin: A Handbook of the Forty-Sixth Annual Co-operative Congress Whitsuntide, 1914* (Manchester: Co-operative Wholesale Society Limited, 1914), p. 39.
48 Patrick Bolger, *The Irish Co-operative Movement: Its History and Development* (Dublin: Institute of Public Administration, 1977), p. 1.
49 Quoted in Fergus Campbell, 'The social dynamics of nationalist politics in the west of Ireland 1898–1918', *Past and Present* 182:1 (February 2004), p. 203.
50 Emmet O'Connor, *Syndicalism in Ireland, 1917–1923* (Cork: Cork University Press, 1988), p. 22.
51 O'Connor, *Waterford*, p. 141.

8

Employers *and* workers: conflicting identities over women's wages in the co-operative movement, 1906–18

Rachael Vorberg-Rugh

> Co-operation is a many-sided reform, and Co-operators can look at themselves from various points of view. We may see ourselves as a crowd of purchasers, as an army of workers, as a band of citizens – and as *Employers*.[1]

The co-operative movement at the turn of the twentieth century encompassed multiple identities. It was a movement of organised consumers, whose aim was the gradual replacement of capitalism with a collectively owned and democratically-governed 'Co-operative Commonwealth'.[2] At the same time, co-operation was a major business concern, responsible for between 6 and 7 per cent of the nation's total retail sales.[3] Nationally, many leading co-operators were active social reformers, while locally co-operatives provided numerous educational and social opportunities. But for most, the 'Co-op' was simply a fixture of working-class life – a place to shop, earn a dividend and invest their small savings.

The question of a minimum wage for women workers employed in co-operative stores and factories stood at the confluence of these multiple identities. Between 1906 and 1918, co-operators engaged in a protracted debate about setting a minimum wage for the movement's female employees. By the outbreak of war, this issue was the source of considerable labour unrest, leading ultimately to a series of strikes against co-operative stores and factories by the Amalgamated Union of Co-operative Employees (AUCE). These developments took place concurrently with a period of numerical and economic expansion in the movement – and co-operators often found themselves torn between their social ideals and their economic gains. The question of women's wages became a polarising issue at the centre of these conflicts.

As economists Deborah Figart, Ellen Mutari and Marilyn Power noted in their recent work on American minimum-wage legislation, the wages that a particular set of workers receive are based on more than an economic calculation of profit and loss. Wages also reflect commonly held views about the relative worth of different groups, often in the areas of class, ethnicity and gender.[4] Particularly among the British working classes of this era, 'skill' was a very loaded term. The controversy over the wages of female co-operative workers illustrates the premise that wage setting is a social practice that can be used to reinforce, and sometimes reinterpret, women's status in the workplace.

The status of female employees was a key issue underlying the minimum-wage debate – but it was not the only concern. The question also touched on ongoing tensions over the proper relationship between trade unions and co-operation, the ties between national co-operative bodies and local societies and whether the movement should prioritise its business activities or its social ideals. As historian Peter Gurney rightly points out, 'any critical historical assessment of the movement . . . must necessarily confront the fact that the co-operative project was deeply marked by theoretical and ideological silences and tensions'.[5] Nor was the question divorced from the wider social questions of the day – most notably, the rise of new unionism and the widespread concern over wages and working conditions in what were termed 'sweated industries'.

Co-operation in the early twentieth century

The co-operative movement at the turn of the century was growing rapidly in membership, in social influence and in economic power. By 1905, Great Britain boasted over 2.25 million members in nearly 1,600 autonomous societies.[6] The Co-operative Wholesale Society (CWS) in England and Wales and its Scottish counterpart (SCWS) produced nearly £5 million worth of foodstuffs and household goods in factories across the country.[7]

At the same time, co-operative stores and factories were struggling to compete in a rapidly evolving and increasingly competitive retail environment. As economic historian James Jefferys noted in his seminal work on retail trading in Britain, the years from 1875 to the First World War saw 'a transformation of the distributive trades comparable in many ways to the revolutionary changes that had taken place in the industrial structure of the country in the previous century'.[8] The advent of large-scale retailing also had enormous consequences for retail employment, among them questions of labour costs, wages and working conditions, the 'de-skilling' of shop work and trade-union organisation.[9] While co-operators were broadly committed to improving the position of labour, like their counterparts in private industries, co-operative management committees faced significant pressures to reduce wage costs through the introduction of cheaper juvenile or female labour.[10] Reduced costs could mean higher dividends for members – and many co-operators believed that putting the 'divi' in the hands of the members was the most effective means of achieving social change. As Gurney notes, 'the dividend itself was an "ideal"'.[11]

In 1905, the co-operative movement employed around 100,000 workers.

While the majority worked in the distributive sector, about 40 per cent were employed in the productive factories associated with large societies or the Wholesales.[12] Most employees in distributive stores were male, but co-operative factories were far more likely to employ female labour. For example, a 1906 article on the CWS Pickle and Preserve Works in Middleton noted that, of the 400 workers, 'women and girls naturally form the greater number of employees, being in proportion to the men and boys of about 2 to 1'.[13]

Consumers' co-operation, organised as a democracy of purchasers, had few avenues for employee involvement.[14] By 1906, increasing numbers of co-operative employees sought a different kind of voice in co-operative affairs – through trades unions. Initially, unionisation was confined to skilled male labourers in co-operative factories, who joined the union of their respective craft – for instance, workers in the CWS boot works at Leicester might join their local branch of the Boot and Shoe Operatives. Most craft unions did not admit unskilled men, and even fewer accepted women workers. On the distributive side, until the 1890s no trades unions existed for male or female shop workers, who were considered semi-skilled or unskilled. Founded in 1895, the Amalgamated Union of Co-operative Employees (AUCE) sought to organise co-operative employees, not by trade, but across co-operative industries.[15] Another union founded around the same time, the National Union of Shop Assistants, recruited some of its members from co-operative stores – but this chapter deals exclusively with the AUCE.[16]

On the surface, the AUCE accorded female employees a high degree of equality with their male counterparts. There were no union restrictions on female membership or on the types of work women might engage in. Men and women were organised in the same branches and received the same benefits. In practice, however, the AUCE made few efforts to recruit women workers to its ranks in its first two decades.[17] In 1906, fewer than 500 of the AUCE's 15,000 members were female.[18]

In outlook, the AUCE had much in common with the 'new unionism' of the period, although in its early years it was far from a militant body. Many co-operative societies prided themselves on being model employers and most trade unionists agreed that the working conditions of co-operative employees were considerably better than those of their counterparts in private trade. However, the AUCE maintained that some co-operative societies were far below the model. Before 1911, the union did not engage in strikes or collective bargaining, focusing its efforts on gathering information about hours and wages and developing educational campaigns to improve working conditions.[19] Still, as its membership and organisation grew, the AUCE became an increasingly significant voice on questions of hours and wages.

The relationship between trades unions and the co-operative movement

Table 8.1 *Female AUCE membership as per cent of total, 1900–18*

Year	Total members	Female members	% female
1900	6,276	171	2.7
1901	7,338	228	3.1
1902	8,294	229	2.8
1903	9,404	393	4.2
1904	10,535	406	3.9
1905	11,779	489	4.2
1906	13,150	498	3.8
1907	17,287	650	3.8
1908	22,998	1,020	4.4
1909	26,883	1,581	5.9
1910	29,273	2,070	7.1
1911	30,394	2,775	9.1
1912	32,367	2,895	8.9
1913	40,583	–	–
1914	44,538	6,000*	13.5
1915	50,950	–	–
1916	59,752	–	–
1917	73,263	25,941	35.4
1918	81,149	32,351	39.9

Note:

* Because AUCE annual reports did not collect statistics on female membership for 1913–16, the 1914 statistics on female members are an estimate, printed in 'Notes and News', *Co-operative News* (15 October 1917), p. 977.

Source: AUCE annual reports (Manchester: AUCE, 1901–19). Irish statistics are omitted.

was a complicated one. On the local level, many co-operative store members were trade unionists, as were many of the elected members of co-operative management committees, who determined the wages of their employees. During local disputes, co-operative stores often donated funds and supplies to trade-union relief committees. Nationally, co-operative and trade unionist delegates attended each others' congresses, and throughout the early twentieth century several attempts were made to strengthen the formal ties between the two. Yet tensions also existed. At the heart of the matter was a fundamental disagreement over the best means by which to improve the condition of the working classes. As one speaker at a Co-operative Congress put it: 'They were like travellers who had started on a railway, the lines of which diverged, and they got further from each other as they proceeded. The one started from the point of view of the consumer, and the other from the point of view of the producer.'[20] While trade unionists and co-operators were in broad agreement about the ideals of the Co-operative Commonwealth, they often disagreed on how best to achieve it.

The final organisation in the debate over the female minimum wage was the English Women's Co-operative Guild (WCG). In 1906 the Guild claimed over 21,000 members, and another 8,700 were members of its sister organisation in Scotland.[21] The Guild sought to organise women through the power of their market baskets. Since women were the primary consumers within the working-class family, and co-operatives produced and sold basic household goods, the movement's financial health depended on its ability to attract and sustain a female customer base. Despite their 'basket power', however, few women rose to positions of leadership within the movement before the Guild's foundation in 1883. As an auxiliary organisation, the Guild aimed to promote the involvement of women in the co-operative movement and to improve the position of working-class women generally. While the Guild's membership represented only a tiny minority of women members, it served as the primary voice for the interests of women co-operators.[22]

Under the leadership of Margaret Llewelyn Davies, the Guild's general secretary from 1889–1922, the WCG took particular interest in the welfare of women workers. In all its campaigns, the Guild sought to connect women's role as purchasers of household goods with the conditions under which those products were made. The Guild developed close ties with anti-sweating campaigns and the Women's Trade Union Association (WTUA), while other Guildswomen helped form the Women's Industrial Council in 1894.[23] Throughout the 1890s, the Guild used the 'Women's Corner' of the *Co-operative News* to campaign against sweated labour, in favour of a trade-union label and in support of early closing in co-operative stores. In 1896, the Guild conducted investigations into women's conditions in CWS clothing factories and the distributive stores. The following year, the Guild published the first pamphlets and articles suggesting the need for a minimum wage for female co-operative employees.[24]

Male and female minimums

At the turn of the twentieth century, the concept of a minimum wage had become a matter of public debate. As early as 1897, social reformers including J.A. Hobson and Sidney and Beatrice Webb called for a national minimum wage as a solution to the problem of sweated industries. By 1906, with a new Liberal government in power and the Sweated Industries Exhibition drawing huge crowds in London and Manchester, anti-sweating campaigns were much on the minds of working-class reformers. While some advocated national minimums and some backed Sir Charles Dilke's compromise measure of Trade Boards, trade unionists proceeded to fight for minimum wages workplace by workplace.[25] Female trade-union organisations also grew substantially in this period, as social reformers and trade-union leaders of both sexes sought to address the problems presented by low-paid female labour. Although there were only 167,000 trade union women in 1906, organisations like the Women's Trade Union League (WTUL) and the Federation of Women Workers engaged in active propaganda and lobbing efforts to improve women's wages.[26]

From its formation the AUCE promoted a minimum wage of twenty-four shillings per week for adult male employees, conducting its first agitation on the topic in 1897.[27] However, the union's small size and conciliatory stance meant that little progress was made before 1906. The AUCE based its arguments on ethical grounds, arguing that a minimum wage was necessary for male employees to support their families and maintain their own health. Moreover, AUCE leaders argued, by serving as a model employer the movement could attract more workers – particularly trade unionists and their wives – to the stores.[28]

The first major victory for the male minimum wage came with a resolution in its favour at the 1906 Co-operative Congress. Then, in August 1907, the CWS board agreed to adopt the minimum for its adult male employees. Yet the battle was far from won. It was one thing to pass a resolution at Congress, but quite another to gain the support of local management committees, many of whom viewed the non-binding recommendations as 'of no importance to them'.[29] Three years after the first Congress resolution, and twelve years after the first AUCE campaign, just over one-third of the 1,400 societies had adopted the male minimum.[30]

Throughout the pre-war period, the AUCE continued to agitate for the minimum wage, society by society. As the union moved toward a more militant stance, its tactics evolved. In the spring of 1909, the union increased its staff of paid organisers from one to three. Next, the AUCE organised public demonstrations in several towns, putting pressure on societies – and their trade-unionist members – to adopt rules requiring payment of trade-union rates.[31] When the AUCE created a strike fund in 1911, it was guaranteed that wages would be a central issue for the movement.

Meanwhile, the question of women's wages in the co-operative movement moved to the top of the agenda for the first time at the 1906 WCG Congress. The programme included a 'sweated goods' exhibition and an evening lecture from Gertrude Tuckwell, then president of the WTUL.[32] During the Congress sessions, a paper on 'The Protection of Women Workers' led to a resolution calling for joint AUCE and Guild action for a female minimum wage.[33] The following year, the 1907 Co-operative Congress approved the principle of a minimum wage for both men and women. Shortly thereafter, representatives

Table 8.2 *Minimum-wage scale agreed by 1909 Co-operative Congress*

Age	14	15	16	17	18	19	20	21
Male wages (shillings/week)	6	8	10	12	15	18	21	24
Female wages	5	7	9	11	13	15	17	17

Note: Under the scale, adult males were defined as 21 years or older; adult females were defined as 20 years or older.

Source: R.B. Padley, *Newcastle Congress and After* (Manchester: Co-operative Newspaper Society Ltd, 1909), p. 4.

of the Co-operative Union, the AUCE and the WCG (but, curiously, *not* the Wholesales) met to devise a minimum scale.[34] In 1908, and at every subsequent meeting until 1912, the Co-operative Congress approved the scale of wages they devised.[35]

Although a minority of Guild and AUCE leaders argued in favour of equal pay for male and female employees, the Guild's leadership recognised that even a modest, lower minimum wage for women would come up against stiff resistance from management committees and CWS directors. All parties were well aware of the widely publicised Board of Trade report showing that nearly one-third of all working women earned less than twelve shillings per week.[36] Guild leaders were also keenly aware of the need to protect adult women's earnings, understanding that if the minimum wage for adult women was set too high, co-operative employers might be tempted to replace them with younger workers at lower wages.

In their campaign, the WCG continued the trend set by the AUCE a few years earlier, arguing the need for a living wage on ethical grounds. Both inside and outside the movement, employers assumed that male employees needed wages that would support their families. In most regions, women workers were expected to leave the workforce upon marriage, and rely on their families for support until that time. While men needed a family wage, the argument ran, women worked for 'pin-money'. The Guild pointed out that this was often not the case, citing examples of adult women who were attempting to support dependents on ten to twelve shillings a week.[37]

Thus, Margaret Llewelyn Davies wrote that the scale put forward was 'based on the barest physical needs of an independent human machine. No woman of eighteen can live a healthy, self-respecting life on less than 13 shillings a week . . . Such wage allows for no saving, no subscriptions, no recreation, no education, no extras of any kind.'[38] The Guild also tried to counter notions that female labour had less value due to women's lesser physical strength. An article in the 'Women's Corner' commented wryly: 'We have to open our minds to a new principle, and that is very difficult for Englishmen. It must be accepted that girl's or women's labour is always "worth" a living wage'.[39] The Guild appealed to co-operators' ideals and working-class identity, noting that the movement's focus on dividends was always intended as a means to an end: 'the elevation of the economic and social condition of the workers by a policy of mutual aid'.[40] And, particularly after the CWS had accepted the male minimum, Davies pointed out the hypocrisy of denying a minimum wage to women.[41]

Once the 1908 Co-operative Congress adopted the minimum scale, the Guild campaign swung into high gear. That summer, the Guild loaned personnel to the AUCE to assist in encouraging female co-operative employees to join the union.[42] The AUCE and the Guild formed both national and regional committees to carry out joint actions. Guild branches were encouraged to help the AUCE arrange socials to 'make the Union known amongst female employés'.[43] The Guild's 1910 annual report noted that 157 branches had held 191 meetings with special speakers, while fourteen district conferences were arranged to discuss the minimum wage and trade unionism for female employees.[44]

There was evidence of some success. A speech by one Guildswoman led to the formation of an AUCE branch in Melton Mobray, which all the women employees joined. In Birmingham, local Guild efforts led to the adoption of the female minimum, while resolutions at quarterly meetings in Lincoln and Gloucester 'were largely due to the initiative and support of Guild members'.[45] But successes were hard to come by. In 1910, while 500 local societies had adopted the men's minimum, just thirty-six honoured the full Congress scale.[46]

Why was progress so slow? Certainly the women's-minimum campaign faced the same difficulty as that of the men: minimum wage scales had to be adopted in each local society. Then, too, raising the very low wages of women to the standard set by the minimum scale involved a much more sizeable leap than the rise required for men. Management committees complained that they could not afford the addition to their wages bill without raising prices or lowering dividends. This sentiment was coupled with the continuing perception that women's 'unskilled' labour was simply less valuable. The Blaydon Society, for instance, paid the scale to men and boys, but stated that, 'as regards girls, except in exceptional cases, the scale is more than ordinary girls are worth'.[47]

Other evidence suggests that there were tensions between male and female workers in the rank and file. Writing in the *Co-operative Employé*, Stratford co-operator J. Baldwin condemned the apathy of many women workers toward unionisation, commenting that 'the attitude of the majority [is] expressed as follows: "Oh, I shall be married soon, and the Union would be of no use to me then."[48] Sunderland AUCE member W.T. Scott also acknowledged the difficulties of encouraging union members to organise their female co-workers, writing:

> If unity is strength – and we often boast this fact – why do we as branches keep the ladies back, who are our fellow employés? For while some of our branches have grasped the importance of this, there are others, large and small, who have persistently refused, or neglected to canvass, or in any way endeavour to enlist the sympathy and co-operation of the other sex.[49]

Despite areas of conflict, the Guild and the AUCE continued to work together with some success. By 1914, the union included 6,000 female members, making up 13.5 per cent of the total membership – up from 3.8 per cent in 1906.[50] Some of the increase can be attributed to the Union's inclusion as an approved society in the National Insurance Act of 1911, but the joint action of the AUCE and the Guild nevertheless played a key role in bringing women to the union.

In 1910, although branches of both organisations continued local efforts to obtain a female minimum in the stores, the Guild's leaders turned their attention to the single largest co-operative employer: the CWS. Their efforts began with a petition to the CWS board, signed by over half of the Guild's 26,000 members. Throughout 1911/12 they engaged in a vigorous lobbying campaign to win over delegates to CWS quarterly meetings.

While CWS directors agreed that a female minimum wage was a worthy goal, they echoed store managers' arguments that the economic impact of such a move would be detrimental to the financial health of the movement. Raising wages might mean raising prices on co-operative goods, which would divert trade to private manufacturers and ultimately lead to redundancies among the very co-operative workers the AUCE and the Guild were endeavouring to help. They maintained that a fixed rate across trades and localities was inflexible, and complained that they had not been involved in setting up the Congress scale and that they considered it only a recommendation.[51] Rather than lobbying for a co-operative minimum, the CWS directors argued, the movement should focus its attention on a legal minimum wage that would apply to all employers. In the meantime, said the directors in a 1911 report, co-operators should have 'confidence that our deliberations and actions will be in the best and truest interests of the society and its employés'.[52]

Needless to say, after five years of battling management committees, neither the AUCE nor the Guild trusted the CWS to maintain the best interests of female employees. Following a defeat by over 500 votes at the December 1911 CWS delegate meeting, the Guild made the adoption of the female minimum wage the centrepiece of its 1912 programme. Rank-and-file Guildswomen were urged to distribute leaflets, lobby management committees and get themselves appointed as delegates to the next quarterly meeting.[53] After a year and a half of lobbying, the campaign worked: the following year the CWS quarterly meeting voted to adopt the minimum-wage scale in all its departments by 1914, this time by a margin of 139 votes.[54]

Emboldened by their success, the Guild and the AUCE continued to lobby local co-operative societies, increasing the number of stores adopting the female minimum to 240 by 1914.[55] Yet on the eve of the First World War, only 16 per cent of co-operative societies had adopted the full minimum-wage scale – suggesting that a broad divide could and did exist between official co-operative policy and actual practice.[56] Arguments over the role of trade unions and female labour continued throughout the country, and the coming war would only accentuate these divides.

Separate minimums, substitute workers and equal pay

Between 1906 and 1914, the co-operative movement experienced substantial growth, adding nearly a million members and more than 40,000 employees to its ranks. The WCG also saw their membership numbers rise. During the war years, membership continued to expand, as co-operators added another half million members to their ranks by 1918. The war years were particularly good to the AUCE, which saw its total membership double and its female membership quadruple. Only the WCG experienced slight declines during the war years, which were rapidly reversed after war's end.[57]

Wartime conditions accentuated the growing divisions between local management committees, CWS directors and the AUCE. Even before the war, co-operative managers viewed increasing AUCE militancy with alarm. A 1913 *Wheatsheaf* article complained: 'Co-operative stores soon will be expected to work under conditions that never have been dreamt of by the employee in the multiple shops. Because it is hard to get better conditions from the capitalists, and comparatively easy to win them from co-operators, catch-as-catch-can!'[58] Moreover, work stoppages became more common between 1911 and 1914, as the AUCE exercised its newly created strike fund at the CWS Bristol flour mill, the Leicester boot works and in sporadic disputes with local stores.[59] The Co-operative Union responded by setting up Conciliation Boards in 1914 to reduce conflict between committees and the AUCE.[60] The shortage of male labour brought about by wartime enlistment, and later conscription, introduced a further divisive element. As the male labour crunch worsened in 1915, tensions increased.

That summer, unions including the AUCE introduced a new category of female employee. Women who replaced men lost to military service were referred to as 'substitute' workers, whose conditions of employment included the provision that they would be discharged at war's end. Yet the traditionally lower wages of women workers who were now entering into 'male' occupations were a source of great concern to male trade unionists. If substituted women performed the same work as men for lower wages, unions feared employers would not return to male wage standards after the war. Suddenly, male trade union leaders inside and outside the movement began to advocate what had previously been a radical concept: equal pay for equal work.

Some Guildswomen were elated at the unexpected turn of events brought about by male trade unionists' qualified acceptance of equal pay, while others expressed annoyance. One WCG member wrote 'the proposals of the AUCE, in spite of seeming justice to women, are in reality made mainly in the interests of men'.[61] Nevertheless, the Guild continued to work with the AUCE, particularly after the appointment of its first female organiser in 1915. Ellen Wilkinson, the future Labour MP, started a 'Women's Department' in the union shortly after her arrival.[62]

As co-operative societies began to lose male employees to enlistment, the AUCE drafted its policy for substituted women. They firmly stated that male workers would be reinstated in their positions and that substituted females were to be regarded as temporary. The union required that substituted workers join a trade union. They declared that 'the principle of equal pay for equal work should be rigidly maintained', conceding only that women might receive the lesser Congress scale during a month's probation period.[63]

The issue of substituted female labour was contentious enough to cause a near strike at Sheffield's Brightside and Carbrook Society later that summer. The *Co-operative News* reported that the society's conference 'appeared to take the view that women workers were not equal to men, but believed, on the other hand, that there should be equal pay for equal work', clearly basing their argument on the need to protect male wages after the war.[64]

The controversy over substituted women also had an impact on existing female employees, as the *Co-operative News* pointed out: 'A female worker, new to the work and new to the service of the society, will thus be in receipt of wages which be 5s. to 10s. higher per week than other female employés who may have been with the society for many years, and who, by the way, may be longstanding members of the AUCE.'[65] In response, union organiser L. Lumley stated somewhat unconvincingly that the existing employees were not applying for vacancies because they preferred permanent positions to temporary ones, even at higher wages.[66]

The AUCE policy raised a firestorm of protest in some areas, as evidenced by the rhetoric at a North West sectional meeting. One speaker stated unequivocally: 'They at Carnsforth believed the women were not equal to men. Why, then, should they be called upon to pay them the same wages?' Others protested the implication that unskilled women could be trained to take over for skilled men in just months. Mr Hall, of East Yorkshire, felt: 'Anyone with experience of the grocery trade would know that it would take three inexperienced women to do the work of one efficient and well-trained man.' A South Yorkshireman reflected the hardening opinion of many co-operators when he stated: 'They had got to fight the AUCE . . . the movement must put its foot down firmly.'[67]

Relations were not much better with the CWS. At a 1915 quarterly meeting, its directors described a strategy clearly designed to get around union policy about substitution, noting: 'In no case was the woman doing precisely the same work, and in no case was she receiving the same rate of pay, but that work was given to women which was suitable to them.'[68] Articles in the *Wheatsheaf* grew ever more critical of union developments. The comments of a Bolton editor are characteristic of hardening CWS attitudes:

> We confess we look upon these concessions to employees with apprehension . . . We believe the members should rule in all matters pertaining to their own society. We believe, too, that the employees should be content with the decisions of their own employers. We believe, further, that there never should have been such a thing as a trade union within the co-operative movement. It is an anomaly.[69]

Hostility only increased as the war dragged on, as the AUCE struck on new demands for war bonuses for employees due to the rising cost of living. The *Co-operative News*, recognising the breakdown in relations between the AUCE and the wider movement, editorialised that the situation 'ought never to have existed in a new system of democratic capital and labour. That is why we plead so much for some kind of new machinery to deal with the differences between committees, officials, and labour'.[70]

The Co-operative Union's Central Board evidently agreed that matters were coming to a head. In 1916, the Board put forward a Congress resolution establishing a defence fund for co-operative societies, which raised £427,000. Although Conciliation Boards were already in place, societies were advised to establish district Hours and Wages Boards as a new mechanism for settling disputes between societies and trade unions, and the Co-operative Union added a paid labour advisor to its staff. Wages and Hours Boards spread during 1917/18 to nearly all of the sixty-two districts in England, Scotland and Wales.[71] As G.D.H. Cole put it, co-operative societies formed 'what amounted to an employers' federation to resist the AUCE'.[72]

Even with all this machinery in place, however, union militancy did not dissipate. The AUCE engaged in more than seventy strikes against local co-operative societies on the subject of wages in the period 1914–18. Evidence suggests that, while the AUCE supported female wage increases, equal pay was far from a reality in many areas. In her 1920 history of women and trade unionism, Barbara Drake noted of the AUCE: 'Definite progress was made during the war, although advances of wages varied considerably from one district to another.' At the end of 1918, war bonuses for men and women in the West Riding were over twenty-two shillings, although women often received seven shillings less than men in wages. Evidence of wages across the movement is difficult to come by for this period, but suggests that separate male and female minimums remained common, with equal pay most frequently applying to store management positions.[73]

The minimum-wage debates offer historians a unique view of the fault lines running through the co-operative movement of the early twentieth century. Gender was certainly a key area of conflict. Those campaigning for female minimum wages or equal pay had to contend with entrenched perceptions that female labour was of lesser value. While many recognised that cheaper female labour could undercut male wages, even during the war years it was difficult to overcome the idea that women workers were worth less than their male counterparts.

In debating women's wages, the movement revealed other divisions within the Co-operative Commonwealth. The minimum-wage question brought the ongoing tension between the movement's increasing economic power and its social ideals into the forefront. It also revealed the ambivalence underlying the often close relationship between the co-operative and trade union movements. It is particularly striking that the wartime period of labour unrest took place at the very time that rationing, claims of unfair treatment and profiteering by private businessmen, and government taxes on dividends led to a heightened sense of working-class identity among co-operators of all stripes.[74] Yet many co-operators expressed concern at increasing union militancy, particularly when it was aimed at their stores and factories, and questioned the ability of trade unions to achieve broader social and political aims. The new sense of class-consciousness co-existed uneasily with the legacy of wartime labour disputes.

The Women's Guild, however, showed no such ambivalence. Throughout the period the Guild clearly identified itself with trade unionism through its minimum-wage campaign and its ties to women's labour organisations, and as a consistent advocate of a political 'fusion of forces' between co-operation and trade unions. While historians of the WCG have focused much of their attention on its ability to use its 'basket power' to achieve its aims, the extent to which the Guild allied itself with organised labour in the minimum-wage campaign has been largely overlooked.[75] The Guild joined its consumer-organising tactics with those of a quasi-political pressure group, allying with idealist co-operative leaders and the AUCE to push for co-operative policy changes. Their efforts achieved notable successes, and cemented the Guild's reputation as a progressive force. As one *Wheatsheaf* correspondent put it, 'what the women determine to-day the movement accepts tomorrow'.[76]

While pressure-group tactics worked in some instances, the minimum-wage story also demonstrates the limitations of the Guild's position. With few women in positions of leadership on co-operative boards and management committees, and no formal representation at Co-operative Congresses, the WCG had to achieve most of their aims through indirect means. Whether lobbying the CWS, the Co-operative Union or the AUCE, the Guild's position as an independent auxiliary body meant that it could act as a 'bully pulpit' but had only indirect decision-making power.

Notes

1 Women's Co-operative Guild (hereafter WCG), *A Co-operative Standard for Women Workers* (Kirkby Lonsdale: WCG, 1908), p. 1.

2 Other forms of co-operation, including worker co-operatives, were active in this period. This essay focuses solely on consumer co-operatives.

3 James B. Jefferys, *Retail Trading in Britain, 1850–1950* (Cambridge: Cambridge University Press, 1954), p. 19.

4 Deborah Figart, Ellen Mutari and Marilyn Power, *Living Wages, Equal Wages: Gender and Labor Market Policies in the United States* (London and New York: Routledge, 2002), p. 5.

5 Peter Gurney, *Co-operative Culture and the Politics of Consumption in England, 1870–1930* (Manchester: Manchester University Press, 1996), p. 231.

6 Throughout this chapter, 'Great Britain' will be used to denote England, Scotland and Wales. Irish figures have been removed from all statistical information. Co-operative Union (hereafter CU), *Thirty-eighth Annual Congress Report* (Manchester: CU, 1906), pp. 548–59.

7 Gurney, *Co-operative Culture*, p. 20.

8 Jefferys, *Retail Trading in Britain*, p. 6.

9 Ibid., p. xvi.

10 See Michael J. Winstanley, *The Shopkeeper's World, 1830–1914* (Manchester: Manchester University Press, 1983).

11 Gurney, *Co-operative Culture*, p. 10.

12 CU, *Thirty-eighth Annual Congress Report*, pp. 550–1.

13 'The Middleton preserve and pickle works: concluded', *Wheatsheaf* (October 1906), p. 58.

14 As late as 1921 most co-operative societies banned employees from seeking election to management committees. Sidney and Beatrice Webb, *The Consumer's Co-operative Movement* (London: Longman's, Green and Co., 1921), pp. 30–1.

15 A. Hewitt, 'The old brigade: the AUCE: origination and amalgamation', *Co-operative Employé* (Jan 1909), pp. 12–15. For the early history of the Amalgamated Union of Co-operative Employees (hereafter AUCE), see also G.D.H. Cole, *A Century of Co-operation* (Manchester: CU, 1944) pp. 335–51, and Sir William Richardson, *A Union of Many Trades: The History of USDAW* (Manchester: Union of Shop, Distributive and Allied Workers, c.1979), pp. 13–54.

16 See Lee Holcombe, *Victorian Ladies at Work: Middle Class Working Women in England and Wales 1850–1914* (Newton Abbot: David & Charles Holdings, 1973), pp. 103–40; Cole, *A Century of Co-operation* pp. 335–51; and Richardson, *A Union of Many Trades.*

17 Holcombe, *Victorian Ladies at Work*, pp. 120–1.

18 AUCE, *Fifteenth Annual Report* (Manchester: AUCE, 1906), pp. 22–3.

19 Webb and Webb, *Consumer's Co-operative Movement*, pp. 194–5.

20 'Sparks from the anvil', *Shop Life Reform* (10 June 1891), p. 251.

21 WCG, *Twenty-third Annual Report* (Co-operative Wholesale Society [hereafter CWS]: Manchester, 1906), p. 5; Scottish Women's Co-operative Guild (hereafter SWCG), *Fourteenth Annual Report* (Glasgow: Scottish Co-operative Wholesale Society [hereafter SCWS], 1906), p. 6.

22 For two different approaches to the WCG, see Gillian Scott, *Feminism and the Politics of Working Women: Women's Co-operative Guild, 1880s to the Second World War* (London: UCL Press, 1998) and Barbara Blaszak, *The Matriarchs of England's Co-operative Movement: A Study in Gender Politics and Female Leadership, 1883–1921* (Westport, CT and London: Greenwood, 2000).

23 Cole, *A Century of Co-operation*, p 339.

24 Lilian Harris, *The Treatment of Women Employees in Co-operative Stores* (Kirkby Lonsdale: WCG, 1897).

25 See Sheila Blackburn, 'Ideology and social policy: the origins of the Trade Boards Act', *Historical Journal* 34:1 (1991), pp. 43–64.

26 Barbara Drake, *Women in Trade Unions* (London: Labour Research Department, 1920), p. 30.

27 J.A. Woodbridge, 'The minimum wage', *Co-operative Employé* (July 1909), p. 5.

28 E.R.S. Mundy, 'Whatsoever is right will I pay thee', *Co-operative Employé* (December 1908), p. 17.

29 L. Lumley, 'Rebuffed at Rishton', *Co-operative Employé* (June 1910), p. 5.

30 Woodbridge, *Co-operative Employé* (July 1909), p. 5.

31 'Minutes of Executive Council', *Co-operative Employé* (March 1909), pp. 10–11; 'Stafford Co-operative Society', *Co-operative Employé* (July 1909), p. 21; 'Resolutions adopted', *Co-operative Employé* (November 1910), p. 17; L. Lumley, 'Co-operators and collective bargaining', *Co-operative Employé* (August 1910), p. 13.

32 'The Guild Congress at Ipswich', *Wheatsheaf* (August 1906), p. 22.

33 WCG, *Twenty-third Annual Report* (Manchester: CWS, 1906), p. 6.

34 A. Hewitt, 'The minimum wage movement', *Co-operative Employé* (July 1908), p. 5.

35 R.B. Padley, *Newcastle Congress and After* (Manchester: Co-operative Newspaper Society Ltd, 1909), p. 4.

36 Drake, *Women in Trade Unions*, p. 44.

37 WCG, *A Co-operative Standard for Women Workers*, p. 3.

38 Margaret Llewelyn Davies (hereafter MLD), 'The women's minimum wage campaign', *Co-operative News* (1 April 1911), p. 403.

39 MLD, 'The women's minimum wage campaign', *Co-operative News* (21 January 1911), p. 61.

40 'Women's wages in the co-operative movement', *Co-operative News* (3 June 1911), p. 678.

41 MLD, *Co-operative News* (21 January 1911), p. 61.

42 'Executive Council', *Co-operative Employé* (July 1908), p. 11.

43 WCG Central Committee, 'The Women's Guild and the AUCE', *Co-operative Employé* (December 1909), p. 22.

44 WCG, *Twenty-seventh Annual Report* (London: WCG, 1910), p. 7.

45 WCG Central Committee, *Co-operative Employé* (December 1909), p. 22.

46 Catherine Webb, 'The Women's Congress at Oxford', *Wheatsheaf* (September 1910), p. 46.

47 'Congress and the minimum wage', *Co-operative Employé* (June 1910), p. 9.

48 J. Baldwin, 'Our women-folk and trade unionism', *Co-operative Employé* (February 1910), p. 10.

49 W.T. Scott, 'The AUCE and female employees', *Co-operative Employé* (September 1908), p. 15.

50 'Notes and news', *Co-operative News* (13 October 1917), p. 977; AUCE, *Fifteenth Annual Report*, pp. 22–3; AUCE, *Twenty-third Annual Report* (Manchester: AUCE, 1914), p. 42.

51 Percy Redfern, *The Story of the CWS: The Jubilee History of the Co-operative Wholesale Society Limited, 1863–1913* (Manchester: CWS, 1913), pp. 360–61.

52 'The CWS and the minimum wage', *Co-operative News* (11 November 1911), p. 1423.

53 'Not words, but deeds: the Guild's campaign for the coming winter', *Co-operative News* (16 September 1911), p. 1200.

54 'Women workers,' *Co-operative News* (28 December 1912), p. 1622.

55 Drake, *Women in Trade Unions*, p. 56.

56 CU, *Forty-sixth Annual Congress Report* (Manchester: CU, 1915), p. 696.

57 *Forty-sixth Annual Congress Report*, pp. 696–7; CU, *Fiftieth Annual Congress Report* (Manchester: CU, 1919), pp. 742–3; AUCE, *Twenty-Third Annual Report*, p. 42; AUCE, *Twenty-seventh Annual Report* (Manchester: AUCE, 1918), p. 36; WCG, *Thirty-second Annual Report* (London: WCG, 1915), p. 3; *Thirty-sixth Annual Report* (London: WCG, 1919), p. 3; and K.M. Callen, *History of the Scottish Co-operative Women's Guild* (Glasgow: SCWS, 1952), p. 31.

58 P.R., 'Trade unionism and co-operation', *Wheatsheaf* (May 1913), p. 166.

59 P.R., 'Co-operators, the AUCE, and the Shop Assistants' Union', *Wheatsheaf* (December 1913), p. 94; 'The strike at the CWS Works', *Wheatsheaf* (May 1913), p. 162.

60 Cole, *A Century of Co-operation*, p. 342.

61 Cicely Ford, 'Injustice to Women', *Co-operative News* (30 October 1915), p. 1460.

62 Drake, *Women in Trade Unions*, pp. 167–8.

63 'Co-operation and the war?', *Co-operative News* (19 June 1915), p. 841.

64 'Co-operative female labour', *Co-operative News* (28 August 1915), p. 1149.

65 'Co-operative female workers' wages', *Co-operative News* (28 August 1915), p. 1156.

66 'Men's wages for women workers', *Co-operative News* (18 September 1915), p. 1241.

67 'Critics of the AUCE', *Co-operative News* (9 October 1915), p. 1350.

68 'Women's opportunities in wartime', *Co-operative News* (27 March 1915), p. 418.

69 Quoted in B.P., 'A reader's notes on Wheatsheaf local pages', *Wheatsheaf* (July 1915), p. 1.

70 'Female war labour in the movement', *Co-operative News* (9 October 1915), p. 1352.

71 Webb and Webb, *Consumer's Co-operative Movement*, pp. 221–2.

72 Cole, *A Century of Co-operation*, p. 342.

73 Drake, *Women in Trade Unions*, pp. 90, 168–9.

74 See Cole, *A Century of Co-operation*, pp. 264–70.

75 For example, Gillian Scott directly connects the Guild's 'basket power' to the minimum-wage campaign. See Scott, 'Basket power and market forces: the Women's Co-operative Guild 1883–1920', in Barbara Einhorn and Eileen Janes Yeo (eds), *Women and Market Societies: Crisis and Opportunity* (Aldershot: Edward Elgar, 1995), p. 34.

76 B.P., 'It appears to me: notes on Wheatsheaf local pages', *Wheatsheaf* (February 1911), p. 114.

9

'Mothers for Peace', co-operation, feminism and peace: the Women's Co-operative Guild and the antiwar movement between the wars

Andrew Flinn

[Women co-operators] were to demand peace and disarmament and the spread of Co-operative principles, not only among the working people of Great Britain, but among the nations of the world. And the force that lay behind their speeches and drove them home beyond the reach of eloquence was compact of many things – of men with whips, of sick rooms where match-boxes were made, of hunger and cold, of many and difficult child-births, of much scrubbing and washing up, of reading Shelley and William Morris and Samuel Butler over the kitchen table, of weekly meetings of the Women's Guild . . . (Virginia Woolf, 1931)[1]

In the introduction to a volume of the memories of co-operative women published in 1931, Virginia Woolf focused on the growth and strength of the Women's Co-operative Guild (WCG), and in doing so emphasised the importance of the interlocking principles of co-operation, internationalism, feminism, and the desire for peace in motivating Guild activists. This chapter will examine the WCG in the inter-war period, in particular its opposition to war in the 1930s, and, following on from Woolf, assess to what extent the uncompromising pacifism of most of its leaders and many of its most active members was the result of a combination of class, maternalist feminism and co-operative internationalism.

Under its pioneering leader, Margaret Llewelyn Davies (General Secretary 1889–1921), the WCG developed into a radical organisation which campaigned on a wide range of what might be termed 'gendered' issues such as childcare, maternal mortality, equal pay, family allowances, birth control, abortion and divorce reform, as well as seeking to advocate and educate on behalf of the Co-operative (and often Labour) movements. In this period, peace propaganda and opposition to war was only one facet of the Guild's activities but it was consistent with the rest of the organisation's agenda. The Guild's radical outlook developed because, uniquely, it was 'at the centre of three overlapping spheres: Co-operation, feminism and the Labour movement'.[2] The Guild was a part of all these movements, but operating across these boundaries also afforded the organisation and its leaders a degree of independence and space not available to other Co-operative- or Labour-movement organisations. In the 1930s the WCG continued to grow in terms of branches and members, peaking in 1939, but at the same time Guild influence in the wider co-operative and labour movements was in decline and, according to some commentators, its radicalism and independence were also significantly diluted.[3] Nevertheless this chapter argues that the Guild remained an organisation with radical instincts, that these instincts were best exemplified by the commitment of its leaders to absolute pacifism, and that it was this very radicalism, unpopular and some would say unrealistic in the face of the political realties of the late 1930s, that led to its isolation and declining influence among its natural allies in the Labour and Co-operative movements.

In common with other aspects of the history of the co-operative movement in Britain, the WCG has perhaps not received as much attention as it deserves from historians. However there have been a number of useful studies, including a centenary history, *Caring and Sharing* published in 1983. Useful references can be found in works examining women's history generally or women in the labour movement.[4] There have also been important examinations of the Guild's activities within the peace movement by Black, Liddington, Morrison and others.[5] But the most detailed, engaging and stimulating has been the work of Gillian Scott.[6]

Scott argues that under the 'pivotal' leadership of Llewelyn Davies the Guild developed into a radical and independent women's working-class organisation articulating a socialist-feminist agenda which she describes as a 'militant proletarian feminity' including co-operation, workers' rights and women's rights. However, Scott argues that after Davies stepped down as Guild secretary in 1921, leaders such as Eleanor Barton (General Secretary, 1925–37) 'whose first loyalty was to the Labour and Co-operative Parties' oversaw the centralisation of the organisation's federal and democratic structures and diluted the radical socialist-feminist campaigns in favour of a more moderate and electorally focused 'Labourist' approach. Scott sees as evidence of this shift the Guild's downplaying of controversial subjects such as reproductive rights as well as the curtailment of Guild democracy, notably the exclusion of Communists from office within the WCG.[7] Both these positions can be interpreted as Guild leaders demonstrating 'a strong identification with the sectional interests of labour' and in particular with the orthodox positions associated with the Labour movement leadership in the late 1920s and 1930s – witness the Labour Party's efforts to silence debate on divisive issues such as divorce and reproductive rights and the attempted bans on Communists' membership of Labour Party, trade unions and trades councils. Scott is also critical of the Guild's uncompromising advocacy of pacifism in the 1930s, believing that this stance was partly responsible for the organisation's decline during and after the Second World War, and arguing that the Guild had been 'captured by a pacifist sect as part of its slide into ever greater sclerosis.'[8]

This chapter will take Scott's arguments, in particular in relation to the Guild's identification of war and peace as the dominant issue of the period and its advocacy of a pacifist position as the starting point. While there is some evidence to suggest that the Guild did continue to campaign on controversial topics such as birth control and abortion, Scott's general thesis has much to commend it. But this chapter differs in one important aspect by suggesting that rather than being an aberration, pacifism was for a generation of Guild leaders and activists a core component of the very socialist-feminist tradition that Scott believes was otherwise abandoned by the same Guild leadership. The peace campaigns might be judged to have overly dominated the Guild's campaigning as the decade wore on, at the expense of other important feminist issues, but that is surely understandable in the wider context of the period. Equally, pacifism might also be condemned – as it was by many critics within and without the Guild – for being unrealistic and damaging in the face of the threat posed by fascism. Nevertheless this chapter will argue that the WCG's stance can only be really understood as a manifestation of the organisation's development into a radical, working-class and feminist organisation at the time of the First World War in which the interplay between international co-operation, socialism and feminism was crucial.

The Women's Co-operative Guild: a brief history

The Guild had been founded in 1883 in London by Mrs Acland and Mrs Lawrenson, and generally drew its membership from middle-aged, married, 'respectable' working-class women, few of whom were in paid employment but who were active in the co-operative movement. It was originally intended as a propaganda and educational body aimed at extending public understanding of co-operative principles. According to the Guild's rules, members were to be dedicated to promoting 'a new social order in which co-operation shall replace capitalism and women have equal opportunities with men'. Elsewhere members were urged to struggle until they had built Jerusalem.[9] But under Llewellyn Davies the Guild broadened its concerns, becoming what she called a 'trade union for married women'. As well as seeking to popularise the idea of the 'Co-operative Commonwealth' via educational activities such as debates, short courses and public speaking, the Guild also became increasingly involved in non-cooperative issues such as divorce-law reform, birth control and family allowances.[10] Like the rest of the Co-operative movement, the inter-war period was one of growth and expansion for the Guild (even if this growth masked some long-term difficulties) and the WCG doubled in size in the inter-war years, peaking at 87,246 members organised in 1,819 branches in 1939. Nevertheless these activists were a fraction of the wider Co-operative movement's nine million members.

As with the wider co-operative movement, the Guild developed a federal, self-governing structure. Crucially, although the Guild was part of the wider movement and received financial support from the Co-operative Union, it was not directly governed by the movement. With the Guild having stood firm in the disputes with the Union over its advocacy of divorce-law reform during the First World War, when under pressure from the Catholic Church the Co-operative Union withheld the Guild's grant, the Guild was able to maintain and extend its autonomy.[11] Branches were attached to the local society, but a democratic structure left most decision-making processes at the local or district level. However, the expansion of the numbers of branches and members throughout the 1920s and 1930s meant that the suitability of these structures for running such a large organisation came into question. As a result, the governance of the Guild became increasingly centralised and dominated by 'a bureaucratic, elite leadership' on the Central Committee (CC), and some commentators suggest that this contributed to the compromising of the force and uniqueness of the Guild's original radical voice.[12]

The Guild emerged from the First World War and the dispute over divorce-law reform as an independent and self-confident organisation with its own distinct political agenda, which sometimes complemented and sometimes conflicted (as in the case of demands for lower prices and higher wages for co-operative workers or campaigns for birth control) with the orthodoxies of the wider co-operative and labour movement. It is not the focus of this chapter to detail all the aspects of the Guild's campaigning during this period; however, it does seem that, despite a clear shift of emphasis and diminution of active campaigning in the 1930s on what might be termed a socialist-feminist agenda, there is evidence that the Guild was still active on issues that might be labelled 'the politics of motherhood' – such as malnutrition, the cost of living, health, housing and maternal mortality.[13] In addition, although it may not have had the priority of earlier periods, the Guild's actions were in stark contrast to the silence of other working-class women's organisations such as Labour women's sections by being one of the only organisations still prepared to put forward initiatives for the reform of the law with regard to birth control and abortion. At its 1934 Congress the Guild became one of the first women's organisations to publicly call for the legalisation of abortion and some members continued to link such campaigns to Guild ideals in explicitly feminist terms, arguing that a 'woman must have control of her own body if she is to gain the complete emancipation that the guild stands for'.[14] It is certainly true that such language was rarer in the 1930s than in earlier periods, but the Guild was by no means unique in this shift, and many other working-class women's and feminist organisations responded to the political and economic challenges of the period by similarly altering their priorities and the language they used.

Peace movements in the 1930s: peace and gender

The revival of a mass-based peace movement in Britain in the late 1970s and early 1980s was accompanied by a growing focus among both activists and academics on the history of the peace movement in general and on the role of women and gender in understanding antiwar and antimilitarist movements in particular. Among the most detailed and significant studies of nineteenth- and twentieth-century British peace movements are those by Martin Ceadel. His work seeks to identify and distinguish the many different beliefs and tendencies that have characterised antiwar and peace campaigns, most notably between the minority absolute pacifists, and the majority whom he terms 'pacificists'. The former generally held to their 'absolutist' stance out of moral or religious conviction, while the latter group campaigned for peace but were, by the late 1930s at least, prepared to accept the use of force as a last resort in preventing wider conflict. Furthermore, among the pacificists, there were also profound divisions between the socialists, the liberals and the radicals over the causes of war, notably the responsibility of capitalism and imperialism and the distinctions between a 'just' revolutionary or class war and unjust imperialist or nationalist conflicts.[15] In the late 1920s and early 1930s, the distinction between revolutionary socialist and non-socialist antiwar groups was probably more fundamental than the differences between the pacifists and the non-pacifists. The mainstream peace movement sought to preserve peace through negotiated disarmament and international co-operation via the League of Nations, an institution rejected by many on the revolutionary left as imperialist. However, the growing threat of fascism and aggressor nations in the 1930s, evident in conflicts in Abyssinia, China and Spain, according to Ceadel destroyed 'the long-standing compatibility between pacifism and the needs of the socialist movement'.[16] While absolute pacifists remained committed to a complete opposition to war, long before September 1939 the majority of British peace campaigners within the labour movement had come to accept the necessity of the threat of aggressive action and then war itself in order to defeat fascism. Reflecting on this shift after the war had broken out, the Guild argued that it was tragic that

> the Labour Movement of Britain has forgotten all it owes to the teachings of Keir Hardie and the other pioneers and repeats its blunders of 1914, lining up with capitalism in the waging of a war to defend Imperial interests.[17]

But in contrast to the much broader networks of socialist, feminist and moral or religious opposition to the First World War, opposition to the 1939–45 war came only from a rather disparate collection of individual moral pacifists, revolutionary socialists and pro-fascists. The Women's Co-operative Guild, along with the Woodcraft Folk, were the only significant organisations within the labour and co-operative movements to maintain a consistent pacifist position. As a result of this the Guild was increasingly isolated from its natural allies within the labour movement and beset by internal dissent.

There is an apparent contradiction here. How can the view that the Guild was transformed in the inter-war period from a radical 'social' feminist organisation to a more moderate, labourist, electorally focused one be reconciled with its consistent avowal of an extremely controversial peace policy which isolated Guild leaders from the very Labour and Co-operative Parties that they were otherwise seeking to support? Scott argues that the Guild's retreat from advocating a social feminist agenda can be understood in that its 'commitment to parliamentarism meant that Guild policy, indeed its whole conception of the "woman question" was effectively limited to what the leadership of the labour movement would find acceptable'. But this explanation cannot incorporate or explain the equally 'unacceptable' espousal of pacifism, and Scott has to argue that this is a largely personal, ethical and moral aberration, whereby Guild leaders 'cast aside their loyalty to labour to put absolute pacifism ahead of all other considerations'. She explicitly rejects the suggestion that this might be best understood as a feminist pacifism on the grounds that Guild propaganda tended not to articulate 'women's innate aversion to war' but to focus on an economic analysis in its understanding of the causes of war.[18] However, following Black, another solution to this apparent contradiction is to view the Guild's pacifism and its antiwar rhetoric (including references to motherhood and gender as well as opposition to capitalist competition) as resulting from its articulation of a maternalist feminism, and a working-class and international co-operative identity.[19]

The Guild was keenly aware of the contradictions and problems that its pacifism caused, in particular in relation to its traditional allies. Many members, especially younger ones and those closely associated with parties of the left, strongly opposed the policy and, although it became increasingly unsustainable intellectually, the leadership sought to hold the broader peace movement together by embracing contradictory pacifist and non-pacifist tendencies. But in the end, the leadership and many activists remained true to their principles and refused to abandon absolute pacifism. This cannot be explained in terms of the organisation being captured by a pacifist 'sect', but rather that this pacifism was a core component of their feminist, co-operative and internationalist identity.

In developing its independent, campaigning identity before 1914 the Guild had concentrated on questions regarding women's role and place in society. However the experiences of the First World War made a huge difference to the priorities of the movement and many of its members. The war transformed the gendered politics of peace, not just in the Guild but also in the Women's International League for Peace and Freedom and the Women's Peace Crusade as well as more broadly in the non-gendered Union of Democratic Control (UDC) and the No Conscription Fellowship (NCO). The images and rhetoric of maternal feminity were used not only by the state, which stressed women's maternal duties in raising soldiers and then supporting the men at the front, but also by women who opposed the conflict. The language of maternity thus encompassed both a conservative and a radical intent. The latter drew upon and expressed the individual and collective experience of loss.[20]

The experience of loss was hugely important, in terms both of the tragedy of the personal loss of fathers, husbands and children but also of a collective, communal loss, experienced by nearly all within society and resulting in a widespread and popular feeling of 'never again' in response to war and militarism. The experience of the 'mass slaughter of the First World War' explained the 'visceral' antiwar convictions of many of the prominent Guild leaders, and this was clearly expressed in gendered language of womanhood and motherhood adopted in the Guild and elsewhere by the radical opponents of the war, which contrasted women as creators and nurturers with the destroyers of life. As one guildswoman put it in *Life as We Have Known It*, there would have been no war if women had got the vote before 1914, as 'there's no mother or wife in England nor Germany that would give their loved one to be killed'.[21] Rose Simpson, Eleanor Barton's niece and the Guild's general secretary in the late 1930s, received her political education in antiwar ILP circles at the end of First World War as assistant to the activist and writer Katharine Bruce Glasier on *The Labour Leader*. Simpson echoed Bruce Glasier's combination of maternalist feminism, socialism and internationalism by urging women 'not [to] bear children to be used by governments as cannon fodder'.[22] The report of the controversial discussion and reaffirmation of the Guild's pacifist policy at its 1938 Congress expressed the 'deep conviction that pervades the whole of the guild membership that the mothers of one land cannot countenance, in any circumstances, for any reason, the wholesale murder of the children of another nation'. Guild banners on Co-operative demonstrations declared 'Mothers for Peace'.[23]

These arguments articulated a social, maternalist feminist connection between gender and war and peace, asserting that certain maternal values (nurturing, co-operation) were absent or subordinated in a male-dominated world, and which, if promoted, had the potential to transform an otherwise defective society. This meant that the Guild, unlike other pacifist organisations such as the Peace Army, did not actively promote passive or non-violent resistance to war. Rather they sought to prevent war by embracing peace propaganda and education. In particular for maternalist feminists like the

Guild, their belief that 'character was made chiefly by the womenfolk, the mothers and the teachers' pointed to the role that could be played by women in the socialisation of children against war, and in the creation of a 'peace mind'. In 1934 demands for a more militant peace strategy were rejected by the leadership who insisted on educational programmes, propaganda events such as Peace Plays and the Peace Pledge, opposition to the promotion of militarism in schools and militaristic organisations such as the Boy Scouts and the Girl Guides (hence the foundation in 1925 and the strong support offered to the Woodcraft Folk by the Guild) and demands that Empire Days in schools be replaced by Peace Days.[24]

The Guild's most famous and long-lasting contribution to the Peace movement, the white poppy, symbolised 'a firm determination to use every effort to end the evil of war', and was part of a campaign to reinvent Armistice Day as a Peace Day. First adopted in 1933, sales of the White Poppy rose to more than 85,000 in five years, and it remains to this day a symbol of peace and peace protest, though now administered by the Peace Pledge Union (PPU) rather than the Guild. Initially the money raised through sales was intended for the peace work or for the Guild's maternity work as a 'contribution to the preservation of life rather than its destruction', though controversy soon forced an announcement that the poppies were not to be used for fundraising. Wearing a white poppy was a potentially dangerous act. The white poppy was strongly opposed by the British Legion and dubbed by the press the 'coward's poppy'. Some individuals were physically attacked, and others lost their jobs. The poppy and pacifism were also controversial, even unpopular within the co-operative movement. Concerned about the possibility of a consumer boycott being organised against co-operative shops, the Co-operative Union sought unsuccessfully to put pressure on the Guild to retreat. Strong criticism was voiced in the movement's conferences and publications.[25] Nevertheless for many Guildswomen, their absolute opposition to conflict was not just shaped by gender or motherhood but also rooted in an internationalism and a belief in co-operative principles.

Co-operative internationalism

The experience of the First World War not only framed a feminist or gendered critique of war, but for many in the Co-operative movement an analysis of the roots of the conflict which focused on capitalism, imperialism and the competition for resources gave even greater force to the belief that international co-operation offered an alternative means of peacefully organising society for the benefit of all. On the eve of the First World War, the International Co-operative Alliance (ICA) spoke of its hope that 'international conflicts will disappear as the social and economic life of every nation becomes organised according to co-operative principles'. With the foundation of the International Women's Co-operative Guild (ICWG), also known as the Mothers' International, in 1921, guildswomen sought an end to conflict, not only by education and socialisation but also by substituting co-operation for capitalist competition as the fundamental principle of international relations. The role of the international co-operative organisations was to support and encourage the spread of co-operative principles worldwide as well as seeking to coordinate national movements. In this context the international dimension meant that, rather than just supporting the peace campaigns of others, the Guild developed their own distinctive perspective on peace and international relations. Although it is difficult to gauge the depth of support for a co-operative (as opposed to, for instance, a socialist) transformation of society and for an international rather than a national dimension to co-operation, the international co-operative commonwealth remained a central part of the movement's rhetoric and propaganda throughout the inter-war period. Co-operative-movement pageants such as one held in Wembley Stadium to celebrate International Co-operators Day in 1938 and including many guildswomen among the cast, portrayed this transformation as the triumph of a peaceful and plentiful international co-operative commonwealth over a capitalist system which had brought only inequality, poverty and war.[26]

The ICWG's and the British Guild's gendered and co-operative understanding of the roots of conflict informed their view that a more equal redistribution of the world's resources was alongside international disarmament the key to a long-term and sustainable peace. The Guild argued that the failure of the League of Nations and the ongoing conflicts which characterised the 1930s were caused by an unfair domination of the League and global markets by those powers who had dictated the peace terms at the end of the First World War. Guild leaders argued that these conflicts would be best resolved by a World Conference on Territories to examine the redistribution of raw materials and markets to ensure 'justice and equity for all nations' and the establishment of a fair system of international justice. In the context of the late 1930s this analysis of the causes and solutions of conflict inclined advocates not only to take a pacifist position but also to accept some of the grievances of the aggressor powers as legitimate and justified, and to adopt a position not dissimilar to appeasement. Not everyone within the co-operative movement or indeed in the Guild accepted the logic of this reasoning, and many felt that such an analysis was not applicable to the fascist threat posed in particular by Germany. The imprisonment of Emmy Freundlich, the Austrian president of the ICWG, in 1934 and her subsequent escape to Britain in 1939, as well as the fate of co-operators and other labour-movement activists in Germany, all received prominent coverage within the co-operative press. The awareness of the threat of fascism underpinned the conclusion by a significant proportion of the membership that pacifism and appeasement were no longer appropriate to the present international circumstances.[27]

Fractured movements and personal pacifism

So the Guild's pacifism, however inspired and genuinely held, became increasingly controversial both within the co-operative movement including the Guild itself and within the broader 'progressive' peace movement. To some extent the conflict with the wider co-operative movement reflected old tensions about the Guild's autonomy and campaigning on non-co-operative issues (divorce law, peace, abortion reform) and the detrimental commercial effects that such controversy might have on the movement, although on this occasion the Guild's grant was not withheld. In addition to commercial sensitivities there was also a widespread rejection of pacifism as an appropriate response to fascism.

Since the Co-operative Party's formation in 1917, the Guild had been one of the party's strongest supporters, but relations between the two organisations became increasingly strained over this issue. At the 1937 Co-operative Party conference, one party delegate, William Nally from Manchester, attacked the Guild's pacifism as 'emotional' and urged guildswomen to 'embrace the real world'. The conference overwhelmingly passed a policy in favour of collective security, later endorsed by the full Co-operative Congress. The Guild responded with an unconvincing compromise designed to preserve the movement's unity; the next Guild congress reaffirmed support for absolute pacifism but it also declared support for the movement's official pacificist policy of collective security.[28] Against the backdrop of escalating conflict in Spain and China, many Guildswomen, particularly but not exclusively younger women, began to criticise publicly the official policy. One correspondent to the *Co-operative News*, Ellen Jarman, criticised leading Guild advocates of pacifism like Lillian Harris, Margaret Llewelyn Davies and Rose Simpson, and the contradictions in Guild policy, saying that '[she was] not willing to run down the collective security policy of the Co-operative Party in the guildroom and openly support it outside. That, to [her, was] hypocrisy'.[29] She further called for a ballot of the whole membership on the pacifist policy and predicted that many guildswomen like her would resign over the issue. Although many individuals in co-operative and labour movements were still pacifists at this time, by the end of 1937 the Guild recognised that the tide was turning within the movement and that many members had abandoned pacifism and had accepted the necessity of 'armed preparedness to resist fascist aggression'.[30]

The next year, with the broader shift within the co-operative movement to embracing collective security and the Peace Alliance becoming ever more pronounced, the dispute came to a head at the 1938 Guild congress.

The leadership's motion which called for total disarmament, the replacement of the National government with a Co-operative and Labour one, 'the establishment of a policy of International Peace and Friendship based upon International Co-operative Trade between nations', and which reaffirmed the Guild's peace policy as an 'absolutist pacifist policy' was adopted but only by the comparatively narrow margin of 897 votes to 623. Again the main opposition was said to come from younger left-wing delegates.[31] The only other organisation within the co-operative movement to take a similar stand was the Woodcraft Folk which was 'pledged not to fight for King and country', a stance that provoked censure from the Co-operative Union but was supported by the Guild. Despite the pressure from the Union, both the Guild's and the Woodcraft Folks' struggle to resolve the contradiction between pacifism and anti-fascism continued into the Second World War. Given that both organisations had very similar ideological histories (founded within but autonomous from the co-operative movement, closely associated with the antiwar socialism of the Independent Labour Party (ILP) and opposed to glorification of militarism), it is hardly surprising that they were so close and had many of the same internal difficulties with this issue.[32]

Guild pacifists were also increasingly isolated within the broader labour movement. Historically the Guild's closest allies had been the ethical socialists and antiwar activists of the ILP and the No More War Movement (NMWM), relationships which were forged in the antiwar movement of 1914–18. However, during the course of the 1930s, the ILP had turned to the left, with various groupings and factions embracing revolutionary class conflict and advocating working-class opposition to fascism. Within the Labour Party, the Guild identified most closely with the Christian-socialist pacifism personified by George Lansbury. However, the threat of fascist aggression in Abyssinia and the labour movement's support for economic and military sanctions against Italy to deter such aggression resulted in the resignation of Lansbury as Labour leader, the marginalisation of the pacifist tendency within the party and, outside the left, a widespread acceptance of the need to prepare for war.[33]

Before the Abyssinian crisis, the Guild and other Labour pacificists could unite in support the League of Nations, if allied to a programme of negotiated disarmament, without having to acknowledge what were the real implications of sanctions and collective security. After 1935 it was accepted by the majority of the labour movement that only international collective security backed up by a credible threat to use force would be enough to prevent further fascist aggression. The Guild, however, followed Lansbury in concentrating on seeking to remove the causes of conflict, competition for resources, by redistributing those resources from those who monopolised them to those who claimed they had been excluded.[34]

For the rest of the decade, the gap widened between the Guild and its natural allies in the labour and co-operative movements, with those who held to an absolute pacifist position increasingly isolated even within the antiwar movement. The initial response of Guild leaders to these developments was to fudge the issue, embracing both pacifism and the wider movement's acceptance of collective security. This inherently contradictory stance was never likely to be sustainable. By 1939 it unravelled under pressure of events, and the Guild retreated into a more individualised and voluntary absolute pacifism, in which as an organisation it refused to take part in any activities which could be deemed as contributing to the war effort but left individuals to make up their own decisions on the basis of conscience.

Absolute pacifism and personal witness?

In its original formulation, the Guild's peace-campaign strategy combined advocacy for the international co-operative commonwealth (seeking to undermine the chief cause of war, capitalist and imperialist competition for resources and markets) with seeking to bring about an individual and collective 'peace mind' in society, especially among children via education and propaganda (opposing the glorification of militarism and empire in schools, demonstrating for peace on Armistice Day, promoting learning of languages and respect for other cultures in guild meetings, staging peace plays). Until 1935 or 1936, the Guild's pacifism sat fairly comfortably with its allies in the wider labour and co-operative movements who also wished to prevent another war and, revolutionary socialists aside, hoped that this might be achieved through international disarmament negotiations and co-operation rather than the use of force administered by international organisations such as the League of Nations. However, the failure of international co-operation in the face of the fascist threat meant that this common ground disappeared, and the Guild found itself criticised by its closest political allies. In response to these criticisms, including some guildswomen, the Guild's pacifism was increasingly articulated as an individual and personal commitment, more in line with the Peace Pledge Union and religious objection than with a collective response. In the difficult conditions that pertained after war began in September 1939, the Guild retained a rhetorical focus on education and international co-operation, calling for a negotiated peace and for a post-war co-operative order to prevent further hostilities, but in practical terms its campaigns were limited to individual acts of conviction and support for those victimised, particularly co-operative employees, for their beliefs.[35]

The early war years saw the Guild's membership declining steeply, falling from 87,000 in 1939 to just over 49,000 in 1941. Certainly the difficulties of operating under wartime conditions were responsible for a significant part of these membership losses. In some cases attendances at even previously well-attended branches fell into single figures before gradually recovering. However, it is probable that other factors were at work as well. Scott and others argue that pacifism split the organisation and drove members away. In particular the Guild's decision to not support at an organisational level the Government's evacuation scheme or the Women's Volunteer Service, but to leave participation up to the conscience of individual members, may have angered many and encouraged them to let their membership lapse. Guildswomen would often be members of a number of different organisations (Labour women's sections, local social organisations, etc.), and many women may have simply shifted the main focus of their activity to the organisations which best represented their current interests without making any great statement of explanation or resignation. Nevertheless some Guild leaders such as Cecily Cook (General Secretary, 1940–53) apparently welcomed the losses, referring to those who had left as a purging of 'dead wood'. Despite sentiments such as this, it seems unfair to characterise this process as one by which the Guild was 'captured by a pacifist sect', for it would seem that for many in the Guild, perhaps the majority, pacifism was a consistent and long-held belief, a result of their identity as women co-operators.[36]

There is another factor which should be taken into account. Although the immediate post-war years saw a limited recovery in Guild membership, continuous decline set in again in the 1950s. According to one historian of the co-operative movement, growth in the membership of co-operative societies and guilds in the 1930s masked a decline in active participation and the appeal of co-operation, especially amongst the young.[37] This would suggest that, although the movement retained an important place in working-class life for many decades to come, the roots of its long-term decline can actually be found in the period of its greatest size. Perhaps the Guild's membership decline was not really the result of official advocacy of pacifism but of a wider stagnation. Certainly the Guild was concerned by the threat to its own continuing survival if younger generations were not attracted to the ideals of co-operation.[38]

This generational focus was also central to understanding the Guild's pacifism and the disputes that surrounded it. The Guild's membership and certainly its leadership in this period was drawn from mostly older, middle-aged women with strong memories of the First World War, which were of course not shared by younger members who in the context of a growing fascist threat were often seen as being the strongest critics of the pacifist policy.[39]

For this older generation of guildswomen, their pacifism was closest to and often overlapped with a religious or morally inspired pacifism, but resulting from the combination of co-operation and feminism was actually a more secular pacifism. The Guild's pacifism was a factor which excluded the organisation from political influence, and perhaps it did fail to engage with the political realities of the period; but it was an important and genuine belief based on a commitment to international co-operation as a solution to the world's problems, and by maternalist experience of individual and collective loss in 1914–18. In this sense the continued advocacy of a pacifist position by Guild leaders was not an aberration but central to understanding their identity.

The Guild's co-operative inspired pacifism meant a rejection of the possibility of seeing war, including class war and violent revolution, as motor for positive change and transformation. This had implications for the Guild's understanding of the struggle for peace, but inevitably also for transformation of society based on equality, collaboration and co-operation. The divisive policy of blacklisting and excluding of communists from the guild office needs to be considered within this context. Scott sees the attack on communists as part of Barton's ultra-loyal adherence to the labour leadership and as a betrayal of the Guild's best democratic, non-sectarian and radical traditions. While this is certainly plausible, the Guild's ideological antipathy to communism should also be acknowledged as a factor in justifying these exclusions. While the Guild denounced capitalism, it sought a peaceful transition to the co-operative commonwealth. Many of its leaders were ambivalent to even the concept of a class war. Despite the Guild defining its agenda in terms of class and a critique of capitalism, the 1939 congress only narrowly rejected a resolution which repudiated the concept of 'class war' entirely. The Communist party's advocacy of revolutionary change including the necessary use of force was viewed by Guild leaders as the antithesis of their support for the gradual and peaceful transformation of society and thus, perhaps, a reason for seeking to exclude them from holding office in the organisation.[40]

The pacifism espoused by the Guild's dominant faction should not be seen as aberrant but as a set of beliefs that comes directly from the organisation's radical, socialist, internationalist and maternalist feminist past. Leaders like Eleanor Barton and Cecily Cook were mainstream labour-movement figures but like many others they had their political roots in the war-time ILP. While many, often younger, women rejected pacifism as incompatible with the threat from fascism, this elder cohort of Guild activists remained true to their identity. Whatever the viability of seeking to oppose fascism with pacifism, it is possible that in a world in which conflict over scarce resources may be ever more common in the future, a re-evaluation of the role of international co-operation in preventing such conflicts may be very timely.

Notes

1 V. Woolf, 'Introductory Letter', in M. Llewelyn Davies (ed.), *Life As We Have Known It* (London: Virago, 1977 originally 1931), pp. xxxviii–ix.

2 M. Pugh, *Women and the Women's Movement in Britain, 1914–1959* (Basingstoke: Macmillan, 1992), p. 230.

3 Guild membership in 1919–20 stood at 44,500, organised in 783 branches; it peaked in 1939 at 87,246 members in 1,819 branches. See J. Gaffin and D. Thoms, *Caring and Sharing* (Manchester: Co-operative Union, 1983), p. 268.

4 Gaffin and Thoms, *Caring and Sharing*; J. Gaffin, 'Women and Co-operation', in L. Middleton (ed.), *Women in the Labour Movement* (London: Croom Helm, 1977); J. Purvis (ed.), *Women's History: Britain, 1850–1945* (London: UCL Press, 1995); S. Rowbotham, *A Century of Women* (London: Viking, 1997); P. Graves, *Labour Women: Women in British Working-class Politics 1918–1939* (Cambridge: Cambridge University Press, 1994); J. Hannan and K. Hunt, *Socialist Women: Britain, 1880s to 1920s* (London: Routledge, 2002).

5 N. Black, 'The Mothers' International: the Women's Co-operative Guild and feminism pacifism', *Women's Studies International Forum*, 7 (1984); J. Liddington, *The Long Road to Greenham: Feminism and Anti-militarism in Britain since 1820* (London: Virago, 1989); C. Morrison, 'The Women's Co-operative Guild: campaigns for peace 1918–1939', in B. Lancaster and P. Maguire (eds), *Towards the Co-operative Commonwealth: Essays in the History of Co-operation* (Loughborough: Co-operative College, 1996).

6 G. Scott, *Feminism and the Politics of Working Women* (London: UCL Press, 1998); Scott, '"As a war-horse to the beat of drums": representations of working-class feminity in the Women's Co-operative Guild, 1880s to the Second World War', in E. Yeo (ed.), *Radical Feminity: Women's Self-representation in the Public Sphere* (Manchester: Manchester University Press, 1998); and Scott, 'A "trade union for married women": The Women's Co-operative Guild 1914–1920', in S. Oldfield (ed.), *This Working-Day World: Women's Lives and Culture(s) in Britain 1914–1945* (London: Taylor & Francis, 1994).

7 Scott, *Feminism*, pp. 4–7, 160 and 184; 'As a war-horse', pp. 211–12.

8 Scott, *Feminism*, pp. 5, 221–2.

9 WCG rules 1935, *Reynold's News* (23 June 1935).

10 G. Scott, 'Women's autonomy and divorce law reform', in S. Yeo, *New Views of Co-operation* (London: Routledge, 1988), p. 132.

11 Gaffin and Thoms, *Caring and Sharing*, pp. 47–52.

12 Scott, *Feminism*, p. 269.

13 Rowbotham, *Century of Women*, pp 126–7; *Women's Outlook* (January 1935); Gaffin and Thoms, *Caring and Sharing*, pp. 104–8.

14 Graves, *Labour women*, pp. 195–9; Pugh, *Women and the Women's Movement*, pp. 116, 249–57; Rowbotham, *A Century of Women*, pp. 193–4; *Women's Co-operative Guild Annual Report* 1935 (1934 congress decisions); WCG CC minutes 22 March 1937 and *Co-operative News* (16 June and 4 August 1934).

15 M. Ceadel, *Pacifism in Britain, 1914–1945* (Oxford: Clarendon, 1980), pp. 1–8; M. Ceadel, *Thinking About Peace and War* (Oxford: Oxford University Press, 1987); M. Ceadel 'The peace movement between the wars: problems of definition', in R. Taylor and N. Young (eds), *Campaigns for Peace: British Peace Movements in the Twentieth Century* (Manchester: Manchester University Press, 1987) p. 74; M.

Ceadel, *Semi-Detached Idealists: The British Peace Movement and International Relations, 1854–1945* (Oxford: Oxford University Press, 2000).

16 Ceadel, *Thinking About Peace*, pp. 73–96; M. Shaw, 'War, peace and British Marxism 1895–1945', in Taylor and Young, *Campaigns for Peace*, pp. 49–68; A. Flinn and G. Cohen, 'The Abyssinia crisis, British labour and the fracturing of the anti-war movement', *Socialist History* 28 (2006), 36–59.

17 Brynmor Jones Library, Hull University, Women's Co-operative Guild Central Committee (CC) minutes, DCW1/12, 'Statement on the outbreak of war', September 1939.

18 Scott, *Feminism*, pp. 5, 222–3; Scott, 'As a war-horse', pp. 212, 215–16.

19 Black 'The Mothers' International', p. 167.

20 J. Elgin, 'Women and peace: from suffragists to Greenham women', in Taylor and Young (eds), *Campaigns for Peace*, pp. 226–32; Liddington, *The Long Road*; S. Grayzel, *Women's Identities at War: Gender, Motherhood and Politics in Britain and France during the First World War* (London: University of North Carolina Press, 1999).

21 Gaffin and Thomas, *Caring and Sharing*, p. 109; Scott, *Feminism*, pp. 222–3; Liddington, *The Long Road*, pp. 159–61; International Co-operative Women's Guild circular letter, 'Women and peace', 1936 DCX/8/1; Davies, *Life as We Have Known It*, p. 65.

22 Women's Co-operative Guild General Secretaries candidate biographies, DCW/8/3, 1937; Hannan and Hunt, *Socialist Women*, pp. 185, 192. Before becoming General Secretary of the WCG in 1937 at the age of 39, Rose Simpson had only been involved in the Guild for four years, working as a sub-editor and writing articles for *Women's Outlook* and the women's page of *Co-operative News* as well as being active in Manchester peace groups and Co-operative Education classes. As General Secretary in the last years before the war she was one of the most public and uncompromising advocates of pacifism within the Guild, joining the executive of the short-lived No Conscription League in 1939. Her time as General Secretary was short-lived and ended in controversy when she was forced to resign at the end of 1939 after criticisms of her management style and allegations of financial irregularities emerged.

23 *Women's Outlook* (7 July 1934, 30 March 1935 and 16 July 1938).

24 Black, 'The Mothers' International', pp. 468, 472; Liddington, *The Long Road*, p. 148; *Co-operative News* (9 June 1934 and 21 November 1936); *Women's Outlook* (28 April 1934 and 22 February 1936); Bishopsgate Institute, High Wycombe WCG minutes, 3 April 1933, WCG/8/47/5.

25 Morrison, 'The Women's Co-operative Guild: Campaigns for Peace 1918–1939' pp. 92–3; *Co-operative News* (24 November 1934, 23 March 1935, 4 June and 20 November 1937); WCG CC minutes 13 March and 3 October 1933, 7 May and 22 November 1934; *Women's Outlook* (8 December 1934, 18 December and 25 December 1937); WCG *Annual Report* 1935 and 1939.

26 J. Birchall, *The International Co-operative Movement* (Manchester: Manchester University Press 1997), pp. 46–7; P. Gurney, *Co-operative Culture and the Politics of Consumption in England, 1870–1930* (Manchester: Manchester University

Press, 1996), pp. 107, 110; *Towards Tomorrow: Pageant of Co-operation*, film of Wembley pageant on International Co-operation Day, London Co-operative Society, 1938, available at the British Film Institute.

27 Black, 'The Mothers' International', p. 471; ICWG Resolution on Peace November 1935, DCX/8/1; file on arrest of ICWG president Emmy Freundlich, DCX/7/1; ICWG 'Basis for an international peace programme', *c*.1935, LSE Woodcraft Folk Archives, YMA/WF/129; *WCG Annual Report* 1936; *Co-operative News* (20 June and 18 July 1936).

28 *Co-operative News* (3 April and 4 June 1937); *Women's Outlook* (15 May and 7 August 1937); *Co-operative Party Conference Report* 1937; *Co-operative Congress Annual Report* 1937.

29 *Co-operative News* (20 November 1937).

30 *Co-operative News* (18 and 25 December 1937); *Women's Outlook* (25 December 1937).

31 Liddington, *The Long Road*, pp. 163–6, WCG 56 *Annual Report* 1938–1939; *Women's Outlook* (16 July 1938).

32 M. Davis, *Fashioning a New World: A History of the Woodcraft Folk* (Loughborough: Holyoake Books, 2000) pp. 45, 68–72 and 78–81; Co-operative Congress, *Annual Report* 1938; WCG 56 *Annual Report* 1938–1939.

33 Flinn and Cohen, 'The Abyssinia crisis'.

34 WCG *53 Annual Report* 1935–1936; WCG CC minutes 7 October 1935.

35 Scott, 'As a war-horse', pp. 215–16; WCG CC minutes 25 September 1939; WCG Congress resolutions and amendments, 1940; *Women's Outlook* (30 September 1939).

36 Scott, *Feminism*, pp. 5 and 222–3; Rowbotham, *Century of Women*, pp. 178–9; Graves, *Labour Women*, p. 210; WCG 56 *Annual Report* 1938–1939 and *58 Annual Report* 1940–1941.

37 Gurney, *Co-operative Culture*, pp. 233–7.

38 *Co-operative News* (5 March 1938); *Women's Outlook* (7 January 1939).

39 *Women's Outlook* (20 March 1937 and 16 July 1938).

40 Scott, *Feminism*, pp 203–13; *Co-operative News* (17 June 1939).

Part III

Consumerism and material culture

10

The commemorative urge: the co-operative movement's collective memory

Chris Wrigley

The pioneer co-operators' early endeavours are reverentially recorded in a large body of commemorative literature. Though unsurprisingly on a vastly lower key than books of saints or Foxe's *Book Of Martyrs*, the books often have in places a similar tone. They often celebrate mini-epics of self-help, with earnest working men and women overcoming economic adversity and human adversaries in the form of powerful bodies of shopkeepers.

Often the pioneers' endeavours were perceived as part of a wider working-class struggle to achieve a good standard of life in the face of urban and rural adversities. In the case of the Lincoln society, its historian quoted approvingly from a trade-union journal, 'The tyranny of the village shopkeeper is often as great as that of the farmer'.[1] In the textile urban areas shopkeepers were often also seen as oppressors, while the cotton famine of the early 1860s and the downturns in the trade cycles added to any dissatisfaction with employers. A frequent theme was that the co-operators were public-spirited people who sought 'to extend justice and fair dealing to the worker, and to prevent the exploitation of the consumer by the predatory profiteer'.[2] The Bradford centenary volume expressed their aims in an older, idealistic phraseology, 'These early co-operators . . . were seeking social salvation and meant to secure it by their own means'.[3]

Much has been written in recent years on commemoration of the First World War or of other wars, and also on radical and other political memorials. There is also much enthusiasm for collecting china and glass commemorating royalty, politicians or major events. Lincoln Hallinan, in his book *British Commemoratives: Royalty, Politics, War and Sport* (1995), observed that '[the] purpose of a commemorative is to record, in permanent form, events and individuals who played an important part in the life of the nation'.[4] Co-operative commemoratives fell beyond the parameters of his book, yet commemorative china, glass and decorated tins as well as books are readily to be found in antique shops and second-hand bookstores. Although important in the history of the co-operative movement, including its business history, such items have been largely neglected, with Peter Gurney's excellent

Co-operative Culture and the Politics of Consumption in England being the exception.[5]

Gurney has observed that 'the jubilee histories constitute an important and largely forgotten genre of "people's history" . . . Between 1897 and the end of the First World War at least seventy-five were produced in England'.[6] There were a lot of commemoratives for fiftieth or sixtieth anniversaries for societies founded in 1859–62. Plates also marked this era. For example, a large commemorative plate which depicted all the Society's presidents was issued by the Manchester and Salford Co-op to mark 1859–1909. Other societies marked their celebrations in the inter-war period. These included the London Co-operative Society, 1828–1928, and Liverpool, where various societies had existed, 1829–1929. For an example in the area of other memorabilia, the Heckmondwyke Co-operative Society issued a large bowl to mark 1860–1930. In very broad terms the commemorative books and memorabilia were intended as propaganda. They existed to give one or more messages about the co-operative movement, and some of these changed over time.

The books and memorabilia linked directly to one of the central business issues facing co-operative societies from their beginnings: confidence. In the societies rested many hopes and aspirations of their members, but high among these was a safe means of financial betterment. Quite apart from the divi (dividend), for many people a sound co-op society represented a safe location for savings. This was well illustrated during the 1883 Weavers' strike in West Yorkshire. The Huddersfield Industrial Society permitted members to withdraw their capital without the usual notice, thereby enabling many families to survive. The official history noted that '[p]robably, had it not been for the existence of the Society, this capital would not have been available to fall back upon'. It added that instead of the Society's capital increasing by about £7,000, in this period it decreased by £3,000.[7]

Notwithstanding the problem of facing the calumnies of shopkeepers and others hostile to co-operation, the leaders of the co-operative movement believed that one of the biggest threats to confidence in the viability of co-op societies was the giving of credit to members. This was the ruin among others of some Edinburgh societies and the Liverpool Equitable Society, as well as various other Victorian savings institutions. While it is well known that the Rochdale Pioneers' Society arose during a textile strike, it is less well known that the Pioneers' early success was aided by the failure of the Rochdale Savings Bank in 1849 and, in contrast, by the Rochdale co-operative's pledge not to give credit.[8] Many co-operative societies before the First World War made their refusal to give credit a major feature of their claims to members' confidence in the soundness of their business. This was emphasised in the jubilee and centenary histories where the policy had been operated from the early days. For instance, in the case of the Derby Society in 1861, George Jacob Holyoake wrote that

> two members of the committee were requested to resign for allowing, or offering to allow, credit. This was an act of principle to forbid credit in a co-operative society, which has honour because it inculcates thrift, teaches thrift and seeks to deliver its members from the degradation and slavery of debt.

Similarly, some forty years later George Harwood, the Liberal MP for Bolton, observed that co-operation 'had taught the working classes of England one invaluable lesson, namely the lesson to pay ready money'. As a result, 'They were ceasing to be one week behind and so escaped the pawnbrokers.'[9] So, the policy of no credit had two sides: security for thrifty members and the enforcement of moral improvement on those who desired to live on 'tick' yet avail themselves of the co-operative stores.

Yet it seems that the majority of co-operative societies did give credit and did not go bankrupt. However, here the official historians of the Edwardian era presented such practices as aberrations of the early days, with credit often continued by members' meeting votes in spite of the elected officers' urging otherwise. In the case of the Ripley Society, the giving of credit as early as 1863 was ascribed to the widespread practice of the area:

> 'shop books' and 'tallymen's cards' were only too often in evidence in the workers' homes, shopkeepers offering every inducement to enable their customers to obtain goods on easy terms, so that it must have been the desire of the Society to conform to the custom of the locality and offer equal, or perhaps better, facilities to the members to enable them to get 'just a week behind'.

It was also believed that Ripley members needed credit 'with members living so far away from the Stores and requiring their goods in large quantities'.[10] Nevertheless, the authors of the jubilee history were explicit as to their views on credit, describing it as 'this evil' and noting that the level of credit, which had been the equivalent of seventeen shillings (85p) per member in 1870, had risen to one pound three shillings (£1.15) by 1876, but thereafter dwindled and was being eliminated in stages from 1902.[11] In the case of St Cuthbert's Co-operative Association, Edinburgh, the committee succeeded in capping the amount of credit at fifteen shillings (75p) per pound of share capital. The author of that society's jubilee history praised the society's leaders for being advocates of ready cash, and was blunt that the giving of credit was ruinous.[12]

The York Society also struggled to eliminate credit. In spite of the Society's resolving in 1890 to end giving credit that December, the practice took years to eliminate. In 1890 the amount owed equalled 'about one-seventh' of the capital. George Briggs, the Secretary of the York Society in 1909, wrote vehemently of the old bad ways:

It will be evident from this (a) that the Society was losing the use of 14 per cent of its capital; (b) that the cost of keeping accounts was increased, owing to the extra labour involved; (c) that 5 per cent interest was actually being paid on share capital to members who were owing money to the Society, which was manifestly unfair to the other members; (d) that restrictions had to be placed on withdrawals of share capital to meet probable chances of loss; (e) that losses were imminent, hence the County Court proceedings, also loss of trade often occurs through the displeasure incurred in enforcing payment; (f) that the Committee were involved in needless care and anxiety, and could better employ their time and energies in developing the Society; (g) that it was a departure from the lofty ideals of its founders and did not really benefit those who obtained credit, also it was contrary to rule; (h) that losses incurred had to be borne by those who paid ready money and were loyal to the Society and its rules.[13]

Readers of the jubilee history were intended to be under no doubt that the society was then (1908) under a more rigorous and prudent regime. Similarly, as reported in the Bolton history, James Barlow JP, chairing an 1879 meeting, declared that 'it was an utter impossibility, so long as the Society was well looked after, that a Society like this could come to a crash'.[14]

Yet, as Paul Johnson has emphasised, the pressures of life on working-class families made many ordinary co-operators insist on credit. In 1886, 54 per cent of the 946 industrial and provident societies gave credit, by 1911 this had risen to 82 per cent. Thus there was a mismatch between the ideals expressed and promoted by the movement's leaders and what was happening under consumer pressure. This became even more marked with the spread of attractive hire-purchase and other credit arrangements after the First and Second World Wars.[15] In terms of this chapter, it is very notable that the histories expressed the dominant view of the co-operative leadership. Where the practices of the societies were at variance, then credit was noted but deplored.

Nevertheless, the issue of credit highlights the propaganda nature of the jubilee histories. They were there not just to celebrate but to propagate ideals, and, as argued here, the propaganda on this theme was in essence to give the all-important message of confidence in the financial stability of the societies.

Confidence in the viability of the co-operative societies depended for many years on their not only avoiding the risks of giving credit but also being long-established, solid and reliable businesses which had a track record of steady growth. The publication of the histories celebrated the heroic triumphs over adversity of the pioneers and the wise and prudent management of the societies, providing overall an 'Upward and Onward' (as one jubilee history entitled a chapter) sense of destiny.[16] Many of the jubilee history books of the late nineteenth and early twentieth centuries were published by the CWS's printing works in two standard formats. These books contributed to the co-operative movement's brand name and to the suggestion of the strength of a large and growing organisation. The books helped promote the movement's ethical consumer aspirations, expressed by Holyoake in his history of the Derby Society, as the stores 'are pledged not only to honesty in measure, but to purity in all commodities'.[17]

The strength derived from being parts of a bigger movement was clearly indicated in many societies' histories. Part of this strength came from clusters of societies, with the later ones benefiting from drawing on the experience of societies established earlier. Hence, the co-operative societies often provide an example of a recent major interest of business historians: the benefits to businesses in being parts of clusters. In such studies, careful consideration is given to such matters as whether there is synergy stemming from clusters of firms and whether such clusters support growth and boost others in the same lines of business.[18]

The value of the experience of earlier co-operative societies to new ones was a feature of many society histories. One important area for new societies was the diffusion of business information on finance, management skills and products. In the case of the Long Eaton Working Men's Co-operative Society, it benefited from its proximity to the Derby Society and at the outset adopted the Derby Society's rules.[19] In Bradford, the man designated to be first manager of the co-operative society began his training as follows:

> Mr Howarth's first grocery lesson was derived from the manager of the Leeds Society, with whom he spent four days, getting to know things and being introduced to various tradesmen: also how and what to buy. In this connection he went with the Leeds manager to the Otley market to study the manner of buying the best butter, a very important duty in that day...[20]

As well as recording the diffusion of business knowledge, the histories often showed how clusters helped to deepen the market. A repeated feature of the early days of co-operative societies before the CWS was the considerable benefit of neighbouring co-operatives taking, for example, part of a mill's capacity on a regular basis or, alternatively, providing orders for co-operative mills, factories or workshops. The Long Eaton history made it clear that the society's early success was assisted by a cluster of supportive villages and small towns with co-operative branches.[21]

Related to the potential benefits of clusters was a more general source of strength in the widespread nature of the co-operative movement. The jubilee histories underlined the ways that societies benefited from one another, disseminating ideas and best practice. The Gloucester history, for instance, highlighted how the co-operative message had arrived from northern England. It noted that after the Rochdale Pioneers:

The idea had spread to other towns in Yorkshire and Lancashire, the newspapers and periodicals of that day were beginning to record its progress, railwaymen then as now, were removed from town to town in the course of their occupation, and they naturally took with them the knowledge they had been gaining of this new society . . .

Benjamin Brook, at that time a fitter on the Great Western Railway, came from Halifax . . . William Priestley from Huddersfield, William Pollard from Burnley, and many others whose names could be mentioned came from the 'North Country', and either by living together or living near, or both, were able to form a community of ideas or rather, perhaps a reciprocity of thought.[22]

The Gloucester Society sent to Rochdale for a copy of its rules in 1863 when revising their own. They sought further informed advice directly:

Mr Brook took his annual leave and went to Queensborough [Queensbury], near his home, where there was a flourishing society. He returned full of practical information both of what to do and what not to do. Mr Priestley himself wrote to Halifax, numbering among his friends Mr Horsefall who was the architect of a large store built for the Halifax Society.[23]

The Queensbury Society also provided a source of informed inspiration for the Bradford Society. Its jubilee history colourfully observed that '[d]ocumentary and other evidence can be produced to show that co-operation in that district took its rise high up on the hills at Queensbury, then like a stream trickled down to Great Horton. Some time afterwards it sprang up in two distinct places in Bradford.' Two of the key figures in the Bradford Society came from Harden, just south-west of Bingley, where another co-operative society was established. One of the two men 'got a situation at Queensbury, where he came in direct contact with the active workers of the successful society which had been established there'.[24] Readers of the jubilee histories – mostly members of those societies – could not but realise their society was part of a much greater movement and that their society had benefited from the co-operative network which transmitted the wisdom of experience.

As well as contributing to confidence in the business stability of the co-operative movement, the jubilee histories and memorabilia were very much part of the societies' propaganda and advertising. In the late nineteenth and early twentieth centuries the co-operative societies were on the offensive, not defensive as a century later. The societies were often fired up with a missionary zeal to spread the good news of co-operation. They also looked back to the great fervour of the pioneering days. The Gloucester jubilee history included the comment that its authors 'would have liked to have made more than a passing allusion to the great work done by the society and its leading members in propaganda work in all parts of the country, and especially in Wales, but the death of most of the older members who took part in this has removed the chief source of information and made it difficult to know for certain what particular societies were started and assisted'.[25]

Yet a solid, urban-based society such as Lincoln could look back on its less hard-headed predecessors in its rural hinterland. In recording the changes in the nature of the rural Lincolnshire co-operatives, it was very clear that the jubilee volume heralded the economic solidity provided by the later city body. Duncan McInnes, author of the jubilee volume, noted that in the mid-1860s the Labourers' League movement

> became for a few years very powerful in the county among cottagers and agricultural day-wage workers. It was a curious compound of trade unionism and Co-operation, distributive and productive. The labourers were led by the promoters to believe that the establishment of a Co-operative store must follow the opening of a branch of the League, and that from subscriptions and from profits of trading the outgrowth would speedily be farms worked Co-operatively all over the agricultural counties.

For good measure, McInnes also gave as an explanation for the problems of such rural-initiated co-operation as stemming from the alleged slower-working minds, secretive natures and greater individualism of the agricultural workers.[26] His stereotyping was picked up and approvingly reprinted fifty years later in the centenary volume. However, in contrast to the oddities of the early rural movement, the authors of the centenary volume could point to the Lincoln society's successful 'invasion' of the countryside, noting that

> [it] was in 1877 that the society adopted a definite plan of propaganda and development for village co-operation, and that plan was pursued without interruption for many years until a trading area of scores of square miles – today it is 2,000 square miles – was added to the society's territory.[27]

The co-operative societies also staked out territory, as much as markets, with their careful choices of location of shops. In setting up a shop in some working-class areas the motivation often included aspirations of elevating the moral character of the inhabitants of the neighbourhood with self-help and even self-respect, moving people away from living in near penury and frequent dependency on pawnbrokers. The society histories recorded several such claims to altruism in the making of commercial decisions. The York Society's history, for instance, recorded that

> [f]or some time past the Directors had been on the lookout for property in the Walmgate district, with a view to seeing what could be done to bring Co-operation to the doors of the people who needed it most, that is, those who had little money and who had to make it go as far as possible.
>
> A public house, called the Albert Inn, at the corner of Albert Street and George Street, having lost its licence was for sale, and, as it was in the midst of

a network of streets of small houses it presented the desired opportunity and was bought for £470.[28]

The societies' histories also recorded how, like Anglican churches, the co-operatives were eager to set up in new centres of population. For example, the Bristol Society's history recorded that 'with the rapid growth of population on the newly-developed Coldharbour Estate it soon became evident that the Society must have its own stock of goods on the spot'.[29]

In this way co-operation spread through working-class areas, a presence which reached more women and a broader spectrum of men than trade unionism. In reaching so many, its success rivalled that of the Friendly Societies. While the co-operatives were rarely involved in politics before the First World War, they nevertheless represented an alternative ethos to the private enterprise of the small shopkeepers.

The hostility of the local shopkeepers was a frequent and major theme of the societies' histories. They were presented as a major obstacle for the co-operative pilgrims' progress. They were the evil hobgoblins in the near morality tales that were part of the genre. William Maxwell JP, in the preface to his account of St Cuthbert's history, expressed the hope that in its account of 'the many difficulties . . . surmounted', 'the reminiscences may encourage working-men to hold fast to the principles of Co-operation, and face with confidence any difficulties that may confront them'.[30]

Yet the jubilee histories do remind the reader that the co-operative societies were a challenge to a substantial vested interest. As Peter Gurney has commented, the intermittent challenges of shopkeepers to the co-operative stores has not received much attention from historians, with Geoffrey Crossick's and Michael Winstanley's work remaining early major exceptions.[31]

The co-operators' provision of goods challenged social relationships in town and country. The Bradford Society history commented, 'Working men were mentally realising the possibility of becoming the masters instead of the slaves of capital'.[32] In the early days the co-operators and their shops were smeared as unrespectable subversives. F.W. Peaples wrote of the Bolton Society:

Opposition was rife on every hand, more particularly among the local shop-keepers, who did all they could to foster this spirit, and used every means (as is the case now) to bring discredit on the movement. They did succeed in arous-ing a spirit of suspicion in the minds of many – a thing easily done then – so much so that the parents of James Yates, who was the first shop boy employed by the Society, considered it was hardly respectable enough for him, so he was taken away and obtained a situation in the Bolton Public Library, from which, after thirteen years' service, he got appointed to the Public Library at Leeds as Chief Librarian.

After twenty-five years, the Secretary of the Bolton Society could conclude
that

> [at] one time members of the Society incurred thereby a certain amount of
> reproach and odium. Now to be a member of the Bolton Co-operative society
> is looked upon as a sign of respectability, and I always think a Co-operative
> almanac hung up in a house is a sign that the tenant of that house is a thrifty,
> ready-money person.[33]

Bolton was one of the areas where the private shopkeepers were most out-
raged at the challenge to their 'birthright'. In 1894 when a Bolton and District
Grocers and Provision Dealers' Association was set up, John F. Steele, its
prime promoter, complained that 'the old respectable tradesman of fifty years
ago, who was looked up to as an authority on all things, and held one of the
most respectable positions in the community, was rapidly becoming extinct
and his place was being taken by the large capitalist with his numerous branch
shops trading on cash lines, or the Co-operative Society, which had got such
a hold among English operatives'. Steele went on to claim that the co-op did
three quarters of Bolton's trade and evaded much taxation, so 'the Society
which robbed him of his birthright was wallowing in more money than
they knew what to do with'. There were also determined campaigns against
co-operators in Glasgow, Barrhead and other parts of Scotland, with a few
employers dismissing workers for being co-operators.[34]

There were later assaults on co-operation in other parts of the country. In
York, Plymouth and elsewhere there was a co-ordinated campaign in 1905–6,
with *The Tradesman and Shopkeeper* at its core. It lessened after the Plymouth
Society was awarded £5,000 damages when it took the paper to court. George
Briggs wrote of the 1905–6 anti-co-operative campaign in York:

> Sandwich men were sent round with samples and prices of goods alleged to be
> sold at the Stores. The Traders' Defence Association, which in itself was a form
> of Co-operation, but with the essential difference, that it was Co-operation
> for private gain, was formed. Pressure was brought to bear upon employers to
> inquire where their employees spent their money. Threats of discharge, and
> even notice to terminate their employment, were resorted to, with the result in
> one case . . . of the person under notice finding a better and more remunerative
> situation within the Society. Lodgers were even asked to find out whether their
> landladies traded at the Stores. Professional and business men were circular-
> ised, pointed out the error of their ways and the consequences which would
> follow.

However, he concluded, 'Reviewing the attack as a whole, there is very little
doubt that ultimately it proved a good and cheap advertisement for the
society.'[35]

Big industrial disputes also featured in the histories as adversities in which the co-operatives assisted their members or other working people. The great mining lock-out of 1893 was a major example. At Ripley the co-operative members voted £150 a week for six weeks for soup, as well as giving the miners free use of the co-operative hall. The co-operative activists formed relief committees and during the dispute collected and distributed £1,170 9*s*. 4*d*., with more than 20,000 relief tickets given out. At Barnsley the co-operative society paid out over £4,000 in relief grants, while members withdrew £67,000.[36]

Other co-operative societies also recorded their help in 1893 to the miners. The Bristol history recounted how the Bedminster co-operators 'saw the grim spectre of hunger and cold' among the Somerset miners' families and successfully sought relief from the £5,000 allocated for this purpose by the Co-operative Wholesale Society. The Hyde society gave a hundred 4 lb loaves to the Miners' Relief Soup Kitchen. In the case of the Bolton jubilee history, the generous donations of the public were noted, but the dispute gave an opportunity for lengthy didactic reflections on co-operation. These began:

> Everybody was feeling the pinch of the coal struggle. The poorest, of course, were experiencing its effects most. Millions of money were being lost, homes brought to destitution, women and children were starving, and working people paying famine prices for coal – and all for what? Because people are not yet wise enough to throw over the competitive system for the better plan of Co-operation . . . Combinations among employers and employed are teaching the law of mutual dependence.[37]

While this was notably explicit, it was but one example of the propaganda role served by the jubilee histories.

While the 1893 coal dispute affected a large number of co-operatives, other strikes and lock-outs were more local and received notice in the histories of the areas affected. For instance, during the famous Manningham Mills dispute of 1890–91, the Bradford society set up collecting boxes in its stores after its chairman ruled that a motion passed voting £200 toward the fund for the families of those affected was illegal. Similarly, £20 voted by the Huddersfield Co-operative Society was also ruled illegal, with the Co-operative Union backing an unsuccessful appeal to the High Court of Justice in London. The Bristol Society, however, had no legal difficulties in 1901 when it distributed £5 of goods among the families of locked-out tram workers.[38]

After the First World War the co-operatives continued to play a major part in mining areas in sustaining the families of strikers. This became a concern for Lloyd George's government in 1921, and for several co-operative societies which found it took years to recover credit given to the miners, in some instances up to the next major dispute in 1926. Assistance was also given to other workers in dispute, such as iron moulders by the Ipswich Society in 1919.[39] The recording of such endeavours indicated the co-operative movement's support for working people and reinforced the message of such volumes that the co-operative movement was a major player in society.

The jubilee histories also recalled that co-operative idealism was wider than just national concerns, and, as one successor of early nineteenth-century radicalism, it had international horizons and some international interests. While many of the international connections and interests were fostered by co-operation's national bodies, the various societies were pleased to record their occasional international interests. The Bradford Co-operative Society's history looked back to the late 1850s, observing that

> [w]orking men in Bradford, as elsewhere, were awakening to a clearer sense of their own powers and importance. M. Louis Blanc, the French reformer, had fanned the flame by an eloquent address in the Temperance Hall on 'Co-operation', in which he related to a crowded audience, chiefly composed of the working class, the steps taken by the workers of France to realise among themselves the principles of co-operation which he described as one of the most practical and permanent results of the French Revolution of 1848.

Louis Blanc was also a supporter of the 1869 Co-operative Congress in London.[40] The Cambridge society was associated with the co-operative congresses, with Aneurin Williams helping Eduard Bernstein, the SPD leader, in the translation of speeches given at the International Co-operative Congress at Hamburg in 1910.[41]

The co-operative-society histories also recalled the societies' support for various liberal causes. The Hyde Society's history commented, 'It may be of interest to many to know that a collection was made amongst the society's employees for the Bulgarian Relief Fund in September 1876.' Support for such causes continued, with perhaps the widest support coming in the 1930s with the Spanish Civil War, including raising funds for Spanish refugees.[42]

The commemorative volumes contained much reflection on the aims and ideals of co-operation as well as taking the opportunity 'to rejoice' at past achievements.[43] Indeed, they often contained what one might call harder-line propaganda. Written by long-serving senior elected officials of the societies or by committed writers such as George Jacob Holyoake (see Table 10.1, appended), they often had within them not only a dominant narrative of brave persistence overcoming adversity and a Whig celebration of how the vicissitudes of the past led to the glorious present, but also some strongly made messages about the moral values they believed were embedded in co-operation. The voice (or voices) in such histories were of the activists who insisted on the self-help and community-minded (as opposed to individualistic) values of co-operation. In the case of the moral desirability of ready money, not credit, the membership was at odds with the leaders and, in due course, the spread of hire-purchase and other credit systems resulted in this appearing a Canutestyle struggle. Yet, as argued here, the no-credit policy was also about a central issue for co-operatives: confidence in their viability.

The histories also represented a softer-line propaganda. They advertised the longevity and the strengths of the co-operatives, not least in being parts of a greater whole. They met a commemorative urge: to celebrate and to pay homage to the work and lives of those who had gone before while advertising the collectivist yet self-help values of the co-operatives in providing goods at competitive prices at usually a reliable quality. This unusual combination of collective activity yet self-help was expressed in some of the histories. The point was made that the late nineteenth-century capitalist trusts operated for private gain, whereas the co-ops were a form of trust but operated for a collective good.[44]

The histories and other memorabilia were also propaganda in the form of advertising. They marked and celebrated successful businesses. They also were part of several actions which showed the local co-operative movement was a force in its community. One notable way of achieving both advertising and a sense of solidarity among members was the holding of parades led by bands at notable co-operative occasions, such as the laying of the foundation stone of a new store. For instance in Huddersfield in July 1876, Jackson's band led a procession half a mile from the centre to Marsh to mark the laying of the corner stone for a new store.[45]

In Lancashire where there was much working-class support for the Conservatives in the late nineteenth century, the movement generally took care not to alienate potential supporters by partisan politics. The Bolton jubilee history included the observation that '[c]o-operation was one of those movements that happily needed no party'.[46] Elsewhere the co-operative leaders asserted their role in the community by becoming Justices of the Peace or by standing and being elected as poor-law guardians or as members of school boards. More rarely they stood as co-operators in municipal elections. In York in 1900 W.H. Shaw, a director, was elected with co-op support for Micklegate ward, while T. Anderson, another director, was elected an Independent. However, the York members later declined to fund other candidates and leading co-operators who sought to be councillors had, as in the past, to secure other sponsors.[47]

The histories were written mostly by men, very frequently major players in the co-operative societies celebrated (see Table 10.1). In some histories women were nearly invisible. In the case of the Bolton volume, it is dedicated to Mrs Mary Ann Ashton, a publican, who fostered co-operation and was a key pioneer. In the Ten Acres and Stirchley Society the emergence of women in the society is a clear strand in the celebratory story. Most have sections on the Women's Guild but, by and large, the commemorative urge was by males about male achievements in providing quality goods for 'the woman with the basket'.

Table 10.1 *Some jubilee and centenary authors*

50 years

Derby 1850–1900	George Jacob Holyoake	Major co-operator plus writer of histories
	Amos Scotton	President 1875–77, Secretary editor of *Monthly Record* 1886–92, presided over 1884 national co-op congress (Derby) and C.W.S. director 1891–1904
York 1858–1908	George Briggs, JP	Secretary from 1893 (a public auditor)
Bolton 1859–1909	F.W. Peaples	Assistant Secretary (author of local history, whose bird-egg collection ended up in Bolton museums)
St Cuthbert's, Edinburgh 1859–1909	William Maxwell, JP	Secretary 1878–82
Bradford 1860–1910	Joseph Bennett and John Baldwin	Secretary since 1894 Committee since 1901 (previously on committee of West Bowling Society)
Gloucester 1860–1910	Francis Purnell and Henry W. Williams	Secretary from 1903, employee since 1878 General Committee 1900–4 and 1905–6
Huddersfield 1860–1910	Owen Balmforth	Chairman of Education Committee, 1893–1902
Ripley 1860–1910	William R.A. Pilcher and Harry N. Bridge	Auditor since 1884 Son of the Secretary of 1875 onward
Barrhead, Paisley 1861–1911	Robert Murray, JP	Former member of Board of Management and director of SCWS, 1880
Lincoln 1861–1911	Duncan McInnes, JP	Secretary 1882–1903
Hyde 1862–1912	Thomas Jones and Joseph Rhodes	Committee member since 1901 Employee member of Jubilee Committee
Birmingham 1881–1931	TS [Thomas Stokes]	Ten years on Education Committee

Table 10.1 (continued)

30, 60, 70 and 75 years		
Bristol [1881–1911]	Edward Jackson	Education Committee member
Ipswich 1868–1928	[Thomas Bird]	Committee 1911–23, minute secretary 1914–23, later publicity manager
Long Eaton 1868–1928	Gertrude R. Lane and Robert Rowley	
Cambridge 1868–1938	W. Henry Brown	Author of numerous co-op books
Derby 1850–1925	W. Leslie Unsworth	Journalist, son of a director (elected since 1908)
Ten Acres and Stirchley, Birmingham 1875–1950	Harry M. Vickrage, JP	Secretary of Education Committee since 1946, author of 75th-anniversary history of Birmingham Society and author of a thesis for Co-operative Honours Diploma
100 years		
London [1824–1927]	W. Henry Brown	Author of co-operative histories
Liverpool 1829–1929	W. Henry Brown	Secretary and Chief Executive Officer since 1947
Halstead 1860–1960	A.E. Hodginson, JP	Secretary since 1947
Lincoln 1861–1961	Frank Bruckshaw and Duncan McNab	
Nottingham 1863–1963	Francis W. Leeman	Former director and Vice President
Ipswich 1868–1968	[William Knowles, with others]	Co-operative and Labour Party activist

The various commemoratives were intended both to celebrate the achievements of the past and to nudge the present and the future more toward co-operative ideals and endeavours. Were they effective? This is hard to answer, even impressionistically. The plates and glass (like the earlier almanacs) were on display in many co-operators' houses. Quite probably so were many of the jubilee and other histories, especially the fine products of the late Victorian and Edwardian era. Those that are in circulation appear to have been well read, a contrast to the uncut pages of many books emerging from the break-up of stately and country-house libraries. Perhaps the readers were active members rather than the general membership. Yet, there was much earnest book reading among many skilled and some unskilled workers and for some the free copies may have been appreciated. However, later, in the age of radio, television and many attractive specialist journals, the commemorative format was less popular, while the local history market for attractively presented photographs proved co-op histories in that format could be popular when sold via the co-ops' connections. This is well illustrated by the Ipswich and Norwich millennium commemorative volume, *People and Places: A Pictorial History* (2000), which was 'quite deliberately' prepared for 'the nostalgia market'. It sold well, nearly 10,000 copies quickly, being marketed via milk rounds.[48]

The commemoratives paid homage to the movement's past. They offered its collective memory, but a selective memory. The jubilee histories in particular pressed co-operative ideals, even some which were dated and being rejected by the majority of the members. They were part of the societies' propaganda. The earlier volumes and other memorabilia have a certain brash Whig-style confidence: the future as well as the past belongs to them. Later, the hope expressed in them is more that the future will maintain, or return to, past successes.

Notes

1 Quoting *Labourers' Union Chronicle* (30 June 1877). Frank Bruckshaw and Duncan McNab, *A Century of Achievement: The Story of Lincoln Co-operative Society* (Lincoln, [1961]), p. 76. (The various commemorative histories were published by the societies.)

2 W.H. Adsett, 'Foreward', [T. Bird], *Through Sixty Years: Diamond Jubilee of the Ipswich Industrial Co operative Society Limited, 1868–1928* (Ipswich, 1928), p. 8.

3 Joseph Bennett and John Baldwin, *City of Bradford Co-operative Society Limited: Jubilee History 1860–1910* (Bradford, 1910), p. 58.

4 Lincoln Hallinan, *British Commemoratives: Royalty, Politics, War and Sport* (London: Antique Collectors' Club, 1995).

5 Peter Gurney, *Co-operative Culture and the Politics of Consumption in England, 1870–1930* (Manchester: Manchester University Press, 1996), especially pp. 128–36.

6 Ibid., p. 128.

7 Owen Balmforth, *The Huddersfield Industrial Society Ltd: History of Fifty Years' Progress, 1860–1910* (Manchester, 1910), p. 111.

8 Lee E. Grugel, *George Jacob Holyoake* (Philadelphia: Porcupine Press, 1976), p. 130.

9 George Jacob Holyoake, *Jubilee History Of The Derby Co-operative Provident Society Ltd, 1850–1908* (Manchester, 1900), p. 62; F.W. Peaples, *History of the Great and Little Bolton Co-operative Society Ltd Showing Fifty Years' Progress, 1859–1909* (Bolton, 1909), p. 264.

10 William R.A. Pilcher and Harry N. Bridge, *The Jubilee History of the Ripley Provident Industrial and Co-operative Society Ltd* (Manchester, 1910), pp. 25, 51.
11 Ibid., pp. 25, 44, 52, 100, 109, 118.
12 William Maxwell JP (ed.), *First Fifty Years of St Cuthbert's Co-operative Association Limited 1859–1909* (Edinburgh, 1909), pp. 88–90, 53.
13 George Briggs, JP, *Jubilee History of the York Equitable Industrial Society Limited* (Manchester, 1909), pp. 77–8.
14 Peaples, *Bolton*, pp. 114–15.
15 Paul Johnson, *Saving and Spending: The Working Class Economy in Britain 1870–1939* (Oxford: Clarendon, 1985), pp. 131–42. For an overview of the changes in US shopping (which spread to the UK) see Margaret Walsh, 'The Organization of American Consumption', in G. Thompson (ed.), *The United States in the Twentieth Century*, Vol. 2 (London: Hodder and Stoughton, 2000), pp. 7–34.
16 Maxwell, *St Cuthbert's*, pp. 218–36. In similar vein a history of the Cambridge Society reported that it had 'strode forward steadily, and surely'. W. Henry Brown, *Co-operation in a University Town* (Cambridge, 1938), p. 25.
17 Holyoake, *Derby*, p. 19.
18 A. Popp and J. Wilson (eds), 'Introduction', *Industrial Clusters and Regional Business Networks in England 1750–1970* (Aldershot: Ashgate, 2003).
19 Gertrude R. Lane and Robert Bowley, *Through Six Decades: The Story of Co-operation in Long Eaton and District, 1868–1928* (Manchester, 1929), p. 22.
20 Bennett and Baldwin, *Bradford*, p. 19. Howarth then worked for eight days in the business of a friend in Keighley.
21 Lane and Bowley, *Through Six Decades*.
22 Francis Purnell and Henry W. Williams, *Jubilee History of the Gloucester Co-operative and Industrial Society Limited* (Gloucester, 1910), p. 2. Five of the local pioneers all lived in Ryecroft Street.
23 Ibid., pp. 27 and 18. The Barrhead, Halstead and Lincoln societies also sent for the Rochdale rules (and for others). Robert Murphy, *History of Barrhead Co-operative Society Limited* (Barrhead, 1911), p. 5; A.E. Hodgkinson, JP, *The Great Adventure: Halstead Co-operative Society Limited* (Halstead, 1960), p. 6. Frank Bruckshaw and Duncan McNab, *A Century of Achievement: The Story of Lincoln Co-operative Society* (Lincoln, n.d. [1961]), p. 19.
24 Bennett and Baldwin, *Bradford*, pp. 4–5.
25 Purnell and Williams, 'Preface', *Gloucester*, p. v.
26 Duncan McInnes, JP, *History of Co-operation in Lincoln, 1861–1911* (Manchester, 1911), pp. 41–5.
27 Bruckshaw and McNab, *A Century of Achievement*, p. 75.
28 Briggs, *York*, p. 178.
29 Edward Jackson, *A Study in Democracy, being An Account of The Rise and Progress of Industrial Co-operation in Bristol* (Manchester, 1911), p. 391.
30 Maxwell, *St Cuthbert's*, p. v.
31 Burney, *Co-operative Culture*, pp. 199–202; G. Crossick, 'Shopkeepers and the State in Britain 1870–1914', in G. Crossick and G. Haupt (eds), *Shopkeepers and Master Artisans in Nineteenth Century Europe* (London: Methuen, 1984); Michael

Winstanley, *The Shopkeeper's World, 1830–1914* (Manchester: Manchester University Press, 1983).

32 Bennett and Baldwin, *Bradford*, p. 14.

33 Peaples, *Bolton*, pp. 33 and 142.

34 *The Grocer*, quoted in Peaples, *Bolton*, pp. 183–4, reporting a meeting of grocers in Bolton, 10 January 1894. In 1897 the Bolton Grocers' Association had 56 members and subscription income of £14 per annum. Ibid., p. 207. Murray, *Barrhead*, pp. 84–5.

35 Briggs, *York*, pp. 187–94. See also, for example, attacks on co-operation in Bristol in 1896–7; Jackson, *Bristol*, pp. 113–14. The CWS launched a £50,000 boycott (of co-ops) defence fund in 1902. The Ripley Society, for instance, donated £200; Pilcher and Bridge, *Ripley*, p. 120.

36 Pilcher and Bridge, *Ripley*, pp. 90–1. On Barnsley, see Gurney, *Co-operative Culture*, p. 137.

37 Peaples, *Bolton*, p. 173.

38 Bennett and Baldwin, *Bradford*, pp. 177–9. Balmforth, *Huddersfield*, pp. 137–8. A rule change did enable the Huddersfield Society to vote £100 to the families of miners killed in the Thornhill Colliery explosion in 1893. Ibid., p. 142. Jackson, *Bristol*, p. 148.

39 C. Wrigley, *Lloyd George and the Challenge of Labour* (Hemel Hempstead: Harvester Wheatsheaf, 1990), pp. 160, 164, 198. For one example on 1926 see T. Stokes, *History of the Birmingham Co-operative Society Limited, 1881–1931* (Birmingham, 1931), pp. 145–9, 153.

40 Bennett and Baldwin, *Bradford*, p. 2; Brown, *London*, pp. 50–1. Louis Blanc (1811–82) had served in the 1848 Provisional Government in France before going into exile in London until 1870.

41 Brown, *Cambridge*, pp. 104–8.

42 Thomas Jones and Joseph Rhodes, *Jubilee History of the Hyde Equitable Co-operative Society Limited, 1862–1912* (Manchester, 1912), p. 51; Brown, *Cambridge*, p. 74; Tom Buchanan, *The Spanish Civil War and the British Labour Movement* (Cambridge: Cambridge University Press, 1991), pp. 118–20, 155–6.

43 Hodgkinson, *Halstead*, p. 5.

44 For example, in the Barnsley history; quoted in Gurney, *Co-operative Culture*, pp. 137–8.

45 Balmforth, *Huddersfield*, pp. 81–2.

46 Peaples, *Bolton*, p. 262.

47 Briggs, *York*, pp. 131, 139, 151.

48 Its title and cover are not obviously those of a co-op history. An attractive photographic volume, its contents are of wider cultural and political interest than the traditional co-op history, with the entertainers Jimmy Edwards and Dick Emery opening stores and the politicians Aneurin Bevan and Hugh Gaitskell speaking. Mrs Beryl Fulcher, the President, in her foreword enquired if the reader has a family photograph album and then observed, 'Well, this is our album . . . In some ways our co-op is like a family.' On its print run of 5,000, plus a further 5,000, and sales, W. Knowles to author, 29 May 2005.

11

Promoting product quality: the Co-op and the Council of Industrial Design

Lesley Whitworth

It is clear from the substantial writings of recent and earlier commentators that the co-operative movement faced a multiplicity of challenges over the course of the twentieth century.[1] At times severe, these challenges ranged from its own internal structural difficulties to the impacts of demographic change, affluence, urban redevelopment, commercial obstruction, political intransigence, and growing community disengagement with its wider aims. Alongside these, and notwithstanding the profound nature of the difficulties they represented, the observation that the Co-op was failing to adapt to the needs of a more fashion-conscious shopper has been a frequent one. Indeed it has become a commonplace of much commentary on the post-war decline of the co-operative movement. Yet in contrast to the effort expended on analysing the former of these issues, the aspect of consumer engagement has been treated relatively slightly. Even writers who have striven to overcome the acknowledged difficulty of locating sources suitable for the study of shopping experience have drawn a line at Co-op shoppers. Andrew Alexander writes that the 'potentially unique relationship between the Movement and some of its members . . . requires separate study'.[2]

Fashion itself is too readily asserted as an uncomplicated phenomenon, when its myriad forms and complex influences require thorough and sustained interrogation. In relation to the Co-op, 'fashion' is posited as antithetical to homespun co-operative values, but this is a false dichotomy. Clearly there was some engagement between the two, for it is the assertion of the Co-op doing fashion badly that recurs in the literature. In reality, fashion is referenced in these accounts as crude shorthand for the absence of a progressive, modernising relationship between the movement and its followers, and other customers beside. The responsiveness to changing consumer needs, and the freedom to develop 'new products and new services in every field' trumpeted in co-operative literature, bore slight resemblance to the stagnating product ranges, store layouts and sales techniques observable in its shops.[3]

The material environment of Co-op retail and other spaces has seldom been the focus of sustained attention.[4] There are exceptions. Eileen Yeo's sensitive work on co-operative tea-rooms, and on the absorption of the streets into the Co-op infrastructure through the prominence of its administrative and warehouse buildings, and the performative aspects of processions and festivals, is one such.[5] Another is Martin Purvis's careful analysis of the impact of modernist architectural thinking on the design of a significant number of inter-war co-operative department stores.[6] In her work on the Manchester and Salford Equitable Co-operative Society, Victoria Kelley draws attention to its attempts to generate advertising banners and placards that would compete with those of its commercial competitors, and enliven the interiors of its shops.[7]

It is equally true that we know perilously little about what it was like to work in many capacities for the Co-op, and how that might have impacted directly or indirectly on the customer's shopping experience. As Peter Gurney writes: 'we need to know far more about the movement's internal difficulties, which undoubtedly contributed to its eventual decline', citing in particular difficult labour relations within co-operative enterprises, and 'the inability to confront properly an often rather ascetic approach to the world of goods'.[8] Examining an episode of shared campaigning for improved product standards in co-operative (and other) goods provides a means of recovering one aspect of the Movement's faltering attempt to improve its engagement with its customer base. Using records generated through a period of engagement between the Co-op and the Council of Industrial Design, a body founded a century almost to the day after the Rochdale Pioneers opened their doors, this chapter will contribute to a better understanding of some of the internal difficulties Gurney identifies. By drawing attention to the importance of first co-operation and then Co-operation to the newborn CoID, it is the intention of this contribution to reveal a possibly unanticipated pattern of co-operative activity.

Co-operation and co-operation

The announcement of the formation of the Council of Industrial Design (CoID) was made to the House of Commons on 19 December 1944 by Hugh Dalton, President of its sponsoring ministry, the Board of Trade. This development followed on more than a century of official concern about the quality of design evident in British manufactured goods, and the form that it finally took owed a great deal to a succession of determined individuals whose vision was given significance by the looming economic crisis faced by Britain at war's end.[9]

Intended to 'promote by all practicable means the improvement of design in the products of British industry', the Council was conceptualised from the outset as a body that needed to embrace the broadest possible constituencies of interest in order to bring about the deep-seated shift necessary in commercial, industrial and popular attitudes to design standards.[10] 'Co-operation' was the means by which the shift was to be effected. Endowed with no power other than the force of its persuasion, the Council was heavily reliant on forming strong associative bonds, and winning over hearts and minds. The proposition of widespread co-operation was a key precept in the delivery of the Council's aims.

It would be necessary for the Council to 'co-operate with the Education Authorities' in order to stimulate changes in the training of industrial designers and to orchestrate its work 'in co-operation with industry' in order to encourage the adoption of design strategies (see Figure 11.1).[11] Within firms, 'co-operation between the designer, the production engineer and the salesman' would be essential to the delivery of design policy outcomes, and in the wider world 'co-operation with local Chambers of Commerce and Trade, FBI branches, Municipal Councils, and press' would be vital to the dissemination of information about Council initiatives.[12] The 'cordial co-operation' of all government departments was to be 'taken for granted' and the sympathetic engagement of 'influential interests, such as . . . the Royal Institute of British Architects, with whom the Council will have to co-operate' was to be assiduously cultivated.[13] Council objectives were to be achieved through 'consumer co-operation' and with 'the co-operation of retailers' Council displays could be sited on the high street.[14] 'A co-operative personality' was said to be 'one of the greatest assets to a successful designer'.[15]

Deliberations concerning occupancy of the modest number of places available at the Council's 'high table' were complex and protracted, but there seems from the outset to have been a measure of agreement that the co-operative movement should have a seat. In this it was consistent with the pattern established by a pre-war counterpart of the Council's, the Council for Art and Industry, which had included J.T. Davis, a CWS Director.[16] On this occasion, however, following a glancing reference to Leslie Wainwright as a possible representative of the Co-operative's retailing side, R.S. Edwards of the CWS quickly emerged as 'the likeliest of the men in the Co-operative Movement'.[17] Meanwhile Co-operator Mrs Margaret Allen found a place ostensibly representing women's interests.[18]

Two out of 19 members of the very first Council of Industrial Design therefore shared a co-operative background. Margaret Allen was a member of the management committee of the Watford Co-operative Society Ltd, of the Central Board of the Co-operative Union, and of the Women's Co-operative Guild. Dr Edwards, a physicist, was a Director of the Co-operative Wholesale Society, and had experience as a temporary wartime civil servant in the Board of Trade. Mrs Allen was put in charge of one of the Council's most important early initiatives, its far-sighted but short-lived consumer-focused Housewives'

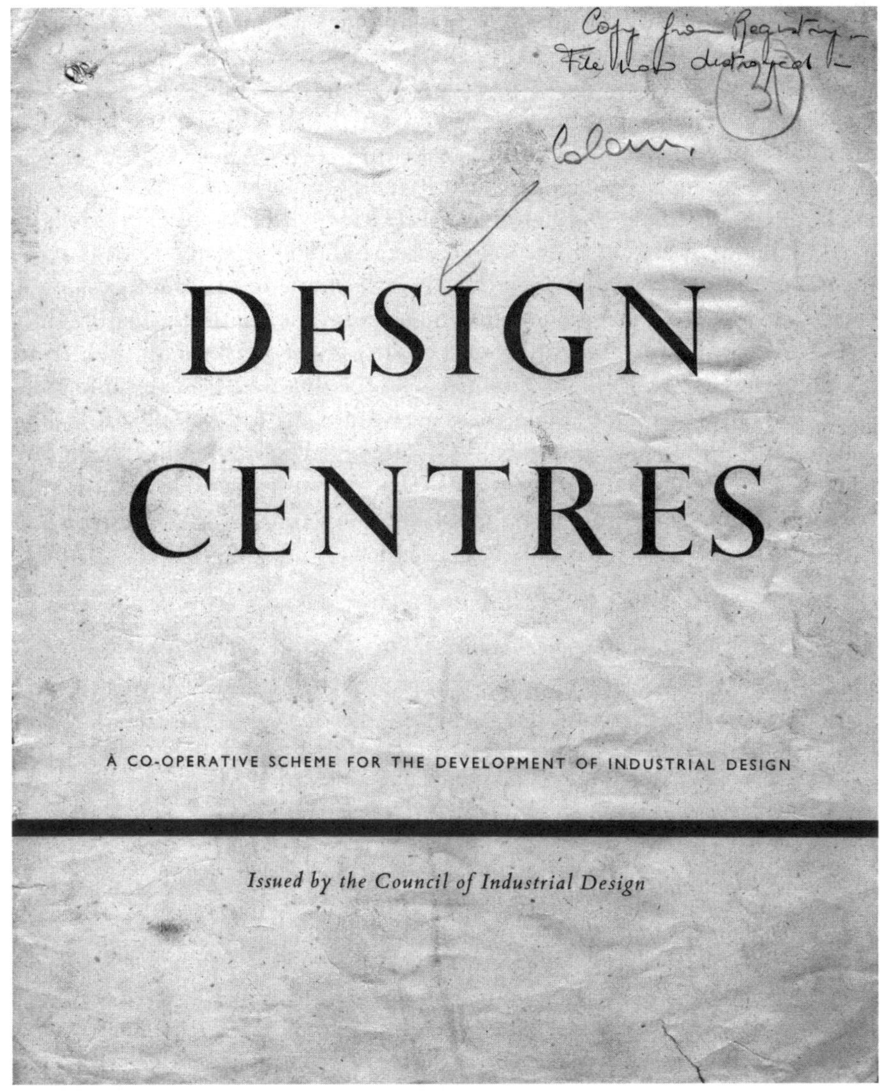

Figure 11.1 Draft cover, CoID Design Centre leaflet, 1945 (Design Archives, University of Brighton)

Committee.[19] She completed her term in December 1947 and retired. At the same time, however, Dr Edwards became the Council's second Chairman, a role he maintained until 1953 when appointment to the Chairmanship of the North Eastern Regional Gas Board precluded its continuation.[20] In Spring 1951 Edwards was joined on the Council by A.N. Silver, Dry Goods Trade Manager of the London Co-operative Society, who remained until 1954, after which three years elapsed during which no one with a co-operative associa-tion served. In 1957 the pattern re-established itself with the appointment of Kenneth Noble, another Director of the Co-operative Wholesale Society, who was reappointed no fewer than three times, not finally retiring until 1966 after nine years' unbroken contribution.

The continuing presence of co-operative figures on the Council's govern-ing body during this founding period is striking when the other component parts of that body are considered. It was a core and oft-repeated value that the many interest groups with which the Council sought to maintain a dialogue could not hope for continuous representation on the relatively small, tightly configured committee. Serving members were chosen instead for their com-bined interests and individual qualities, and the Board of Trade went to great lengths to ensure balance and fairness over time, across different sectors and constituencies.[21] The scope of the Co-op's involvement in retail, distribution, wholesale and manufacture ensured its relevance in such circumstances, and goes some way to explaining its high profile.

The progression of a shared agenda, I

At the Council's first showcase event, the Britain Can Make It exhibition of 1946, Co-operative products were in evidence throughout.[22] Included were gardening equipment, bed linen, a vacuum cleaner (see Figure 11.2), shoes, handbags and several furniture items, for example.[23] Immediately prior to his departure in 1947, the first Director, S.C. Leslie, wrote a memorandum laying down the areas in which he hoped the Council would make rapid progress:

> I hope it may be possible to establish closer relations with this great movement, representing as it does so large a fraction of the country's trade. It might . . . be possible to establish friendly relations, perhaps through the formation of a consultative committee on design jointly sponsored by the Council, the CWS, and, if thought appropriate, by the retail societies. No doubt we shall find in the Co-operative Movement the same receptivity, and readiness to meet and exchange ideas as has been evinced by the engineering industries.[24]

This marked the first occasion on which a design advisory body for the Co-op was mooted by the Council. The CWS was among several bodies with which the Council held early discussions about the need for 'fundamental research' into the physiological and performance requirements of certain commodities, including investigation of the population's distribution 'by sizes and types'.[25] Good evidence exists of a burgeoning relationship between the two organi-sations from this time. Relatively few issues of the CoID's monthly *Design Newsletter* appeared without some reference to joint CU-CoID initiatives. The fruits of this engagement – events, forums, publications, educational tools

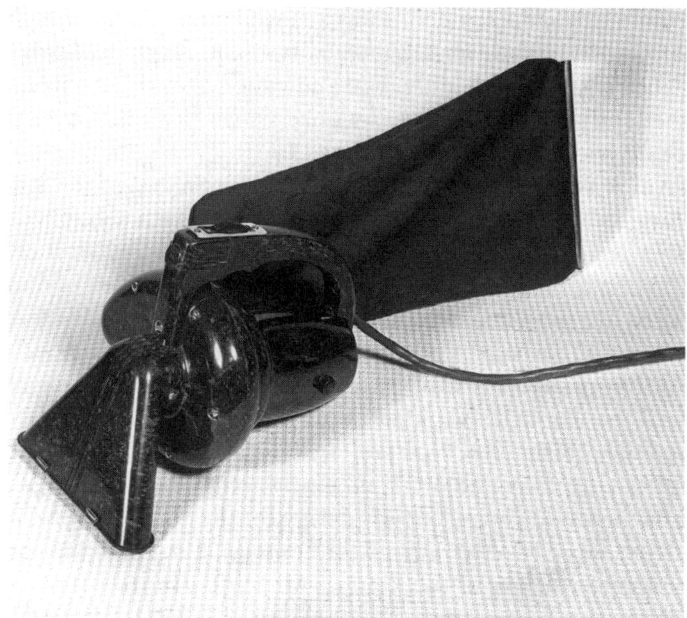

Figure 11.2 CWS hand-held vacuum cleaner, 1946 (Design Archives, University of Brighton)

– are delineated below to characterise the shared sense of 'mission', its broad geographical spread, and the increasing tempo of the exchange.

In 1948 a two-day programme was planned for thirty to forty CWS designers, at the request of Roger Edwards. Training for furniture salesmen was also requested by the London Co-operative Society. The stated aims of the resulting residential course were couched in the following terms: (1) 'to point out the changing needs of Society', (2) 'to broaden the approach of its staff, encouraging them to demand better standards for their customers from the suppliers', and (3) 'to develop with the salesmen the idea that they are providing a social service by advising their members, discovering and meeting their real domestic needs rather than merely supplying them with three-piece suites'.[26] The definition of this agenda was of a piece with the holistic, liberating, social-democratic idealism of the Council at this date. Achieving the right equipment for people's homes would improve the quality of lives, while at the same time contributing to the sustenance of steady economic growth and the expansion of employment opportunities. Seeking to ascertain 'real needs' was an early preoccupation of the Council's, the basis of the distinction it foregrounded between consumer research and market research, and evident in the deliberations of its Housewives' Committee as well as policy discussions about the formation of industry and sector-specific design centres. The encouragement of a more critically engaged and discriminating shopping public was a central mechanism through which it hoped to progress the drive for higher quality and product standards in British goods, to the benefit of both individual and nation.[27] In this it naturally found a sympathetic ally in the Co-op whose concern historically had been the provision of keenly priced goods of definite quality.

The Royal Arsenal Society ran a lecture series on design for the home in Surbiton and Bexley Heath in early 1951, covering such subjects as 'what is good design', 'shapes and size' and 'colours and materials', and concluding with a 'design quiz'.[28] St Albans Co-operative Society was one of four sources of goods used in a show house designed by the CoID for Hatfield Development Corporation. The terraced property demonstrated 'what can be achieved today, within very strict limits of space and money, in the planning of a home', and showed the Council's work at its most practical.[29] The May *Newsletter* announced that 'Design Appreciation' was to be a project of the co-operative movement during 1951 and 1952; members, employees and organisations, particularly the Guilds, were to study design for the home using a CU-written and CoID-produced booklet 'Design for Discussion'.[30] There was further collaboration in the delivery of two courses for traders in the summer months. Local co-operative groups were supplied with visual aids to raise awareness of design issues, and the co-operative press was said to be ready to support the campaign to raise design standards. Reprising what was coming to be an entrenched CoID view, but with the suggestion of CU compliance and enthusiasm, the September *Newsletter* said that

> [the] Co-operative Movement is well placed to exert a direct influence on the design of innumerable household products, for it comprises manufacturers, retailers and consumers. Some co-operators are already expressing a demand for higher standards in design; and the Co-operative Union believes that now is the time to take a more definite attitude and to intensify its work in the field of design.[31]

Lecture courses were held during August at Bexhill and at Stanford Hall.[32] About forty co-operators including men and women from the Guilds and retail staff attended each. The programme was based on the booklet, each talk being followed by small-group discussion and feedback in open session. At the conclusion of each course suggestions for future action were gathered as an aid to planning. The October *Newsletter* trumpeted publication of a generously illustrated 100-page booklet 'Design and our Homes', written by Margaret Llewellyn as a CU-CoID production and intended for wide distribution. Providing a straightforward introduction to the practice of design with suggestions for discussion, it was hoped that the format, on sale priced one shilling, would be popular among the eleven million members of the co-operative movement.[33]

In January 1952, future use of this booklet was the focus of a conference at North Berwick organised by CoID's Scottish Committee in association with the CU Scottish education section. Fifty representatives of Co-op Education Committees attended, and one outcome was a course dedicated to the booklet's use held at Seamhill, Ayrshire, to which Co-op discussion group leaders were invited.[34] In February, the CoID held three residential courses for Co-operative Society furniture salesmen in Ilminster. The CoID Retail Section reported enthusiastically that these had stimulated much valuable discussion of design problems.[35]

Building on the success of two earlier summer schools and good continuing sales of 'Design and our Homes', the CU's Education Department arranged a third school at Stanford Hall in 1952, at which the following topics were discussed:

> The home from early times to the present day; what we mean by good design; furniture design and construction; room planning; colour, light and wall decoration; pattern and furnishing fabrics; common-sense in the kitchen; our shops – what they sell and how they display it.[36]

Thus the case for a design policy was broadened out from products to promotion. Later that year, the Royal Arsenal Co-operative Society's Abbey Wood guesthouse in South East London was the location for two CU-CoID events. In October, furniture sales staffs attended a residential course on furniture design where speakers included the CU's Chief Education Officer R.L. Marshall, the Council's Director Gordon Russell and Co-operator and Council member A.N. Silver. A conference for departmental managers to discuss design problems with special reference to co-operative opportunities was scheduled after this, and on this occasion the lecturers included George Breeze of Lewis's.[37] Breeze's view was that

> [the] retailer . . . cannot hope to increase his trade in better-designed things unless great care is taken in the layout of his showrooms, the display of his goods . . . the make-up of newspaper advertisements and such incidentals as the lettering of posters and permanent notices.

He also stressed 'the importance of staff training and of close contact between retail buyers and product designers'.[38]

In the autumn no fewer than six retail societies – London, Grays, Stockton, Sheffield, Rotherham and Chesterfield – announced or commenced lectures or courses on design for the home. Grays in Essex even undertook to deliver their programme of three sessions at each of the twelve locations at which it operated. The CoID's November *Newsletter* recorded these activities as 'signs of a growing interest in design problems within the Co-operative Movement', other pointers to which were said to be

the showing of a CoID touring exhibition by the Worcester Society last
summer; the opening of a permanent display of contemporary furnishings at
Huddersfield; a group discussion of design problems by Young Co-operators
in their summer school last July; a forthcoming conference in London for
Co-operative managers; and a careful survey by the Movement's newspaper,
"Co-operative News", of the extent to which societies are handling contemporary furnishings.

Furthermore, after an initial sale of 10,000 copies, 'Design and Our Homes'
was reprinted.[39]

A residential course for salesmen, departmental heads and managers
from Scotland and the North of England was held in North Berwick in
association with a small exhibition of contemporary furnishings in January
1953.[40] That year the South Suburban Co-operative Society, with the assistance of Christina Brock of the London Co-operative Society, produced
a filmstrip on design for the home. It compared good and bad product
design, and was accompanied by a sound tape. On its being shown to
branches of the Women's Co-operative Guild and the British Federation
of Young Co-operators, Guild members were also invited to enter an essay
competition penning their responses to the filmstrip, and the contemporary furnishings and household accessories it illustrated.[41] Also in Spring
1953, three regional conferences in Bath, Harrogate and London brought
together managers responsible for soft furnishings or furniture with the
aim of stimulating interest in contemporary furnishings and showing how
good design could be part of business policy.[42] At a residential course for
sales staff at Attingham Park in February 1954, the speaker on 'The retailer's
responsibility and Co-operative Opportunities' was the Huddersfield &
District Society's own H.L. Midgley, a fact that strongly suggests the Co-op's
internalisation of CoID's oft-repeated message.[43]

In early 1956, shortly before the Council's groundbreaking Design Centre
opened in London's Haymarket, a vibrant 'new age' was heralded in Margaret
Llewellyn's *Colour and Pattern in your Home*, a further CU-CoID publication.
Aimed at the amateur in an era of 'do it yourself', it showed the impact of
scale, proportion, pattern, colour and light on decorative schemes, and concluded with practical advice.[44] At the end of the year, a new colour filmstrip
by the same name was launched with accompanying lecture notes for group
purchase, and it was suggested that this was a popular discussion subject. The
accompanying statement that '[p]art of the responsibility of a movement of
consumers is to organise education on planning and decorating the home'
is again indicative of at least partial absorption by the CU of the Council's
message that design advice was another 'social service' the Co-op owed to its
members.[45]

The challenge of CWS production

The CWS was founded in 1863 'by the joint action of retail co-operative societies throughout the country' as a 'bulk-buying agency', and took on the role of production in 1873.[46] Toward the end of the nineteenth century, heavy investment was made in productive capacity and, by the mid-1950s, the CWS owned more than 200 manufacturing plants. Notwithstanding this, four-fifths of the goods sold in the co-operative movement were not produced by the CWS, and approximately 70 per cent of CWS supplies to retail societies still comprised groceries and provisions, with 'dry goods' (clothing, furniture, hardware, drapery, etc.) lagging a long way behind.[47]

Throughout May and June of 1957, Industrial Officers of the CoID made a series of prearranged visits to CWS factories at the organisation's request.[48] Records of these site visits are revelatory of the conditions pertaining in the productive units of 'Britain's biggest business', and disclose how far from an integrated, systematised model of production the CWS manufacturing operation really was. While variations existed in the functioning of each of the works, none could be described as in any way satisfactory. A high proportion of questions included on the visitors' schedule were rendered futile by dint of the discovery that 'in fact no design policy existed' for them to interrogate.[49] The CWS Scale Works at Birmingham received a broadly positive evaluation: the worst that was said here was that 'their own patterns [tend] to be average and always a bit behind [those of] some of their competitors'. However, against this it had to be noted that none of the output was actually destined for the domestic consumer. At the Enfield Clock Depot, only 10 per cent of stock consisted of CWS-manufactured goods, and these relied on clock movements bought in from Smiths. High-pressure advertising by specialist clock manufacturers was felt to present insuperable difficulties for 'Federal' (CWS) clocks. The modesty of the CWS advertising budget, coupled with the lack of a large, efficient production line in a large factory, meant that poor imitation at a lower cost was all that was aimed for. Here the Industrial Officers recommended ceasing manufacture.

Competition from equivalent branded products was also an inhibiting factor at the Cycle Factory at Tyseley in Birmingham, where again 'the majority of products [consisted of] the assembly of ready-made components'. There 'seemed to be no attempt to stimulate sales either by employing a designer or by presenting them attractively in the showroom', and although design suggestions originated almost exclusively from buyers and retail groups, it was 'rare for stock to be held by the Societies'. Regrettably, retail sales were often conducted by staff from the hardware or furniture departments who lacked specialised knowledge, and the 'lack of proper retail sales and after sales service by the Co-operative Societies' was felt to be one of the main reasons behind falling demand for the products of this factory. Industrial Officers 'gained the impression that this factory is capable of turning out well made cycles and that efficient automatic machinery is available, but was in fact not in use owing to the smallness of the runs being put through. Work was therefore being carried out by hand.'

Another facility where the plant was not in itself felt to be a problem was the Dudley National Works responsible for hollowware, shelving, steel office furniture and vacuum cleaners. Built in 1920, although apparently untouched over the intervening years, the site operated multiple machine shops that generated small simultaneous runs of a wide variety of products where sales growth might have been anticipated in this period.[50] The officer observed that '[the] factory itself has an excellent production potential. It is equipped with a generous allowance of machinery and the labour standard is reasonable'. This, however, proved not to be the whole story, for 'no-one seemed to know from day to day what quantities would be required':

> It is quite well laid out; equipped with reasonable plant and machinery and seemed to be in a permanent state of idleness. Components and finished products filled the assembly shops, but no human element seemed at work to manufacture the former and assemble the latter; although I was assured that the day of my visit was no different to any other normal working day.[51]

The problem was a familiar one. Demand from CWS buyers of various departments was signalled through a sample or illustration which the works was asked to reproduce at a cheaper price, but without any guarantee of sales. Uncertainty produced two contrasting effects. Anachronistic high-end products such as the Invincible washing machine were the result of unwillingness to gamble on investment in a press tool. They were effectively hand-made: the top plate was an aluminium sand casting hand-finished to a mirror polish. The responsible designer was 'justifiably proud' of this item which the visitor judged was 'very much ahead, in design and quality, of any other product made by the factory'. On the other hand, with planning impossible and quantity production uneconomic, pressure existed to reduce parts so that the product suffered. 'The cheaper vacuum cleaner and the electric fire were very badly made and were decidedly dangerous.' In between, there were plenty of items which were 'on the whole well made and finished and the design standards average', although 'as with other CWS manufactures certainly not of a high standard'.[52] The detail was said to follow trends that were 'currently popular' but with 'little evidence of originality'. Lighting fittings 'attempted to be fashionable [but] were in fact out of fashion'. In every case the brevity of the runs militated against effective cost reduction.

Unsurprisingly, the CoID officer concluded that although a design department could make a significant difference in a factory of this type, both to product development and to production management, it would be wasted as things were. The lack of even a rudimentary marketing system made it impossible to foresee effective competition with other branded goods. Notwithstanding the factory manager's conviction that Dudley could manufacture a vacuum cleaner to equal any then available in quality and price, the entire workforce struggled under the dispiriting knowledge that Electrolux would always be chosen in preference by the CWS Depot. Some sales of the Dudley cleaner were felt to be better than none at all, though production was unjustifiable from an economic standpoint. Blame was attached to retail-outlet managers seeking to maximise their profit-sensitive salaries, and hence keen to take advantage of national advertising campaigns and trained personnel made available by Hoover to run in-store demonstrations; also to wholesale managers dissatisfied with margins that did no more than cover their Depot's running costs. These tensions within the co-operative 'family' undoubtedly deserve closer scrutiny.

No attempt had been made to display the products from the factory. There was no showroom at the leather-goods factory, and in the china and earthenware factories sales areas were dull, uninspiring and even dirty. At the Enfield Clock Depot there was a newly constructed and decorated showroom, but in contradistinction to usual sales practice there were no photographs or samples available to buyers. At the cotton textile factories in Broughton and Radcliffe there was 'no correlation of product design, packaging, showroom or factory planning', pointing to another significant area of deficiency. Here the officer 'was shown one item of improved, but not very good, packaging which had been fought for by Group'. He noted that packaging 'seemed to be a shared responsibility between the buyer, group and factory management and the CWS Publicity Department'. Similarly, standards of advertising material at the Lincoln Road Cabinet and Bedding factory in Enfield were low. The showcards, pelmets and other items seen by the visitor were 'incredibly dull, of a 1930 circa' type. Here the problem appeared to be a 'Printing Works Manager who permitted no interference from the furniture factory management or the furniture designer'.

Deprived of a raft of supporting materials with which to inspire sales, staff at the ceramic factories were not alone in bemoaning the absence of any opportunity to directly enthuse those further along the chain. Factory visits from buyers were rare; the majority used their local depot instead. There was therefore 'no briefing of the salesmen on new designs. The designer or decorator can but seldom sell his designs to buyers'. This was hard because the demand for new lines was excessive and irrational. Prodigious numbers of designs were required from the decorating managers, who nevertheless were rarely given the opportunity to work on new body shapes. Buyers were responsible for diverse kinds of goods and rarely possessed any specialist knowledge. The size of the productive units and the age of the equipment militated against economic quantity production and hence any kind of realistic competition with other commercial interests. Sourcing from outside CWS production was the norm. Constant turnover of designs, with none surviving longer than six months regardless of success, and obsessive regard for price as the determining factor, made the establishment of successful innovative lines, capable of consistent sales and future development, utterly unlikely. There was no promotion of new lines, the concept of merchandising seeming alien, and retail displays were utilitarian and uninspiring. Staff were demoralised, and consciousness of the hopeless situation soured the working atmosphere.

In the same way, short production runs of six months were usual at the Lincoln Road Cabinet and Bedding factory in Enfield. Here market-research resources were known of but had not been used. Instead there was reliance on twice-yearly meetings of five section heads, and buyers took the lead in determining what went into production. Choices were based largely on criteria of cost, so that of 300 or so designs put forward in a year, almost all were rejected on these grounds. Only 40 per cent of stock was CWS-made. Attitudes toward good, contemporary design were disparaging. The quality of the materials and the finish of the goods were a cause for concern to the visitors.

CWS cotton textile products were felt to be 'up to the average in the industry', but

> [t]here was no evidence of experimental or designs of an advanced nature because of (1) the difficulty in selling such designs to the buyers (2) the pressure from group and the mill manager for minimum quantities (3) the freedom given to buyers to go outside the movement for small lots of novelty lines.

On the sales side 'there was little evidence of market research', and there was no centralised control over the production of particular lines or the presentation of products. Remarkably, given the scope of co-operative operations, the Industrial Officer felt that 'healthy influence derived from direct contact with the retail trade was absent', and that 'the existing set up of a rigid channel of distribution, factory – wholesale buyer – retail buyer – member, has inevitably a throttling effect on design initiative'.

At the Birmingham Aluminium Works there was 'no evidence of any attempt to design any article systematically', and no evidence of a designer being brought in on any of the products manufactured there. In fact, there seemed 'little understanding as to the real meaning of "designed" products', those for which all aspects of manufacture, promotion and function were considered. The impression gained was that 'design meant novelty'.[53]

Before concluding this section, we must in fairness turn our attention to the exceptional case of the CWS leather-goods factory, where an enthusiastic and capable new factory manager had refocused production and, keeping himself up to date on home and continental developments, was overseeing the manufacture of well-designed ranges of fashion and travel goods. Here the problem was one of buyer lethargy owing to the earlier predominance of poor standards. The retail buyers were described as 'truculent', although the section heads at Newcastle, Manchester, Cardiff, Bristol and London were said to be 'very helpful'. Since this manager was acutely conscious of the 'highly competitive and fashion conscious market' in which they were operating, the main worry was whether he could sustain his present level of input into the design process, as well as attending to his other responsibilities, without standards beginning to slip again.

While CoID visitors noticed elsewhere that 'most promotion to executive positions is made from within the Works', with all the insularity of outlook which that implies, this was certainly not the case here. The new manager had formerly been with Michelin, and had joined CWS two years earlier. In this time he had succeeded in bringing the unit's sales deficit down from £96,000 to £16,000, had reorganised the factory 'from top to bottom' and was buying in new machinery. The Sales Manager was formerly with Belstaff clothing, and there was a new young designer from Germany, with an impeccable training and employment record from top-flight German institutions.

Even the normally lamentable labelling attracted positive approbation and significantly, the CWS name had been omitted from the labels on travel goods because of the high level of sales through private enterprise. Advertisements in the trade press had brought in orders from Africa and Ceylon, and enquiries from Canada, Ghana, Italy and France. At that particular time there was insufficient money for national advertising, but this was an aspiration for the future. Staggeringly, the market-research department had been asked for assistance, but the resulting report omitted information on such salient features as colour, price ranges and preferred sizes of luggage.[54] The pro-market research manager gave as the reason for this that

> [the] Department is not regarded within the Movement as of any importance and therefore the staff is rather small and when they are asked to produce a report, they are inclined to take a long time, often too long, and by that time, the information given is out of date.

In the meantime, and at a distance to these exchanges and their reportage, the head of CoID's Industrial Division was asked to maintain a watching brief on CWS submissions to the Council's Design Index of approved products, so that Kenneth Noble could be kept informed. Noble hoped for a monthly update, but was notified that it was doubtful 'whether we have had even one submission a month from the various factories'.[55] The resulting lists showed the hit-and-miss nature of CWS results: for example the 'Defiant' Consolette Radiogram (R107) was accepted by the Design Review Committee on 28

January 1958, whereas the 'Defiant' Radio (MSH 356) had been rejected on 26 June 1956. Worse still, CWS practices worked counter to any kudos that might have resulted from admission to the Index: its 'Windsor' bone-china teaware (187/60) was accepted in April 1955 but production was discontinued in July the same year.

The progression of a shared agenda, II

The co-operative movement was not removed from the general run of debate and development within UK retailing. At a 1957 conference on 'Planning for Progress in Retailing' organised by the British Institute of Management, two out of ten speakers were representatives: one of the CWS, and one of the Nottingham Society.[56] The presentation made by the manager of the CWS market-research department, F. Lambert, revealed how significant its contribution had been in the process of store conversion to the wholly innovative self-service model adopted from America. This revelation came in the very same year as the lamentable state of market-research resources available to CWS manufacturers became obvious to CoID. At the most basic level, it was suggested that

> Investigation should be carried out into the purchasing power of the CWS customer. The economic structure which exists today is . . . vastly different to that which existed in the years following the founding of the Society. The CWS customer will purchase a £60 washing machine or refrigerator manufactured by a well-known company.

This begged the even more fundamental question 'Does the CWS want to market its own products in competition with non-Society manufacturers?' CoID reports were redolent with a sense of abandonment of the movement's manufacturing aspect. Capacity was under-developed or left standing, buyers were described as 'truculent'. This seems all the more remarkable given the convictions underpinning the original investment, and the obstruction the Co-op continued to face from other suppliers. If 'fashion' was an uncomfortable bedfellow, it still remains an open question why CWS rejected the possibility of achieving high standards and scale outputs in the provision of a range of household equipment including desirable consumer durables. Instead, a stultifying sense of inertia was apparent; a pervasive and corrosive acceptance of a rhetoric of 'adequacy'.

Lacking the ambition to be anything other than middle-of-the-road – in fact, aiming precisely for the middle of the road – CWS output would always be vulnerable to the machinations of trend-setters. Apart from the leather factory there had been complete abrogation of the responsibility to innovate. Product development (though no such concept had a meaningful existence) needed to be wrested from the hands of works managers whose attributes, though many and varied, tended to be of a technical or practical nature, and whose status had been steadily accrued through diligent long service, rather than expansive thinking, or responsiveness to new stimuli. The Industrial Officers felt that 'The CWS Directorate would have to encourage, even insist on, a small proportion of frankly experimental production to build up prestige for the movement in forward looking, high quality merchandise'.[57] And then too, it would 'need the enthusiasm of the buyers and proper display in the retail shops to combat competition from outside the movement'. Under the existing arrangements 'Loyalty to the Society is probably [the store manager's] last consideration'. Whereas the conditions prevailing in workshops, factories, showrooms and stores were arguably no worse than in many other independent distribution outlets, the degree of crude vertical integration made the Co-op peculiarly susceptible to the cumulative effects of each of the weaknesses. The failings at each level of the organisation undermined and eroded the edifice of co-operative distribution. The whole was the sum of its imperfect parts.

A modest renaissance and a conclusion

A.N. Silver made a prescient contribution to the 1952 Co-operative Management conference 'Design and the Co-operative Movement' which accurately prefigured many of the issues laid bare by the factory visits carried out five years later. His experience before becoming Dry Goods Trade Manager of the London Co-operative Society, the Society that initiated the self-service revolution, included graduation from Jesus College Cambridge and time with Marks & Spencer. But by 1954 he had moved on to the employ of the London Export Corporation and ceased his involvement with the Council. Unlike Silver, Kenneth Noble's whole working life had been spent with the co-operative movement. Appointed to the Council of Industrial Design in the year that it delivered its laboriously crafted and softened report to the CWS, it was not he who had commissioned the investigation.[58] Nevertheless, it was with him that Gordon Russell sought personal talks on the suggestion of a Design Director for the organisation. What appears to re-emerge in Noble's mid-1960s CWS initiative is the conviction to be a manufacturer of repute.

Notwithstanding the break in Co-op representation on the Council, the 1960s were a period of continuing engagement between the two organisations, marked by a series of bold in-store events and a further publication.[59] In 1963 the London Design Centre 'Came to Plymouth', occupying 4,000 square feet of sales space in Co-operative House between 3 October and 2 November. There were 400 exhibits from Design Index, the Council's listing of 'approved' goods, and 60,000 people viewed them. In 1965 the pattern was repeated in

Scunthorpe, occupying 2,400 square feet of sales space between 30 September and 30 October. This time, room settings were deployed to display products from Design Index sold by the store. Again in 1967 the 'Design Centre Came to Peterborough' between 19 April and 27 May. The displays covered an area of 3,500 square feet and featured six room settings as well as displays of 500 products from Design Index sold by the store. When the exhibition closed it had been extended by two weeks and seen by approximately 17,330 people, strongly indicating the existence of an appreciative audience for such endeavours.[60]

A major innovation came at the conclusion of Noble's own long stint on the Council. The CWS Design Panel announced in 1966 was intended 'to coordinate and develop all aspects of the society's design activities. It will initiate studies into architecture, vehicle liveries, uniforms, packaging, print, etc.' The breadth of this conception was underlined by Noble's statement that '[the] task of the new panel will be to keep under continuous review what might be described as all visual contact between the CWS and the public'.[61] As might be expected the Council welcomed the announcement warmly, pausing only to plead that 'Co-op', 'the one word that is already established in the public's mind as referring to the whole co-operative movement', be urgently reconsidered as the most powerful brand name available to them.[62] Besides Noble, the panel consisted of eight CWS executives and three outside members, one of whom was *Woman* editor Mary Grieve, with whom he had served on the Council. His investment in the proposition is clear from his stout defence of the formula in an exchange of letters published soon afterward in *Design*.[63] By 1967 the CWS had a design officer, Peter Craymer, and by 1968 new ranges were being announced which were intended to 'establish the CWS as a manufacturer whose products sell not only to Co-op stores but competitively to all domestic and export markets' (see Figure 11.3).[64]

While it proved necessary for the Council to make the explicit suggestion of design leadership to the Co-op on at least three occasions separated by many years,[65] and to nurture its representatives' interest over the long term, it would be quite erroneous to aver a wholesale failing, if the pun can be pardoned, on CWS' part to recognise the importance of the appearance of its goods, its stores and its marketing mechanisms. Rather, its engagement over this period should be characterised as a series of uneven 'pulses'.

The classes and discussion groups, the film strips and publications all represented a significant investment by the Education Committee of the Co-operative Union. The conscientious effort made to imbue the movement with a degree of design awareness is worthy of note, and we might commend, and be surprised by, the investigative action reflected by the factory visits initiated and ongoing while the Co-operative Independent Commission completed its business. For its own part, despite the difficulties of some experimental interventions,[66] CoID maintained a long relationship with the Co-op;

Figure 11.3 CWS Agincourt tableware and Sapphire Nova cutlery, 1968
(Design Archives, University of Brighton)

cultivated dialogue with staff at all levels including fabricators, buyers, sales staff and management; identified examples of the CWS succeeding in fashion (the leather factory); kept the issue of visual imagery and its own-brand identity constantly before it; and gave a platform to those who recognised that 'today's experiment is tomorrow's bread and butter'.[67]

What the two organisations seemed unable to do after 1950 was to unite in order to formulate and propagate a set of quality standards across a broad range of products including an expanding number of new consumer durables. Although Black asserts that '*Which?* tests were mostly positive about Co-op products', a survey of editions from the later 1960s arguably presents a more complicated picture, in which the categories within which CWS goods were not included are as revealing as the instances in which they receive relatively good reports.[68] By this time *Which?* was routinely cross-referring its readers to those products that also appeared on the CoID's Design Index; and products submitted for inclusion on the Index needed to comply with relevant BSI standards where such existed. In addition, Gordon Russell was an Honorary Vice President of the Consumers' Association, and consumer champions like Mary Adams, Deputy Chair of the Consumers' Association, and Elaine Burton, then Baroness Burton of Coventry, had served terms on the Council.[69]

To conclude, we might contemplate Gordon Russell's closing comments to the BIM conference mentioned above, and consider their significance for the partner the Council so assiduously cultivated over more than two decades: '[A] design policy cannot pay dividends unless it is intelligible, consistent, sustained and backed by enthusiasm. Then it is an irresistible ally.'[70]

Notes

1 Recent accounts include P. Gurney, *Co-operative Culture and the Politics of Consumption in England, 1870–1930* (Manchester: Manchester University Press, 1996); P. Gurney, 'The battle of the consumer in postwar Britain', *Journal of Modern History* 77:4 (2005), pp. 956–87; M. Hilton, *Consumerism in Twentieth Century Britain* (Cambridge: Cambridge University Press, 2003) and J. Birchall, *Co-op: The People's Business* (Manchester: Manchester University Press, 1994).

2 A. Alexander, 'Retailing and consumption: evidence from wartime Britain', *International Review of Retail, Distribution and Consumer Research* 12:1 (2002), pp. 39–57, 40.

3 'CWS: The world's largest co-operative trading organisation', CWS leaflet (n.d. *c.*1956).

4 Arguably we know more about Women's Co-operative Guild campaigns for better domestic spaces and equipment: see G. Scott, 'Workshops fit for home-workers: the Women's Co-operative Guild and housing reform in mid-twentieth century Britain', in E. Darling and L. Whitworth (eds), *Women and the Making of Built Space in England, 1870–1950* (Aldershot: Ashgate, 2007), pp. 162–79; although on CIC responses to Co-op stores see Black, Chapter 3 in this volume.

5 E. Yeo, 'Rival town halls and tearooms in the second city of the Empire: the Scottish Co-operative movement's architectural encounters', paper delivered to 'Taking Stock: the co-operative movement in British history' (People's History Museum, Manchester, 13–14 May 2005).

6 M. Purvis, 'Spectacular shopping at the great democratic stores: co-operative department stores in inter-war Britain', paper delivered to 'Retail trading in Britain: 2006 CHORD conference' (University of Wolverhampton, 20 September, 2006).

7   V. Kelley, 'The equitable consumer: shopping at the Co-op in Manchester', *Journal of Design History* 11:4 (1998) pp. 295–310.

8   Gurney, 'Battle of the consumer', p. 984.

9   See Council of Industrial Design, *First Annual Report, 1945–46* (HMSO: London, 1946). M. Farr, *Design in British Industry: A Mid-century Survey* (Cambridge: Cambridge University Press, 1955); A. Coulson, *A Bibliography of Design in Britain, 1851–1970* (London: Design Council, 1979). For the importance of businessmen civil servants to the progression of a design agenda within the wartime Board of Trade see L. Whitworth, 'Inscribing design on the nation: the creators of the British Council of Industrial Design', *Business and Economic History On-line*, 3 (2005) http://www.thebhc.org.publications/BEHonline/2005/whitworth.pdf.

10 Dalton to Barlow, 19 December 1944; letter reproduced in CoID *First Annual Report*.

11 Ibid., Board of Trade records, National Archives (Kew, hereafter NA): BT 64/2430. Helmore to Edwards, 13 June 1949.

12 Records of the Council of Industrial Design (now Design Council), Design Council Archive, University of Brighton (hereafter DCA); DCA 1/1946 Minutes of Council Meetings, 1946; Report on the Training of the Industrial Designer, July 1946 C(46)22; DCA 1/1946 Minutes of Council Meetings, 1946; The Council's Forward Programme: Note by the Director C(46)29.

13 NA: BT 64/5172. Lintott to Kilroy, 28 November 1944; NA: BT 64/5171. 'Central Design Council', 30 August [1944].

14 DCA 1/1947 Minutes of Council Meetings, 1947; Report by the Director and Deputy Director to the meeting of Council on 13 June 1947; DCA 189 Public Relations Policy. Appendix A to C(45)25.

15 DCA 1/1946 Minutes of Council Meetings, 1946; Report on the Training of the Industrial Designer, July 1946 C(46)22.

16 The Council for Art and Industry was suspended at the commencement of hostilities. A letter to the Board of Trade from the Parliamentary Committee of the Co-operative Congress urged Davis's continued involvement, but the President was said to favour 'new blood'. NA: BT64/5173; letters dated 6 October 1944 and 27 October 1944.

17 NA: BT 64/5173; Newman to Carruthers, 7 September 1944 and R.S. Edwards to Newman 8 September 1944.

18 Though this was not mentioned in Council statements, she was also a leading light in the Standing Joint Committee of Working Women's Organisations. For more on Allen see L. Whitworth, 'A brief episode of domestic reconnoitring: the Housewives' Committee of the Council of Industrial Design', in Darling and Whitworth (eds), *Women*, pp. 180–96.

19 For a fuller account of this important initiative see Whitworth, 'A brief episode'.

20 The Director, furniture designer Gordon Russell, described him as an 'admirable' Chairman, who was 'exceedingly keen' on the Council's work. NA: BT 64/2410; Confidential memorandum initialled E.L.K.R., 11 May 1949.

21 See for example NA: BT 64/5173 and 64/2410–11.

22 On the exhibition see P.J. Maguire and J.M. Woodham (eds), *Design and Cultural*

Politics in Britain: The Britain Can Make It Exhibition of 1946 (London: Leicester University Press, 1997).

23	See Britain Can Make It *Exhibition Catalogue* and *Supplement* (London: HMSO, 1946).

24	DCA 1/1947: Memorandum from the Director (C(47)19), included with the papers for the meeting of Council held on 13 June 1947. The view expressed was in line with that of the think-tank Political and Economic Planning with which Leslie and the Council's Chairman, Thomas Barlow, were associated.

25	CoID, *2nd Annual Report, 1946–1947* (HMSO: London, 1947), p. 17.

26	DCA 357: Memorandum from Beresford Evans to Gordon Russell, 31 December 1947; TM(48)1 Minutes of the 10 meeting of the Training Committee, 7 January 1948; Training Section: Report for the period ending 31 January 1948.

27	See L. Whitworth, 'Anticipating affluence: skill, judgement and the problems of aesthetic tutelage', in L. Black and H. Pemberton (eds), *An Affluent Society? Britain's Post-War 'Golden Age' Revisited* (Aldershot: Ashgate, 2004) pp. 167–83.

28	*Design Newsletter* No. 24, January 1951.

29	*Design Newsletter* No. 27, April 1951.

30	*Design Newsletter* No. 28, May 1951.

31	*Design Newsletter* No. 31, September 1951. See also Paul Reilly's editorial in the Council's journal *Design*, December 1951, in which similar sentiments were expressed.

32	Stanford Hall is the name of the Co-operative Union's premises near Loughborough.

33	*Design Newsletter* No. 32, October 1951.

34	*Design Newsletter* No. 36, February 1952.

35	*Design Newsletter* No. 37, March 1952.

36	*Design Newsletter* No. 40, June 1952.

37	*Design Newsletter* No. 42, September 1952.

38	G. Breeze speaking to CoID Scottish Committee, reported in *Design Newsletter* No. 46, January 1953. Gurney notes the competition between the Co-op and Lewis's; see Gurney, *Co-operative Culture*, pp. 233–4.

39	*Design Newsletter* No. 44, November 1952.

40	*Design Newsletter* No. 46, January 1953.

41	*Design Newsletter* No. 47, February 1953.

42	*Design Newsletter* No. 49, April 1953.

43	*Design Newsletter* No. 57, February 1954.

44	*Design Newsletter* No. 79, February 1956.

45	*Design Newsletter* No. 89, December 1956.

46	'The world's largest co-operative trading organisation'. Fuller accounts of its evolution are contained in Gurney, *Co-operative Culture,* and Birchall, *Co-op.*

47	R.S. Edwards at the conclusion of *Design and the Co-operative Movement.* Co-operative Management Conference, Harrogate, 1952 (Manchester: CU/CoID, 1952), p. 19. 'The world's largest co-operative trading organisation leaflet'.

48	These were the two Longton (Stoke) Potteries; the Weaving Mills (Cotton), Broughton, Salford; Birmingham Aluminium Works, Tyseley; Ilford Radio

Depot; the Furniture Factories, Enfield; Birmingham Cycle Factory, Tyseley; Birmingham Scales Factory; Dudley National Works (Office Furniture and Appliances); and the London Clock Depot, Enfield.

49 Quotations throughout this section and the following one are taken from the site reports and various versions of the draft commentary filed at DCA 819/3.

50 The full range included galvanised hollowware – dustbins, pails, buckets, watering cans; steel office equipment – metal desks, filing cabinets, cash boxes, safes, chairs (only available in olive green drab); lighting fittings – fluorescent industrial and commercial fittings; domestic appliances – washing machines, irons, vacuum cleaners, and electric fires.

51 The Unity (cutlery) works in Sheffield was also regarded as 'reasonably large and comparatively modern', but here too there was an 'air of leisure amounting almost to torpor'.

52 Production of two electric irons was also out-sourced to a firm who applied the CWS nameplate.

53 This is in stark contrast to the sophisticated systematisation of design methods evolved by theorists such as L. Bruce Archer by this date. See 'Systematic method for designers', Parts 1–7 in *Design*, 172, 174, 176, 179 (1963); 181, 185 and 188 (1964); and *Systematic Method for Designers* (London: CoID, 1965).

54 This lends support to A.N. Silver's view that CWS market research was oriented more toward store location and patterns of patronage than to product investigation, *Design and the Co-operative Movement*, p. 16.

55 DCA 819/3: A. Gardner Medwin to K. Noble, letter dated 9 September 1957.

56 British Institute of Management, *Planning for Progress in Retailing* (London: BIM, 1957). Gordon Russell, CoID Director, also spoke at the event.

57 This was said explicitly in relation to cotton products, but clearly had wider application.

58 Formally this request came from H. Buckley, Secretary and Executive Officer of the Co-operative Wholesale Society.

59 Henry Stephenson and Lillian Stephenson, *Eating, Sleeping and Living* (Manchester: CU/CoID, 1964).

60 CoID, *19th Annual Report, 1963–1964* (London: HMSO, 1964), p. 22; CoID, *21st Annual Report, 1965–1966* (London: HMSO, 1966), p. 37; CoID, *23rd Annual Report, 1967–1968* (London: HMSO, 1968), p. 33. The *19th Annual Report* also carried images of Scunthorpe Co-operative Society's new house style as applied to vehicle livery and stationery, indicating that studies of individual societies' responses to such challenges may yield new insights.

61 See *Design* 207 (1966), p. 69.

62 'Creating a design policy for the Co-op', *Design* 208 (1966), p. 19. A variety of other names were being considered at the time.

63 See *Design* 210 (1966), p. 67 and *Design* 211 (1966), p. 71.

64 See *Design* 219 (1967) p. 57 and *Design* 232 (1968), p. 64.

65 These were in Leslie's 1947 memorandum, during the 1952 Co-operative Management conference, and in the response to the 1957 factory visits.

66 Described by J. Woodham in 'An episode in post-Utility design management:

the Council of Industrial Design and the Co-operative Wholesale Society', in J. Attfield (ed.), *Utility Reassessed: The Role of Ethics in the Practice of Good Design* (Manchester: Manchester University Press, 1999), pp. 39–57.
67 A.N. Silver at the 1952 Co-operative Management Conference, *Design and the Co-operative Movement*, p. 14.
68 L. Black, 'The impression of affluence: political culture in the 1950s and 1960s', in Black and Pemberton (eds), *An Affluent Society*, p. 97.
69 Adams and Burton were appointed in January 1963. Adams served until 1966 and Burton until 1968.
70 BIM, *Planning for Progress in Retailing*, p. 26.

12

Innovation, modernisation, consumerism: the co-operative movement and the making of British advertising and marketing culture, 1890s–1960s

Stefan Schwarzkopf

The development of personality does not dispose of an advertising budget. (Sidney Pollard, *The Co-operatives at the Crossroads*, 1964)

We live in an age of trusted brands and communities . . . Few commercial communities have as distinguished a history as the Co-op. This doesn't mean it can beat the global buying power of Tesco. But there is a growing community of ethical shoppers for whom the Co-op is a natural partner. It deserves to succeed. (*Guardian*, 4 September 2006)

Branding the unbrandable?

The co-operative movement and modern advertising seem to be two subjects which do not go together very easily. On the one hand, there is a large-scale grass-roots network of consumers and producers, which was formed in the belief that branding and advertising were an unnecessary burden on those who produced, distributed and purchased consumer goods. In the world of co-operators, advertising was a costly means of communication which created fictitious values, and which sustained a purely competitive mindset that divided society into the 'haves' and the 'have nots'. On the other hand, the *raison d'être* of modern advertising is based on a diametrically opposed system of beliefs. In the world of late nineteenth-century advertising agents, newspaper and magazine publishers or salesmen, nationally advertised consumer brands were a boon to economy and society as they stimulated and stabilised demand, provided reassurance to consumers as to the quality and origin of products and allowed manufacturers to reap the rewards of launching innovative products.

When the chairman of the Co-operative Wholesale Societies (CWS), J.T.W. Mitchell, addressed a quarterly meeting of the movement in 1880, he described the practice of advertising all out as the 'Barnum wickedness of the competitive world'.[1] This statement is often quoted as summing up the unwillingness and – crucially – the inability of the co-operative movement to engage with the challenges as well as the opportunities of modern marketing. In particular, Peter Gurney has suggested that advertising exposed a 'fundamental clash' between the 'moral economy' of the co-operative movement and its dependence on active, politicised membership on the one side and the capitalist interest in forming a mass of passive, susceptible consumers on the other. According to Gurney and earlier authors on the subject, such as Arnold Bonner and the French co-operator Professor Charles Gide, the co-operative movement's political culture was in a sense an essential barrier to innovations in advertising and marketing, since this culture revolved around rational notions of universal provisioning, thrift and utility rather than around target markets, emotional 'identity brands' or the creation of artificial needs.[2]

In this chapter, I introduce three arguments with respect to the difficult relationship between the co-operative movement and modern advertising, marketing and brand management. First, I attempt show that there was no such essential or insurmountable cultural gulf between the co-operative movement and modern advertising practices. In contrast, I suggest that a young generation of co-operative managers after 1900 exhibited a great deal of enthusiasm about the opportunities offered by publicity for the movement. Secondly, I argue that this enthusiasm, in turn, resulted in a number of innovations which shaped the making of modern advertising practices in the United Kingdom as a whole. Thus, rather than being shaken off by the rapid modernisation of advertising in the early twentieth century, the co-operative movement was an essential part of that story of modernisation.

Thirdly, I argue that in some sense the co-operative movement was a victim of its own success in trying to put the consumer on the map of British businesses. One of the major contributions of the movement, for example, was to push forward modes of production and retailing which relied heavily on economies of scale in generic goods and staple foods, high profits per unit through distribution of large volumes of goods, customer retention through profit-sharing schemes and the focus on communicating the CWS *brand* as a reassurance for consumers as regards the value, reliability and safety of products. These areas – the economies of large-scale production, large-scale retailing of bulk, branding and consumer trust – came to define 'modern' marketing strategy in the late nineteenth century and served as the co-operative's main sources of competitive advantage against Lever, Lipton's and Sainsbury's. After the Second World War, however, the movement's earlier enthusiasm for innovations in marketing vanished and caused the movement to decline in a world characterised by the emergence of highly segmented markets and new forms of brand management.

Innovation and modernisation

The co-operative movement in Britain needs to be ranked among the main initiators of the marketing of branded goods and the use of the brand as a communicative device to add value to products which were difficult to differentiate in the mind of consumers. Advertisements by a number of co-operative productive societies around 1900 stressed this idea of customer value and focused on tangible product advantages and the high quality of co-operatively produced goods. Products carrying the 'CWS' brand were said to stand for 'contented workers, wholesome and reliable goods' and 'satisfied consumers' (Figure 12.1).[3] Advertisements published by various productive and wholesale societies around 1900 followed a style which was typical for their period. A 1909 advertisement for 'Anchor' boots and shoes, for example, stressed the uses of the product: boots for school girls and boys (Figure 12.2). Also in line with Victorian and Edwardian advertising design, this advertisement used an attractive and pleasing picture to attract and keep the eyes of potential customers. A 1903 piano advertisement published by the Bristol Co-operative Pianoforte Productive Society offered the product on the hire-purchase system, a financing system that was often criticised by contemporaries as the very opposite of restraint and thrift (Figure 12.3).

Stressing the uses of products in advertisements was the most common approach to advertising communication between the mid-nineteenth century and the mid-1920s.[4] In this era of eye-catching designs and 'reason-why copy', the co-operative movement executed this approach to the marketing of products not only very efficiently but also on the same level of design proficiency achieved by its capitalist rivals. In 1916, in the middle of a major war that saw food rationing and decreased consumer spending power, the CWS put out full-colour advertisements for their mustard (Figure 12.4). In this advertisement, the brand, its quality ('Double Superfine') and its uses (table, kitchen, bath and sickroom) are being stressed. What is remarkable is that the imagined target group of this product is presented in the advertisement as well. Yet this target group does not at all seem to be the oppressed rural or town worker, but the middle-class gentleman who is able to afford a dinner lady and a butler. In this design, the CWS of course used one of the oldest tools of persuasion in advertising – that is, surrounding the product with an aura of social achievement and prestige.[5]

Before the First World War, co-op members and leaders discussed advertising more as part of the general educative and propaganda work of the movement. For this purpose, a Joint Propaganda Committee at the Manchester headquarters decided on propaganda and canvassing strategies, helped with the organisation of large-scale meetings, secured the production of lantern slides for lecture evenings and supported the production of leaflets and

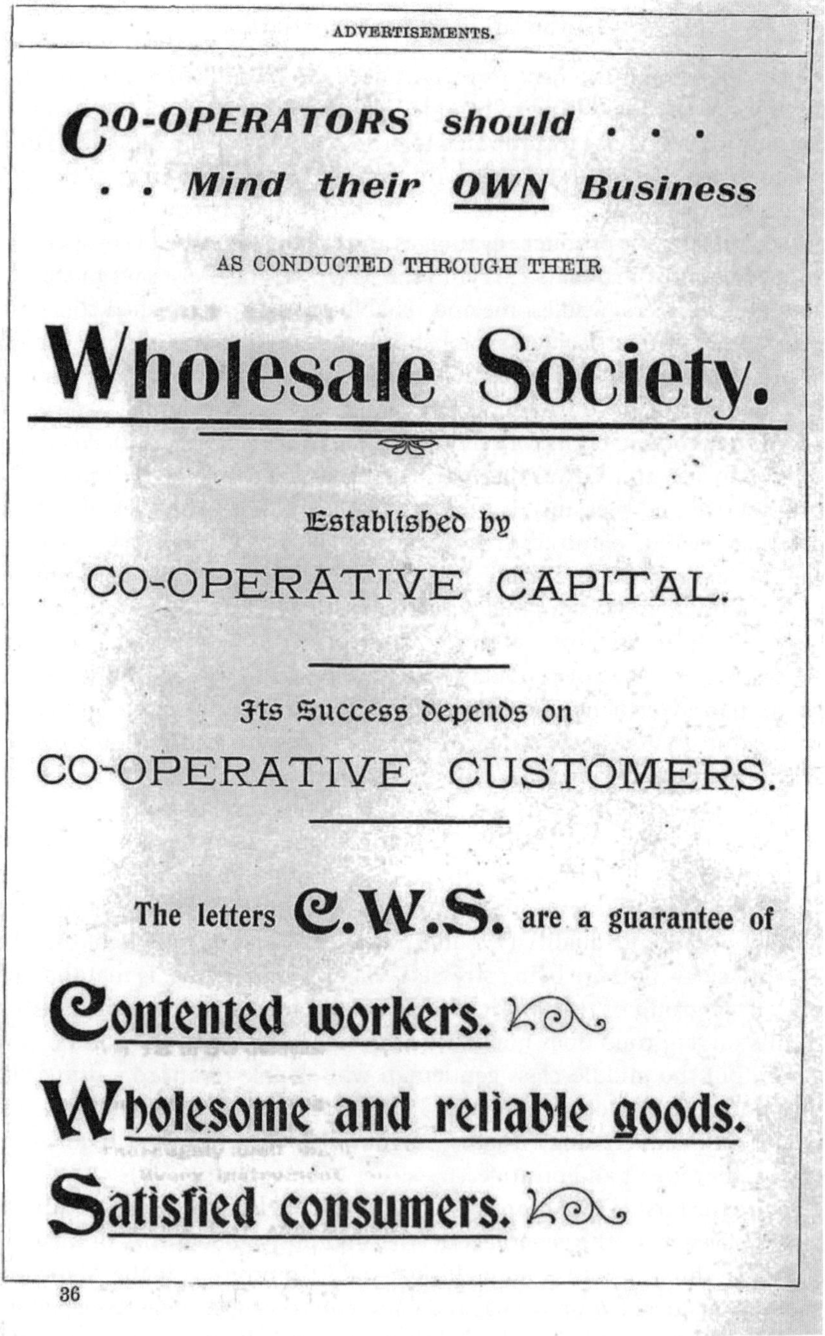

Figure 12.1 CWS: A guarantee label

Figure 12.2 Anchor boots

Figure 12.3 Bristol piano advertisement

Figure 12.4 CWS Mustard, 1916

pamphlets such as 'How to take a town (co-operatively) by storm' (1904). In 1908 alone, the Co-operative Union's Lantern Department issued some 19,000 lantern slides to member societies in the country (e.g. 'Little grey brother' targeted at children and teenagers). These activities were said to be essentially about education, but it was recognised that it was this commercial propaganda which helped 'qualify ourselves to meet the competition in the open market'.[6] It was the educative, propagandist drive which ensured that the movement was often ahead of its time as regards modern means of commercial mass communication. Co-operative societies not only employed traditional publicity tools, such as handbills, advertisements, posters, magic-lantern slide lectures, trade and product exhibitions, pamphlets, circulars, theatre shows, trade pageants and periodical publications (local *Wheatsheafs* and *Co-operative News*). As Alan Burton has shown, the CWS was the first organisation in the United Kingdom to utilise the new technique of moving pictures as part of their lectures, community evenings and trade exhibitions.[7]

While Burton interprets these early beginnings of the co-op film movement as part of the history of British *film*, contemporaries such as Sidney Box pointed out that these CWS commercials were indeed 'Britain's first advertising films'.[8] The first co-operative films were screened in 1899 and showed the soap, starch and candle works at Irlam, the biscuit factory at Crumpsall and the London tea warehouse.[9] The first advertising movies by the co-operatives' capitalist competitors appeared after that and also focused on factories and ways of production rather than on specific products. The CWS, Britain's first film advertiser, produced about forty such small feature films between 1899 and 1914. Sidney Box, quoted above, was associated with the CWS through a firm called Publicity Films Ltd, which in 1928 produced the movement's first product-centred commercial, 'The magic basket'. This commercial followed an initiative that was started in 1927 to modernise CWS publicity. In that year, the movement's first annual National Propaganda Campaign had been launched and a 'Special conference on methods of co-operative propaganda and education' had been held at Stockholm.[10] Following the advice given in the report of the conference proceedings, the CWS employed Publicity Films Ltd in late 1927, which produced ten silent advertising movies for the CSW between 1928 and 1930. These included 'The magic basket' (1928) on shopping and life in a 'co-operative' way, 'The cup that cheers' (1928) about CWS tea, and a number of other commercials about co-operative soap, polishes, shoes, biscuits, flour and preserves.[11]

In 1930, the CWS and Publicity Film Ltd produced the movement's first 'talkie' ('Her Dress Allowance'), which sold the advantages of shopping at co-operative draperies. In the same year, the CWS showed its advertising movies at the Ideal Home Exhibition in London.[12] By the early 1930s, the CWS employed a fleet of demonstration vans touring the country which offered

Figure 12.5 Co-op 1935 Tea demonstration van

a selection of co-operative products and screened sound feature films in the open air. This was a remarkably modern form of sales promotion which introduced thousands of consumers to the variety and quality of co-operatively produced goods.[13]

The evidence from the history of co-operative film publicity suggests that around the turn of the last century a new generation of co-operators was taking over the steering of the movement. A whole number of pamphlets and articles were published by the Co-operative Union and the Wholesale Society at that time, calling for more and better co-operative advertising. In 1903, for example, a pamphlet on 'Co-operative advertising' written by James Cheyne voiced a common concern that the movement lagged behind in the field of publicity. Cheyne demanded a vigorous propaganda and advertising campaign to check 'the advance of the combines'.[14] In 1913, the author of a similar pamphlet advised that the movement should spend pounds on advertising 'where it now spends pennies only'. He called for more moving-picture films and well-illustrated booklets 'in bright and glowing styles'.[15] In 1924, the publicity organiser of the Manchester and Salford Society, Charles Smethurst, too, called on his fellow co-operators to develop a more 'aggressive attitude' in using advertising to attract new members instead of preaching to the converted.[16] Two years later, the *Co-operative Official* reminded its readers that 'if the movement desires to maintain and extend its business it must resort to advertising methods'.[17]

Some of these voices acknowledged that 'bright' advertising for co-operative products of course had to be paid for by someone, and warned that posters, showcards, films and colourful magazine advertisements could be seen as a contradiction of co-operative principles. Alanson Sessions, of the Pacific Co-operative Society in San Francisco, told his British fellow co-operators that advertising was no less than a 'curse of the consumer'.[18] Thus, from the earliest moments of co-operative advertising, it turned out to be very difficult to negotiate a credible and sustainable position for the CWS between the commercial pressure to attract customers and the principles of enlightened consumerism. A speaker at the 1915 meeting of the National Co-operative Managers' Association, for example, argued that

> [t]here is now actually a very live advertising department at Balloon Street, who are only prevented from showing the retail societies how co-operators ought to advertise by a section, who are afraid that they are going too fast in that direction, and perhaps they also remember some of the things that they have said in days gone by about our competitors adding the cost of advertising to the articles they had to sell.[19]

A number of articles appearing in the co-operative press also called on this new generation of people who were not 'afraid' to advertise as their forefathers in the 'days gone by'. One article appearing in September 1907 in the *Co-operative News* asked its readers

> Why is it that the majority of co-operative stores are not advertised? On every hand we see the private trader advertising his business – whether large or small. You must not forget that in order to gain more members and do more trade, your doings must be told to those outside the movement. You must interest the general public in your stores and the advantages gained by becoming members. Why not using the local newspapers for blowing your own trumpet? The private trader, as a rule, makes good use of this, why not the co-operative societies?[20]

The co-operative advertising machinery

It was during the Edwardian period that the co-operative movement indeed began to realise and appreciate the powers of advertising if taken into their own hands. At the same time, the Co-operative Headquarters in Manchester began to modernise its publicity apparatus. Since 1863, there had been in existence a Co-operative Publicity Department in charge of general publicity on behalf of the co-operative movement. This department published the monthly *Wheatsheaf* and organised co-operative trade exhibitions and CWS exhibits at agricultural shows. This department grew rapidly from a staff of eight in 1913 to a publicity staff of 100 in 1938. In 1916, in response to attacks on the co-operative movement in the press, a more specialised Co-operative Press Agency was formed under James Haslam, the father of many of the earlier CWS advertising campaigns. The Press Agency was put in charge of sending out press reports to newsrooms, the drafting and placing of advertisements and the drafting and publication of pamphlets. The enormous growth of the Co-operative's publicity activities immediately after the First World War eventually necessitated the merger of these bureaus and departments under the umbrella of one Publicity Department in 1926. Director of the department became James Haslam, who was later replaced by Percy Redfern and C.E. Tomlinson.[21] The advertising posters produced by this department throughout the 1920s and 1930s were characterised by a visual appeal second to none of the capitalist firms' advertising campaigns at that time (Figure 12.6). In the late 1930s, the department was able to win Britain's foremost poster designer at that time, Abram Games, to produce a number of posters for the Co-operative Permanent Building Society (Figure 12.7).

One year after the foundation of the Press Agency, in 1917, a Survey Committee started its work and recommended in its report to the Annual Co-operative Congress to organise national advertising schemes worth £100,000 to £200,000 every year.[22] It took almost ten years, however, before these recommendations were implemented. In 1927, the CWS began to launch Annual Propaganda Campaigns – usually running for two or three weeks in February – which were aimed at publicising the movement and attracting new members. For the 1927 Annual Propaganda Campaign alone, 14 million leaflets, 45,000 posters and 30,000 window bills were produced by the Publicity Department's photographers, copy writers and editors. Advertisements for co-operative products such as soap were placed in more than 400 newspapers each year and were supported by millions of posters, window bills, showcards, picture postcards and advertising novelties, such as toys or serviettes bearing CWS brand names.[23] In 1928, one poster had been prepared with the slogan 'Buy at the Co-op. and watch your savings mount up!' Specially designed leaflets not only promised 'More money for you!' but also an answer to the problem 'What women want'.[24] On a more critical note, however, Carr-Saunders's study of the British co-operative movement showed that in 1936, out of the 1,777 societies included in the Co-operative Union only 144 were actually participating in the collective advertising scheme.[25]

The larger and more important societies often joined the publicity machinery enthusiastically. In 1928 alone the Scottish Co-operative Wholesale Society in Glasgow erected electric advertising signs in various inner-city places, purchased illuminated poster spaces in tramcars and buses and spent some £1,400 on adapting "The Magic Basket" film in order to make it suitable for the Scottish market.[26] Local organisers of co-operative advertising campaigns in the 1920s and 1930s were issued with booklets on how to run them successfully and efficiently. One 'Handbook for propagandists and canvassers' included a chapter on 'The psychological moment' and

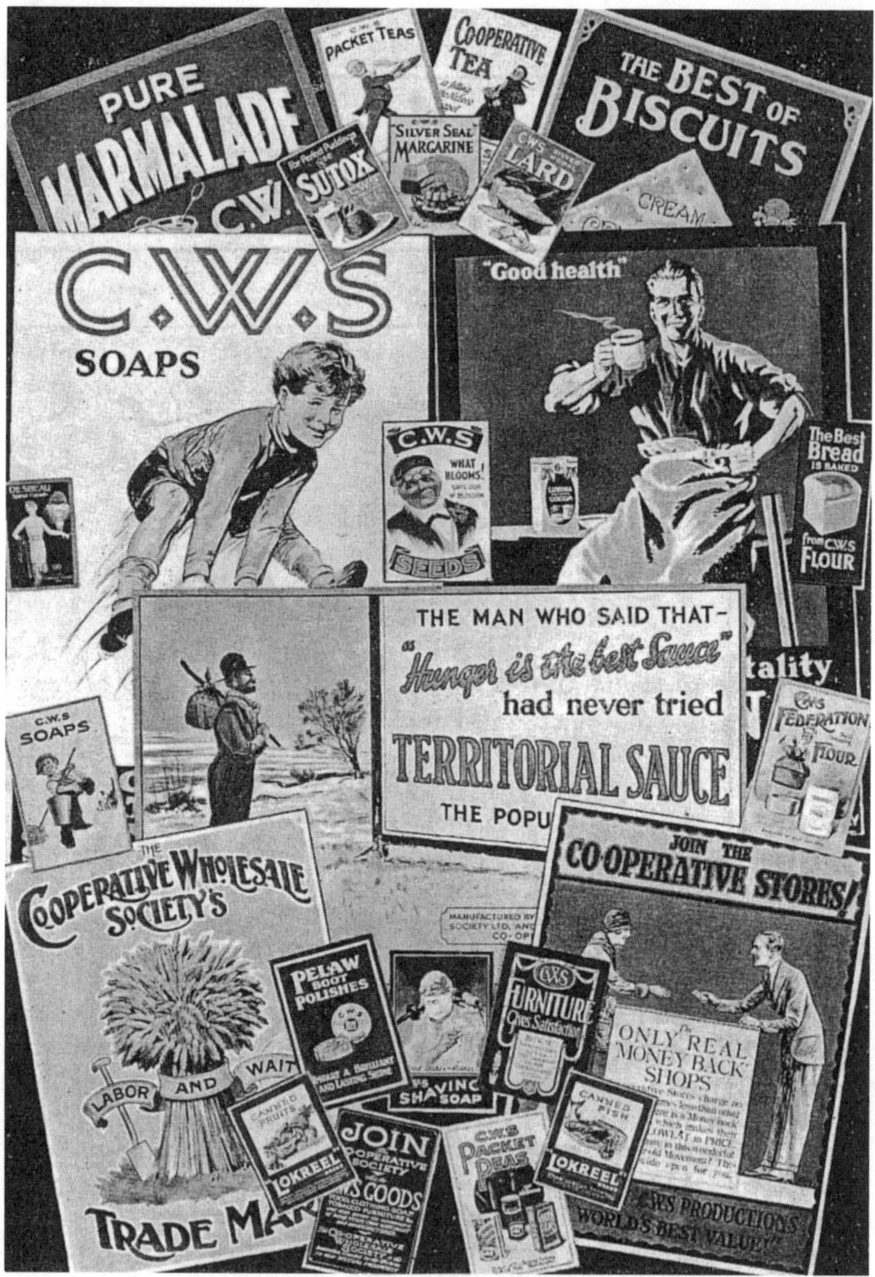

Figure 12.6 Example of posters designed by Publicity Department

Figure 12.7 CPBS Posters, 1938–39

explained for local society managers how to order advertising material from the Manchester CWS headquarters, how to conduct door-to-door canvassing and how to write reports to the local press.[27] At that time, the CWS and the Co-operative Union also began to offer classes and correspondence courses on advertising, and the film work of the movement saw its most rapid expansion. The total advertising expenditure of the CWS, however, was still comparatively small. In 1933, the co-operative movement spent only around £657,000 on advertising altogether. This needs to be compared to the £1.1 million which was spent alone on soap advertising in Britain annually in the mid-1930s.[28]

The most important change to co-operative advertising policy in the inter-war years, however, took place in the target group chosen by the wholesale and retail societies. While before the 1930s many co-operators confined themselves to the working-class consumer buying those goods that were needed, the 1930s saw a change of advertising policy toward targeting the young and wealthy middle classes who consumed for pleasure and aspiration. A booklet on co-operative advertising guidelines published in 1937 called on the movement to face the reality that the Co-op had to attract masses of disconnected and rather passive consumers and that only large advertising schemes could help in breaking through the apathy to attract young families and middle-class consumers. The author of the booklet called on the movement to make allowance for the changed desires of a new generation of potential co-operators: 'Young people in particular are open to the lure of the newer types of multiple and departmental stores, mass-production tailors, hire-purchase furniture dealers and the glitter of Neon lights and stainless steel fascias.'[29]

This change of emphasis is exemplified in a direct-mail campaign launched by the Co-operative Union in 1934. Thousands of letters directed at middle-class families in Britain were sent out bearing the slogan 'The mystery of the next door neighbour'. On the back of the letter was printed 'Can you solve this?' as an invitation to people to open the mysterious letter. Inside the letter was a leaflet which told the story of two families, the Blacks and the Whites. While both families were members of a local co-operative society, the Blacks bought all their goods, footwear, clothing, furniture and hardware from the co-operative store, not just groceries as the White family did. This meant that the Blacks received more than double the co-operative dividend of the Whites. Unlike the Whites, the Blacks therefore enjoyed a summer holiday every year (Figure 12.8).[30]

This advertising letter also exemplifies the co-operative movement's vision of the political economy of consumer desire. It introduces stereotypically middle-class families as co-operators. The dress code of both husband and wife, the summer holiday as a consumer product, the semi-detached suburban house shown on the outside of the letter – everything pointed at the movement's belief that it now represented middle-class England. At the same time, of course, George Orwell's novels *Keep the Aspidistra Flying* (1936) and *Coming up for Air* (1939) described the co-operative stores as the natural ally of poverty-stricken working-class communities. Moreover, the advertising letter introduces the children of the White family, who bought only their groceries at the Co-op, as slightly better dressed than the children of the Blacks, who bought their clothing at the Co-op stores. The admission that co-operatively produced clothing might be less fashionable or up-to-date than dresses, trousers and shirts produced by capitalist firms points right at the heart of the movement's troublesome relationship with consumers' innate irrationality. This advertisement actually needs to be read as a warning to consumers not to fall for their desire to seek instant gratification but instead to adopt a strategy of deferred gratification. Clearly recognising that capitalist firms often offered more fashionable clothing, furniture or white consumer goods, this co-operative advertisement spelled out the advantages of co-operative consumerism. By accepting slightly less fashionable clothing, for example, consumers could enjoy a higher standard of life in the long term.

The new strategy of targeting middle-class consumers, a strategy that had been introduced by the 1919 Co-operative Development Plan, permeated a number of co-operative marketing campaigns in the inter-war period. In the

THE BLACKS LIVE NEXT DOOR TO THE WHITES

Mr. Black earns the same weekly wage as his friend Mr. White;

Mrs. Black gets the same housekeeping allowance as Mrs. White;

Tom and Mary Black are just as well dressed as their next-door playmates, Jack and Nellie White—slightly better, if anything;

Both families, in fact, live in practically equal circumstances;

Yet the Blacks go away every summer, while the Whites have to stay at home.

How do the Blacks do it?

Here is the Answer:

Mrs. White is quite a wise woman. Like so many of us nowadays she finds it difficult to make ends meet.

Naturally, she buys all her groceries from the Co-operative Stores. The pure, wholesome foods help to keep her family fit and strong.

And the dividend comes in so useful for shoe repairs, and gas and electricity bills. She says with a smile that co-operative shopping is her only "saving" grace.

But, somehow, she never seems to be able to save up enough to take the family away during the holidays.

Mrs. Black is wiser still. Like her neighbour, she gets her groceries from the "Stores," but that is not all.

All the footwear, clothing, hardware, and furnishings—and many more things, too—in the Blacks home come from the Co-operative Society.

The quality of co-operative productions is absolutely dependable and the price is reasonable.

Besides, from this added value the Blacks get more than twice as much dividend as the Whites. It pays for their quarterly bills and a summer holiday as well.

CO-OPERATIVE QUALITY COUNTS

—and you can always bank on your dividend

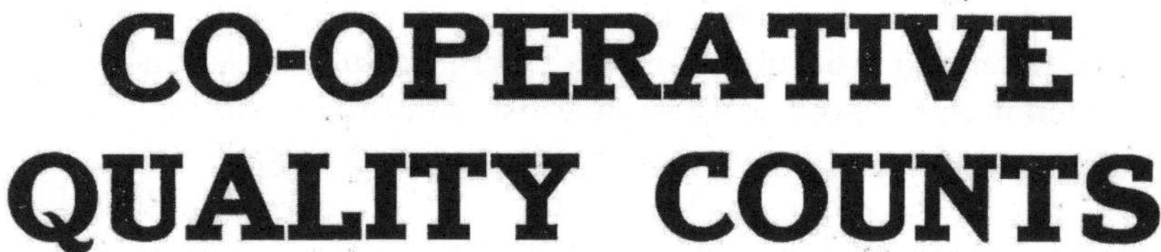

Figure 12.8 Direct-mail campaign 1934

late 1920s, the *Wheatsheaf* issued an annual 'Holiday Guide' printed in full colour, which contained travel advice and thousands of holiday addresses on more than 200 pages. Similar holiday guides were issued annually by British insurance and railway companies, which again shows that the co-operative movement strove hard to keep fully up-to-date with the modernisation of British consumer lifestyles.

For various reasons, the co-operative movement was at the forefront of a number of mid-twentieth-century innovations in marketing and retailing. In 1939, for example, the CWS formed a Market Research Department at a time when the techniques of market and consumer research were still relatively young and untried.[31] The outbreak of war prevented the Department from becoming very active in the early 1940s, but by the early 1950s it conducted up to 25,000 interviews each year using samples ranging from 500 to 2,000 consumers. The Department tested consumers' reactions to new products and it studied consumer reactions to self-service shops. In other studies, it measured consumers' attitudes to existing and proposed CWS brands and, by proposing changes to existing products, it ultimately became a useful tool for the CWS to determine brand policy.[32] Another important innovation in British retailing after the Second World War was the introduction of self-service shops. Here, too, the co-operative movement played an important role by erecting Britain's first self-service supermarket in Romford (Essex) in 1942.[33]

A new type of 'consumerism'

The enthusiasm for the opportunities of modern advertising methods as well as the sobering sense of realism as to the target group of consumers the Co-ops had to compete for seem to have been lost after the war. Throughout the 1950s, the co-operative movement faced new challenges on a scale unknown before. These included the so-called 'advertising wars' which it had to fight out with Unilever and Procter & Gamble ('detergent war', 'margarine war'). The introduction in 1955 of television advertising in Britain through ITV posed severe technical and financial challenges to the CWS. Initially, the CWS tried to take part in the exciting new medium of TV advertising and produced a number of commercials advertising either the co-operative stores ('Co-op for Value'; 'Co-op Shopping') or specific brands, such as 'Blue Bell Margarine' or 'Lofty Cakes'. Yet it soon became clear to observers within and outside the co-operative movement that the advertising expenditure of the private manufacturers such as Unilever (detergents), Imperial Tobacco (cigarettes), Heinz (foodstuffs) and Cadbury's (confectionery) crowded the CWS out of the market.[34] In their 1962 study on 'Advertising in Action', the two right-wing 'free-market' economists Ralph Harris and Arthur Seldon concluded that the failure of the CWS to employ advertising and sales promotion on a larger scale was the major reason for its failure to establish its detergent brand 'Spel' on the market. Where Unilever spent almost £1.5 million on advertising its 'Persil' brand alone, most of it on television, the CWS promotional budget for 'Spel' never exceeded £300,000 in any one year. Again, the autonomy of the local co-operative societies was seen as the main barrier to the implementation of a concentrated national promotion campaign for 'Spel'.[35]

The advertising wars of the 1950s also exposed major gaps within the movement as regards the organisational capabilities required for the running of large-scale promotional campaigns. The 760 or so independent societies that had emerged by the mid-1960s continued to enjoy growing membership numbers. Yet, their independence did not facilitate a level of co-ordinated market and consumer research which allowed for example Unilever to successfully position its products. By 1960, the CWS produced more than 100 brands which all needed careful marketing stewardship in order to occupy meaningful positions in the minds of consumers. However, at no point in the post-war period was there such a stewardship, and Carr-Saunders's pre-war criticism of a lack of a holistic co-operative marketing policy conducted in a 'specialised and scientific manner' simply returned some 30 years later in a damning report written under the auspices of the CWS's Chief Executive Philip Thomas.[36] Thomas had been the first 'outsider' CEO appointed at the CWS in January 1967. He instigated a radical and wide-ranging modernisation programme ('Operation Facelift') which mainly focused on the marketing and distribution side of the CWS. Thomas's report in 1967 led to the adoption of a new 'Co-op' symbol and the unified Co-op brand, which replaced the dozens of disparate 'Wheatsheaf' and 'CWS' brand names that were in use until then. Thomas also ordered a £1.3 million promotional campaign which included the standardisation of shop-fronts, product designs and pricing. The untimely death of the 43-year-old Thomas in a plane crash in spring 1968 prevented the CWS from implementing important parts of these measures.[37]

In addition, the post-war period saw the return of the original hostility against brands and marketing within the co-operative movement. This hostility needs to be understood as part of a wider left-wing criticism of affluence and acquisitiveness.[38] Adding to this sense of social alienation was the fact that the Co-op's essentially working-class-based idea of consumers' protection from adulterated and overprized foodstuffs became replaced by an essentially middle-class-based idea of consumer interest, which tended to stress better choice and protection through independent information, competitive product testing and standardised labelling.[39] This 'new consumerism' meant that the Webbian vision of co-operation as a socialist community of producers and consumers found itself even more under threat.[40] Sidney Pollard summarised these multiple challenges when he warned the movement in 1964 that

> [the] local societies, as retailing organisations, have to stand up in bitter com-
> petitive battle to opponents who are all organised for rapid and ruthless deci-
> sion-making, while they themselves are subject to the most direct democratic
> control with all its delays and frustrations – a form of democracy, moreover,
> which permits narrow sectional and local interests to defeat measures for the
> common benefit of the whole Movement.[41]

By the late 1960s, a lot of commentators agreed that the heydays of the Co-op stores were over. In that decade alone, the Co-op's share of the retail trade fell by 25 per cent.[42] What had been the strength of the movement, namely the autonomy of its local retail co-operative societies, became a major burden. While the movement's top management favoured stronger centralisation and a merger of wholesale and retail societies, many members on the ground feared this could negatively impact on the democratic nature of the co-operative system. This struggle between forces favouring centralisation and those in favour of decentralisation created immense barriers to the modernisation especially of the retail side of the movement. It also created opportunity costs which the highly centralised competitors such as British Home Stores, Boots or Sainsbury's did not have to face.

The biggest challenge to the marketing and advertising of the co-operative movement came from the growing realisation that by the end of the 1950s, the United Kingdom was not any longer an undifferentiated mass market of consumers shopping for staple foods such as eggs, bacon, butter and tea. In contrast, marketers realised that this 'mass' now consisted of diverse segments. The knowledge about an increasingly segmented consumer market spilled over into popular culture and language, with people talking about the 'Pepsi Generation' or the 'teenage consumer'.[43] These different market segments made it ever more necessary to keep up with differentiated tastes and rapidly changing consumer demand for fashion goods in particular. Here, the co-operative movement began to lose out long before the rejection of the Gaitskell Commission Report in 1958 and the abolition of Retail Price Maintenance in 1964.[44]

While the CWS advertisements between 1900 and the 1930s were at the vanguard of their time as regards design and the use of photographs and colour, post-war CWS advertisements at times unnecessarily supported a negative image about the Co-op as a daft, grey and boring organisation for daft, grey and boring people. When the magazine *Picture Post* celebrated the coronation of Elizabeth II in its June issue in 1953, it carried numerous stylish, colourful and attractive advertisements by producers of cars, butter and cigarettes which all had a coronation theme. The CWS, too, placed an advertisement celebrating the accession of the young Queen. It was, however, a black-and-white advertisement and lacked any consumer appeal (Figure 12.9). Instead of tomorrow, the advertisement mainly talked about yesterday

Figure 12.9 CWS advertisement 1953

and stressed the pride of the co-operative movement in being Britain's largest business.

A 'new civilisation' that nobody noticed

The history of the relationship between the co-operative movement and modern advertising reflects and complicates a number of historical narratives. Some of these narratives for example see co-operation as a form of 'moral economy' and as such essentially incompatible with the means and aims of modern marketing. Inevitably, these narratives also paint a historical picture of modern marketing and advertising as driven only by private capitalist brands and following a path of 'Americanisation'. This picture is as incomplete as it is insincere, since the vital contribution of the co-operative movement has effectively been taken out of British marketing and advertising history. The case presented above also complicates wider narratives of Britain's political-economic history, which see the consumer as dangling passively between two active forces: the state and the market. Yet, organised consumerism in the form of retail co-operation was a proactive force in the shaping of Britain as a modern consumer society.[45] The ultimate decline of the co-operative movement, however, also seems to support those historians who have argued that the twentieth century saw the marginalisation of civil society owing to the rising power of corporate interests in the market and a state actually favouring these interests over those of citizens' and consumers' self-organisation.

I argue that the central place of the co-operative movement within the modernisation of British advertising, marketing and retailing stemmed from exactly those factors which some commentators have identified as the reasons for the movement's competitive disadvantage – i.e. its ethical stance and its care for excluded sections of society. Co-operative values always placed much emphasis on knowing and trusting the sources of product supply, on using consumer power against unfair trade conditions and unethical economic practices, on reducing advertising that targets groups of vulnerable consumers, on issues of sustainability and on responsible retailing. Surprisingly, the concept of maintaining wider social welfare before short-term profit interests is at the heart of today's marketing theories. Marketing textbooks used at European business schools know this principle as the 'Societal Marketing Concept', and European consumers have discovered their preference for ethically sourced foodstuffs, furniture and clothing coming from fair-trade producer communities around the world.[46] High-street retailers like Marks & Spencer, Waitrose, John Lewis and even ASDA pride themselves for their attractiveness to the ethical consumer.[47] The Co-op stores were part of this change from the very beginning of the 'ethical hype', but their shyness at using large-scale advertising and PR campaigns made sure that no one noticed, and that the likes of Marks & Spencer and Waitrose reaped most of the benefit coming from the rise of ethical consumerism.

The track record of the Co-op brand in pushing fair-trade products, responsible retailing and advertising self-regulation on the agenda of British marketing culture is outstanding. In January 2000, the first bananas carrying the 'Fairtrade' mark were launched in more than 1,000 Co-op stores, a move which forced Tesco and Sainsbury's to follow suit. In March 2000, the Co-op launched Britain's first supermarket own-label fair-trade mark product, a milk-chocolate bar. The Co-op was the first supermarket to launch an own-label fairly traded wine with the Co-op Chilean Carmenere in 2001. In 2002, the Co-op became 'Multiple Retailer of the Year' at the Retail Industry Awards, partly due to its commitment to fair trade. In September 2002, the first supermarket own-label instant coffee granules carrying the 'Fairtrade' mark were launched by Co-op. In November 2002, the Co-op switched all of its own-brand chocolate to 'Fairtrade'. In December the same year, the world's first 'Fairtrade' pineapples went on sale in Co-op stores. Since 2000, the Co-op has started a number of initiatives on reducing the amount of product lines with high sugar, salt and fat content carried in stores ('Responsible Retailing'). It has forced the marketing industry into reviewing its policies on advertising these products to children.[48] This list is incomplete, of course, and only serves to show again that the co-operative movement played an enormously important role in modernising retailing and marketing in Britain from a non-capitalist vantage point. Without the Co-op stores leading the way in the early 2000s, it is questionable whether their competitors would have realised that it is possible to be profitable *and* ethically sound in today's marketing environment. What the Co-operative Union said of its stores in 1924 could not be truer today: 'The co-operative store is in reality the outpost of a new civilisation.'[49] It is therefore time that historians, and perhaps co-operators themselves, noticed.

Notes

1   *Co-operative News* (11 December 1880), p. 809.
2   Peter Gurney, *Co-operative Culture and the Politics of Consumption in England, 1870–1930* (Manchester: Manchester University Press: 1996), pp. 195–8; Peter Gurney, 'Heads, hands and the co-operative utopia: an essay in historiography', *North West Labour History* 19 (1994/95), pp. 3–23; Arnold Bonner, *British Co-operation: The History, Principle, and Organisation of the British Co-operative Movement* (Manchester: Co-operative Union, 1970), pp. 307, 474–6.
3   The Co-operative Union also issued advertisements calling on consumers to buy only Co-op goods that bore a trade-union label, which ensured products were not manufactured under 'sweated' conditions. Margaret Llewelyn Davies, *The*

Women's Co-operative Guild, 1883–1904 (Kirkby: Women's Co-operative Guild, 1904), pp. 122–4.

4 For the product-oriented approach to advertising and a model of the historical development of advertising communication, see William Leiss et al., *Social Communication in Advertising: Consumption in the Market Place* (London: Routledge, 2005), pp. 153–5.

5 John O'Shaughnessy and Nicholas O'Shaughnessy, *Persuasion in Advertising* (London: Routledge, 2004), pp. 80–3.

6 Percy Redfern, *The Story of the C.W.S. The Jubilee History of the Co-operative Wholesale Society Limited, 1863–1913* (London: Co-operative Wholesale Society, 1913), pp. 219–21; Percy Redfern, *The New History of the C.W.S.* (London: Dent, 1938), pp. 452–60; Sidney Webb and Beatrice Webb, *The Consumer's Co-operative Movement* (London: Longman's, 1921), pp. 87–9, 114–15, 143; *Report of the 35th Annual Co-operative Congress* (Manchester, 1903), pp. 345–7; *Report of the 38th Annual Co-operative Congress* (Manchester, 1906), pp. 101–3; *Report of the 40th Annual Co-operative Congress* (Manchester, 1908), p. 75.

7 Alan Burton, *The People's Cinema: Film and the Co-operative Movement* (London: National Film Theatre, 1994), pp. 10–39; Alan Burton, 'The people's cinemas: the picture houses of the co-operative movement', *North West Labour History* 19 (1994/95), pp. 31–47; Alan Burton, *The British Consumer Co-operative Movement and Film, 1890s–1960s* (Manchester: Manchester University Press, 2005), pp. 80–146.

8 'Britain's first advertising films were shown in 1899: CWS first in the field', *Advertiser's Weekly* (13 February 1936), p. 234.

9 *Co-operative News* (15 December 1900), p. 1440; (21 December 1901), p. 1544; (8 March 1902), 279.

10 Fred Hall and William Watkins, *Co-operation* (Manchester: Co-operative Union, 1937), pp. 331–2; *Report of the Proceedings of the Twelfth International Co-operative Congress* (London, 1927), pp. 253–7.

11 'The Magic Basket film', *Co-operative News* (28 January 1928), p. 11; 'The hand of power: The Magic Basket', *The Wheatsheaf* (February 1928), pp. 23–4; 'Scenes from the screen: a pictorial supplement from the CWS films', *The Wheatsheaf* [Pictorial Supplement] (February 1930), pp. i–iv.

12 *Co-operative News* (27 December 1930), p. 4; 'CWS at Olympia', *Co-operative News* (29 March 1930), p. 1.

13 James Haslam, 'How the co-operative movement uses the films', *Advertiser's Weekly* (May 30 1930), p. 276; James Haslam, 'Why the C.W.S uses films', *Advertiser's Weekly* (January 12 1933), p. 51.

14 James Cheyne, *Co-operative Advertising* (Glasgow 1903), p. 11.

15 Charles Rockley, *The Necessity for Advertising the Co-operative Movement, and How to Do it!* (London, 1913), pp. 8–12.

16 'Our publicity policy: are co-operators missing their opportunities?', *Manchester & Salford Monthly Herald*, 36:430 (September 1924), pp. 161f. and Smethurst's letter to the editor 'Advertise', *Co-operative News* (September 13 1924), p. 10.

17 David Rhydderch, 'Advertising and the co-operative movement', *The Co-operative Official* 8:79 (October 1926), p. 328.

18 Alanson Sessions, 'Advertising: the curse of the consumer', *The Co-operative Official* 1:7 (May 1920), pp. 155f.

19 A.J. Jones, 'Co-operative societies and advertising' (Paper read at the Annual Meeting of the National Co-operative Managers' Association, 24 May 1915), p. 1 (Copy at the National Co-operative Archive, Manchester).

20 George Colpus, 'Should we advertise?', *Co-operative News* (September 14 1907), p. 1136.

21 Redfern, *New History*, pp. 429–31; 'CWS publicity department staff shuffle', *Advertiser's Weekly* (September 28 1933), p. 471.

22 A. Barrett, *An Advertising Policy for the Co-operative Movement* (Manchester: Co-operative Union, 1926), pp. 19–23.

23 F.C. Crowther, *The Co-operative Movement and Advertising* (Manchester: Co-operative Union, 1927), pp. 4–6; *Co-operative Publicity in Britain: A Souvenir Booklet Prepared for the International Co-operative Exhibition* (Manchester: Co-operative Union, 1927), pp. 9–12.

24 *Second Annual National Co-operative Propaganda Campaign* (Manchester 1927), p. 14.

25 Alexander Carr-Saunders, P. Sargant Florence and Robert Peers, *Consumers' Co-operation in Great Britain: an Examination of the British Co-operative Movement* (London: Allen & Unwin, 1938).

26 Scottish Co-operative Wholesale Society, Minutes 1928, see Meetings 20 January, 27 January, 17 February, 8 June, 2 November 1928 (Mitchell Library, Archives of the Scottish Co-operative Wholesale Society, CWS 1/1/263).

27 George Griffiths, *Co-operative Propaganda: a Handbook for Propagandists and Canvassers* (Manchester: Co-operative Union, 1926), pp. 29ff.; pp. 77ff.

28 E. Topham, *Co-operative Publicity and Advertising* (Manchester: Co-operative Union, 1937), p. 9.

29 Ibid., pp. 12–16; quote on p. 16.

30 Copy at the National Co-operative Archive, Manchester.

31 For the early history of market research in the UK, see Paul Redmayne and Hugh Weeks, *Market Research* (London: Butterworth, 1931); Ian Blythe, *The Making of an Industry: The Market Research Society, 1946–1986* (London: Market Research Society, 2005); John Downham, *British Market Research Bureau: The First Sixty Years, 1933–1993* (London: BMRB, 1993).

32 'Attracting Brains', *Co-operative News* (29 September 1945), p. 8; F. Lambert, 'Techniques for competitive trading', *Markets and People* (May 1951), pp. 12–14; CWS Publicity Department (ed.), *A Consumer's Democracy* (Manchester: Co-operative Union, 1951), pp. 136–41.

33 'The small food shop is on its way out in the United States', *Co-operative News* (June 30 1951), p. 13. For the rise of self-service co-operative supermarkets, see John Benson, *The Rise of Consumer Society in Britain, 1880–1980* (London: Longman, 1994), pp. 59–71; Martin J. Purvis, 'Co-operative retailing in Britain', in John Benson and Gareth Shaw (eds), *The Evolution of Retail Systems, ca. 1800–1914* (Leicester: Leicester University Press, 1992), pp. 107–34; Martin Purvis, 'Co-operative department stores in interwar Britain'; and Gareth Shaw and

Andrew Alexander, 'The Co-ops as retail innovators', papers given at the 2006 Annual Conference of the Centre for the History of Retailing and Distribution (CHORD), Wolverhampton University, September 21 2006; Gareth Shaw, Louise Curth and Andrew Alexander, 'Selling self-service and the supermarket: the Americanisation of food retailing in Britain, 1945–1960', *Business History* 46:4 (2004), pp. 568–80; Gareth Shaw, 'Transferring a retail innovation: the early stages of supermarket development in post-war Britain', *Economic History Yearbook* 2 (2005), pp. 57–70.

34 See *Co-operative News* (January 26 1952), p. 4; (December 27 1952), p. 2; Bob Millar, 'Ethics and economics of advertising', *Co-operative News* (June 20 1953), p. 3; and the excellent study by Peter Gurney, 'The battle of the consumer in post-war Britain', *Journal of Modern History* 77:4 (December 2005), pp. 956–87.

35 Ralph Harris and Arthur Seldon, *Advertising in Action* (London: Hutchinson, 1962), pp. 151–3, 331; 'Much interest in "Spel" film', *Co-operative News* (9 January 1954), p. 6.

36 For the pre-war criticism see Carr-Saunders et al., *Consumers' Co-operation*; 'Co-operatives: propaganda for ideas before goods. Lack of scientific advertising and salesmanship alleged', *Advertising World* (March 1938), pp. 35, 76.

37 See Thomas appearing in the 15-minute propaganda movie 'The NEW Co-op' (1967) explaining the changes to the Co-op brand (copy at British Film Institute Archive); 'Co-op's new selling image', *The Times* (December 14 1967), p. 23.

38 Lawrence Black, *The Political Culture of the Left in Affluent Britain, 1951–1964* (Basingstoke: Palgrave, 2003), pp. 114–15; Sidney Pollard, *Co-operatives at the Cross-roads* (London: Fabian Society, 1965) pp. 13–14; Alan Sinfield, *Literature, Politics and Culture in Postwar Britain* (Oxford: Blackwell, 1989), pp. 41–59, 105–15.

39 Pollard, *Co-operatives*, p. 22; Elaine Burton, *The Battle of the Consumer* (London: Labour Party, 1955), pp. 19–23; Matthew Hilton, *Consumerism in Twentieth-century Britain: the Search for a Historical Movement* (Cambridge: Cambridge University Press, 2003), pp. 167–93.

40 Webb and Webb, *Consumers' Co-operative Movement*.

41 Pollard, *Co-operatives*, p. 1.

42 'Trying to become more co-operative', *The Times* (May 28 1969), p. 23.

43 Richard Tedlow, *New and Improved: the Story of Mass Marketing in America* (New York: Heinemann, 1990), pp. 4–12; Mark Abrams, *The Teenage Consumer* (London: London Press Exchange, 1959). The co-operative journal *Home Magazine*, for example, published a 'Teenage Number' in July 1961.

44 Hugh Gaitskell, *Co-operative Independent Commission Report* (Manchester: Co-operative Press, 1958).

45 Hilton, *Consumerism*; Frank Trentmann, 'Beyond consumerism: new historical perspectives on consumption', *Journal of Contemporary History* 39:3 (2004), pp. 373–401; Frédéric Lebaron, 'The state and the market: the rise of the economic rationale', *Contemporary European History* 9 (2000), pp. 463–73.

46 Philip Kotler et al., *Principles of Marketing* (Harlow: Pearson-Prentice Hall,

2005), pp. 17–20; Andrew Crane and Dirk Matten, *Business Ethics* (Oxford: Oxford University Press, 2007), pp. 313–51.

47 *Guardian G2* (1 February 2007), pp. 19f.

48 Co-operative Wholesale Society (ed.), *Blackmail: the Ethics of Modern Food Production and Advertising* (Manchester: Co-operative Union, July 2000).

49 Quoted in Burton, *British Consumer Co-operative Movement and Film*, p. vi.

13

'Co-operation: the hope of the consumer'? The co-operative movement and consumer protection, 1914–60

Nicole Robertson

The co-operative movement is the largest consumer wholesale/retailing organisation in the world. It self-consciously represents consumer interests, especially those of the working classes. The development of consumer protection groups has been a feature of twentieth-century Western society, and the work of Ralph Nader and the Consumers' Advisory Council are well documented. Yet the co-operative movement's efforts to promote the interests of consumers, whether co-operative members or not, have largely gone unreported and unrecognised by historians.

The co-operative movement's organisers, its members and at least some of its working-class customers very much saw defending consumer interests as a distinctive role of the co-operative movement. In the nineteenth century, the movement was founded to provide wholesome, unadulterated food for its customer-members. Protecting the consumer in this way remained a central concern during the first half of the twentieth century. Its literature, both national and local, was very explicit on its self-perception as an organisation that used the power of association to satisfy and protect rather than exploit the needs of consumers. This can be seen in work published during the early part of the century, for example Emerson R. Harris, *Co-operation: the hope of the consumer*,[1] as well as literature published in the 1960s, for example J.M. Wood, *Protecting the Consumer*.[2]

This chapter examines the movement's work to promote and safeguard the interests of consumers during the period 1914–60, in both war and peace. It incorporates a discussion of campaigns and examples at a local level, drawing on the experiences of individual societies.[3] Initially, consideration is given to the co-operative method of organising trade and the way in which this was said to empower the consumer. Unlike advisory organisations designed to promote consumer interests, the co-operative movement operated in the trading sphere and was thus able to implement the actions and policies it was promoting. This chapter, therefore, will discuss the pragmatic measures introduced by the co-operative retail and wholesaling societies, as well as the work of the Co-operative Party. The movement also worked in association with other bodies designed to protect the interests of consumers, and this aspect of the movement's work is also discussed.

The principles of the co-operative movement and the consumer

The co-operative movement was based on the notion that all consumers had a common interest in, and a need for, food, clothing, houses and all the things which go to make a home, and that these things should be adequately provided. The concept central to the consumers' co-operative movement, which made this organisation different from other types of businesses, was that, by association, consumers could generate economic power.[4] Through the concept of 'economic democracy', the co-operative movement placed 'into the hands of the people the *ownership* of their own food, clothing, houses and other commodities necessary to life'.[5] The movement was established to promote the interests of consumers, each of whom could purchase his or her own share in its business activities.

The structure and business ethos of the organisation was designed specifically to benefit the consumer. A unique feature of the co-operative movement is its federal structure. Individual co-operative societies composed of individual members represented the first stage of co-operative association. These primary associations, which were established to satisfy the common needs of their individual members, could form higher associations between themselves, and by so doing were able to meet their common needs.[6] The significance and purpose of this federal structure was 'to place at the disposal of its smallest component units all the benefits normally conferred by large-scale financial, administrative and technical concentration'.[7] Thus individual households formed the membership of each retail co-operative society. These societies in turn were incorporated into a national and international organisation. It was argued that the co-operative method of organising trade empowered the consumer because 'co-operation locates the origin and the exercise of power at the very origin of needs; man then remains his own master, and the organisation is his servant'.[8]

Inter-co-operative relations (i.e. those between producer societies or agricultural co-operative societies) and distributive co-operative organisations had economic advantages. Direct contact between these organisations was said to eliminate superfluous expenditure as it formed an 'uninterrupted and complete chain of provisions which extended from the place of production to the household of the consumer'.[9] By adopting the principle of self-supply, the co-operative movement was said to be able to 'by-pass the middle man, [and] go direct to the source of supply'.[10] Bridging the gap between the producer and the consumer in this way enabled the co-operative movement to offer financial benefits to the customer-member. These wholesaling and productive activities of the co-operative movement enabled consumers to control the production and distribution of a wide variety of goods and services.[11] Most notably, it enabled co-operative retail societies to acquire produce at less than market prices. The advantages to the consumer were demonstrated, for example, during the First World War. With the onset of the war, some private flour millers ended all contracts. The Co-operative Wholesale Society (CWS), however, honoured all its contracts. What is more, it sold a little over one million sacks of flour during the first six months at less than market prices (either ignoring small market advances or selling at a reduced rate).[12]

Protecting the consumer in the 'competitive arena'

Involvement in the wholesale and productive business, as well as in the distributive trade, not only secured economic advantages for the consumer by eliminating superfluous expenditure and honouring existing contracts during times of crisis, but was also said to be an advantage with regards to 'genuineness and hygiene in the trade of foodstuffs'.[13] For newly formed retail societies in the nineteenth century, the CWS was of great importance. As one pioneer co-operator stated, 'we never knew the bottom price. We would buy "best" and the trader would send "twixt and tween". We were always paying for firsts and getting seconds'.[14] The CWS was said to put an end to these worries as 'it gave an honest deal to its members and, as CWS operations extended more deeply into the produce markets, it gave knowledgeable and informed guidance on buying.'[15]

The role of the co-operative movement in providing consumers with pure food remained of central concern to co-operative organisations in the twentieth century, just as it had been during the earlier period. Protecting the consumer from being exploited by other business enterprises was a message that was made explicitly clear in co-operative sources. The commitment to selling only goods that were pure and of a high quality was visually portrayed in cartoon drawings in the *Co-operative News*. One such image depicted a 'wise consumer' witnessing the adulteration of food by those who wanted to make as much profit as possible. This was accompanied by the caption, 'By co-operation only can the people be assured of getting pure and wholesome food'.[16] The purity and quality of co-operative products was also emphasised to the consumer in the advertisements produced by individual retail societies.[17] Literature distributed to the members of individual societies also included articles which explicitly stated how the rights of consumers were defended by their co-operative society, as it protected members against fraud and adulteration in the sale and distribution of commodities.[18]

As J.M. Wood emphasised, unlike many other consumer organisations whose main function was advisory, the co-operative movement was in a position to enforce the policies it was supporting. Wood argued that

> a Co-operative Society exists to protect and promote the interests of its members, and so far as the greater part of the British Movement is concerned, those members are consumers . . . [A]fter more than a century it remains the greatest consumers' organisation, and indeed the only one that is *actively engaged in the competitive arena*.[19]

The pragmatic measures introduced by the co-operative movement to promote and safeguard consumers can be clearly seen during periods of war. During the First World War, there is evidence to suggest that within some localities, the co-operative movement was identified by consumers as a key organisation defending their interests. Julia Bush's work on East London highlights how the practical measures taken by co-operative societies (for example, refusing to raise prices on its own foodstuffs already in stock) received much public support.[20]

Although the government controlled the distribution to wholesalers and retailers of a large number of the principal food commodities, co-operative retail societies were critical of the fact that the Government did not regulate the supply of all staple foodstuffs to the public. Concerned about inequitable food supply, and the absence of a comprehensive Government rationing scheme, many retail societies devised their own rationing system to ensure supplies were shared out fairly and equally. Such schemes were implemented some months before any Government-organised scheme came into operation.[21]

During this national crisis, the co-operative movement was also concerned with stabilising the price of essential commodities, and campaigned against deliberate profiteering on foodstuffs during the war. The Co-op claimed that only in its stores was it possible 'to buy food and other necessaries at the bare cost of production and distribution'.[22] To a certain extent, the consumer was able to avoid monopolist prices by purchasing through a co-operative store, for 'even where the advertised prices obtaining in the general market [were] charged the purchaser [received] a varying rebate in the form of dividend'.[23]

Likewise during the Second World War, retail societies continued to give the dividend on purchases, and advertised this as an advantage to consumers who traded with the Co-op during wartime as it was not available elsewhere.[24] During the Second World War, a quarter of the total civilian population received their main food commodities from co-operative sources. In terms of consumer protection the role played by the co-operative movement during this period extended beyond providing the consumer with a good deal on foodstuffs. As the pamphlet entitled *Battle for Output: A Consumers' View* emphasised, the co-operative movement was not just a business, but a movement which realised its social obligations.[25] The author, Bert Oram (the Co-operative Party Research Officer, who later became a Labour MP 1971/4 and was appointed to the House of Lords), drew attention to the fact that the co-operative societies were the vanguard of those urging early and widespread rationing of all scarce foods. A rationing scheme was considered an important element in protecting the consumer, and criticism was made against those who opposed such schemes; for example,

> attacks on controls, rationing and subsidies are easily made by those whose irresponsibility is matched by their lack of genuine concern for the working-class standard of life. Inasmuch as controls and rationing are the consequences of shortages, they are a matter of regret for all; they were preferable, however, to the alternative method of restricting consumption by means of price increase such as we saw in the period of the first world war.[26]

Work to defend and promote the interests of consumers during wartime was also carried out within the localities. Individual retail societies protested strongly against food profiteering and kept consumers updated on rationing developments. Individual societies kept members informed of the movement's work to bring about an improvement in the allocation of foodstuffs, and sent resolutions to various bodies appealing for the revision of certain rationing schemes. The Kettering Society, for example, was one of the many societies that sent resolutions to the Co-operative Milk Trade Association supporting its actions to devise a better milk allocation system.[27] Matters such as the shortage of certain food supplies were discussed at members' meetings, and the work of national figures, like A.V. Alexander, was discussed.[28]

The price charged for goods, especially foodstuffs, was of foremost importance to the consumer. During normal trading conditions, co-operative retail societies did not seek to sell goods at a considerably lower price than that of other shopkeepers in the local area. The original rules of the Rochdale Pioneers specifically stated that goods would be sold at prevailing local prices.[29] The incentive behind establishing co-operative retail societies was not to undercut other businesses. Rather it was intended that co-operative retail societies would differ from other stores, not in the price of goods, but in what the consumer received for this price. Consumers would pay prevailing local prices for goods, but they could be assured that the goods they purchased were pure, unadulterated and of a high quality. Customer-members also received the 'dividend' (a share of profits distributed to members in proportion to goods purchased), a policy unique to co-operative societies.

What becomes clear is that co-operative retail societies were not only concerned with promoting and defending the interests of a certain group of consumers. Often representing the consumer in this way was not dependent upon whether they were members or not: sources published by the co-operative movement were keen to emphasise that the way in which the movement controlled prices in the interest of their members also had a restraining effect on the prices of goods sold by other shopkeepers in the area. This market effect thus helped the general public, notwithstanding other shopkeepers. The co-operative movement was criticised, however, for failing to protect or promote the interests of the poorest members of the community. In 1921, an article published in *The New Dawn* (the newspaper of the National Union of Distributive and Allied Workers) strongly criticised the co-operative move-ment for having 'no concern for the bottom dog'. It argued that, especially during periods of economic hardship, the payment of the dividend enabled the multiple shop to cut prices and secure the trade of this poorer group of consumers. To this group of consumers, belonging to their local co-operative society did not serve their best interest because those 'whose earnings are precarious, and who, in consequence, must get the biggest immediate return for their money . . . cannot await the benefits of Co-operative dividend three months hence'.[30] It was suggested that the introduction of a non-dividend system of trading should be worked in some branches and departments. It was claimed that one society ran one of its grocery shops along this line, although such a method of trading was not prevalent, as the central ethos of co-operation revolved around the notion of sharing the 'profits' among members in the form of a dividend. It could also be argued, however, that the so-called 'bottom dogs' also needed to buy children's shoes or desired a day's holiday, and the dividend could prove a valuable contribution toward the costs of these items.

Within the movement itself, the relationship between the price of goods sold by the retail societies and the dividend was an area of some debate. Literature published by individual societies expressed concern that the movement was 'becoming more and more a dividend making concern'. Consequently, it was argued that 'a great many of the poorest are finding it very difficult to trade with the movement because of the high prices charged to maintain a big dividend'.[31] Beatrice Webb, in the pamphlet *The Discovery of the Consumer*, refuted the notion that dividends on purchases had been pro-vided in advance by the customers at unnecessarily high prices. She argued the retail prices charged by co-operative societies were very strictly control-led by those charged by the profit-making shopkeepers, in that they were competing for the same business. If co-operative societies sold their products above the current retail prices for equal quality, argued Webb, people would not shop at the 'co-op'.[32] To an extent this is certainly true, yet the records of individual societies did contain details of complaints by customers regard-ing the prices of goods sold by co-operative retail societies. Management boards dismissed some of these complaints as being factually wrong, while dismissing others because they were viewed as being of a general nature rather providing specific comparisons with goods sold by other local shopkeepers.[33]

Nonetheless, this indicates that there does appear to have been some dissatisfaction among customers.

By the 1950s, individual managers of local societies also expressed some concern to committee members that their pricing policy was not as competitive as the cut-price policies of their competitors.[34] It was argued that the majority of co-operative members were no longer interested in securing a high rate of dividend on purchases. In contrast to expectations in previous periods, during these 'easier times' the consumer sought moderate prices and quick service.[35] An article that appeared in the *Co-operative Review* went as far as to claim that one reason for a lack of progress of retail co-operative societies in dry goods was their failure to meet the price competition of more progressive private traders.[36] There were reports of instances where the 'recommended' retail prices suggested by the wholesale society were exceeded, and consequently the consumer failed to benefit.[37] Reports also exist of cases where societies had failed to pass on price reductions to the consumer due to a desire to secure a high dividend on purchases. These cases were condemned not only as being wrong in principle, but also for potentially losing trade to the private-trade multiples.[38]

During the 1950s, the market share of both the multiples and co-operative societies continued to increase, at the expense of the independent shopkeepers. It was not until the 1960s that the multiples continued to increase their share of total retail trade at the expense of both the independent shopkeepers *and* the co-operative societies.[39] The records of individual co-operative societies, however, reveal that in the age of affluence the co-operative societies were increasingly unable to compete effectively with their multiple counterparts.

The parliamentary work of the co-operative movement

In considering the extent to which, and ways in which, the co-operative movement promoted the interests of consumers, it is important to examine the work of the Co-operative Party and its role as a consumer pressure group. In 1917, the co-operative movement decided to seek direct representation in Parliament. This was significant considering the movement had initially been pledged to political neutrality. This decision was prompted by a number of factors. One of these was the notion that during the First World War the co-operative movement's ability to defend and promote consumers' interests was limited by the fact that it did not have a political presence.[40]

The work of the Co-operative Party as a consumer pressure group has often been overlooked. For example, R.T. McKenzie states that the 'work of the Co-operative Party cannot be dealt with in detail', and therefore only refers to it 'in its relations with the Labour Party'.[41] In his work on British pressure groups, J.D. Stewart emphasised the importance of the Co-operative MPs as representatives of a pressure group which scrutinise legislation, defend the rights of the consumer, and ensure that, whatever Government is in power, the voice of the organised consumers is heard.[42] However, he focuses upon the Co-operative Party's organisation and structure rather than on the effectiveness of its campaigns. Yet the Party's work to defend the interests of consumers, regardless of whether they were members of a co-operative society, deserves attention.

One important aspect of the Co-operative Party's work was to campaign to give statutory effects to practices in the interest of the consumer that were already in use by the Movement. For example, selling tea by its net weight was a long-standing practice in co-operative stores, and it was promoted as a benefit associated with buying CWS tea. In 1922, against a strong attempt by the trade to maintain the practice of gross-weight packing of tea, co-operative pressure ensured that the Sale of Tea Act was passed. This required all traders to pack tea by net weight, and thus 'the consumer has not, therefore, any longer to pay the price of tea for paper and lead foil, and is saving in that respect approximately £4,000,000 per annum'.[43]

The Co-operative Party also sought to complement the work carried out by the wider movement. For example, co-operative organisations paid particular attention to the quality and cleanliness of milk. The work of F.B. Smith,[44] Peter Atkins[45] and Jim Phillips and Michael French[46] emphasise the continuing dangers of milk during the inter-war period. Milk was recognised by the Local Government Board as the single most adulterated item of food or drink.[47] Individual co-operative societies made efforts to educate their members in the dangers of unclean milk, and arranged for experts to give talks on the process and advantages of pasteurisation.[48] The Co-operative Party formed an important component in this campaign for improvements in the hygiene and safety of milk. In 1923, for example, the Party was involved in the campaign to alter the pasteurisation regulations of milk, resulting in the Milk (special Designations) Orders. This Order modified the 1922 Milk and Dairies Amendment Act by placing the series of licensed designations (enabling producers to sell milk as 'Certified') on a permanent legislative footing, and was welcomed by health campaigners.[49]

Another important function of the Co-operative Party was to improve legislation that protected the vulnerability of consumers from business malpractice. In 1926, Co-operative MPs were instrumental in the introduction of the Sale of Food (Weights and Measures) Act, which replaced an earlier 1878 Act. This was of great importance in protecting the consumer. It compelled all traders to sell a number of pre-packed goods by quantity, and penalised those who sold food in short weights and measures.[50] During the debate to discuss this Bill in the House of Commons, Alfred Barnes (a Co-operative MP) proposed an Amendment which would place a limit on the weight of the paper used for articles that would be weighed for sale in the wrapper. A clause to this effect was incorporated into the 1926 Act, although it did not incorporate the exact weights that Barnes had specified.[51]

The relationship between pressure groups and political parties is particularly important when considering the case of the co-operative movement. Indeed, when discussing the effectiveness of the Co-operative Party as a consumer pressure group, it is necessary to consider how this role was affected by its relationship with the Labour Party.[52] Writing in 1925, Barnes stated that the Co-operative and the Labour parties are 'organically related' and 'complementary to one another'. He also emphasised that he did not find that 'the growth of the Labour Party has led to any reduction in the importance of the co-operative movement'.[53] However, this had not always been the case. In 1917, the co-operative movement withdrew its representatives from the War Emergency: Workers' National Committee (WNC).[54] It did so because there were those within the co-operative movement who felt that 'the two committees [i.e. the WNC and Co-op] were crossing each other's lines of their work',[55] and feared that the WNC was becoming 'too well recognized as Labour's voice on consumer issues'.[56] The effectiveness of the co-operative movement as a consumer pressure group in Parliament had, at times, been hindered by its relationship with the Labour Party. Indeed, Wyn Grant argued that overly close links between a pressure group and one political party would be counterproductive, as it would mean that the group would only be influential when that party was in power.[57] Such links seem to have affected the Co-operative Party's position. For example, A.V. Alexander (a prominent Co-op MP and a minister in Churchill's coalition government of 1940–45) campaigned to establish a Consumers' Council.[58] It was hoped that such a Council would enquire into the operations of trading associations alleged to be operating against the interests of the public, and form a valuable 'weapon in the hands of consumers'.[59] Although the 1930 Consumers' Bill passed its initial reading in the Commons, in 1931 when Labour suffered one of the most catastrophic defeats in its history the Co-operative Party's position in Parliament also suffered, and this bill disappeared. Matthew Hilton has also highlighted the problems that could arise when the championing of the consumer clashed with Labour's concern for the trade unionist.[60]

Despite this, however, it is also important to recognise that the Co-operative Party benefited from its association with the Labour Party. The co-operative movement needed a 'voice' in Parliament because neither the Liberals (who supported the private traders – often to the detriment of co-operative organisations) nor the Tories (who were allied with the shopkeepers) took notice of co-operative grievances and concerns. Thus although the Co-operative Party's association with the Labour Party made the Liberals and Tories more hostile to it, the relationship with the Labour Party ensured that issues raised by the co-operators were given a stronger voice. For example, during the 1924 Labour Ministry, co-operators were consulted on consumer issues and obtained direct representation on all important committees (such as the Royal Commission on Food Prices) to the extent that A.V. Alexander declared 'Co-operation has been recognised as it never was before'.[61] Furthermore, it was extremely unlikely that the Co-operative Party would have got anywhere had they run candidates against Labour.

Associations with other consumer organisations

In its efforts to promote and safeguard the interests of consumers, the co-operative movement worked alongside other agencies involved in consumer protection. Working in association with other organisations was a feature throughout the period 1914–60, most prominently during periods of war.

Co-operative representatives, for example, were present on the Consumers' Council. This Council, created in 1918 and consisting of men and women from working-class bodies and food producers' offices, acted as a consultative body to the Ministry of Food. A Co-operative Wholesale Society director, Sir Thomas Allen, became its deputy chairman. It was intended that this Council representing the organised working classes would 'see with an eye of the consumer whether the interests and rights of consumers are being properly watched or not'.[62] Although its actions were limited by the fact that it had no legal power to enforce measures in the consumers' interests, the Council's efforts to get subsidies and controls extended were credited with slowing down the price increases toward the end of the war.[63]

Representatives from individual co-operative societies were also represented on the local food-control committees. These were a feature of both World Wars and were established to supervise general consumer and trade interests in the event of war. Such representation was said to be 'official recognition of the capacity of the movement to serve the consumer'.[64]

Efforts to promote the interests of consumers did not only focus upon issues concerning foodstuffs. It was also extended to cover broader consumer issues. In December 1939, the *Co-operative News* reported on a new venture for the defence of civil rights and the provision of personal advice on wartime problems. This venture was lead by the Co-operative Party and the Guilds in collaboration with various 'citizen service' bodies. For example, within the Midlands, individual advisory committees were established at Nottingham, Leicester and Birmingham. These advised people on various issues: pension and allowance for dependants of men serving with the Forces; questions relating to the relief which the law permitted with regard to mortgage payments, hire-purchase agreements, rent restrictions and pensions; and compensation for civilians injured or killed during air raids or during war operations.[65]

The period after the Second World War saw an increase in the number of organisations that provided an advisory service for the consumer.[66] Providing consumers with information and advice on the products they had purchased (or were considering buying) had always been an important aspect of work carried out by the co-operative movement. The task of providing the consumer with information regarding the preparation and nutritional value of foodstuffs had been undertaken by co-operative organisations in many countries.[67]

The co-operative movement actively supported these organisations that emerged to protect consumers and offer them advice and guidance. In 1952, when the Government abandoned the Utility Schemes,[68] the British Standards Institution (BSI) developed the Kite-Mark Scheme in an effort to provide a standard mark of quality. The journal of the Co-operative Union (the *Co-operative Review*) declared that it was imperative that the co-operative movement associate itself with the consumer-information activities of the BSI, stating that the movement could not 'afford to neglect participation in this contemporary method of educating and informing the shopper'.[69] It fully supported the BSI's Kite-Mark scheme, and invited BSI lecturers to attend Co-operative Summer Schools.[70]

In 1955, the BSI founded the Advisory Council of Consumer Goods. Articles in co-operative publications urged all retail co-operative societies and auxiliary organisations to become interested in the activities of the BSI's Consumer Council.[71] In 1957, this Council established an associate membership scheme whereby members received the bulletin *Shopper's Guide* (a bulletin written without technical jargon, allowing members to make factual comparison of different brands). Representatives from the co-operative movement became involved with this publication.[72] In this way, the co-operative movement not only supported these organisations, but also was actively involved in their work designed to educate and inform consumers.

One of the most significant of these projects was *The Consumer and the Law*, written by Harvey Cole and Aubrey Diamond. This was the first-ever book that sought to explain to consumers their legal rights, and was sponsored and published by the Co-operative Union. Set out in a clear, straightforward manner, it sought to reveal rights which consumers might not have suspected they possessed.[73] Inspired by the notion that 'an informed consumer is important for raising the general standards of trade and commerce in the country', it provided information on topics including 'the shopper and the law', 'the householder and the law' and 'the family and the law'. It also gave advice on holidays, hire purchase and rental agreements.[74] Although out of print by 1962, *The Consumer and the Law* set an important precedent. It had highlighted the need for books of this kind and provided the impetus for the Consumers' Association's 1962 publication *The Law for Consumers*, which was the first in a long series of Consumer Publications.[75]

Complaints against co-operative societies

Although the co-operative movement claimed to speak for consumers and safeguard their rights, on occasions societies were found to be guilty of the very things they criticised other businesses for doing. The movement centred upon the commitment to sell only pure, unadulterated and high-quality goods. There is evidence, however, that consumers were not completely satisfied with the service they received from their local co-operative retail outlet. Such problems concerned the cleanliness of the shops, overcharging (with prosecutions taking place), and individual retail societies selling food which was of poor quality or contaminated.[76]

The records of individual co-operative societies reveal a number of problems concerning the products that they sold. A proportion of these were attributed to mistakes or lack of diligence by staff employed in the various retail outlets. During the 1920s, for example, the Kettering Society experienced problems with employees in its Bakery Department. Various complaints were made about this department: bread was sold in short weight and it was reportedly 'bad in colour and streaky'.[77] These problems were blamed on the staff working in the Bakery Department, and at numerous times throughout this period the board of directors told the Bakery Manager that changes in the staff would have to be made if these types of incident continued to occur.[78] Incompetence by employees when they handled or prepared foodstuffs (often leading to complaints by customers or prosecution) were treated as serious acts of misconduct. The board of directors of the Kettering Society suspended an employee for smoking while weighing up sugar.[79] A prominent example of a case of this nature and the impact it had on a co-operative society can be seen in 1914 in Nottingham. Members of the Nottingham Society were 'startled and shocked by the disclosure in the Summons Court regarding the condition of certain goods in [their] slaughter-house at Egerton Street'.[80] The Society reported that it was humiliated by this experience as it occurred while celebrating its jubilee. The Society had just held an exhibition, presented members with a souvenir emphasising a glowing future when 'there burst in upon [the society] a terrible revelation in regard to bad meat, and a heavy bulk of it'.[81] The Society acknowledged that this meat had been discovered by the butchery committee. It claimed, however, that this was ordered to be destroyed, but that this order was disobeyed by some of the staff. Consequently, the Society was fined. The incident received coverage in the local press and it was feared that this episode shook the confidence of the members in buying goods from the butchery department.[82]

Aside from the incompetence of certain employees, complaints regarding the standard of products sold by the retail societies were also attributed to the poor quality of products as received from the supplier. On occasions, the supplier of such products was actually the CWS.[83] There were incidents of poor-quality products (such as bread) made so because of old or broken machinery being used.[84] When problems did arise, individual retail societies were quick to defend their position. Shortcomings were often acknowledged, with measures taken to prevent the incident from recurring. In 1956, for example, a customer discovered a mouse in a bottle of milk sold by the Skegness Co-operative Society (which had been amalgamated with the Nottingham Society in 1927). The Society was prosecuted and the managing secretary acknowledged that there was no adequate means of safeguarding the Society or customer against foreign matter being in bottles at the time of sale, but a prototype electronic scanner was in the process of being erected.[85]

Those outside of the movement were also sceptical of the extent to which the co-operative movement was recognised as the prominent mouthpiece voicing consumers' concerns and protecting their interests. An enquiry by the Research Institute for Consumer Affairs (RICA) stated that when people speak of the rise of the militant consumer, rather than referring to the co-operative movement, 'it is reasonably safe to assume that, pressed for evidence, they would point to the growth of the Consumers' Association, to the publication of the Molony Report and the establishment of the Consumer council, and to the current claim of all the political parties to be the consumer's true friend'.[86]

Conclusion

The question of why the co-operative movement's contribution to consumer protection has not been more widely recognised in literature focusing on consumerism was raised in a pamphlet published by the Co-operative Union. It was suggested in this pamphlet that this was partly the fault of the movement itself because it had not been sufficiently concerned about its public image. The hostile attitude of the Press was also blamed, as it was felt that the Press tended 'to find news value only in those events that denigrate the Movement, while a section of it has for many years been actively hostile'.[87] It can also, perhaps, be attributed to the fact that the bodies upon which it worked were not given sufficient recognition. Notably, J.R. Clynes stated that the Consumers' Council (on which co-operative representatives played an important role) 'rendered such service to the country that it deserved more credit than it ever received'.[88]

Yet throughout the period examined in this chapter, the co-operative movement used a variety of methods to promote and protect the consumer. As a movement of and for consumers, its business ethos and federal structure was organised to empower them. In addition to the work carried out by retailing and wholesaling facets of the movement, the Co-operative Party undertook various campaigns to safeguard consumer interest.

Despite certain limitations in its work, the co-operative movement aired major consumer issues and, on occasions, pressed the Government to act. It campaigned to improve the quality and cleanliness of foodstuffs, such as milk, and promoted legislation designed to protect the consumer from business malpractice. During periods of war, the movement's achievements included promoting (and implementing) equitable rationing systems and protesting against food profiteering. The movement's activities during the period 1914–60 did not, however, solely focus on issues concerning foodstuffs. Various facets of the co-operative movement worked alongside other organisations to provide a range of services. These included providing advice on compensation entitlements for civilians injured during war operations, supporting the BSI's Kite-Mark scheme, and collaborating to publish the first book that explained to consumers their legal rights.

For historians exploring consumerism, the co-operative movement is of notable interest in that it occupied a unique position as an organisation which worked in an advisory capacity to safeguard consumer interests (whether co-operative members or not) and, as J.M. Wood highlighted, was also engaged in the competitive arena.[89] Thus the movement was (and still is) able to implement pragmatic measures to safeguard and assist the consumer. In this way, the scope of the movement's activities gave it the capacity to promote consumer interests in both the high street and the House of Commons.

Notes

The author wishes to acknowledge the Economic History Society, in conjunction with the Institute of Historical Research, for awarding the R.H. Tawney Fellowship, which funded the period of research during which this chapter was written.

1 Emerson P. Harris, *Co-operation: The Hope of the Consumer* (New York: Macmillan, 1919).

2 J.M. Wood, *Protecting the Consumer* (Manchester: Co-operative Party, 1963). J. M. Wood joined the Parliamentary Committee of the Co-operative Union in 1934. He became Secretary of this Committee in 1956. He wrote in many Co-operative journals on topics such as monopolies and restrictive practices, consumer protection, and the distributive trades.

3 Little has been published on the experiences of these societies. See Nicole Robertson, '"A good deal … and a good deal more": the impact of the co-operative movement on communities in the Midlands, 1914–60' (PhD dissertation, 2006).

4 British Federation of Co-operative Youth, *Talking to Some Purpose: Discussion Booklet Number 2* (London, c.1940), p. 6.

5 *Co-operative News* (1 January 1921), p. 2 (my italics).

6 International Labour Office (hereafter ILO), *Co-operative Organisations and Post-war Relief* (Montreal: ILO 1944), p. 6.

7 Ibid., pp. 88–9.

8 G. Fauquet, *Le Secteur coopératif: essai sur la place de l'homme dans les institutions coopératives et de celles-ci dans l'économie* (Brussels, 1942), cited in ILO, *Co-operative Organisations and Post-war Relief*, p. 10.

9 ILO, *The Co-operative Movement and Better Nutrition* (Geneva: ILO 1937), p. 11.

10 Sir William Richardson, *The CWS in War and Peace 1938–1976* (Manchester: Co-operative Wholesale Society, 1977), p. 46.

11 Harvey R. Cole and Aubrey L. Diamond, *The Consumer and the Law* (Loughborough: Co-operative Union, 1960), p. 123.

12 Percy Redfern, *Told in Brief: The History and Purpose of the CWS* (Manchester, c.1932), p. 26.

13 ILO, *Co-operative Movement and Better Nutrition*, p. 11.

14 Richardson, *The CWS in War and Peace*, p. 46.

15 Ibid.

16 *Co-operative News* (14 February 1914), p. 210.

17 For example, an advertisement for the Birmingham Co-operative Bakeries stated: 'we guarantee all bread manufactured by the society to be ABSOLUTELY PURE. All flour used is guaranteed PURE and UNADULTERATED, and free from all chemicals'. (Birmingham Co-operative Society (BCS) Half-yearly Report, October 1926. Birmingham Central Library, Co-operative Bibliographies.)

18 *Wheatsheaf* (Nottingham edn) (August 1926) (Nottinghamshire Archives, DD/GN), pp. i–ii.

19 Wood, *Protecting the Consumer*, p. 7 (my italics).

20 Julia Bush, *Behind The Lines: East London Labour 1914–1919* (London: Merlin 1984), pp. 42, 84.

21 T. Smith, *The Story of the Birmingham Co-operative Society* (Birmingham, 1951), p. 26; T. Smith, *History of Birmingham Co-operative Society, 1881–1931* (Birmingham, 1931), pp. 91–4; Leicester Co-operative Society (LCS) Board Minutes, 7 November 1917 (National Co-operative Archive).

22 Co-operative Wholesale Society, *People's Year Book* (Manchester: Co-operative Wholesale Society, 1916), p. 515.

23 Ibid., p. 517.

24 BCS Quarterly Report, 7 October 1939.

25 A.E. Oram, *Battle for Output: A Consumer's View* (London: Reynolds News, 1947), p. 21.

26 Ibid., p. 12.

27 Kettering Industrial Co-operative Society (KICS) Board Minutes, 3 December 1941 (National Co-operative Archive).

28 Leicester Members' Meeting Minutes, 13 November 1939 (National Co-operative Archive).

29 Jack Bailey, *The British Co-operative Movement*, rev. edn (London: Hutchinson, 1960), p. 20.

30 J.T. Cairns, 'Trade without dividend: a suggestion to the co-operative movement', *New Dawn* (12 November 1921), p. 8.

31 *Nottingham District Co-operative Record*, July 1915 (Nottinghamshire Archives, DD/GN), p. v.

32 Beatrice Webb, *The Discovery of the Consumer* (London: Ernest Benn, 1928), pp. 19–20.

33 KICS Board Minutes, 30 November 1927.

34 Ibid., 23 July 1958.

35 *Co-operative Review* (October 1957), p. 237.

36 Ibid.

37 Ibid.

38 *Co-operative Review* (January 1958), p. 8.

39 Data from Arnold Bonner, *British Co-operation*, rev. edn (Manchester: Co-operative Union, 1970), p. 245.

40 Other important factors which played a role in the decision to enter politics were the way the co-operative movement had been penalised by rationing in favour of private traders, the Excess Profits Tax, and the ratio of co-operative employees called for military service when compared with employees in the private sector. On these points, see S. Pollard, 'The foundation of the Co-operative Party', in A. Briggs and J. Saville (eds), *Essays in Labour History, 1886–1923* (London: Macmillan, 1971), and Tony Adams, 'The formation of the Co-operative Party re-considered', *International Review of Social History* 32 (1987).

41 R.T. McKenzie, *British Political Parties* (London, 1963), p. 529.

42 J.D. Stewart, *British Pressure Groups* (Oxford, 1958), p. 182.

43 A.V. Alexander, *The Business Value of Political Action to the Co-operative Movement* (Manchester: Co-operative Union, 1928), p. 7.

44 F.B. Smith, *The Retreat of Tuberculosis, 1850–1951* (London: Croom Helm, 1988).

45 P.J. Atkins, 'Sophistication detected: or, the adulteration of the milk supply, 1850–1914', *Social History* 16 (1991).

46 Jim Phillips and Michael French, 'State regulation and the hazards of milk, 1900–1930', *The Society for the Social History of Medicine* 12:3 (1999).

47 Ibid., pp. 371–2.

48 KICS Board Minutes, 10 March and 3 April 1926.

49 Jim Phillips and Michael French, *Cheated not Poisoned? Food Regulation in the United Kingdom, 1875–1938* (Manchester: Manchester University Press, 2000), p. 172.

50 Alexander, *The Business Value of Political Action*, p. 5; R. Cranston, *Consumers and the Law* (London, 1978), p. 263.

51 The Parliamentary Debates, 200 *H C Deb.* 5s, c.2142–2148, 9 December 1926.

52 An electoral agreement (the Cheltenham Agreement) formalising the relationship between the two parties was first passed in 1927. This made provisions for a joint sub-committee to be established, and ruled that local Co-operative parties were to be eligible for affiliation to the divisional Labour parties, but stated explicitly that this was not intended to interfere with pre-existing arrangements within individual localities. (*Co-operative Congress Report*, 1927, pp. 95–6.)

53 Alfred Barnes, *Co-operative Aims in Politics* (Manchester: Co-operative Union,1925), p. 5.

54 The WNC was formed in 1914 in order to 'mitigate the destitution which will inevitably overtake our working people whilst the state of war lasts' (Arthur Henderson, cited in Chris Wrigley, *Arthur Henderson* (Cardiff: GPC Books, 1990), p. 78. The WNC comprised members of the Co-operative Union, Co-operative Wholesale Society, Labour Party, Parliamentary Committee of the Trade Union Congress, the General Federation of Trade Unions, and a host of other labour and socialist bodies. It was involved in a variety of issues relating to consumption.

55 *Co-operative News* (29 September, 1917), quoted in J.M. Winter, *Socialism and the Challenge of War: Ideas and Politics in Britain, 1912–18* (London: Routledge & Kegan Paul, 1974), p. 205.

56 In Winter, *Socialism and the Challenge of War*, pp. 205–6. In addition, co-operators criticised the WNC because it was self-appointed and not responsible to any electorate, and also because members of the committee were known to be pacifists.

57 Wyn Grant, *Pressure Groups, Politics and Democracy in Britain* (London: Harvester Wheatsheaf, 1995), p. 83.

58 T. Carbery, *Consumers in Politics* (Manchester: Manchester University Press, 1969), p. 189.

59 F. Hayward, *The Co-operative Boycott and its Political Implications* (Manchester: Co-operative Union, 1930), p. 13.

60 Matthew Hilton, *Consumerism in 20th-century Britain* (Cambridge: Cambridge University Press, 2003), p. 87.

61 Alexander, *The Business Value of Political Action*, p. 8.

62 W.H. Beveridge, *British Food Control* (*Economic and Social History of the World War*, British series) (Oxford: Milford, 1928), p. 71.

63 L.M. Barnett, *British Food Policy During the First World War* (London: Allen & Unwin, 1985), p. 154.

64 *Wheatsheaf* (Birmingham edn) (October 1939), p. vii (Birmingham Central Library, Co-operative Bibliographies). It can be argued that involving the co-operative movement, as a body representing consumer interest, in this way was sensible and essential policy during these periods. In this respect, comparisons can be drawn with the Government's recognition of trade-union influence during wartime. See for example Chris Wrigley, *British Trade Unions Since 1933* (Cambridge: Cambridge University Press, 2002), pp. 14–15.

65 *Co-operative News* (30 December 1939), p. 4.

66 See for example Hilton, *Consumerism in 20th-Century Britain*, p. 167.

67 For example, the Co-operative Union of Britain organised demonstrations and displays which sought to educate the public in the preparation of food products. The Swedish Co-operative Wholesale Society, one of the most advanced in developing a consumer-advisory service, published a whole series of books focusing on food, health and the nourishment needs of the human body. These publications were used as the basis of discussion groups. By 1937, 300 of these study groups

(with about 3,600 members) existed. (ILO, *The Co-operative Movement and Better Nutrition*, pp. 60–4.)

68 Utility Schemes were introduced during the Second World War on a variety of goods, including clothing and furniture, to ensure a supply of goods of the best quality were available at controlled prices.

69 *Co-operative Review* (January 1958), p. 17.

70 Ibid., p. 18.

71 Ibid., pp. 17–18.

72 In 1962, the Consumer Advisory Trust was established to publish *Shopper's Guide*. The editorial Advisory Council of this publication consisted of members drawn from the Consumer Advisory Council and included a CWS director – Mrs Eva Dodds (Wood, *Protecting the Consumer*, pp. 21–2).

73 Cole and Diamond, *The Consumer and the Law.*

74 Ibid., Authors' Foreword.

75 Eirlys Roberts, *Which? Consumers' Association 1957–1982* (London: Consumers' Association, 1982), pp. 84–7.

76 Some examples: it was reported that some of the shops owned by certain co-operative societies were in a 'very dirty condition … [and] stock in an awful state' (KICS Board Minutes, 10 September 1930). The Price Regulation Committee prosecuted other societies for overcharging (Nottingham Co-operative Society [NCS] Directors' Meeting, 7 June 1943). Loaves of bread sold by some co-operative societies were 'quite black and dirty'(KICS Board Minutes, 18 May 1931). Some milk was deemed 'unfit for human consumption' (NCS Directors' Meeting, 22 January 1954).

77 KICS Board Minutes, 6 July 1927 and 21 September 1928.

78 Ibid., 14 June 1922, 5 March 1923 and 6 July 1927.

79 Ibid., 17 June 1925.

80 *Nottingham District Co-operative Record* (January 1914), p. 2.

81 Ibid.

82 Ibid.

83 KICS Board Minutes, 11 July 1931.

84 Ibid., 21 October 1925.

85 NCS Directors' Meeting, 24 February 1956.

86 Research Institute for Consumer Affairs, *British Co-operatives: A Consumers' Movement?* (1964), p. 3.

87 Wood, *Protecting the Consumer*, p. 8.

88 J.R. Clynes, *Memoirs, 1869–1924* (London: Hutchinson, 1937), p. 237.

89 Wood, *Protecting the Consumer*, p. 7.

14

'Cost of a cup of tea': Fair Trade and the British co-operative movement, *c*.1960–2000

Matthew Anderson

In recent years, the Co-op has claimed to be the 'Champion of Fairtrade' in the mainstream.[1] The figures go some way to supporting this claim: in 2004, the Co-operative Group accounted for one third of all Fairtrade sales through grocery outlets and sold more Fairtrade coffee than any other supermarket retailer in the UK.[2] Total Fairtrade sales at the Co-op have risen from £100,000 in 1998 to £21 million in 2004. In recent years, this has contributed to returning £1.25 million annually in Fairtrade premiums to the producers. The Co-operative Group has also been clear about its future commitment: 'Our goal is that, eventually all Co-op products from developing countries will be fairly traded and that fair trade ingredients are used more and more in our standard products.'[3] From the early 1990s, Fairtrade has been central to identifying the 'Co-operative difference' and promoting a market position separate from that of the supermarkets.

The influence of the co-operative model on the Fair Trade movement can be seen in a number of ways.[4] Most clearly this is through the Co-operative Group's retail support for the Fairtrade label, but also in the Fairtrade Foundation's preference for supporting producer co-operatives. At the more abstract level the apparent ethical and moral links between the original principles of the Rochdale Pioneers and Fair Trade values have been emphasised. Given that the co-operative movement is now at the heart of the Fair Trade movement and has been identified by some commentators as 'naturally sympathetic', it would seem reasonable to suppose that the co-operative movement would have been a pioneer of alternative – or Fair – Trade when it developed in the 1960s and 1970s.[5] But, as this chapter will argue, the idea of the co-operative movement as 'naturally sympathetic' to Fair Trade overlooks the internal contradictions and debates within the movement that took place during the 1960s and 1970s.

In exploring the co-operative movement's response to issues of Fair Trade, this chapter will address themes that have clear parallels with the discussions found in earlier chapters. For example, the question of a minimum wage for female employees and the debates over Co-op employee workplace representation both demonstrated the tensions that existed over labour relations in British co-operative retail societies. By incorporating an international dimension into this field of research, this chapter will widen this discussion to take account of the Co-op's treatment of workers employed in the global South. The tensions between the national leadership and the ancillaries of the movement, particularly the Women's Co-operative Guild (WCG), is also a theme developed in several chapters. The WCG's advocacy of absolute pacifism and its support for a minimum wage for women both showed the ability of the WCG to draw on the ideals of the movement in order to promote a 'radical' or 'socially progressive' campaign. This chapter will highlight the role of the WCG in the consumer campaigns of the 1960s and 1970s and show that the WCG was at the forefront in campaigning for fair tea prices and in calling for a boycott of the apartheid regime in South Africa.

This chapter will demonstrate that, from the outset, tensions existed within the co-operative movement over how it should conduct its international trading. From the late nineteenth century, the consumer co-operative members of the International Co-operative Alliance (ICA), such as the British movement, expressed a desire to realise the ideals of international co-operation. But when it came to a choice between demonstrating solidarity with producer co-operatives from the South and maintaining the consumer dividend, invariably it was the producer co-operatives that lost out. In practice, the British movement was operating its trading ventures along the same lines as any other major commercial importer. It was not until the early 1990s that the Co-op management recognised that Fair Trade was a viable proposition and would allow them to conduct international trade in a manner that was compatible with the ideals of the movement.

What is required, in light of the emergence of the 'ethical consumer' and the Fair Trade movement, is a reassessment of the co-operative movement's values and principles in its international development and trading programme from the 1960s. The Co-op's capacity to support ethical consumerism during this period was limited by four factors: first, its focus on competition from the supermarkets; secondly, its complex structure with numerous independent individual societies; thirdly, its failure to recognise the significance of the consumer-producer dynamics within the movement; and finally, its lack of communication with its membership. From the early 1980s it was the Co-op's ability to positively address these same factors that allowed it to realise the potential of Fair Trade in defining the 'Co-operative difference'. Ultimately it was the realisation of the presence of 'ethical consumers' within the Co-op membership and in society as a whole that demonstrated a potential market for ethical banking and retailing, and persuaded the Co-op management that it could be commercially viable.

The 'Co-operative commonwealth' revisited

There has yet to be a historically focused academic assessment of the co-operative movement's approach to ethical – or fair – trade in the twentieth century. In part this is maybe a reflection of the limited academic attention to the Co-op more generally. Some within the movement have argued that this was a reflection of the declining dynamism of the Co-op. Rita Rhodes, Education Officer of the ICA, stated that 'in terms of [both] trading practices and democratic appeal, the movement is not seen to be as radical as once it was. Increasing academic indifference reflects this.'[6] Studying the Co-op in relation to the emerging Fair Trade movement in the 1960s and 1970s provides an opportunity to explore further an under-researched aspect of the Co-op, the significance of co-operative values and principles in its international trade relations with developing countries.

By the early twentieth century the established opinion among scholars on the left was that the co-operative movement had arrived at a position quite different from the idea with which it had begun. Fabians such as Sidney and Beatrice Webb argued that the movement had grown on the basis of self-interest and had idealism grafted on to it.[7] This opinion was reinforced by G.D.H. Cole who believed that the Co-op was, 'a satisfactory grocer's shop and a good savings-bank, but no self-respecting revolutionary would believe that it would ever make a breach in the walls of capitalism'.[8] Sidney Pollard developed this critique when he identified two distinct phases of co-operation.[9] The first, 1820 to 1846, was dominated by Robert Owen and his commitment to establishing the Co-operative Commonwealth that would form the basis of a 'new moral world'. The second phase was initiated by the Rochdale Pioneers and was characterised by a drift from the ideal of the Co-operative Commonwealth and a preoccupation with shopkeeping and the principle of the consumer dividend.

In recent years, the Fabian interpretation of the Co-op has been increasingly challenged. Stephen Yeo has argued that the fact the world did not go the co-operators' way was not academic justification to dismiss their commitment to a 'world-making' project.[10] Yeo showed that as late as 1893 co-operators such as Holyoake were committed to the practical realisation of the Co-operative Commonwealth. And Peter Gurney has argued that co-operative ideals were not squeezed out of the movement as a result of the success of the dividend. He maintained that, 'late nineteenth century co-operation produced its own brand of utopianism based on the principle of the dividend'.[11]

These debates over the ideals of the Co-op have so far focused almost exclusively on the domestic situation of the movement and have neglected a thorough assessment of the international 'world-making' potential of the original ideals. The concept of international co-operation between co-operatives is essential to linkages between the co-operative movement and Fair Trade, and is an area that remains under-researched. Other work has looked at how different strands of co-operation (consumer, worker, credit) have developed throughout the world to form an international movement; but they have not engaged with this debate over the extent of idealism within the movement.[12] W.P. Watkins looks more thoroughly at the international links between co-operatives, but has not extended this assessment past the 1970s.[13] Contemporary literature on political consumption has to some extent recognised a role for the co-operative movement in the emergence of the 'ethical consumer' in the late twentieth century, but that role is yet to be fully defined and these linkages require further research, particularly in relation to the Fair Trade movement in the 1960s and 1970s.[14]

CWS plantations and the campaign for fair tea prices

Tea was virtually the only product imported by the Co-op from developing countries where the Co-operative Wholesale Society (CWS) maintained direct control over the entire supply chain. In 1902, The Co-operative Tea Society (CTS) purchased estates in Sri Lanka, and tea soon became a major import. By 1972 the CTS was making a profit on all its operations of £1.1 million and paid a dividend to the Co-operative Wholesale Society and the Scottish CWS of £650,000. This gave tea a particular significance within the movement and made it the clearest example of the Co-op's international trading principles in practice. So, when the conditions on CWS tea plantations in Sri Lanka and India were openly criticised in the media, in the mid-1970s, many ordinary co-operative members were shocked by the allegations and some were jolted from their complacency into action. Tea became the focus of consumer campaigns – led by non-governmental organisations (NGOs) and joined by many Co-op members – for fair wages for the tea pickers. The politicisation of tea led to a wider questioning of international trade relations, which in turn dealt with many of the issues relevant to the emerging Fair Trade ideology.

The CWS tea plantations were forced onto the agenda by the public outcry in response to a 1973 World in Action television programme 'Cost of a cup of tea'.[15] The programme was an exposé of the intolerable working conditions on the tea plantations in Sri Lanka, owned by many of the household brands including the CWS. The programme stated that, in 1973, tea was about the only item on the shopping list that was still as cheap as in 1970; World in Action set out to 'investigate what it costs others to keep the cost of a packet of tea unchanged'.[16] The Mahouvilla estate, owned by the Co-operative Tea

Society, was identified by World in Action as having housing that was 'marginally worse' than the Brooke Bond estates, and similarly poor wages and living conditions that resulted in malnutrition, hook worm, vitamin deficiency and high child mortality.[17]

It seems that the international trading obligations and responsibilities of the co-operative movement had for some time been misunderstood, or idealised, by the membership. One Society member stated that he had, 'always understood that it was in order to ensure that our tea workers were properly paid that the co-ops were obliged to purchase from their own tea plantations'.[18] This, unfortunately, was never the case; primarily, any obligation to buy from CWS plantations came from the commercial motivation to maintain a consistent supply of cheap tea. Co-op members believed that the CWS should operate its trading practices in keeping with Co-op values and principles and not be dragged down by competition with big business. One member responded, 'These are slave conditions which we expect from capitalism and private enterprise, but to see them linked with the co-operative movement is something which just cannot be left without violent protest.'[19] The scandal of the Sri Lankan tea plantations led to the realisation among some members of the true priorities of the CWS and they responded, 'we don't want cheap "99" tea at that price!'[20]

During the 1970s the conditions on tea plantations proved a significant convergence issue for many consumer activists and NGOs (and ten years later coffee would play a similar role). Several reports were published exposing the poor working conditions on tea plantations, particularly in Sri Lanka.[21] All the big household names came in for serious criticism including the Co-operative Wholesale Society. The activist group, War on Want, called for British manufactures, retailers and consumers to 'accept responsibility for the conditions which estate workers have to endure'.[22] In 1977 an Oxfam report, 'A bitter taste to your cuppa', was featured in the ICA journal, *Consumer Affairs Bulletin*.[23] The report described how thousands of housewives all over Britain had signed a petition declaring their willingness to pay 'a fair price for tea in order to help poor people in tea growing countries'.[24] Oxfam further stated that public opinion in Britain was sending a message to the government that 'the days of cheap tea at the expense of the poor should be over for good'.[25]

The Co-operative seemed a natural ally for NGOs and consumer activists looking to restructure traditional supply chains, since the 'Co-operative difference' meant that it controlled its own brand products from raw material to shelf. The Co-op claimed that 'no other retailer had the same degree of control over the source of its product'.[26] But despite calls for fairer prices for tea, the Co-op, in order to compete with the supermarkets, continued a policy of price cutting. In November 1977 they cut tea prices by 6p per lb, and again in March

1978.[27] At the time their advertisements ran with the slogan 'The Co-op: the place to go for a bargain beverage'.[28] As the World Development Movement (WDM) found, the Co-op's price cutting policy was not easy to align with an ethical trading programme. They commented that '[it] has not proved any easier to change the policies of the Co-operative Wholesale Society'.[29] After numerous requests from the WDM and pressure from Co-operative members, the CWS finally met with the WDM in November 1980. But the meeting achieved little. The WDM were left with the impression that by this stage the Co-op simply wanted to 'get rid of its estates and responsibilities as soon as possible'.[30]

As shown above, the politicisation of tea played an import role in the wider understanding of ethical trade issues among members of the co-operative movement. In the objections they raised about conditions on CWS tea plantations, Co-op members frequently focused on the trading values and principles as established by nineteenth-century co-operators such as Robert Owen and the Rochdale Pioneers, and emphasised how the movement had departed from these ideals. But did conditions on CWS tea plantations in the 1970s genuinely demonstrate a break from established co-operative values and principles? Or was this critique the result of an idealised notion of the origins of the co-operative movement's international-trading philosophy? What is needed in order to explore these questions further is a reassessment of the nineteenth-century international trade relations between the British Co-op and co-operatives in developing countries.

International co-operative trade and the ICA, 1895–1970

The British co-operative movement was a founding member of the International Co-operative Alliance (ICA) in 1895 and, for the first 50 years, was the dominant force in the organisation. By 1907, more than half the affiliated societies were British, and they provided more than three-fifths of the ICA's income.[31] The ICA was established as a networking organisation designed to promote co-operation between co-operatives. Membership of the ICA brought the British consumer co-operative into direct contact with other forms of co-operative, including worker and agricultural co-operatives. It was this networking between consumer and producer co-operatives that had the potential to become a model for Fair Trade, had it been given the opportunity to further develop in the 1960s and 1970s.

At the Paris Congress in 1896 it was agreed by ICA delegates that consumer societies should give preference to industrial and agricultural co-ops when purchasing supplies, provided that quality and prices were the same.[32] The International Co-operative Wholesale Society (ICWS), established in 1924, marked the first serious attempt by the ICA to facilitate international trade in the twentieth century (previous attempts had been hampered by political and economic instability, the result of war and economic depression).[33] But the ICWS was not itself an active trading organisation – it remained solely as a facility for information exchange. Albin Johansson, an ICA delegate, was frustrated at the ICA's inability to challenge capitalism's dominance in international economics. He believed that the ICA had to 'take a step forward from the passing of resolutions to true international constructive work'.[34]

Margaret Digby, Co-op historian and secretary of the Plunkett Foundation, shared Johansson's belief in the potential of international co-operative trade.[35] In 1928, Digby argued for the 'complete interlocking of the trading interests of producers and consumers,' whereby, 'no consumers' society would purchase goods "outside the movement" while there existed a co-operative marketing society capable of supplying them'.[36] Digby found that, for the most part, a full assessment of the origins of goods imported by the British co-operative movement was restricted by the inadequacy of the record-keeping. She concluded that, with the exception of tea, it was 'impossible to say how many may be of co-operative origin; others must be from private sources'.[37] The very fact that the CWS were not distinguishing between imports from private suppliers and those from co-operatives demonstrates in itself that, in practice, the philosophy of international co-operative collaboration was not prioritised by CWS buyers. This discrepancy between ideology and practice in the CWS' international trade relations was evidence of the failure to overcome the consumer-producer dichotomy within the movement. Digby argued that nationally the issue of relations between the two sides was being tentatively worked out, but she acknowledged that, 'internationally, it has got little further than the stage of discussion'.[38]

In 1938 the ICA established the International Co-operative Trading Agency (ICTA). This was a direct trading body, but it only traded for two years before the onset of war forced it to suspend business. After the war the ICTA merged with the ICWS and resumed business in 1946. But in May 1952 the ICTA ceased trading; it had not been receiving sufficient support from its members to cover its expenses.[39] Despite these setbacks the idea of international co-operative trade remained appealing to many within the ICA and at the 1954 ICA Congress in Paris one of the major themes was: 'International Co-operative Trade, the Possibilities of Practical Collaboration between National Organisations and its Development by the Alliance.'[40] In 1966, at the Vienna Conference, the ICA renewed its commitment to international co-operative collaboration.[41] But these statements of intent meant nothing without the support of the ICA's membership, particularly the British movement.[42] In practice, by the end of the 1960s international co-op to co-op trade between ICA members was still very limited.

Multinational co-operatives: an alternative to multinational corporations

The Co-op's trading policy during the 1970s was characterised by attempts to increase efficiency and drive down costs in response to increased competition from supermarkets and multinational corporations (MNCs). But a different response to the MNCs was also considered by the co-operative movement that could have led to greater co-op to co-op trade and a genuine structure for 'alternative trade'. Johann Brazda has argued that rapidly integrating markets and fierce retail competition might have provoked, 'a new era of international co-operation, with the most active movements engaging in rescue operations for their most endangered counterparts'.[43] For instance, at the ICA's 1972 congress in Warsaw, in response to the growing economic power of MNCs, delegates resolved to 'explore the concept of expanding multinational co-operatives to handle commodities in international trade so as to more closely link producer and consumer co-operatives'.[44]

Some within the British movement believed that the co-operatives' own-label goods could provide the model for restructuring the movement.[45] For instance, in 1972, the CWS own-label food range extended to more than 665 varieties and had sales of £106 million at wholesale prices. Thirty-five of these varieties were made in CWS factories.[46] Charles Job, Director of Royal Arsenal Co-operative Society, argued that the Co-op was undermining itself by stocking numerous goods made by multinationals when CWS alternatives were available. He pointed out that the Co-op's own-label instant coffee, which was a best-seller, was actually made by Tenco, a subsidiary of the US giant Coca-Cola. He voiced his concern at Congress that this was not 'a policy which indicates a move towards a Co-operative Commonwealth'.[47] His solution was for the CWS to manufacture more or buy more from co-operatively owned enterprises abroad.

It seemed that despite initial optimism the practical realities of international co-operative trade were not to be easily realised. One of the main reasons identified by the ICA for the slow growth of inter-co-operative trade was, 'the lack of interest shown by co-operatives in developed countries in finding co-operative trade partners from developing countries'.[48] Some international co-op to co-op trade took place, but consumer societies, such as the British Co-op, tended to deal solely with producer co-operatives from developed countries. For instance, there were long-standing trade links between the CWS and the New Zealand Dairy Co-operatives.[49] One exception was the Japanese consumer co-operative which 'voluntarily sought out trade partners from within the co-operative movement' and 'helped developing co-operatives to improve their international trading capabilities'.[50] For instance, in 1962 UNICOOP Japan agreed on a trading arrangement to import Thai maize from the Thailand COPRODUCT (Bangkok Co-operative Farm Product Marketing Society).

The general lack of interest shown by consumer co-ops, including the British Co-op, to deal with co-operatives from developing countries restricted the co-operative movement's ability to form an alternative international trading structure that could challenge the growing influence of MNCs. But despite the lack of commitment shown by the Co-op in supporting developing co-operatives, this did not prevent it becoming a focal point for NGOs and consumer campaigns throughout the 1960s and 1970s.

New internationalism: the 1960s and 1970s

Throughout the 1960s and 1970s, the co-operative ideology and organisation gained many supporters and promoters among civil society, including anti-apartheid campaigners, development NGOs and alternative trading organisations. Each group saw in the values and principles of the co-operative movement an alternative vision of society. In turn they looked to the British co-operative movement, with its 13 million members, for direction and leadership. Many of these groups believed the Co-op would be 'naturally sympathetic' to their cause, but were ultimately to be left disappointed by the Co-op's limited commitment.[51] During this period the Co-op continued to operate much as a commercial business, and prioritised supplying consumers with cheap products over and above ethical trading concerns. The following section will explore why, despite real potential to unite these differing interests, the Co-op failed to show genuine leadership or commitment to these campaigns.

Boycott of South Africa

The calls for a boycott of South Africa were interesting because they allowed different consumer and NGO groups to converge on a single issue and advocate consumption as a political act. The Anti-Apartheid Movement (AAM), the main coordinator of British campaigns, identified the Co-op as potentially sympathetic to their call for sanctions against South Africa. But the Co-operative Union declined to be involved in the AAM's campaign, stating that 'they [did] not think that it [was] practicable or advisable to pursue a policy of boycott of South African goods'.[52] But this did not discourage AAM from trying to gain the support of local co-operative societies, and here they had more success – most notably with the London, Manchester and Surrey Societies. Some Co-op members championed in the Co-operative press the calls for a boycott, and appealed to the ideals of the movement to look beyond the profit motive. They argued that, 'The South African people naturally look to our movement as one that has greater ideals than merely seeking profit and supplying goods whatever the consequences for others less fortunate than ourselves.'[53]

In 1973 the Co-operative Bank's decision to offer its customers Barclaycard credit cards, rather than Access, made it the focus of consumer action. Barclays was one of the biggest banks in South Africa; officially its stance on apartheid was 'neutral', but, in practice, only one in 45 of its clerical bank staff in South Africa were black and it did nothing to oppose apartheid. Activist members of the Co-op stated that, 'Until the bank alters this dangerous decision, we must all refuse to take credit cards through the bank.'[54] This action demonstrated an innovative form of consumer boycott. The *Co-operative News* was also targeted for its continued promotion of South African goods. The CWS had argued that its role was simply to supply a range of goods and let consumers decide what to buy depending on their own criteria. But campaigners argued that adverts for goods such as Outspan Oranges were, 'aimed at creating a need'.[55] Those that wanted a complete boycott believed that an end to advertising was an important first step. They stated, 'To that end, we first . . . want to see an end to promotion of these goods.'[56]

The British co-operative movement, despite considerable pressure from the membership, maintained that, 'it is unfair to ask the movement to take the lead in this matter when many societies are facing trading difficulties'.[57] Ultimately securing a consistent supply of produce and maintaining market share was prioritised over the ethical concerns of trading with the South African apartheid regime. Consumer activism centred on calls for boycotts of South African products increased awareness among some Co-op members of the wider implications of their consumer choices. This same consumer activism would also prove central to demonstrating a demand for Fair Trade goods. This was particularly significant given that neither Fair Trade organisations nor the co-operative movement had either the marketing budgets or the inclination to employ the services of the so-called 'hidden persuaders'.[58] Growing awareness of Fair Trade instead relied on a diverse, if somewhat conservative, range of grass-roots campaign methods from leafleting and letter writing to petitions and public meetings.

Co-operative development and NGOs

Many of the NGOs that were active in campaigns for a boycott of South Africa during this period were shifting their focus from relief aid to long-term development. In an article on the *Role of Voluntary Aid Agencies*, Graham Alder assessed the quantity of funds going toward development projects compared to that for immediate disaster relief.[59] He reported that Christian Aid had increased development funds proportionately from 45.6 per cent in 1968/69 to 55.4 per cent in 1969/70. Cafod, Christian Aid and War on Want were also identified as having shifted attention and funding toward long-term projects.

This shift in thinking led many development NGOs to recognise the potential of supporting co-operative development in the global South.

Oxfam was one of the first NGOs to realise the development opportunities of the co-operative ideal and in 1966 they looked to the British co-operative movement to support a joint venture. The 'Help the Hungry to Help Each Other' campaign was launched on 4 March 1966, in Birmingham.[60] The object of the campaign was to raise money to establish a self-sufficient consumer co-operative in Bechuanaland (Botswana). The plight of Botswana had gained particular attention since it became known that 30,000 men chose to work in South Africa under the conditions of apartheid so that they could send their wages home to their impoverished families.[61] By 1966 Oxfam was already giving development assistance to forty co-operative projects in twenty countries.[62] Bernard Murphy, Liaison Officer for Co-operatives and Trade Unions, stated of the Oxfam programme in 1966 that '[we] do not say that we are the advance guard for co-operative development in the underdeveloped countries but we do say that we have sown the seeds for the nurturing of the co-operative philosophy'.[63] But Oxfam was clear that this was to be a Co-op-led initiative: they announced that, 'it is for the British co-operators to prove the relevance of the co-operative ideal 122 years after the Rochdale Society opened its doors in Toad Lane'.[64]

By 1970 the programme had achieved its main goals, but it had not run completely smoothly.[65] Twenty months after the launch of the campaign, the Co-operative was still short of the £30,000 they had promised Oxfam. Some within the movement, such as Tom Taylor, President of the Scottish CWS, believed that the Co-op's image had been severely tarnished by its half-hearted approach to the joint programme with Oxfam. Taylor stated that the 'co-operative movement should have some concern for our self-respect and the discharge of our moral responsibilities'.[66] It was proposed that individual co-operative societies could allocate a share number to Oxfam, a practical and innovative way to raise funds. It was also acknowledged that it could be valuable for the movement to 'identify itself more positively as an organisation with a social conscience'.[67] But the Co-op management did not share this view of the movement and rejected the plan for an Oxfam dividend. Furthermore, they questioned the feasibility of the whole programme at a time of 'almost unprecedented trading difficulty'.[68] Potentially this could have been a forerunner to the Fairtrade Social Premium, a dividend on purchase to support Oxfam development projects.

The Botswana campaign demonstrated two main features of the Co-op during this period that limited its ability to lead or even work with development NGOs effectively. First, the structure of the movement was such that it made it almost impossible to run a well co-ordinated national campaign. Bernard Murphy, Oxfam's Co-op and Trade Union Liaison Officer, commented that 'despite the fact that (numerically) the Co-operative Movement represents the largest pressure group in the country (13.5 million) it is probably the most difficult to work with'.[69] Secondly, the Co-op management did not seem to be able to give the same level of support to this type of campaign as did the general membership. The ancillaries of the movement, such as the Co-op Party, the Women's Co-operative Guild, the Education Department and the Woodcraft Folk, were all noted by Oxfam for their contributions. But Murphy stated that '[if] there has been cause for thought it has been that the response from Management Committees has, in the main, been very poor.'[70] The reason given for this was that many societies were 'fighting for survival', and managers were forced to concentrate their energies on 'keeping them afloat'.[71]

The Co-op's limited contribution explained: the 1960s and 1970s

Throughout the 1960s and 1970s the Co-op found its market position increasingly undermined by the big supermarkets. In 1961 the Co-op accounted for 10.4 per cent of the total retail turnover, but by 1980 this had fallen to 6.5 per cent.[72] But this increased retail competition did not necessarily lead the Co-op to become isolated from the rest of civil society. As argued above there were other paths that the Co-op could have taken, such as the exploration of 'multinational co-operatives'.[73] It was the assessment of the Co-op's management committees that was responsible for shaping the commercial trading policies of the movement. This resulted in a victory of the 'businessmen' over the 'ideologues'.[74] They believed that they had to compete on the same terms as supermarkets and focused their full attention on cutting the costs of products to the consumer. This commercial outlook prevented the Co-op from connecting with an ethical trading programme or a broader development agenda.

The organisational structure of the movement with individual Societies fiercely protective of their independence meant that it was hard to implement or even devise a national strategy. This proved a significant weakness when the Co-op was discussing possibilities of co-op to co-op trade. Hugh Todner, Chairman of the UK Co-operative Union, commented on the isolation that existed within the national movement, 'Our movement has 38 separate business plans, all with their own separate buying, marketing, administration and transport facilities . . . No two societies operate the same marketing strategy, and as a result we are not achieving the benefit of our size.'[75] This was not a sound basis on which to develop an international trading strategy. The structural organisation of the Co-op also proved a hindrance in its campaign with Oxfam to support co-operatives in Botswana. Bernard Murphy was clearly both surprised and frustrated that no one person in the movement could speak or act on its behalf and that all decisions were taken at management committee level. He remarked, rather disparagingly, that 'any suggestions made on behalf of the movement by the Union Executive can only be suggestions and are not binding on each Society'.[76]

The British Co-operative movement failed to recognise the significance and the extent of the consumer-producer dichotomy within international co-operation. This meant that it was not in a position to attempt to bring together consumer and producer interests. Despite laudable speeches about the merits of international co-operative collaboration and co-op to co-op trade, in practice, co-op to co-op trade remained barely significant. Evidence of the British co-operative movement developing international co-operative trade links is limited to a handful of cases, and none of these involves producer co-operatives in 'Third World' countries. In failing to understand the differing origins of the two sides of the movement (the consumer movement tracing its origins to the Rochdale Pioneers whereas the farming and thrift sectors traced their lineage to Raiffeisen) they were unable to overcome the basic dilemma of price.[77] Dr Saxena, former Director of the ICA, stated in 1996 that '[c]onsumer organisations are generally interested in the lowest prices, while farmers want the highest'.[78] But it seems that, for the most part, the British Co-op continued to conduct international trade at arm's length, and made no attempt to verify whether or not products had come from a co-operative supplier.

Most significantly, the Co-op management, in its failure to communicate with the membership, underestimated the importance individual members attached to the values and principles of the co-operative movement. The management committees believed that the predominantly working-class membership was solely concerned about value for money. This led the management to believe that there was no market for tea that returned a fair price to the producers, that a boycott of South African goods would result in members shopping elsewhere and that the dividend was too precious to give up for an Oxfam campaign. But for a significant number of Co-op members the co-operative values and principles had a growing relevance in the late twentieth century. A greater awareness of these ethically motivated consumers within the Co-op membership would become crucial in motivating the Co-op to reassess its trading priorities.

The 'Co-operative difference', an ethical approach: the 1980s and 1990s

By the early 1980s there was a growing recognition within the co-operative movement that a preoccupation with economic survival had led to neglect of its social roots.[79] Hedley Whitehead, President of the Co-operative Union, called for a 'radical re-thinking of the Movement's social purpose'.[80] He argued that otherwise the Co-op may 'succeed in maintaining a significant stake in UK retailing but on basically no different terms from any of our most prominent competitors'.[81]

An increased awareness within the movement and the general population of environmental issues such as global warming and acid rain proved a
turning point for the Co-op and led them to reposition themselves as 'green'
retailers.[82] They pioneered a number of initiatives such as converting all
aerosol products to CFC-free propellants, phasing out plastic egg boxes and
promoting the use of biodegradable carrier bags. Lloyd Wilkinson, Chief
Executive of the Co-operative Union, stated that 'the issues surrounding
green consumerism give the movement an unrivalled opportunity to show
what "the Co-op difference" really is'.[83] In 1985 the Co-operative Retail
Services adopted a statement of social goals that outlined its determination 'to
do everything in its power to protect the environment and ensure the efficient
use and protection of natural resources'.[84] The Co-op believed that the consumer could be a positive force for change and highlighted the political nature
of consumption. The CWS' *Co-op Action Guide for the Environment* reminded
consumers that 'every time you take your supermarket trolley for a spin you're
taking part in a referendum about the future of the planet'.[85]

For those outside the movement, the Co-op's complex structure continued to prove an obstacle when it came to assessing their green strategies.
For instance, *The Ethical Consumer* in its May/June 1989 edition confirmed
the Co-op as 'the nearest thing we would recommend as a best buy'.[86] But
this praise was somewhat undermined when they conceded that it was hard
to generalise about the Co-op policy or practice because it was 'made up of
about 100 independent Co-operative societies which collectively operate
1,475 supermarkets and 63 superstores'.[87] Peter Crouchman, Co-op Member
Relations Officer and a Friends of the Earth director, also recognised the
shortcomings of the movement's structure. He bemoaned the fact that 'no one
person can co-ordinate what we [the Co-op] do. This leads to missed opportunities when centrally created ideas are lost at the level that matters most –
locally'.[88] As a result the Co-op lost out to the big supermarkets which proved
much more effective at national marketing campaigns that highlighted their
commitment to environmental initiatives.

It was the Co-operative Bank that (re)introduced initiatives that incorporated not only environmental issues but wider social values into the business
practices of the movement. In May 1992 they became the first UK bank to
publish an 'Ethical Policy'. The Ethical Policy stated that 'given our origins as
part of the co-operative movement and its basic values, it is perhaps not surprising that we should be the first bank to respond to people's growing concerns
about the quality of life here and in the rest of the world'.[89] Arguably what was
more surprising, for many Co-op members, was that the Co-operative Bank
had not responded sooner and had through the 1960s and 1970s continued to
operate no differently from their competitors.[90] The Co-operative Bank management was finally convinced of the need to prioritise co-operative values

in its business mission after conducting market research that revealed 84 per cent of their members felt the bank should have a clear ethical policy.[91] The issues of greatest concern were human rights, armament exports and animal experiments, followed by the fur trade and tobacco manufacture.

In May 1992 the Co-op became the first major UK food retailer to stock Cafédirect coffee. Launched in 1992 as a joint initiative by Twin Trading, Traidcraft, Oxfam Trading and Equal Exchange, Cafédirect represented a reassessment in the message behind the sale of coffee toward 'people' and away from an 'origin/cause' profile.[92] It was far from an immediate success; by September 1995 Cafédirect only accounted for 1.8 per cent of CWS Retail's ground-coffee sales and only 0.1 per cent of the instant-coffee market.[93] But despite some doubts the CWS Retail, encouraged by the success of the Co-operative Bank, was convinced that as consumers became more aware of ethical and welfare issues there would be a future for products such as Cafédirect.[94] The Co-op was pioneering the mainstream retailing of fairtrade products. Its support for Cafédirect came two years before the launch of the Fairtrade Mark in the UK and, had the Co-op decided to drop Cafédirect after initial trials, this could have had serious implications for the mainstream viability not only of Cafédirect, but also of the Fairtrade Mark. With the introduction of Fairtrade products into all 1,450 grocery stores, in 1999 the Co-op became the largest stockist of Fairtrade products in Britain.[95] This hugely increased the availability of Fairtrade products and almost overnight propelled Fairtrade from 'the margins to the mainstream'.[96]

Conclusions

The ideology of an international co-operative movement had existed from the early nineteenth century. Robert Owen had declared his ambition for an 'Association of all Classes and all Nations', and in 1895 with the establishment of the ICA it appeared that Owen's vision had become a reality.[97] But early attempts at encouraging international co-op to co-op trade had soon ended in failure, and it was not until the 1960s that there was genuine renewed interest from within the movement and beyond. During this period, the co-operative movement, with the international network of the ICA, had enormous potential to develop an alternative trading policy between consumer societies in the 'developed' countries of Europe and producer co-operatives in 'developing' countries of Africa, Asia and Latin America. But the movement was not able to rationalise the dichotomy between consumer and producer in a way that could make this proposition work. Instead, the British co-operative movement limited its involvement in international co-op to co-op trade to developed countries such as New Zealand.

Despite the limitations of the trading policies adopted by the Co-op management during this period, what remains interesting was the commitment shown by many Co-op members to international co-op to co-op trade along ethical lines. When the Co-op's failings were highlighted by the national media or the Co-operative press there was a strong response from the membership. Here we see a contrast with the nineteenth century where, it has been argued, the leadership held on to co-operative values whereas the average member was more concerned about making ends meet.[98] It seems that in the mid- to late twentieth century, for some members at least, the co-operative values proved increasingly relevant, while for the management (particularly during the 1960s and 1970s) the prime concern was ensuring the survival of the retail store.

From the 1980s the Co-op began to adopt a more clearly ethical stance and connect more closely with civil society. As discussed above, there were a number of factors that led to this change in direction: first, there was an awareness among the Co-operative Union that, as a result of solely focusing on the economic retail competition, it had become distanced from its values and principles; secondly, although there was not a 'single Co-operative Society for the UK', the movement was becoming more streamlined; thirdly, and most significantly there was a genuine effort to understand the ethical opinions of the membership and the wider public. This demonstrated that there was a market for green and ethical products, and from the late 1990s Fairtrade became central to the Co-operative's positioning as a mainstream retailer with a social goal.

With the introduction of Cafédirect into its stores in 1992, the Co-op for the first time was supporting producer co-operatives in the global South including Mexico, Peru and Costa Rica. It is perhaps an indication of the true extent of the Co-op's preoccupation with economic survival during the 1960s and 1970s that Fair Trade (a model of trade that owed so much to the principles of co-operation) was ultimately pioneered by development organisations, Christian agencies and ATOs rather than the ICA. But through its support for the Fairtrade model the Co-op was able to overcome many of the consumer-producer dichotomies that had proved stumbling blocks in the past. And in situating Fairtrade at the heart of its ethical trading policy, the Co-op was able to reconnect the movement with its nineteenth-century ideals of a Co-operative Commonwealth engaged in a 'world-making project'.

Notes

1 'Fairtrade choc', *Co-operative News* (5 April 1994).
2 *Co-operative News* (16 October 2004).
3 'Fair trade: a cooperative revolution', *Cooperatives UK Magazine* (Issue 3, 2004).
4 Fairtrade refers specifically to products that carry the FAIRTRADE Mark. The

FAIRTRADE Mark is an EU-registered trademark. The Fairtrade Foundation (a registered charity) is the UK member of Fairtrade Labelling Organisations International (FLO), and responsible for licensing the FAIRTRADE Mark. Fair Trade or the Fair Trade movement, refers to the wider network of NGOs, religious agencies and campaign groups that developed the concept of alternative – or fair – trade in the 1960s and 1970s. These pioneering organisations continued to be the driving force behind mainstreaming Fair Trade and, in 1992, CAFOD, Christian Aid, New Consumer, Oxfam, Traidcraft and the World Development Movement became founding members of the Fair Trade Foundation. The internationally agreed definition of Fair Trade is: 'Fair Trade is a trading partnership, based on dialogue, transparency and respect, that seeks greater equity in international trade. It contributes to sustainable development by offering better trading conditions to, and securing the rights of, marginalized producers and workers – especially in the South. Fair Trade organisations (backed by consumers) are engaged actively in supporting producers, awareness raising, and in campaigning for changes in the rules and practice of conventional international trade.' This definition of Fair Trade has been agreed by an informal network of the four Fair Trade Organisations below, known by their initials as FINE: Fairtrade Labelling Organisations International (FLO), International Fair Trade Association (IFAT), Network of European World shops (NEWS!), European Fair Trade Association (EFTA).

5 A. Nicholls and C. Opal, *Fair Trade: Market-Driven Ethical Consumption* (London: Sage, 2005), p. 20.

6 'Where have all the academics gone?', *Co-operative News* (6 November 1990).

7 Sidney Webb and Beatrice Webb, *The Consumers' Co-operative Movement* (London: Longman, 1921).

8 *New Statesman* (15 January 1921).

9 S. Pollard, 'Nineteenth-century co-operation: from community building to shopkeeping', in A. Briggs and J. Saville (eds), *Essays in Labour History* (London: Macmillan, 1960).

10 S. Yeo (ed.), *New Views of Co-operation* (London: Routledge, 1988).

11 P. Gurney, *Co-operative Culture and the Politics of Consumption in England, 1870–1930* (Manchester: Manchester University Press, 1996).

12 J. Birchall, *The International Co-operative Movement* (Manchester: Manchester University Press, 1997).

13 W.P. Watkins, *The International Co-operative Alliance, 1895–1970* (London: ICA, 1970).

14 Nicholls and Opal, *Fair Trade*; M. Hilton, *Consumerism in 20th Century Britain* (Cambridge: Cambridge University Press, 2003); R. Harrison, T. Newholm and D. Shaw, *The Ethical Consumer* (London: Sage Publications, 2005).

15 World in Action: *Cost of a Cup of Tea* (Granada: 24 September 1973).

16 Ibid.

17 Ibid.

18 M. Gillard, 'Ceylon's starving tea girls', *Observer* (23 September 1973).

19 'Tea slaves', *Co-operative News* (12 October 1973).

20 'Sri Lanka horror', *Co-operative News* (5 October 1973).

21 War on Want, *The State of Tea* (London: 1974); Cambridge World Development Action Group, *Tea: The Colonial Legacy* (Cambridge: 1975); Oxfam, 'A bitter taste to your cuppa' in *Consumer Affairs Bulletin* (No. 7, 1977); World Development Movement, *The Tea Trade* (London: 1979). In 1976 the idea of an International Tea Agreement was supported by the fourth United Nations Conference on Trade and Development. Tea was included as one of the 18 commodities in its Integrated Commodities programme, which aimed at establishing a stable price on a range of products from developing countries.

22 War on Want, *The State of Tea*.

23 Oxfam, 'A bitter taste to your cuppa' in *Consumer Affairs Bulletin* (No. 7, 1977).

24 Ibid.

25 Ibid.

26 'Biggest ever share of the tea market', *Co-operative News* (16 November 1977).

27 'Tea prices are cut', *Co-operative News* (9 November 1977) and 'Co-op cuts tea price again', *Co-operative News* (8 March 1978).

28 *Co-operative News* (16 November 1977).

29 World Development Movement, *The Tea Trade*, 2nd edn (London: WDM, 1982 [1979]).

30 Ibid.

31 Birchall, *International Co-operative Movement*, p. 46.

32 Ibid., p. 44.

33 Watkins, *International Co-operative Alliance*, p. 143.

34 Ibid.

35 The Plunkett Foundation, established in 1919 by Horace Plunkett, works to support the development of rural co-operatives in the UK and worldwide.

36 M. Digby, 'Producers and consumers', *The Year Book of Agricultural Co-operation in the British Empire* (London: Plunkett Foundation, 1928).

37 Ibid.

38 Ibid.

39 Watkins, *International Co-operative Alliance*, p. 264.

40 Ibid.

41 ICA Conference, Vienna, 1966.

42 'Britain has by far the largest and most powerful co-operative movement in the capitalist world . . . There can be no effective international co-operative alternative to the Multi-national Corporations without the determined and whole-hearted support of the British movement,' in C. Job (Director of Royal Arsenal Co-operative Society), *Multi National Corporations, The Co-operative Alternative* (Warsaw, ICA Congress, October 1972).

43 J. Brazda and R. Schediwy (eds), *Consumer Co-operatives in a Changing World* (Geneva: ICA, 1989).

44 Ibid.

45 Job, *Multi National Corporations*.

46 Ibid.

47 Ibid.

48 M.V. Madane, 'International co-operative trade in Asia: retrospect and prospect',

The Year Book of Agricultural Co-operation (Oxford: ICA and The Plunkett Foundation, 1978).

49 Ibid.

50 Ibid.

51 Nicholls and Opal, *Fair Trade*, p. 20.

52 Bodleian Library, Oxford, MSS.AAM1, 'Letter to Mr Okunnu from J. Bailey Co-operative Union Secretary' (14 July 1959).

53 'Promotion of S. African goods should stop', *Co-operative News* (29 August 1975).

54 'Co-op Bank: supporters of apartheid?', *Co-operative News* (19 January 1973).

55 There are some parallels with V. Packard, *The Hidden Persuaders* (London: Longman, 1957).

56 *Co-operative News* (29 August 1975).

57 'S. African boycott move has mixed reception', *Co-operative News* (4 April 1964).

58 Packard, *The Hidden Persuaders*.

59 G. Alder, 'The role of voluntary aid agencies', *Co-operative Review* (18 March 1972).

60 B. Murphy, *Help the Hungry to Help Each Other* (Manchester: Co-operative Press, 1966).

61 K. Mayhew, *Catholic Herald* (5 August 1966).

62 Oxfam Archive, Bicester (hereafter OXFAM), R1492 27(3) 1, report by the Information Office, 'Oxfam aid to co-operative schemes' (March 1967).

63 Murphy, *Help the Hungry to Help Each Other*.

64 OXFAM, R1492 27(3) 1, report by the Information Office, *An Ideal Lives* (March 1967).

65 OXFAM, BOT 6 2011 vol. 1, report by M.R. Harris, Field Director Central and Southern Africa (2 July 1968).

66 '£21,000 cheque for Oxfam', *Co-operative News* (3 June 1967).

67 'Divided views on Oxfam divi' *Co-operative News* (5 August 1967).

68 *Co-operative News* (3 June 1967).

69 OXFAM, R1492 27 (3) 10, report by B. Murphy, 'Progress report of the Co-operative Project Appeal' (1967).

70 Murphy, *Help the Hungry to Help Each Other*.

71 Murphy, 'Progress report of the Co-operative Project Appeal'.

72 Brazda and Schediwy (eds), *Consumer Co-operatives in a Changing World*.

73 J. Craig, *Multinational Co-operatives: An alternative for World Development* (Saskatoon: Western Producer Prairie Books, 1976).

74 Brazda and Schediwy (eds), *Consumer Co-operatives in a Changing World*.

75 S.K. Saxena, *The World of Co-operative Enterprise* (Oxford: The Plunkett Foundation, 1996).

76 Ibid.

77 In 1864, Friedrich Wilhelm Raiffeisen set up the first thrift and loan Society in Heddesdorf, Germany. This is often credited as being one of the first rural co-operatives. Raiffeisen's *Credit Unions as a Remedy for the Poverty of Rural and*

Industrial Workers and Artisans, published in 1866, was considered by many as the manual for rural co-operative development.

78 Saxena, *World of Co-operative Enterprise*.

79 H.W. Whitehead, 'President's Address' (Co-operative Union Congress, 1981).

80 Ibid.

81 Ibid.

82 Two books particularly influential in promoting environmental awareness and green consumerism were R. Carson, *Silent Spring* (London: Hamish Hamilton, 1963) and J. Elkington and J. Hailes, *The Green Consumer Guide* (London: Gollancz, 1988).

83 'Green Issues: opportunity knocks for the Co-op', *Co-operative News* (16 January 1990).

84 'The Co-op movement and the environment', *Co-operative News* (22 January 1991).

85 *Co-op Action Guide for the Environment* (Manchester: Co-operative Press, 1989).

86 *Ethical Consumer Magazine* (ECRA Publishing Ltd, May/June 1989).

87 Ibid.

88 P. Crouchman, 'Exit the "green" consumer – enter "green" citizens', *Co-operative Retail Marketing and Management* (June 1990), pp. 4–6.

89 'Bank woos the carers', *Co-operative News* (5 May 1992).

90 As was seen in its decision to operate Barclaycard despite pressure from anti-apartheid campaigners.

91 T. Thomas, 'The Co-operative Bank's ethical stance', *Review of International Co-operation* 86:4 (1993), pp. 71–5.

92 OXFAM: Cafédirect file, 'Establishing a new ethical coffee brand for the UK' (1 November 1990).

93 'Customers don't want Fair Trade products', *Co-operative News* (26 September 1995).

94 *Co-operative News* (5 May 1992).

95 CWS, Press Release, 'Co-op boosts Fairtrade products', www.co-op.ac.uk (1999).

96 M. Newman, *The Financial Times* (11 October 1990).

97 Watkins, *International Co-operative Alliance*, p. 3.

98 Pollard, 'Nineteenth-century co-operation: from community building to shopkeeping'.

Index

 Index